Volume 2

Parent/Teacher Handbook

Teaching Younger Children Everything They Need to Know About
Their Christian Heritage

Dr. Edward A. Buchanan

Phyllis Keith
God bless you!
Edward G. Buchanan

To my children and grandchildren:
Roger, Ami, and Connor
Becky, Marshall, and Mia

ACKNOWLEDGEMENTS

In preparing this handbook I have deeply appreciated the help of my student assistants and my secretary. I would like to espress special thanks to Broadman & Holman Publishers and particularly to my editor without whose help this project would not have become a reality.

Edward A. Buchanan
May 2003

0-8054-9397-2

Published by Broadman & Holman Publishers
Nashville, Tennessee

Dewey Decimal Classification: 649
Subject Heading: CHILD REARING \ CHURCH HISTORY \
CHRISTIAN EDUCATION OF CHILDREN

Scripture quotations are taken from the following versions: Holman Christian
Standard Bible® Copyright © 1999, 2000, 2001, 2002, 2003 by Holman Bible
Publishers. Used by permission. The New American Standard, © Lockman
Foundation, 1960, 1962, 1963, 1968, 1971, 1972, 1973, 1975, 1977; used
by permisison. King James Version.

1 2 3 4 5 6 7 8 9 10   09 08 07 06 05 04

Table of Contents

General Introduction for Parents and Teachers

The content for this book grows out of a conviction that we need to provide our children with a greater understanding of the Christian faith. The world is growing increasingly hostile to Christianity and to those who practice their Christian faith. If the next generation of believers will possess faith and be able to articulate that faith, they will need to have a solid foundation of background knowledge about their faith. We must become more intentional about helping our children know what it means to be a Christian and how to tell others about the strength they receive from their faith in Jesus Christ.

Our Culture

We live in a culture where tolerance is accorded to many outlandish and bizarre groups but not to Christians. The exclusivism of the gospel of Jesus Christ is offensive to many in our world. Other religious groups, who are very evangelistic and militant to bring Christian believers into their folds, are bombarding us with their false doctrines. If we care about our children, it is essential that we help them gain an adequate knowledge to combat these influences and ideologies.

As parents, we are often too busy with our own concerns to spend adequate time with our children and oversee their growth and development. We come home frazzled from the hectic pace of work and even from our leisure activities. We fail to nurture our children to hold the values and beliefs that we have found essential to the well-being of our lives. We assume that there will be time, and someday we will help them. Or we believe that the church will be able to teach them all they need to know to become Christians and to grow in their faith.

Our culture works in opposition to many of the things that we believe. It has been estimated that by the time a child graduates from high school, he or she will have watched twice as many hours of television as spent in the classroom. Television homogenizes its viewers. It does not matter whether a child of five or an adult of twenty-five is watching the television screen; both persons see the same things. For the adult, the prominent themes of violence and sex may not be too significant, but to the child of five, these themes can be very harmful. The child may not understand all of the innuendos, the meaning of the language, or the visual scenes, but the impact upon the child is significant. Even children's cartoons are filled with images of violence. Movies provide another source for visual images that may not enhance but cause difficulty for the child to pattern behavior in healthy ways.

Overt sexual themes are also prominent in our television shows and movies. They pose another hazard for our children, who are not equipped to deal with adult scenes, language, and situations. The philosophy of "Just do it!" pervades our culture. The problems reach a zenith in the teenage years with promiscuity, pregnancy, and abortion. Negative role models who support such a philosophy only make these problems more prevalent. Many of the role models come from professional sports figures and rock stars. Often the morals of these persons do not provide healthy lifestyle models for our children and youth.

Our schools are plagued with violence. Frustration and dissatisfaction result in shootings. Schools have become a haven for illegal drugs and alcohol. Suicides have also become a significant problem in many schools. All of these situations are compounded by the fact that the level of learning in schools has continued to drop over the past two decades.

Psychologist David Elkind has observed that while many of these problems may manifest in the adolescent years, the roots for these behaviors stem from childhood. Inappropriate behaviors may be ignored in childhood but cannot be ignored during the adolescent years, when drugs, drinking, and promiscuity take a painful and distorted toll on the lives of our youth.

While we might continue to analyze endlessly the negative aspects of our society and its effects on our children, the question of what a parent can do to counteract these evil forces requires our urgent attention. The first essential is for parents to spend time with their children. At the first and second grade levels, select wholesome materials, like the stories in this and other books, to read aloud. At bedtime, establish a pattern of having your child sit in your lap and read aloud for ten to fifteen minutes. Then discuss what you both have heard. In doing so, you will develop a deeper and more intimate relationship with your child and at the same time provide a healthy basis for your child to withstand the evils of our society.

Helping Your Child Learn

Current research on learning clearly indicates that things can be done to help children develop healthy attitudes, espouse Christian values, and live out these values in appropriate Christian behavior. Perhaps the foremost principle of learning is that a person needs a solid knowledge base of prior learning. For someone to become a Christian and live in accordance with Christian principles, it is imperative to develop a full understanding of Christian faith. It has been estimated that about half of the young people from one of our major denominations lose their faith when they go off to college. Perhaps one of the reasons is that they never had a solid foundation in the first place. They are often ill equipped to face the temptations of college life and the onslaught of a college culture that ridicules their faith and beliefs.

A second principle for effective learning is learning that is presented in a meaningful and structured format. Our learning needs to be

organized. For example, if you were studying the Gospel of Mark, it would be helpful to have a chart of the way in which the Gospel is structured. Such a chart would provide some pegs on which to hang the individual parts of the text. For the Bible, a time line can help us better retain and recall the information that was gained from the study. Such devices will be included in this study to assist your child to better learn the material.

A third principle of learning that is critical is modeling. This means that we learn by observation. Parents provide children with their most important role models. As a result of the amount of time spent with parents, the child will pick up attitudes, values, beliefs, and behaviors from the parent.

Long before these became principles of learning in today's educational context, the Bible described parents teaching children in Deuteronomy 6:7: *"Repeat them to your children. Talk about them when you sit in your house and when you walk along the road, when you lie down and when you get up."* Note that parents are expected to provide instruction in the precepts of God that lead to godly behavior. That has not changed. God is love, but He has set the moral requirements for us to follow and expects obedience. Unless we know what God expects in His moral precepts, we cannot live our lives in accordance with them. Children need to learn God's expectations and follow them. These expectations are not given to limit our behavior unnecessarily. On the contrary, they are provided to help us live lives that are free from guilt and anxiety.

Basic Christian Learning

To help with the process of understanding Christian faith, each person needs some basic knowledge of the Bible, persons, events, terms, symbols, and phrases that may be included under the term *Christian*. This is called Basic Christian Learning. Basic Christian Learning begins with study of Scripture. Scripture is foundational to everything that we believe. Since the Bible is God's message to us, every Christian needs to be thoroughly grounded in the Bible. This study will begin by providing a solid foundation in Scripture.

But Basic Christian Learning includes more than Bible study. Here are some examples of the kinds of items that are included under the heading of Basic Christian Learning. What does a Christian believe? If you are Presbyterian, how did Presbyterianism develop? If you are Baptist, how did you become Baptist? As much as we might wish that each of our denominations came from the New Testament church, there was a historical process that brought about the development of each of the denominations. Some of the cultures of the past have been much more Christian than our present culture. Children, youth, and adults need to understand past Christian cultures. Christianity has not always been ridiculed as it often is today. Some of the greatest works in art, music, and literature have been inspired by the Christian faith. Consider Michelangelo's magnificent ceiling in the Sistine Chapel in Rome. Or consider the inspiration that led to George Handel's great masterpiece, *The Messiah*. Isaac Watts was a hardened and profane slave trader, but his conversion to Christ led to reformation in his life and inspired him to write the great hymn, "Amazing Grace." John Bunyan was not educated, but was inspired by his faith in Christ to write one of the masterpieces of English literature, *Pilgrim's Progress*. Basic Christian Learning includes all of these and many other related topics. It is intended to provide a fundamental understanding of our Christian faith and stir the imagination of our children to live their Christian faith in the midst of a world that needs the good news of the gospel.

With a background in Basic Christian Learning, a child and young person is prepared to face some of the issues of defining, defending, and living the Christian faith inside and outside the church. Teaching in Sunday school and preaching in the church become more meaningful when set against a background of an understanding that Basic

Christian Learning can provide. Common understanding can foster deeper relationships between parents and their children because they share a common bond of understanding of their Christian faith. Witnessing to Christian belief is no longer an onerous task but a joyous privilege. Christian faith is not only to be believed; it is to be practiced. With basic knowledge of Christian behavior, a Christian can respond to the moral and ethical issues of a non-Christian world that one confronts each day. As the missionary William Carey once observed: "Expect great things of God; attempt great things for God!"

About This Book

This handbook has been designed as a resource tool for teachers and parents who would like to get more depth and understanding into the lessons they are teaching. Some of the foundation materials are part of volume 1 but have been carried over into volume 2 for easy reference. This comprehensive volume will help you and your ministry to children by providing interesting information to bring the Bible to life.

The content of this volume includes everything from ancient Bible history to the customs of people in Bible times. You'll understand more about the roles of males and females and how those roles have influenced our lives down through the ages. You'll get a glimpse of the potters and the carpenters and the metal workers of those days and understand more clearly the heritage of Jesus.

Another section of volume 2 will take you through the varied religious practices of worship and the various celebrations of both the Jews and the Christians. You'll get an in-depth look at Christmas and the birth of our Lord Jesus and His family. Children will understand why we put up Christmas trees and why we celebrate the season as we do even today.

Volume 2 will provide you with more materials to share the Easter traditions as well. You'll learn the history behind the original Passover meal that faithful Jews celebrate today. You'll be more prepared to give meaning to the death and resurrection of our Lord Jesus Christ. You'll walk with the women to the tomb and discover with great joy that the Lord is indeed with us still, and you'll be able to share that joy with your students in a more inspired way.

As the church continues to grow and develop, your students will have a better understanding of the evolution that caused so many denominations to be born, and they'll have an opportunity to look at the medieval church and compare it to the more contemporary church. This volume will provide you with the tools for greater understanding of what we believe and why we believe as we do.

Once your students are grounded more thoroughly in their faith, they'll appreciate the diverse ways that Christianity is shared in our culture. We'll give you a glimpse of missions and a greater understanding of the Great Commission.

Since we're surrounded by fine religious art, we'll give you and your students a better sense of how that artwork developed over the centuries and what inspired the masters to create the works that we still stand in awe of today. And finally, we'll take a little peek at Christianity and science and how the two are not necessarily at odds with each other. We live in a world where many scientists admit that their work only enhances their faith in God. Our mission is to enhance and instill that faith in our children, and we thank you for the part you play in getting that work done.

Bible Customs

Life in Bible Times

Life in Palestine for the average person was lived at a much slower pace than life today. Many occupations were necessary for food. These involved sheep herding, farming, fishing, and the domestic life of the average girl or woman in Israel. A boy would learn the responsibilities that his father would teach him. If his father was a farmer, he would most likely become a farmer as well. If you lived in those days, what kind of person would you likely have become? After you have considered the variety of occupations, what sounds interesting to you?

THE SHEPHERD LIFE IN PALESTINE

If you were a boy who lived in Bible times, you might have been a shepherd. You would have learned how to care for sheep at a very young age. Sheep and goats were very important to people in

that day. You would have been in good company. David was a shepherd boy as he grew up. Many people in the Middle East still shepherd flocks today. Many of the Bedouin Arabs still follow the customs of shepherding, as they did in Bible times.

Sheep were used for food. In our day we eat more beef than lamb. We do not usually eat goat. The coats of the sheep were used to provide sheepskins, and warm clothing was made from their wool. Sheep also provided meat and milk. Their horns were used to carry oil and as a musical instrument, the shofar. Both sheep and goats were used for sacrifice to God in the Temple. The goats provided a large quantity of milk for drinking. They also provided milk for cheese and yogurt. Goatskins were used to make leather, sackcloth, and tent coverings. The goat hair was used to stuff pillows. Water bottles were also made from goatskins.

Caring for sheep was one of the oldest occupations in those days. Shepherding is first mentioned in the Bible in Genesis 4:2. Abel raised sheep, and his brother Cain was a farmer. That followed a pattern that was continued in future years. The older sons became farmers and tilled the land. Cain was the older son, so he became a farmer. Abel was the younger son, and he was a shepherd. The life of a shepherd often caused strife between his wandering way of life and that of the more settled farmer. A farmer had to protect his crops from being eaten by the sheep. In later years, the shepherd learned to guide his sheep down a path between the farmer's fields. If the sheep ate of the farmer's crops, a farmer could collect from the shepherd. Similar strife existed in America between the cowboy and farmer during the settling of the West.

The youngest son took the responsibility of caring for the sheep. Remember, David was out in the fields caring for his father's sheep when Samuel came to anoint a new king. Samuel said to David's father, "Are these all of the sons that you have?" They sent to the fields for David. David came, and he was anointed to become the new king. You can find this in 1 Samuel 16:11ff. Many of David's experiences as a shepherd appear in the psalms.

Sheep and Goats

The fat-tailed sheep was very popular in the Middle East. It had a supply of food for energy stored in the tail region. When there was no rain and little to eat, the sheep could still survive. It was similar to the hump on the camel. Contained in the hump of the camel is a supply of food for energy in difficult times. As a result, the fat area of the sheep's tail was very valuable. Sheep were usually white in color. They grazed along the ground. The shepherd had to constantly find new pastureland where his sheep could graze. The sheep did not like the hot summer sun. They liked to stay in the shade during the heat of the day.

The shepherd also herded goats. Goats were valuable for their milk. They also provided food, and their skins were used for making leather. Goats were usually black in color, and they liked to climb on the mountainsides. Goats liked to eat the leaves of branches that were close to the ground and did not mind the hot summer sun. They would graze throughout the day. Sheep and goats would be led into the field together.

In the field, the shepherd would separate the sheep and the goats. The goats would go to graze on the hillside, while the sheep would graze in the pasture. In the Bible, God is compared to the shepherd. The sheep are compared to people who have trusted in God. By contrast, the goats are used often to describe the evil persons (see Matthew 25:32–33).

Caring for the Sheep

During the day the shepherd cared for his flock. He knew each sheep by name. He was able to place each of the lambs with its mother. He taught each sheep to respond to his voice. When several flocks of sheep were together, a shepherd could call his sheep. Only his sheep would come. Jesus compared Himself to the shepherd. Jesus said, "I am the good shepherd. I know My own sheep and they know Me" (John 10:14).

In the Middle East, the shepherd always led his sheep. He did not go behind them and drive them. The shepherd was always out in front of his sheep. This allowed him to find any places of danger before the sheep walked that way. God is often described as the Shepherd of His people. Like the sheep, God's people are helpless without the Shepherd (Numbers 27:17).

The shepherd often used sheepdogs to help him guide the sheep. Sometimes the shepherd had to lead his sheep across a stream. Sheep do not like water that is flowing rapidly, but the shepherd would help them across the stream. When they all reached the other side safely, the sheep would come and surround the shepherd. To the shepherd, it would appear that the sheep were expressing thanks for the protective care of the shepherd.

David expressed this about God. He said that God drew him out of many waters (Psalm 18:19).

The shepherd would lead his sheep to green pastures to graze. Isaiah described God as a Shepherd who led His people (see Isaiah 40:11). He would take them to a quiet pond or stream to drink. David also described God as the Shepherd who led His people to quiet waters to satisfy their thirst (see Psalm 23:2). If a sheep became separated from the flock or lost, the shepherd would go out and search for the lost sheep. Jesus described Himself as the Shepherd who would go out and seek the lost sheep and bring it back to safety. If a lamb were hurt, the shepherd would carry the lamb on his shoulders. The lamb would become very attached to the shepherd.

One of the constant dangers for the sheep was sunstroke. The shepherd would protect his sheep by anointing them by pouring oil on the head of each sheep from a cruse of oil. This was also done for camels. If the shepherd did not do this, the sheep might suffer and even die from the heat. Often the anointing had to be done several times in a day for protection. In the Old Testament, the priest and the king were anointed as they began their work. For them, it carried the idea of dedication to the service of God. In the New Testament, the Holy Spirit anoints and protects the follower of Jesus.

Sometimes the shepherd had too many sheep to care for by himself. He might hire someone to help him. This person was called a hireling. Unlike the shepherd, the hireling would not always care about the sheep. He would not risk his life to protect the sheep as the shepherd would. If wild animals attacked, the shepherd would defend the sheep with his life, but the hireling might run away.

At night the shepherd would take his sheep to a cave or sheepfold. The sheepfold was a pen that was enclosed by a low fence of stones placed on top of one another. Brambles or thorns would be placed on top of the fence to keep wild animals and thieves from stealing the sheep. The shepherd would lie across the opening of the sheepfold with his own body. If a wild animal tried to enter the sheepfold, that animal would have to pass over the shepherd's body.

There were several enemies of the sheep. Lions and bears often would attack them. Before David went to kill the giant Goliath, he told King Saul how he killed the lion and bear while he was shepherding his father's flocks. Lions and bears are no longer found in that part of the world, but there are still many enemies of the sheep. Hyenas, jackals, wolves, and panthers will attack the sheep at night. Thieves are also a menace to the shepherd. He must be on guard to protect his flock from these wild animals. A shepherd must also protect the sheep from people who would hurt or destroy them.

In the Bible, God is described as the One who protects the believer. The world is full of temptations and problems. But God protects His children, just as the shepherd protects his sheep. The follower of God can count on God's protection, just as the sheep could count on the shepherd.

The Shepherd's Clothing and Equipment

The shepherd usually wore a simple tunic of cotton. Over the tunic he might have a sleeveless coat made of sheepskin. It was called a fleece coat. It would protect the shepherd in the heat of the day and gave protection when it rained. It could also serve as a cover at night to keep him warm. In the daytime his head was also covered with a cloth to protect him from the hot rays of the sun. He normally wore sandals on his feet.

He carried a staff, a long pole about five or six feet long. It usually had a crook on the end. It could be used like a walking stick. The staff was not a weapon, although it could be used against animals that would hurt the flock. Its most important use was to help the sheep. The shepherd could use the crook to pull a sheep out of a thicket of briars. He could use the staff to separate the goats and send them to pasture on the hillside. He also used the staff to assist him in counting his flock at night. As they passed under the staff, he made a mark for every tenth sheep.

The rod was another important item that the shepherd carried. The rod was a club. It was made of a hardwood, like oak. On the end it had a knob. In the knob there were many nails. That made the rod a dangerous weapon. The rod was used to defend the sheep from attack. A king or queen used a scepter. It is believed that the scepter had its origin in the shepherd's rod. The king was often characterized as a shepherd to his people. When David described God as Shepherd, he said, "Your rod and Your staff—they comfort me" (Psalm 23:4).

The shepherd also carried a bag called a scrip. It was usually made of dried animal skin. The scrip served as a pouch to carry the food for the shepherd. This included locusts, wild honey, and berries. When David fought against Goliath, he carried his scrip. Instead of food, he placed the stones inside that he planned to use against the giant. That is described in 1 Samuel 17:40.

Another item that the shepherd carried was the sling. This was a very simple but important weapon. It was made of a piece of leather connected with two strings on either end. A smooth stone was placed in the leather pouch. Then the shepherd would swing the strings faster and faster. He would let go of one of the strings, and the stone would fly toward its target. During the many hours of watching the sheep, the shepherd would practice and become very accurate. Shepherds could stop animals that would harm the sheep with this small but powerful weapon. David was able to kill Goliath with a stone from his sling (see 1 Samuel 17:40–49).

The shepherd's job was a lonely one. He spent many long hours alone in the wilderness with his flocks. To entertain himself, he carried a flute. It was a reed pipe. It is quite possible that David composed many of his psalms using the flute. It entertained the shepherd and his sheep. When it was broken, the shepherd would destroy it and make another.

The shepherd often carried a lamp. The lamp was made of parchment. It could be collapsed like an accordion or a Chinese lantern. Using oil in the bottom, it allowed the shepherd to find his way in the dark.

FARMING IN PALESTINE

If you were not a shepherd in Bible times, most likely you were a farmer. Farming was the most common occupation. As more members of the family were added, the youngest would become the shepherd for the family. The older sons would become farmers. This was very hard work.

Although Abraham came from a land that was rich in farming, his wealth consisted mainly of animal livestock. Recall that the Israelites left Palestine for Egypt when Jacob was old. Joseph served there under the pharaoh. Egypt was a rich paradise for growing wheat and vegetables. Each year the Nile River would overflow its banks. It brought rich soil from the upper part of Egypt and watered the plain along its banks. The people were able to plant their crops and did not have to be concerned about the rain. It almost never rained in Egypt. But the water from the Nile was able to provide enough moisture to allow the plants to grow. During their four hundred years in Egypt, the people of Israel learned to enjoy the good food that the Nile provided.

It is not surprising that when the Israelites left Egypt and came into the Promised Land, many settled the land and became farmers. They did not grow corn. Corn was not known in that part of the world. Rather, they raised grain crops of wheat and barley. They also raised millet. Flax was grown in order to make linen. Some vegetables were also raised, such as cucumbers, leeks, peas, onions, and melons. Since they did not eat meat very often, their diet most often was vegetarian (see Ezekiel 4:9).

Three other agricultural crops were also very important to the diet of the Israelites. Olives from the olive tree were squeezed in an olive press. In our country, many people use animal fat to cook their food. The Israelites used oil from the olives in place of animal fat. Olive oil also provided fuel for lamps to help people see at night. Along with the olive tree, another tree that was also grown for food was the fig tree. Figs provided fruit in the diet of the Israelite people.

Pollution in the water supply made grapes another important crop. Grapes were processed into wine for drinking. Grapes provided a sweet jellylike spread that was used on bread. It was called dibs, and it was similar to our grape jam. Grapes were also dried into raisins.

It is not difficult to see how the growing of plants provided one of the most important sources of food for the Israelite. Farming became one of the essential jobs in ancient Israel.

Preparing the Fields for Planting Grain

Planting the grain seeds usually took place in October or November. The farmers in Egypt received a fresh supply of soil every time the Nile flooded. The farmers in Palestine had to wait for rains to make the ground spongy to allow the seed to be planted. This is described in the Bible in Psalm 65:10.

Usually the farmer plowed the field with a team of two oxen. The oxen wore a yoke, which consisted of two neck braces that were connected by a bar. If both oxen were pulling together, they would share the load. A long bar went between the oxen and was fastened to the plow. The plow was a crude tool. It had a handle for the farmer to push the plow into the ground. The plow itself was a pointed stick. Most plows had an iron piece to cut into the ground.

The farmer also carried an ox goad. The goad was a pole about six feet long. At the end of the pole was a sharp point. It was used to keep the oxen moving and pulling the plow. Since the plow was very light, the farmer had to apply pressure to dig into the hard ground. The farmer also had

to keep his eye on the furrow that he was cutting, all the while goading the oxen and pushing down on the plow. He had to watch the places where he was plowing, since there could be rocks in the way. A rock could break the plow. When the farmer had to plow on a hillside, he would use a mattock or hoe (Isaiah 7:25). The oxen could only work on flat ground. Farming was very hard work.

Jesus told many stories about farming. In one of those stories, He said that anyone who began to plow and looked back was not fit for the kingdom of God (Luke 9:62). If a farmer looked back while he was plowing, his row would be crooked.

Planting the Seed

When the farmer had plowed the field and all was ready, the farmer would sow the seed. Wheat was sown first. Then the barley seed would be scattered. The farmer would carry the seed and throw it along the plowed rows.

Jesus used the sower to tell one of His parables. He said that the sower would scatter the seed. Some fell on the rocks. It grew rapidly but could not take root and soon died. Other seed fell among thorns. It was soon choked out and died. Still other seed fell on good ground and grew until it was ready for harvest. Jesus told His followers that spreading God's Word is like the seed. God wants to see the good seed that grows toward harvest (Matthew 13:18–23).

Jesus told another parable in Matthew 13:24–30 about the wheat and the tares. The tares and the wheat grow side by side. Tares are weeds that look like wheat. When they grow, they turn black rather than golden like the wheat. If they are eaten, they will cause sickness.

The farmer's work did not end with the planting. He continued to use the hoe to pull out the weeds. In Palestine this tool was called a mattock. Use of the mattock, or hoeing, had to be done during the winter season, from December through January. The growing season took place from

February into April. The spring rains helped the seed to sprout and grow.

Harvesting the Grain

Flax was harvested first, in March or April. The farmer used his hoe to cut the flax. Next, barley was harvested in April. It was cut with a sickle. Wheat was harvested in the same way. These stalks were cut. Some of the stalk was left on the ground for grazing animals. Some of the grain was left for the poor to gather. The grain and their stalks were bundled into sheaves. The bundled sheaves were taken to the threshing floor by donkey or camel.

There was always danger of fire that could burn the grain. The dry thorns usually were around the grain. They would easily catch fire, and then the grain would burn as well. There was also danger of fire when the sheaves were brought to the threshing floor. This is described in the Bible in Exodus 22:6. Invading armies could bring great hardship upon the people by burning the supply of food. Finally, thieves might steal the grain and cause a great loss of the crop.

Before the grain was harvested, locusts were a constant threat. Locusts were one of the plagues that God sent upon Egypt when He wanted Pharaoh to let His people go. A locust is similar to a large grasshopper. They came by the thousands and ate all of the grain. When they finished, there was nothing of the grain left. Farmers were always afraid of the locusts, which are described as an advancing army in Joel 2:2–9. They must have caused great fear among the people of Israel.

Some of the grain was left in the fields. The poor people could come to the fields and gather grain to meet their needs. When Ruth came back with her mother-in-law, Naomi, they did not have food. Naomi sent Ruth to the fields of Boaz. Boaz treated Ruth kindly and allowed her to glean grain in his fields after the reapers had finished (see Ruth 2:8–17).

Threshing and Winnowing the Grain

Threshing the grain means that the farmer takes the grain to a threshing floor. If only one person did the threshing, that person would use a flail, a wooden tool used to beat the grain kernel out of its shell. Ruth did this with the barley that she gleaned from the field of Boaz (see Ruth 2:17).

For large quantities of grain, the normal means was to use a sledge. This was a wooden beam that had sharp stones or metal to cut the stalks of the grain and free the grain kernels. The farmer would drive his oxen over the grain, using the sledge. They would go around a circle across the grain and the straw stalks. The sledge would cut the straw into small pieces, and the grain kernels would fall to the bottom. Some of the kernels would remain with the straw and be used to feed the animals. The rest would be taken from the threshing floor to the winnowing process.

Winnowing usually took place in the evening. A breeze was usually blowing in the evening. The farmer and his helpers would throw the grain into the air. The chaff, or coverings of the grain, would blow away in the breeze. The heavier grain kernels would fall to the ground and be gathered in the harvest.

The next step was to sift the grain. This was done with a large sieve. The farmer would remove any bits of straw and tares from the barley or wheat. Then the grain would be measured and stored in large earthen jars. Later it would have to be milled or ground into flour. Water was added to the flour and made into dough. Women made the dough and baked the bread. The wealthy people ate bread of wheat, while the poorer people ate bread of barley.

Growing Grapes

Another kind of farming was growing grapes. Grapevines are another important farm product. They require different conditions from growing grains. Grapes were the first product mentioned in the Bible after the Flood. Noah started to farm and planted a vineyard (see Genesis 9:20).

To prepare a new vineyard, the farmer had to find a section on the side of a hill that was well drained. The farmer then used his mattock or hoe to loosen the dirt. Rocks had to be removed from the rows also. Rows of grapes were then placed along the side of the hill. Grapes require the moisture of the dew at night. During the day they need the warm sunshine. They ripen during the dry season.

To keep thieves and wild animals from stealing the grapes, the farmer would build a wall around his grapevines. A tower was built for the farmer to watch over his grapes as they ripened. The farmer might also build a winepress along the vineyard. Jesus described this in His parable of the landowner (see Matthew 21:33).

The grape vineyard was planted from cuttings of grapevines from other vineyards. Once planted, the grapevines continue to provide grapes for years to come. The grapes blossom in April or May. They give off a very fragrant smell at that time. They ripen during the summer and are ready to harvest in late August or early September.

Harvesting the grapes is a happy time. The pickers gather the grapes in baskets and bring them to the winepress. The family participates in tramping on the grapes with their bare feet. They take out the juice. It drains from the winepress into earthen jars that collect the grape juice.

Many of the grapes are eaten fresh during the harvest season. Fresh grapes are often spread on bread. Other grapes are dried in the sun and allowed to become raisins. The raisins are stored for eating later in the year. Grapes are boiled to provide a rich grape syrup, called dibs. Dibs are spread on bread, like jelly.

Olive Trees and Other trees

One of the most important farm products in the Middle East is olive oil. The olive tree does well in the hot dry climate and the rocky soil of Palestine. All through Bible times the olive tree was very common (see Deuteronomy 8:8). Olive oil is taken from the olive berry. Olives are harvested in October. In one season a tree will produce many gallons of olive oil. Gethsemene, where Jesus went to pray before His arrest, was an olive orchard.

The trees were only harvested every other year because the farmers used sticks to knock the berries from the tree. This often damaged the tree and prevented them from producing berries the next year.

After the berries were harvested, they were taken to an olive press. The olive press was a large stone that was rotated over another stone. The berries were crushed between the stones to take out the oil. A donkey would be hitched to the stone wheel of the olive press and would tread around the press to crush the berries. Then the oil was collected in jars.

Some olives were eaten fresh. Others were placed in salt water to preserve them for eating later in the year. But the main crop was the olive oil. Olive oil was used in place of animal fat for cooking. Olive oil was used as a medicine for healing. In the parable of the good Samaritan, Jesus mentioned olive oil as a salve that was placed on the injured man (see Luke 10:34). Olive oil was used to burn in lamps (see Matthew 25:3). Olive oil was used to anoint the hair and skin. In Old Testament times large quantities of olive oil were considered wealth.

Olive oil had a religious use as well. It was used in anointing prophets, priests, and kings. Anointing means to be set apart to God. The Messiah is described as the anointed One (see Luke 4:18). Followers of Jesus are also described as anointed by the Holy Spirit.

Other trees that were important in ancient Palestine were the fig and sycamore trees. Their fruit was a valuable part of the diet of the Israelites. These were summer crops. The fruit was harvested and eaten fresh. It was also dried and preserved for use later in the year.

FISHING IN PALESTINE

Fishing was not an important industry in Palestine until the time of Christ. When the people of Israel were journeying from Egypt to the Promised Land, they were not able to obtain fish. They missed the fish that they ate in Egypt (see Numbers 11:5).

Apparently, some fishing was done on Lake Galilee, in the Jordan River, and along the Mediterranean coast. Almost no fishing was done in the Dead Sea. The high mineral and salt content of the Dead Sea prevents many fish from living in the sea.

In Old Testament times, both Isaiah and Amos mention fishing with line and hook (see Isaiah 19:8 and Amos 4:2). But fishing of this type was not an important industry in Old Testament times. In New Testament times, Jesus told Peter to fish with line and hook in the sea. He caught a fish and pulled a coin from the fish to pay taxes (see Matthew 17:27).

By Jesus' time, fishing on Lake Galilee had become an important industry. Men like Peter, Andrew, James, and John made their livelihood fishing. They used several different kinds of nets. Jesus called these four disciples to follow Him: He said, "Follow Me, and I will make you into fishers of men!" (Mark 1:17).

The Sea of Galilee is not a large lake, but it has a large supply of more than two dozen varieties of fish. Water in the lake is fresh water that is fed from the mountains in the northern part of Palestine. From Galilee, the water flows south in the Jordan River to the Dead Sea. (Look at the map of Palestine at the time of Christ in the previous section to find Galilee, the Jordan River, and the Dead Sea). The Dead Sea has too much salt and mineral content to allow many fish to live in it.

The Sea of Galilee is about seven miles across and thirteen miles long. There are no natural harbors on the lake. It was necessary for the fishermen to build jetties of stone into the lake to protect their fishing boats. The lake is about seven hundred feet below the level of the Mediterranean Sea. The Mediterranean Sea is thirty miles to the west. In between are mountains that rise fifteen hundred feet above sea level. During the day, when the hot sun is beating on the lake, the air over the lake becomes very warm. Sometimes the cold air from the Mediterranean Sea comes across the mountains and from the west. It meets the warm air on the lake and causes wind and violent storms.

This must have happened at the time when Jesus was with His disciples. He was asleep in the boat when the violent storm came across the lake (see Mark 4:35–41).

The fishing boats on the lake were small. A boat similar to the ones that the disciples would have used was found buried in the sand on the shore of the lake in 1948. It was about twenty-four feet in length and seven feet wide and had a large rudder located in the back to steer the boat. It also had a sail in the shape of a triangle that could be moved about to catch the wind.

Fishing was done with three different kinds of nets. Each of these is mentioned in the Gospels. When Jesus called Peter and Andrew, they were using a cast net. This is a net that is about fifteen to twenty feet across. The cast net has metal weights attached to the outside edges. The fisherman would throw the net into the water. Anything under the net would be caught. He would dive into the water and drag the net to shore. Along with the fish, the fisherman would collect garbage from the lake floor. He would separate the fish and throw the garbage back into the lake (see Mark 1:16).

The second type of net used was a dragnet. It was a much larger net and required several fishermen to control it. It measured about one hundred feet long. There were ropes attached to each end of the net. It was drawn by the fishermen to the shore. Usually the dragnet brought in a large number of fish, along with other debris from the lake. This type of net could also be used by a group of fishermen sailing in two boats. They would drag the net between the fishing boats and gather in the fish. In Matthew 13:47–48, Jesus compared the kingdom of God with a dragnet. The good fish are kept, and the useless ones are thrown out.

The trammel net was a combination of three nets. They formed a pocket that served as a kind of funnel to trap the fish. They dragged the net through the water and trapped the fish. In Luke 5:1–11, Jesus told Peter to let down the nets and pull in the fish from the lake. Peter said they had fished all night and had not caught anything. But he and the other fishermen did as Jesus commanded. The catch was so large that the nets began to break.

When the fishing was finished for the day, the fishermen would return to the shore. They would salt the fish to preserve them. Fish would be sold in the market. Because the nets were dragged along the sea bottom, they would become torn. The fishermen would return to their fishing boats and repair the nets for the next day.

FAMILY ROLES FOR GIRLS AND WOMEN

If you were a girl in Bible times, life would be very different from your life today. Your goal in life would be to become a good wife and mother. You would be responsible for your home. Food preparation would consume a large portion of your day. But there were some other things that a woman had to do as well. A woman was admired for her beauty, purity, and her hard work.

Home was built around the family. Men had responsibilities outside the home, such as the occupations that are described in this section. Women ran the home. Life for women in Bible times had its problems. Women did not have as many rights as men. For example, a woman could not divorce her husband, but a man could divorce his wife. Women could not testify in court. A woman called her husband "Master." Women did the chores, like drawing water at the well and bringing it back home. They cared for the cooking, cleaning, washing, and weaving tasks. When a husband traveled with his wife, she walked and he rode.

In many ways life was difficult for women. But for a wife who was loved by her husband, life was not too bad. A woman bore children. A woman believed that God blessed her when she had children. As a mother, she would teach her children and bring them up to love and obey God.

Growing up, girls learned from watching and helping their mothers. They learned how to choose food and cook for the family. They learned how to take sheep's wool and make clothes from it. They learned to dye the strands, card the wool, and spin the wool into thread. Then they learned to use a loom to make cloth.

Sometimes they would work in the field to gather grain. Other times they would tend the flocks and help care for the sheep and goats. Many girls learned to play musical instruments.

Marriage was arranged by the fathers of the bride and the groom. In Bible times, children usually married at a very young age. Usually a boy married when he was thirteen years of age, and a girl married at age twelve. A wedding was a happy event. There were seven days of dancing and celebration.

A price was paid by the groom's family to the bride's family because her family no longer had the help from their daughter. The bride's family paid a dowry, but the groom could not spend it. If the husband died, his wife had her dowry to help her through a difficult time. In the event that the husband divorced his wife, the dowry was returned to her to care for her needs.

In Proverbs 31:10–31, a good wife is described. She loves her husband and helps him. She is a person who works hard. She rises early in the morning to prepare the family for the day ahead. She cares first for her household. If there are others in the family, she will help to meet their needs. She has compassion on the poor and needy. She cares for the clothing needs of her family by providing clothes of linen or wool. She makes more than enough cloth so that she can sell some of the cloth to merchants. She teaches her family and is kind to all. She is a good businesswoman, buying a field and planting a vineyard. She is a woman who loves God and is a blessing to her family.

Responsibilities of women in Jewish religious practices were low. A mother was responsible to light the candles on Sabbath eve. Women were not allowed to go beyond the Court of the Women in the Temple. In the synagogue, women and children watched the service from a balcony. In the early Christian church, women had responsibility to worship in the same manner as men.

The Bible gives some examples of special women whom God used to lead His people. The first three are from the Old Testament. Miriam was one of these women. Miriam was the sister of Moses. As a girl, her mother gave her the responsibility to care for Moses. She helped the daughter of Pharaoh save Moses' life when Pharaoh commanded all male Hebrew children be killed. Later, Miriam helped Moses and Aaron lead the people of Israel toward the Promised Land.

Deborah was one of the judges of Israel. She was married and still became a prophet, judge, and military leader. That was extremely rare for a woman. She held her court under the palm tree of Deborah (Judges 4:4–5). In Judges 4:6–9, she is described as a prophetess to deliver God's people.

Esther was the brave young woman who risked her life to appear before the king on behalf of the Jewish people. Recall the story of the wicked Haman from the biblical text. Esther went to her husband, King Xerxes, and asked for help against Haman's plot to kill all the Jews in Persia. As a result, the Jews were saved and celebrate the Feast of Purim even today.

From the New Testament there are also several special Christian women who have influenced the church. Lydia lived in Philippi. She was a businesswoman who was a seller of purple (see the section about dying cloth under "Cloth Makers" on page 23). She feared God, and when Paul preached the gospel, she became a believer in Christ. She opened her home to Paul and his followers. Then her home became the first meeting place of the church in Macedonia and in Western Europe. She was a woman who demonstrated Christian virtues of generosity, hospitality, and love for others (see Acts 16:40).

Phoebe served in an official capacity in the city of Cenchrea. Phoebe took Paul's letter to Rome. He described her as one who was a sister in the Lord. She served in the ministry of the church. She exercised hospitality and helped Paul and many others. She was one who was an example of what a Christian should be (see Romans 16:1–2).

CRAFTSMEN

As long as the people of Israel were in Egypt, the Egyptians made the articles that were necessary for life in the home. But after the people left Egypt and settled in their new land, they had to learn trades. Articles that were used in the home, such as dishes, pottery, metal pots, jewelry, clothing, and buildings, had to be made in Palestine. Normally, a father would teach his trade to his son, and the son would carry on the work of his father. Recall that Joseph was a carpenter, and Jesus became a carpenter as He grew up as well.

The Clay Potter

A very important occupation in biblical times was the potter. He made clay pots that were used to hold water and grape juice. The potter would also make plates that you might use to hold your meal at dinnertime. Metal containers, like those made of copper, were too expensive for the average person to buy, but pottery was commonly made and inexpensive.

Imagine that you are invited to go with a friend to the shop where the potter works. It will be necessary to go to a particular part of town, since all or most of the potters worked in one area. It was usually in a place that was outside the city wall but near a gate. In

Jerusalem, Jeremiah described the "Potsherd Gate" (Jeremiah 19:1–2). When pottery was broken, it was discarded on piles. These piles were probably located outside the Potsherd Gate. The potters' shops would likely have been near this gate.

Suppose you could visit a potter's shop. Outside you see a kind of box, like a sandbox for play. In the box is a large amount of clay that is loosely piled. That means the potter is preparing this clay for work in his shop. It must be allowed to weather in the sun, wind, and rain before it is ready for the potter to fashion into a clay pot.

As you enter the shop, you see a large, rough wooden table in front of the potter. You notice that the shop is not clean but has a lot of clay spilled on the floor. The shelves behind the potter are also dirty. They are lined with many clay pots and other things that the potter has made. The potter tells you that these pots are drying before they will be taken to the kiln to be fired.

The potter then takes you to his wheel. This is the place where he will make a pot. He takes a lump of clay and begins to turn his stone wheel. You notice that a pole to another wheel on the floor connects to this wheel. The potter turns the wheel on the floor with his feet. As the lump of clay spins on the upper wheel, the potter begins to fashion the clay into a pot. As it spins, he dips his hand into a water pot that is close by. The potter must keep his hands wet to mold the clay. With his left hand, the potter begins to push the clay in the center of the pot and works inside the pot until he is able to get his entire hand into it. He polishes the outside with a piece of wood to smooth the surface. Little by little he continues to form the pot. Once in a while, the clay has some imperfection, and the potter will push the clay back into a lump and start again. When it is finished, it will be stacked alongside the other pots, awaiting firing in the kiln.

To see the rest of the process, we must go outside again. In a nearby building, the potter takes some of the pottery that has dried. He stacks the pottery in the kiln. A brick cover encloses the kiln. The pots will be heated slowly until they are very hot. Then the temperature will be allowed to drop very slowly until the potter can go and get the pots. This usually takes about three days.

Since you cannot stay for the three days to watch the entire process, the potter takes you back into his shop and shows you some pottery that has already been fired. It was done last week and is ready to be sold. Most of the pots have a dull finish. A few have designs and are glazed. There are other things that the potter has made. You notice that there are little clay figures. There are also drinking mugs, plates, and other storage containers.

The potter shows you some potsherds. These are pieces of pottery that have been chipped or broken. They do not go to waste. Some are taken into town to be used to draw water from the well. Others are used to carry hot coals. Still others serve as writing tablets. The potter warns that care must be taken with the pottery. It is brittle, and if it is put down on a table too quickly, it may shatter.

In several places, the Bible talks about the potter and his pottery. In Jeremiah 18:1–6, God told the prophet to go to the potter's house. Jeremiah stood by as the potter molded a pot on the potter's wheel. When the clay did not mold into the kind of pot that the potter wanted, he smashed the clay back into a lump and began to remold it into something that he liked. God told Jeremiah to tell the people that He would do the same thing with the people of Judah.

The Carpenter

Carpentry was another skilled occupation that developed late among the Israelite people. It was a necessary skill for the people when they settled in the land of Palestine. There are not many records of carpenters before the time of the kings. There must have been some limited carpentry skills that developed among the Israelites, since the farmers needed yokes for oxen and plows.

During Solomon's reign as king of Israel, the king of Tyre, or Phoenicia, sent to Solomon cedar and cypress wood that was needed to build the Temple. They floated the cedar and cypress wood as rafts, similar to what loggers do today (see 1 Kings 5:8–10). As the Israelites watched and worked alongside the skilled carpenters from Phoenicia, they learned carpentry skills that were needed in Israel.

The Phoenicians were master shipbuilders. They built the large ships that sailed the Mediterranean Sea. Remember, Jonah fled to Tarshish (Spain) from doing what God told him to do. He boarded a large ship to go across the Mediterranean. This ship was most likely built by the Phoenicians. Ships were made of wood, so the Phoenicians had to be expert woodworkers.

There were two types of ships that they built. The first was a short round ship that was used for normal trade from port to port. The second was a long boat, like the one that Jonah took to Tarshish. This long ship was seaworthy and could withstand the storms at sea. While Solomon was king, he used the seafaring skills of the Phoenicians rather than developing his own navy.

Some of the skill of the Phoenician carpenters must have been brought to the Israelites when the carpenters came to work on the Temple. The people of Judea must have learned some of the skill of the Phoenicians as they built boats from which they could fish in the waters of Lake Galilee. Shipbuilding never became a major occupation among the people of Israel.

But the Israeites developed enough skill in carpentry to use the skill in necessary building projects for generations to come. The skills that were learned then are still being used today. They are used in building construction. Similar to Solomon's Temple, the beams were placed from wall to wall. On these beams were placed mats that served to roof the building. After the Romans came to Palestine, some buildings had curved roofs, which replaced the flat roofs. For these building tasks, the carpenter had to work at the construction site. Carpenters do the same thing today.

One of the most important types of carpentry was making farm equipment. This work was done in the carpenter's shop, which was usually near his home. Shovels were needed for digging in the rocky ground. Ploughs were made with wood and a metal piece at the bottom to furrow the rough ground. Hoes had wooden handles and a metal piece at the bottom also. Yokes for oxen were made of wood and constructed by the carpenter. An old tradition suggests that Jesus' work as a carpenter was making ploughs and yokes. Another tradition suggests that Jesus was present in the rebuilding of one of the Roman cities near Galilee. While helping to rebuild the city, Jesus would have come into contact with Gentiles, or non-Jews.

In his shop, the carpenter also made furniture. He exercised his carpentry skill in doing these projects. Building chests for storing things in the home was a task of the carpenter. Other furniture included tables, chairs, and stools. Window lattices, doors, and doorframes allowed the carpenter to show off his skill in making a home attractive. Wooden locks and keys were other projects that the carpenter would have done in the home. The royal carpenters, who served the king, also showed their skill by making bed frames that were inlaid with ivory.

Musical instruments had parts that required a lot of skill. The carpenter had to shape the instrument in a manner so that the musician could strike the correct note by blowing through the instrument. They also made harps and other instruments. Isaiah 44:13 tells us that some carpenters foolishly made idols of wood. The idols displeased God.

Perhaps the most amazing thing about the carpenter was the primitive tools that he used. A piece of metal was attached to a handle by leather thongs to form an axe. It was dangerous, since the head would sometimes come off. A saw was a metal blade with rough teeth along the cutting edge. Metal chisels and awls were used. A hammer consisted of a piece of stone that was attached to a wooden handle like a mallet. A drill was a piece of metal that was turned by a bow. The carpenter also had a primitive plane to smooth rough wooden edges.

In addition to the tools, the carpenter used a measuring line. He could obtain measurements for his building requirements using this line. He also had a stylus that made a circle. He used a pencil to mark the wood. This is similar to the way a carpenter makes a circle today. In spite of the primitive tools, the carpenter was able to create some very excellent work.

The Metalworkers

Metalwork in Palestine was not native to the Israelites. Metalworking was a very early occupation in the Middle East. In Genesis 4:22, Tubal-Cain was described as a forger of metals. Although iron was known to the Israelites, the Philistines kept the Israelites from forging iron or even sharpening iron axe heads, mattocks, blades for the ploughs, or sickles. Up until Kings David and Solomon, very little metallurgy was done among the Israelites. King Solomon got Huram of Tyre, a worker in bronze, for the metalwork to be done on the Temple (see 1 Kings 7:13–14). Later, King Joash hired workers in bronze and iron to repair the Temple (see 2 Chronicles 24:12). There is also a description that Israelite smiths were carried into exile in Babylon (see 2 Kings 24:14).

To use a metal, the ore had to first be mined or taken out of the earth. This did not require any skill. Slaves and conquered peoples were used to mine the ore. Gold and silver were easily found and mined and were used for jewelry, gold thread, and overlays for wood and other metals.

Copper was more difficult to mine. It was discovered that if some tin were added to the copper, bronze was produced. Bronze had the advantage of being a harder metal and was useful for making shields, doors, and armor. Bronze was also used in the Temple for pots, basins, shovels, and the great molten sea (see 1 Kings 7:23–25).

Iron had the advantage of being even harder than bronze. Iron was plentiful and useful for making nails, bolts, spearheads, axe heads, and heads of hoes.

After the metal was mined, it had to be smelted. Smelting was a process of separating the slag, or waste, from the metal. The slag was poured off and left. There are large deposits of slag today where smelting was done in Bible times. To smelt the metal, it was heated to a high temperature so that the metal became liquid. The metal then hardened into blocks, called ingots. The ingots were sent to the refiner for refining and molding into useful objects, such as shields or hoes.

During the reign of Solomon, smelting copper and iron was done near Ezion-geber. This city was located on the Gulf of Aqaba. Strong winds blew constantly in Ezion-geber. The winds kept the smelting fires burning at high temperatures (see 1 Kings 7:45–46).

Copper was mined in the south of Palestine. It was smelted near the place where it was mined. But to smelt the copper, acacia wood was necessary to keep the fires burning. When the acacia wood supply was used up, the industry did not survive. Copper was not mined in that area again until the Romans came. They had other sources of fuel to smelt the copper.

Metal was refined or purified by heating the ingot and removing more of the impurities. The refiner would then mold the metal into the shape needed. Molding the metal was the last step. Pouring the hot liquid metal into a mold that was made of stone or clay made the cast. If the object to be made were a gold ring, the liquid gold would be poured into a mold. After it hardened, the refiner would take a hammer and break the mold. The ring would be filed and polished to bring out its beauty.

It was more difficult to smelt and refine iron. Iron had to be heated and hammered on an anvil or large piece of metal. The Philistines kept this process secret until David and Solomon defeated them.

The prophets compared the process of smelting and refining to God's purifying Israel (see Zechariah 13:9 and Daniel 11:35).

THE WEAVERS AND TANNERS

Cloth Makers

Cloth making comes from a very ancient period. After Adam and Eve sinned in the Garden of Eden, they had to find clothing (see Genesis 3:7, 21). They first used fig leaves, but those would not last, and God gave them skins to clothe themselves. From that time on, it was necessary to make clothes. It was not possible to go to a clothing or department store. The clothes had to be made by hand.

In the earliest days, the task was the responsibility of the woman of the household. Most clothing was made of wool or linen. Wool came from the coat of the sheep. Linen cloth came from the flax plant. Cotton was not used in Palestine until the time of the prophets. The process the Israelite women used was similar to the way cloth was made in the colonial days of America. You can see these processes in places like Williamsburg, Virginia, or Sturbridge Village, Massachusetts. Women did most of this work in colonial America as well.

To make the cloth, the wool or flax had to be cleaned. This process was known as fullering. Hot water was used to wash the strands. The material was laid out in the sun to be bleached and was beaten to pull out the fibers. Finally, the fibers were combed and carded, or pulled into fine strands, to remove any extra material that was not needed. As the textile industry grew, men got into large vats to carry out this process. There is mention of the "Washerman's Field" in Isaiah 7:3. After the fuller's task became more specialized, the material was boiled in a strong, bad-smelling alkaline solution. When women were responsible for this process at home in the early days, dyeing was very primitive. In later days, a man made this his occupation. A mixture of potash, lime, and water was poured into large clay pots. Both animal skins and fibers were dyed. After the fibers or animal skins were boiled for two days, the dye was added to color the material. Eggs of insects and vegetable leaves were crushed into powder and used to make scarlet dye. Yellow dye came from safflower. Murex shells from the sea were crushed to a powder and cooked in salt to make a purple dye. This color was very expensive to make, and royalty used purple as a sign of their power. Lydia, in the New Testament, was a businesswoman and a seller of purple (see Acts 16:14). After the process was finished, the material was washed in clean water and set out to dry in the sun.

The Bible does not describe the dyeing process, but there are many references to material that had been colored (see Exodus 25:4; Esther 8:15; and Numbers 15:38). Archaeologists are persons who dig up the ruins from the past. In Palestine, they have discovered many places where both the fuller and dyeing industries took place. The large vats and earthenware storage jars for potash and lime have been discovered.

Spinning was the process of twisting the threads of flax or wool together to make thread or yarn. In the Middle East, a spindle was a stick with a hook on one end. As the woman turned the spindle, the strands would be twisted together to make thread or yarn. In colonial America, the spinning wheel was used to do this same process with wool or cotton.

Weaving was done to make the cloth. A loom was used for this process. At first the size of the loom was small. A woman would make the cloth only as large as she could reach. Later, large looms were used to weave the cloth. Goliath's spear is described as a weaver's rod in 1 Samuel 17:7. The shuttle would go over one thread and under the next. Then it would be returned, and the same process would be used with the next thread—over and under.

The same process is used in weaving a pot holder on a small loom. Yarn or cloth is stretched across the loom. Then the yarn or cloth is inserted above one strand and below the next to cross the original strands. This process continues until the loom is full. Then the yarn or cloth is tied, and the pot holder is complete.

From the cloth created on the loom, clothes were made. For men working in the fields, a simple loincloth was worn from the waist across the upper part of the leg. If it were an animal skin, it served as sackcloth. Both men and women wore a tunic. This was a garment that looked like a large shirt. It was made of wool or linen. Clothing was very important in the days of the Old Testament. Samson promised thirty linen wraps and thirty changes of clothes to the one who guessed his riddle (see Judges 14:12). Wealth could be seen in the kinds of clothes that a person wore. The robes worn by royalty were decorated in purple, distinguishing them from the rest of the people.

Leather Tanners and Tent Makers

Leather was an important product to persons in the Middle Eastern world. Leather was used for belts, shoes, water bottles, shields, and slings. Leatherwork involved the use of animal skins. Therefore, it was similar to the work of the fuller or the dyer of cloth. It smelled just as bad as the fuller's work. The skins were boiled and soaked for a long period of time in chemicals and dog manure. The purpose of this process was to remove the hair from the animal's skin. The tanner then rubbed and hammered the skin until the hair was removed. Goatskins made better shoes than sheepskins. But sheepskins were used when goatskins were not available.

The tanner would also dye the skins, similar to the cloth dyer. For shoes, the colors red and yellow were preferred. Remember how terrible the smell of the dyeing cloth was. The same was true for the dyeing of animal skins for the making of leather.

In the Middle East the sun is very hot. To prevent becoming dehydrated (suffering from loss of water), the people of Palestine carried water with them. Goatskins made good water flasks. The tanner would take the entire goatskin and place it on the ground before he began the process of tanning the leather. He would sew the openings for the legs and tail closed. The opening at the neck provided an opening for the water. After the skin was tanned and dyed, a cork was put in the neck of the water flask, and it was ready for use. Leather water flasks are still used in countries like Palestine.

The tanner is mentioned in the Book of Acts. The apostle Peter went to the home of Simon the Tanner in Joppa. While Peter was there praying and seeing the vision of God, messengers came from Cornelius, the Roman centurion (see Acts 10:1–23). The men had no trouble finding Simon the Tanner's home. They could smell his house long before they arrived. Archaeologists have found evidence of tanners in the city of Hebron and Jaffa (the present name for the city that was Joppa in the New Testament).

Related to the leather tanner was the tent maker. The tent maker was also a tanner of animal skins. Tents were important to people in Palestine. In Bible times, as well as today, many people lived in tents in the Middle East. For safety, the tents for a family group would be clustered together. Skilled tentmakers were in demand. They would tan and dye the skins. Then they would cut the skins and sew them together to form the tent.

Paul, the apostle, was a tent maker (see Acts 18:3). A married couple, Priscilla and Aquila, met Paul in Corinth. Since they were all tent makers, Paul stayed with them.

Stonemasons and Bricklayers

When the Hebrew people were in slavery in Egypt, they learned how to make bricks. In fact, their most important work was brick making. The bricks were made of clay. The men would add water and tread on the clay until it was soaked to the right level. To this they would add straw. When the bricks dried, the straw would make the bricks stronger (see Exodus 1:13–14).

Remember that the people of Israel left Egypt on the night of the Passover. God brought them into the wilderness journey through the desert lands. There they stayed for forty years. Only Joshua and Caleb went into the Promised Land of Palestine. Joshua led the Israelites against the people of Jericho. Following God's instruction, they marched around the city, and the walls tumbled down. That happened in other cities as well. The people were very successful at knocking down the cities of the Canaanites. But the people of Israel did not know how to rebuild and fortify the cities that they destroyed.

When Solomon was king of Israel, his friendship with the Hiram, king of Tyre (Phoenicia), helped him to learn about many of the skills that Hebrew tradesmen needed. Stonemasons were very much needed to work on Solomon's building projects. With the help of the skilled craftsmen from Phoenicia, the building projects of Solomon were completed. Solomon compelled thirty thousand Israelites to work in the quarries and to transport stone from Lebanon to build his projects. In addition, he had seventy thousand transporters of stone, eighty thousand cutters of stone, and thirty-three hundred supervisors. The Temple, the palace for his wife from Egypt, and his own palace were built from stone (see 1 Kings 5:13–18 and 7:1–12).

Stone was not used for building homes. Bricks, made from clay and straw, were used for homes of the local people. Stone was used for building the Temple, public buildings, the palace of the king, city walls, tombs carved out of the rock, and for aqueducts to carry water. It was often quarried. Limestone had the advantage of being soft when it was in the ground. It could be quarried and cut to size and shape. When it was brought out of the ground and hit the air, it would harden.

The stonecutters were able to cut so exactly that they did not need to use mortar between the stones to hold them in place. They fit perfectly together. Windows were not usually included in the buildings because they were difficult to place. Without mortar or cement, the stones could not have gaps that the windows required.

The stonemason worked with a trowel, measuring string, plumb line, and a wood square. A plumb line is a cord that has a weight attached to the bottom. It is dropped from the top of a wall to make sure the wall is straight. A stonemason also used chisels to cut the rock to the right size. Skilled stonemasons were most often employed by the king. In Amos 7:7–8, God told the prophet He would use the plumb line to compare the people of Israel with God's laws. God said that the people did not measure up. If they had been a wall, the wall would have been crooked.

Religious Occupations

Religious occupations were a little different from the ones we have looked at in the previous pages. Back at the time of entrance into the Promised Land, the priests and Levites were not given land. They were to make their living from the offerings given by the people from the other tribes. The occupations of priest and Levite were passed down from family to family. The religious groups of the Pharisees, Sadducees, Essenes, and Zealots were voluntary. The people who belonged to these groups were not forced to join but wanted to belong.

PROFESSIONAL RELIGIOUS OCCUPATIONS

The Priests

Priests were responsible for the public worship in ancient Israel. They served in the Tabernacle and later in the Temple. They spoke the Word of the Lord to the people and brought the needs of the people to God.

In the days of Abraham, Isaac, and Jacob, the head of the family served as the priest. He would sacrifice for the sins of his family. He would lead the worship of God for his family.

At the time of Moses that practice changed. Aaron, Moses' brother, was set apart to be a priest. From his family line came the priests for future service in Israel. He and his sons were sanctified, or set apart from the rest of the people to serve God (see Exodus 29:9, 30–37). The priests lived in forty-eight cities throughout Israel. They were supported by the gifts, offerings, and donations of the people.

They had the responsibility to help the people know what was clean and what was unclean. They helped the people to understand what was holy and what was not. They taught the people to obey God and His Laws (see Leviticus 10:8–11). They gave the people the blessing of God. They also served as judges to assure that justice was given to the people of Israel (see Deuteronomy 17:8–13).

They represented God to the people. The priests wore a traditional white robe. The priests were the only ones allowed to touch the holy furniture in the tabernacle and later in the Temple.

Sacrifice was an important part of their task. Each sacrifice resulted in the death of a perfect animal. This may have seemed unfair, but God wanted His people to know that sin can only be atoned for by death. God hates sin. He will not allow it. Each sacrifice showed the people that the penalty for sin is death (see Ezekiel 18:20).

Sadly, the priests did not always keep God's Law themselves. Some of them worshiped idols. Others sinned in other ways, breaking God's Law (see Ezekiel 22:26). The people of Israel lost respect for the priests. The people looked to others for their spiritual welfare. They respected the scribes and the Pharisees. We will talk about them later in this section.

Malachi, God's last prophet at the end of the Old Testament, told the people that God's judgment was coming. God would destroy the Temple, and the priesthood would end. But some of the priests were godly men, like Zechariah, father of John the Baptist.

When Jesus came, the priests opposed Him. The Bible tells us that Jesus became the only One who stands between us and God. Through Jesus' death on the cross, Jesus became our sacrifice for sin. We no longer have to sacrifice animals for our sin as the ancient Israelites did. God provided a sacrifice for us in His own Son, Jesus Christ. Then God raised Jesus from the dead, and Jesus became our Priest to God. We have access to God through Jesus. We simply have to pray to reach God.

The High Priest

The office of the high priest was very special. Aaron was the first high priest. The line passed on to the firstborn son. The high priest was the religious ruler of the people. He was also head of the priests.

To install the priest took a period of seven days. During that time the high priest was set apart to his task of service to the Lord. This took place in the Tabernacle first and later in the Temple. His office lasted for his entire life. He had to keep himself pure and holy to God.

He wore the white robe of the priest, and over it was a blue robe with fringe. There were bells and pomegranates attached. Covering his chest was the breastplate that had twelve stones, one stone for each of the tribes of Israel. On his head he wore a turban with a golden rosette stone in the middle. Written on the turban were these words, "Holy to the LORD" (Exodus 28:36).

The most important task for the high priest was to enter the Holy of Holies in the inner part of the Tabernacle, and later the Temple, each year. On the Day of Atonement, the high priest would take the blood of the goat that was sacrificed for his sins and the sins of all the people of Israel. He would sprinkle the blood in front of the curtain of the sanctuary to atone for sin (see Leviticus 4:3–21).

When David became king, he appointed Zadok to become the high priest in Gibeon (see 1 Chronicles 16:39). Zadok was in the line of Aaron. He crowned Solomon as the next king of Israel (see 1 Kings 1:33–34). Solomon had Zadok installed as high priest in the new Temple. Those who came after Zadok continued to serve as high priest in the Temple until the Jews were taken into captivity in Babylon (see 1 Chronicles 6:1–15).

After the captivity, the line of Zadok continued to be the high priests. Zadok's line finally came to an end. The Syrian king, Antiochus, removed Zadok's line of high priests. He placed his own man as high priest. When Herod the Great came to power, he did the same thing. Later, the Romans followed the same pattern. They installed a person of their choosing as high priest. Caiaphas was appointed by the Roman government. He served as high priest at the trial of Jesus.

After Jesus, there was no longer any need for a high priest. Jesus became our High Priest. Jesus is an eternal Priest. He ministers in heaven itself (see Hebrews 4:14 and 9:11).

Levites

Recall when the Israelites were standing before Mount Sinai. God handed down the tablets of stone on which He had written the Ten Commandments to Moses. But during the forty days that Moses was in the mountain, the people sinned against God. They collected gold, and Aaron helped them make a golden calf idol to worship. When Moses came down from the mountain, he was angry. He broke the tablets of stone and called for those who would stand on God's side to come forward. Only the family of Levi came forward. Even though they had participated in making the idol, they were sorry for what they had done and came to serve God. They did as Moses told them. Moses went back up into the mountain to ask for forgiveness for the people (see Exodus 32:26–28).

God honored the Levites by giving them the responsibility to care for the Tabernacle. They were set apart in a service of dedication. They replaced the need for each firstborn male family member to serve in the Tabernacle (see Numbers 3:12–13, 41). The Levites would begin their service at age twenty-five and continue until age fifty, when they would retire (see Numbers 8:23–26). They were not given an inheritance in the land. They were spread throughout the land of Palestine in the forty-eight designated cities.

During the time of the wilderness wandering, the Levites were assigned to take down the Tabernacle and to transport it to the next location. They also put up the Tabernacle at its new site (see Numbers 1:50–53). The Levites had the responsibility to take care of the furniture in the Tabernacle (see Numbers 3:6–9). Careful instructions were given about the care of the furnishings of the Tabernacle (see Numbers 4:1–33). They also did the baking for the Table of Shewbread.

When King David worked with the Levites, he assigned them four major responsibilities in keeping with what God had commanded of Moses (see 1 Chronicles 24–26 and specifially 23:4–5).

The first responsibility was to care for the Tabernacle, and later the Temple, of the Lord. The Levites were to assist the priests in their service in God's house. They helped the priests with the sacrifices and the rituals. They assisted the worshipers.

A second responsibility was to serve as judges and officials. Many of the Levites studied and became scribes. (See the section that describes the scribes below.) Many served as judges of the Law. They helped the people by interpreting the Law of God and helping them to worship.

The third responsibility was to serve as gatekeepers and keepers of the treasury. When treasure was taken from war, the Levites were responsible to care for the money. They used it to repair the House of the Lord.

Finally, their fourth responsibility was to care for the music of worship. They provided a choir and instruments for the daily services in the House of the Lord. They had trumpeters, players of cymbals, lyres, and harps. They also provided a choir for the worship service. The Levites wrote and sang psalms. Psalm 118 is a good example. The people would respond, "His love endures forever." The Levites who participated in the music were also responsible for music at the many festivals in the House of the Lord.

Prophets

The prophets were a group of people who received a message from God to deliver to His people. Prophecy was not like the priesthood. It was not passed from father to son. God chose the prophet and spoke through the prophet. Some prophets were called for a lifetime, such as Jeremiah (see Jeremiah 1:5). Others were called for a period of time. Prophets came from all walks of life. Amos was a herdsman from Tekoa. Ezekiel came from among the priests.

Authority for the message of the prophet came directly from God (see Ezekiel 7:1). Some prophets were threatened (see Jeremiah 1:7–8). Others did some strange things to gain the attention of the people. Ezekiel lay on his left side three hundred ninety days. He then lay on his right side for forty days.

God called the prophet. The prophet's only authority was based on God's call. The way people could be sure God's message came from the prophet was the test of whether the prophecy came true (see Deuteronomy 18:20–22).

The purpose of the prophet's message to the people was to tell the people they had disobeyed God. They had broken God's Law. God would punish His people if they did not repent and turn away from their sin. It was not a popular message, and many prophets were hurt because they said things the people did not want to hear. The false prophets would say that God promised good things to His people. In saying this, the false prophets would ignore the punishment promised.

There were some mighty prophets. Picture the scene of Elijah on Mount Carmel with all the prophets of Baal (see 1 Kings 18:20–40). Elijah had called the people of Israel and the prophets of Baal together to see if the false God Baal or Jehovah God was more powerful. Elijah also wanted to prove this to King Ahab. Elijah stood alone as the prophet of God. Baal had four hundred fifty prophets to help his cause. Elijah called the people to turn from their idolatry and turn to God, but the people did not answer Elijah.

Elijah then told the people to bring two oxen to sacrifice. The prophets of Baal put one ox on their altar. The other one was placed on the altar dedicated to the Lord God. They agreed not to place any fire under either sacrifice. The test would be to see whose God was the true God. The true God would rain fire from heaven and consume the sacrifice. The people and the prophets of Baal agreed.

The prophets of Baal went first. From morning until noon the prophets of Baal called on their god to burn the sacrifice. Nothing happened. At noon Elijah started to make fun of the prophets of Baal. He told them to call louder. Maybe their god was asleep. So the prophets of Baal called louder and began to cut themselves. Still nothing happened. They carried on until nightfall.

By nightfall, Elijah called the people of Israel to his altar. He took twelve stones, one for each of the tribes of Israel. He built the altar and dug a large trench around the altar. Then he placed the wood on the altar. On top of the wood, Elijah placed the sacrifice. He told the people to pour water on the sacrifice and the altar. They did it three times. The large trench that he had dug was now filled with water, and the sacrifice and wood were wet.

When this was done, Elijah prayed. He said to God, "You are the true God of Israel. I have done this at Your word. Now hear me. Answer me. Send your fire on this sacrifice that the people may see Your power and turn back to You again."

At that exact moment the fire fell from heaven. It consumed the sacrifice. It burned the wood and the stones. It licked up the water in the trenches.

The people fell on their faces. They said, "The Lord, He is God!"

The prophet's word stood. Elijah was the true prophet. The prophets of Baal were false.

Scribes

The office of the scribe, or secretary, probably started sometime during the reign of the kings (see 2 Samuel 8:17). Scribes controlled who was able to see the king. As time passed, the scribes were a group of persons who could read and write. Many served the king. Others drew up contracts and wrote letters even for people in the towns around Palestine.

During the reign of King Hezekiah, the king chose a group of men to copy records for him. These records lasted long after his reign. Included was the copying of even some of the proverbs that Solomon had written when he was still king (see Proverbs 25:1). Late in the period of the kings, Baruch wrote the prophecies of Jeremiah (see Jeremiah 36:4).

After the people of Judah returned from their seventy years of captivity in Babylonia, the scribes took on a much more important role among the Jews. The scribes became the interpreters of God's Law. Remember that the priests were still working in the Temple, but the priests did not do what was right. Remember the prophecy of Malachi. God would take the responsibility for the Law away from the priests. The scribes became the new interpreters of the Law. Ezra, the scribe, read the Book of the Law to the people after their return from Babylon (see Nehemiah 8:1–3). The people listened carefully to the reading of the Law and renewed their promise to obey God. They developed respect for the scribes as the new teachers of the Law.

Following Ezra, the later scribes became concerned about keeping every point of the Law. They became a new upper class of lawyers, a powerful group in Israel. The scribes were not paid for their work. Perhaps this was to prevent them from taking bribes from the people for their legal decisions. Many of the scribes became judges and sat on the Sanhedrin, the supreme court in Jerusalem.

Some of the priests became scribes. But scribes could come from any occupation. Some were carpenters, masons, or tent makers. Their official interpretation of the Law became as important as the Law itself. The majority of the scribes were also Pharisees. On several occasions the Gospel writers referred to the scribes as the scribes of the Pharisees. (You may read about the Pharisees in the next section).

The education of a scribe was very long. He had to learn about the Law and the interpretation of the Law to prepare him to teach. It also would help him to make good decisions as a judge. His education began after the age of fourteen and continued until he was forty. He could be ordained. Scribes became judges, rabbis, or government leaders. The lengthy teachings of the scribes were finally written down. These writings are known as the Mishnah.

During Jesus' ministry, many of the scribes discussed legal issues with Him. One of those issues involved the great commandment of the Law. Jesus told the scribe that one must love God with all the heart, soul, and mind. This is the first commandment. The second is loving your neighbor as you love yourself. The scribe commended Jesus on His insight. Jesus said that the scribe was not far from the kingdom of God (see Mark 12:28–34).

OTHER RELIGIOUS GROUPS

To help you better understand the Bible and the people of New Testament Palestine, there are four Jewish religious groups about whom you should know. The people in these groups earned their livelihood from some other job, but they were distinguished for their role in the religious community. They are the Pharisees, the Sadducees, the Essenes, and the Zealots. Both the Pharisees and the Essenes were religious groups, and the Pharisees had some political power. The Sadducees and the Zealots were somewhat religious but very political.

The Pharisees

The Pharisees were the best-known religious group in Palestine. During the four hundred years between the Old Testament and the New Testament there were several uprisings. The best known of these was the Maccabean Revolt. This is celebrated at the Feast of Hannukah. (You may read about that in the next section, under the Jewish holidays). As a result of the Maccabees, the Jewish people gained their independence and fought off the Syrians. The Pharisees came into being about that time. Originally they were a group of men who lived godly lives.

The Pharisees worked hard to keep every letter of the Law of God given by Moses. They were careful to follow the Law of God. Recall that the scribes were a group of lawyers who carefully interpreted the Law. Remember that many of the scribes came from the party of the Pharisees. In the Gospels, the writers often said, "the scribes and the Pharisees." They were closely united. The Pharisees followed the strict interpretation of the Law. They kept the traditions of the elders. They followed the oral as

well as the written Law. For example, they were careful to observe the Sabbath (see Mark 2:24), to wear the phylacteries and fringes on the prayer cloth (see Matthew 23:5), to tithe, and to perform acts of ritual purity (see Matthew 23:16–19). Tithing and purifying were particularly observed by the Pharisees. The Pharisees also believed in the resurrection and in heaven and hell.

The Pharisees limited their contact with the Gentiles and even other Jews in order not to become unclean. They were common people, but most people respected them for their religious practice. Many of the Pharisees participated on the Sanhedrin, the high court of the Jews. This was an important religious and political group in the New Testament.

In the Gospels, the Pharisees are frequently mentioned. Some were opposed to Jesus' ministry. Jesus condemned many of the Pharisees because their personal pride put their emphasis on being religious for the people, not for God (see Matthew 23).

The Sadducees

The Sadducees are believed to have come from the time of King David. Zadok was the high priest at the time of David (see 2 Samuel 15:24). By the time of Jesus, the Sadducees were wealthy landowners. They were not as zealous as the Pharisees to live according to the Law and the traditions of the elders. They did not follow the oral law or believe in the resurrection. They did not believe in heaven and hell. They only believed in the written Law of Moses.

Many of the priests, particularly the high priest, came from the Sadducees. The priests had been the main interpreters of the Law. But some of the priests had been dishonest in the past. Some took bribes from the people, as did Eli's sons. The people lost respect for the priests. That is why the scribes became the new interpreters of the Law.

The Sadducees opposed Jesus throughout His ministry. They liked to make fun of their opponents, and they tried to embarrass Jesus on several occasions. One of these is recorded in all three Gospels. Because a wife was free to remarry, if she became a widow, they played the game of "What if . . ." with Jesus. They said, "What if a wife was married and her husband died. She remarried. The same thing happened seven times. In the resurrection, whose wife would she be?" Jesus answered that such marriage would not take place in the afterlife. He also criticized the Sadducees for not believing in the resurrection. His words silenced the Sadducees (see Matthew 22:23–33).

The Sadducees played a large role in the crucifixion of Jesus. The trial before the high priest was conducted by the Sadducees (see Mark 14:60–64). They also were responsible for Jesus' condemnation before Pilate (see Mark 15:1–10). Not only did the Sadducees oppose Jesus; they also opposed the early church (see Acts 4:1–3).

The Essenes

The Essenes were a group that had a similar origin to the Pharisees. Like the Pharisees, the Essenes were careful to keep the Law of Moses. To be a member of the Essenes, one had to sell all of his property and join the community. They shared everything in common. There were Essenes in all of the towns in Palestine. They were especially known for hospitality. An Essene, who was traveling, knew that he would find shelter among other Essenes.

They were also known as healers. The word seems to have an origin that is related to the Aramaic word for healing. Even though they were careful to keep the Law, they worshiped God in their own communities and did not go to the Temple. Their practices were similar to the New Testament description of John the Baptist. After the establishment of the church, many of the practices of the Essenes may be found in the practices of the early church.

Many of their practices have been found in the discovery of the *Book of Discipline*. The *Book of Discipline* was a book of instructions for the people of a community next to the Dead Sea. This was believed to be an Essene community. The community was in existence for four hundred years before the beginning of the New Testament church.

The *Book of Discipline* told about the way of life of the people in the community. It was discovered among the Dead Sea Scrolls in 1947. A shepherd boy threw a stone into a cave and heard something that sounded like a clink on a piece of pottery. Going through the small entrance, he was unhappy to find rows of old jars. He told about his discovery, and that led to finding the Dead Sea scrolls that had been there for more than two thousand years. Along with the *Book of Discipline*, some of the oldest manuscripts of the Bible were found—Isaiah, Deuteronomy, and many of the psalms. These are the oldest copies of these books of the Bible that we now have. Along with them, other books were also found.

The Zealots

The last of these groups were those who defended Judaism against the foreign Roman invaders. Simon the Zealot was one of Jesus' twelve apostles (see Luke 6:15). The Zealots wanted to get rid of all foreign armies in their land. They were willing to give their lives to defend the honor of the Lord and used military tactics to carry out this purpose. Similar to the Pharisees, the Zealots were jealous to keep the people of Israel pure and to keep the Law. They opposed paying taxes to a foreign power, such as Herod or Rome.

In the later years they became a group who carried daggers. Whenever they had the opportunity, they would kill a Roman soldier. They helped to cause the war that resulted in the destruction of the Temple in AD 70. Their last stand took place on Masada, a large fortress mountain. It took the Roman army two years to build a causeway to conquer the people at Masada. When the Romans made it onto Masada in AD 73, the Zealots had all killed themselves rather than be taken by the Romans.

Religious Practices of Jews and Christians

INTRODUCTION FOR PARENTS AND TEACHERS

Christian faith rests upon a foundation of specific events that were initiated by God to bring our redemption. These events happened at particular times in history. Taken together they form the heritage of our faith. We celebrate these events of God's love in salvation history through worship and annual commemoration each year.

In response to the love of God in giving us salvation, we express our reverent love, devotion, and adoration to God in worship. Worship is the most important activity that we can render to God. God deserves our worship. The Christian calendar gives honor to God for His gracious activity in sending His Son to earth to conquer sin and death and to give salvation to believers in His church. Worship takes place on each of the three great holidays of the Christian year—Christmas, Easter, and Pentecost. It also takes place each week on the Lord's Day, especially as we remember the resurrection of Jesus Christ. Through that one event, God defeated sin and death and purchased our salvation for all eternity.

Worship is both individual and corporate. Christians pray and study God's Word in the privacy of their own homes. Together, we gather in church to share in the preaching of the Word, in prayer, in thanksgiving, and by singing praise to God expressed through the great hymns of the faith and popular choruses of praise.

Worship focuses upon particular times of the day, week, and year, such as personal devotions each day or weekly church services. Worship takes place in definite places, such as one's home or a church building. Worship looks backward through the events of redemption history to God's intervention on our behalf. Worship looks forward to our future hope of what God will do in us and through His church throughout the world.

The Jews preceded us in worship and thanksgiving for God's faithful love through weekly and yearly observances on Sabbath and the annual festivals. The Jewish holidays are particularly instructive. In Deuteronomy 6 God commanded the remembrance of the great events in order that the people would not forget how the Lord had delivered them. In Psalm 78 there is another reference to remembering the graciousness of God to avoid the sins of the past.

The effectiveness of this approach may be observed in Jewish history. The Jews did not succumb to the betrayal by Haman in Persia or more recently to the horrors of the Holocaust of Hitler. If we expect our children to survive into the coming generations as Christians in a pagan world, we will need to do a better job of teaching them the content and history of our Christian faith.

We live in a culture in which history is shunned. The only time that seems to be important to this present generation is the here and now. But that was not characteristic of the Jewish faith, nor can it be true in the future for the Christian faith. It is evident that God views time, place, redemptive history, and our future hope as important. As a result, we need to perceive time, place, and history as important also. The Jewish calendar of annual celebrations is oriented toward the annual harvests and agriculture. Additional ceremonies are held for Passover and the Day of Atonement. Some examples follow.

Creation, the stories of Adam and Eve, and other events from the Old Testament occurred at specific points in time. After Abraham, many of the events that are described in the Old Testament were remembered through the establishment of a holiday to celebrate that event. After Abraham, the importance of place—the Holy Land—assumed great significance for Jews and continues to captivate worldwide attention even today.

Shabbat, or Sabbath, is a weekly observance for the Jews that recalls God's creation of the world. On the seventh day, God rested. Sabbath observance allows Jews to recall the creation event each week.

Passover is the commemoration of the flight from Egypt under the leadership of Moses. This was the time when God acted on behalf of His people, who were suffering under the cruel hand of Pharaoh. God's chosen people were to sacrifice a lamb and place the blood on the lintel of the doorpost. When the angel of death saw the blood on the post, he would pass by that home. For the Egyptians, the firstborn of every living thing was killed. After the angel passed over, the people of Israel left Egypt and wandered in the wilderness for the next forty years. Then God guided them to establish their home in a particular place that He had promised, the land of Palestine.

For children from Christian families, the celebration of these events can bring life to Old Testament events. We can come to a better understanding of how God acted in times past. The Passover Seder is a good example. As a family or among your students, you may obtain a copy of the Passover Seder from a Christian perspective. Consult various resources for some examples of these materials. The Seder will enrich the understanding of your children and provide a fresh insight for adults into the goodness of God in our history. It will provide us with a fuller appreciation of God's love and mercy.

Christians today have a tendency to overlook many of the Old Testament events and circumstances. But without the Old Testament, we cannot fully understand the New Testament. It builds upon the rich heritage and understanding that comes from the Old Testament teachings. Even though the Jewish festivals may seem foreign to us, they can help us to visualize some of the significant redemptive truths that come to life in the New Testament.

As Christians, we have our own holidays to celebrate. The redemptive work of Jesus Christ is at the heart of the observances that we keep. Each of the Christian holidays has a rich and colorful history that keeps us in touch with the life and ministry of our Lord. Even the Lord's Day observance on Sunday is related to the resurrection of Jesus.

In a culture that tries to ignore history, we need to help our children develop a sense of time, place, redemptive history, and our future hope. To be sure, first and second graders will have difficulty with the concepts of historical sequence. Time lines and historical events will not seem to take on the same meaning that will occur by the time your child becomes a third grader. Even then, historical sequence is only beginning to take shape. But it is important for the child to develop such an understanding. It can be deepened and enriched in future grades.

In this section we will examine the religious practices in worship and the celebration of the weekly and yearly holidays of the Jewish people. These will be instructive to us in the ways that God desired His people to worship Him. Reenactment of some of the Jewish holidays will help our children to know and understand these significant events. The Christian holidays of both Easter and Pentecost are built upon their Old Testament counterparts.

Then we will turn our attention to worship for Christians and the observance of Christian holidays. Our culture has obscured the Christian significance of Christmas and Easter with secular and non-Christian observances. We need to help our children to reclaim their rightful Christian heritage and not be captivated by the temporal allurements of our society. More positively, our instruction will help our children appreciate the great redemptive events that we remember at these holidays. We need to help our children have a new appreciation for Sunday Lord's Day observance and not have it taken away by professional sports, shopping, or other worldly pursuits. Lastly, we will glimpse our future hope to be with God eternally.

Religious Practices

Knowing and understanding God's Word is important to the Christian faith. We looked at the stories from the Old Testament and New Testament that led us to learn about Jesus. We saw the church grow from the preaching of Paul throughout the Roman world. We also looked at the geography of the Holy Land and life in Bible times.

We turn our attention next to the Christian practices that make us distinctive from other religious groups. Worship is the most important thing that a Christian can give to God. Worship begins with loving God with all of our hearts. We express that love through prayer and studying God's Word.

God entered our world in Christ. Time is very important to God. The apostle Paul wrote, "But when the time had fully come, God sent his Son, born of a woman, born under law, to redeem those under law, that we might receive the full rights of sons" (Galatians 4:4–5). That means that God loved us enough to send Jesus to bring us back to Himself and make us part of God's family, if we put our trust in Jesus.

God's redeeming love is expressed in time and in particular places. God's promise to Abraham in the Old Testament was that the Hebrew people would come to the land of Palestine and possess it forever. Within that place, the tabernacle and later the Temple were places where God met His people. While, as Christians, we do not worship in the Temple, we do have specific places where we also meet God. It may be in the privacy of our own homes. It also takes place in church.

Looking over redemptive history, we can see that God used specific times and places to develop His relationship with His people—first the Hebrew people and now His church. History is really His story. We study redemptive history to discover what God has done in the past. Our hope for the future is built upon what God has done in the past.

Finally, we come to our future hope. God is not done with us. Just as He raised Jesus Christ from the dead, He will one day bring us to resurrection to live forever with Him. This is our hope. We see what He did in the past, and we can put our trust in Him for the future.

In this section we will examine God's work with people in the past. We will look first at the worship of Jewish people to give us some clues about Christian worship. We will identify some of the Jewish holidays and their importance for us as Christian believers. As you look at the Jewish holidays, remember that they were built around the farming harvests—the raising of barley, wheat, grapes, and other crops.

We will turn next to Christian worship and Christian holidays. How did we come to our worship in Christian churches? Why do we celebrate three major holidays—Christmas, Easter, and Pentecost? What is the history behind them? Christian holidays have a different purpose. Christian holidays are built around the life and ministry of Jesus Christ. He is the One who provides salvation for us and eternal life with God. Finally, we will look at our future Christian hope. This gives life special meaning.

THE SABBATH

In the ancient Jewish writings of the *Torah*, God promised that if the Jewish people would keep the laws, then He would give them a taste of the world to come. That experience is practiced on the Sabbath. It is a day of peace and quiet and occurs at the end of each week on the seventh day.

No work is done on the Sabbath. Many people do not like the laws against work on the Sabbath, but in continuing to work, they miss the beauty of rest to begin a new week of activity. The usual greeting on Sabbath carries the idea. It is *"Shabbat shalom."* That means, "May you have a Sabbath of peace."

How the Sabbath Was Celebrated in the Old Testament

No one knows when the Sabbath was first celebrated. It is the oldest Jewish holiday. It has been a precious treasure for Jewish people for several thousand years.

Observing the Sabbath was the only celebration that was commanded in the Ten Commandments. God told the people they could work six days each week, but the seventh day was set apart from all to rest. For generations it has been the center of Jewish life. It was and is at the heart of a Jewish person's relationship with God. Jews have given the Sabbath a place of honor in their lives and in worship of God.

The Sabbath was set aside to remember the creation of the world. (Read the Creation story from Genesis 1.) It is not necessary to work constantly. People can enjoy God's creation on the Sabbath. By keeping this day, Jewish people pay honor to God. They show that God is in control of the world. They follow His example, resting on the seventh day. (Read the Ten Commandments.)

The Sabbath also helps Jewish people remember that God freed them from slavery in Egypt. (Read the Exodus story.) This day honors God, but it also supports freedom from human slavery to other people. No work is to be done by any member of the household on Sabbath. Even animals are not pushed to work.

The laws about work on the Sabbath are very strict. The laws are intended to help Jewish people rightly keep this day. However, some things that are allowed on the Sabbath are very important, such as the study of the *Torah*, spending time with family and friends, taking a nap, quiet games, and group singing. These are restful activities and are appropriate.

Through history there have been groups of Jewish people who have not kept the Sabbath, and the Jewish faith suffered. In time, people stopped reading the *Torah* and going to the synagogue. They lost their moral courage. They stopped continuing to be Jewish.

When the Sabbath was kept, Jewish people continued in their Jewish traditions. They read and followed the *Torah*. Children grew up practicing their Jewish ways. Beliefs were strengthened. In spite of persecution, Jews maintained their Jewishness.

How the Sabbath Is Celebrated Today

The Sabbath begins when the sun goes down on Friday evening. (Recall that the Jewish day follows the appearance of the moon). It ends when three stars appear in the sky on Saturday night. God told the Israelite people to practice the Sabbath celebration forever (see Exodus 31:17). The Sabbath serves as a model for all other Jewish holidays.

It is a special occasion and Jewish people prepare for the Sabbath as they would prepare for a special guest. They use fine china and dress up. Even though it comes each week, they treat it differently from the other days of the week.

To begin the Sabbath, the woman of the home lights two candles. Out of respect for God, she covers her head. The candles provide light as the daylight fades. Parents call the family to remember

These are Jewish symbols for celebration of the Sabbath—the Sabbath candles and dish.

God's creation of light, and a blessing is said. Then the table is set for the Sabbath evening dinner.

The family leaves home and attends the synagogue service. This service welcomes the Sabbath. There is a lot of singing on this happy occasion. The joyful mood for the Sabbath is set. The service helps to prepare the people to worship God.

After the service, the family returns home. A cup of grape juice is taken. It is called the *kiddush*. This means "holy." Before taking the *kiddush*, a father will bless his wife, and parents will bless their children. The children are encouraged to be like the great Bible persons, such as Joseph. Drinking and eating supports the joy and happiness of the Sabbath. Another blessing over the *kiddush* is recited.

The kiddush cup is used in the celebration of the Sabbath.

Next, the family eats the special bread. It is twisted egg bread specially made for Sabbath. It is called *challah*. A special blessing is also said over the bread.

Following these traditions, the family eats the the Sabbath meal together. After the meal, a prayer of thanksgiving is offered. Moses had instructed the people, after they had eaten and were satisfied, to bless God (see Deuteronomy 8:10). This is done with the prayer of thanksgiving.

During the Sabbath day celebration, the people attend their synagogue. They are required to read from the *Torah*. Prayers are sung. Choirs also may sing. A sermon is presented by the rabbi. On some Sabbath days there may also be special services, such as *bar mitzvah*. (*Bar mitzvah* you will recall is the service that indicates a male child has turned thirteen and has become an adult in his relationship to God. He must perform the responsibilities of an adult in worship. *Bat mitzvah* is a similar service for girls.) The entire Sabbath service usually lasts about three and one-half hours.

The Sabbath ends at nightfall, when three stars are visible in the sky. The family concludes the Sabbath with the *Habdalah* service. *Habdalah* means "separation," or the separation of the Sabbath from the week to come. It may be done in the home and the synagogue. The special *Habdalah* candle is lighted. The *Habdalah* grape juice brings the Sabbath to a close. Along with the candle and the cup, special sweet-smelling spices like cinnamon, cloves, and nutmeg are presented. Other lights in the house are turned off. Only the *Habdalah* candle sheds its light in the house. The family sings together. They wish a blessing for the week to come in drinking the cup and smelling the fragrance of the spices.

What Christians Can Learn

Christians do not worship on the seventh day of the week. We worship on the first day of the week. This is a remembrance of Jesus' resurrection on the first day of the week. While we do not follow the Jewish law, Christians would do well to consider the holiness of God and the need to set Sunday aside for worship and to keep it holy to the Lord. Notice the activities that are encouraged on the Sabbath. Christians could use the same kinds of activities and honor Sunday.

The use of the cup of grape juice, *kiddush*, and the special bread, *challah*, reminds us of the Lord's Supper. We can learn from the celebration of the Sabbath for our own celebration of Sunday as the Lord's Day.

THE TABERNACLE AND THE TEMPLE

The Tabernacle

When Moses was on Mount Sinai, he received instructions from God on how to build a sanctuary for worship. Since the people of Israel were on the move during the wilderness journey, the sanctuary was portable. The Tabernacle was constructed according to the instructions that God gave (see Exodus 25–27). The area of the Tabernacle was enclosed with a curtain that was held up with poles. Upon entering the enclosure, one faced the high altar. Here the priests conducted the daily sacrifice. Behind the altar was a large laver, or basin, for the priests to wash before coming to God. The Tabernacle itself was behind the laver.

The Tabernacle was a temporary building, constructed of pillars that were covered as a tent. During the wilderness wanderings, the glory of God hovered over the tent. This showed that God's presence was with His people. The first room inside had several pieces of furniture. There was a table of shewbread, an incense altar, and the seven-branched lampstand. At the end of the room was another curtain, which led to the inner sanctuary. In the inner sanctuary was the Holy of Holies. Contained in the Holy of Holies was the ark of the covenant.

The ark was a gold-covered box that originally contained the Ten Commandments, Aaron's rod that had budded, and a pot of manna from the wilderness journey. On top of the ark were two cherubim, or angels. These cherubim formed a throne for God, Who was invisible to the people of Israel. The mercy seat was located between the cherubim. The Tabernacle represented the temple in which God dwells in heaven. No one was allowed to go into the Holy of Holies. On the Day of Atonement, the high priest would take the blood of the sacrificed goat to be placed upon the mercy seat as sacrifice for sin for himself and for the people of Israel.

The people were allowed to enter the outer court of the Tabernacle, where they could pray, worship, and make sacrifice to God. Many of the psalms were written to be used to sing praise to God in the outer court.

The Temple

The first Temple was built by Solomon and served the same purpose as the Tabernacle (see 1 Kings 6).

Instead of a temporary dwelling place, it was a permanent dwelling place. God was present in the Temple and dwelt among His people. The arrangement of the Temple was similar to the Tabernacle. The furniture in the Temple was also similar to the Tabernacle. The Temple was much larger than the Tabernacle however. The Temple on earth was believed to be a copy of the heavenly dwelling place of God.

The Temple built by Solomon lasted more than four hundred years. God called the people of Israel to be holy and not to sin, but they disobeyed. The Temple was a symbol of God dwelling with His people, so God allowed the Temple to be destroyed by Nebuchadnezzar, king of Babylon, after Israel's disobedience. The Babylonians took the gold from the Temple back to Babylon. They also took many of the people of Israel into captivity in Babylon for seventy years.

Finally, Persia conquered Babylonia. Cyrus, king of Persia, sent the people of Israel back to their homeland. Cyrus provided money and materials to rebuild the Temple. Many of the original furnishings of the Temple were also returned with the people of Judah.

Then the second temple was built (see Ezra 3:8–13 and 6:13–18). Jewish sacrifice, prayer, and worship took place in the Temple again. This Temple lasted another five hundred years. Just before the birth of Jesus, Herod the Great began to rebuild the Temple because it was in poor condition. It took eighty-five years to finish. In the year AD 70, the Roman army came to Jerusalem and destroyed the Temple.

The only trace of the Temple that remains today is the Western Wall. It is called the Wailing Wall. It remains the most holy place for Jews. It is still the hope of Jews around the world that the Temple will one day be rebuilt. They look forward to worshiping again in the Temple.

With the Temple gone, sacrifice ended. The priests no longer served. There was no longer any need for priests, and they disappeared. Worship and prayer could no longer be conducted in the Temple. Because the Jewish people had been in captivity outside their homeland, they developed the synagogue. The synagogue is the place of worship for Jews all over the world today.

Synagogue

A synagogue is a place of worship and prayer for Jewish persons. The term *synagogue* means "a place of gathering." When the Jewish people were taken into captivity to Babylon, they would choose a building for worship and study. This became known as the synagogue. Synagogues were well established by the time of Jesus. There were many synagogues across the Roman world and in Jerusalem.

With the destruction of the second Temple in AD 70, the synagogue has even been called the Temple. The synagogue has become more important to Jewish life and worship. Recall that an important part of the Temple service included animal sacrifice. Sacrifice meant that the worshiper gave up something of worth to God. The worshiper gave an animal that was perfect, but God's blessing has greater worth than the near perfect animal. The destruction of the Temple meant the sacrifice of animals was no longer possible. Instead of a sacrifice, the people turned to prayer as their offering to God. This could be done in Babylon, Jerusalem, or Rome.

The synagogue is first a "house of prayer." The religious services of Jewish people take place there. Reading from the *Torah*, singing, listening to a sermon, and prayer are all part of the service in the synagogue.

The synagogue also became a "house of study." For children it was a place where they spent time learning from the *Torah*. Later they studied the oral Law and the other Jewish writings. But study was not limited to children and the synagogue became a place of study for adults.

The synagogue was and is a "house of gathering" a social center where Jewish people gather to relate to one another.

The *Torah* scroll has been placed at the center of attention in the synagogue. This placement shows the *Torah* is central to the Jewish faith. It contains the will of God for the Jewish people. The *Torah* has both the history and the laws of the Jewish faith.

There is a pulpit, or platform, that is raised in the front of the synagogue. This is known as the *bimah*. It faces east toward Jerusalem.

The holy ark is a cabinet in the front of the synagogue. It holds the *Torah*. The holy ark represents the ark of the covenant that was part of the Tabernacle in the wilderness and later the Temple. In front of the holy ark is a curtain covering, or veil. The curtain is made of blue, scarlet, and purple linen.

A lamp or eternal light burns continuously over the holy ark. This is a symbol of the light that burned over the Hebrew people while they wandered in the wilderness. It speaks of the eternal presence of God.

Today a Jewish person joins a synagogue by paying dues each year. There is no ruling group over all synagogues. Each synagogue establishes its own rules and calls its own rabbi.

The Rabbi

The rabbi serves as head of the Jewish community. He is the religious leader, teacher, and one who interprets the Jewish law. He also serves as pastor to the congregation, preacher, counselor, and community leader.

His ordination gives him the responsibility to conduct the Jewish rites. He performs circumcision (recall, that is a rite performed eight days after a Jewish boy is born) and conducts the ceremony for naming a baby. He performs weddings and funerals, and teaches children and adults in the Jewish faith.

After the destruction of the second temple in AD 70, the rabbi replaced the priest as the religious leader among the Jewish congregation. He is a person who has studied Jewish law and practice. He essentially serves as a pastor.

The Cantor

The Cantor, or *hazzan*, serves in a synagogue. He is usually one who is trained in music. He has a good voice and is responsible for leading the congregation in chants of worship. He also leads in singing prayers. His task is to inspire the members of the congregation through music and to bring them closer to God.

Jewish Practices

There are far too many Jewish practices for us to study all of them. However, there are some that would help us better understand Jewish faith and practice. We will look at these more closely.

THE JEWISH NEW YEAR

The Jewish name for the Jewish New Year is *Rosh Hashanah*. It means "head of the year." It is celebrated very differently from our New Year. It is a solemn two-day holiday. We celebrate on January 1 each year with loud parties and fireworks. The Jewish New Year means a returning to God. People wear white clothing to symbolize their purity.

The two-day celebration starts a period that lasts for the next ten days known as the Days of Awe. These days lead to the holiest day of the Jewish year, the Day of Atonement. During the Days of Awe, Jewish people think back over their past year. They try to discover those things that have hurt their relationship with God and with other persons. They ask God for forgiveness. They also seek forgiveness of persons whom they have wronged during the last year.

Celebration in the Old Testament

Unlike other Jewish holidays, the New Year was not caused by a specific historical event. It is, however, associated with Abraham's attempt to sacrifice Isaac. (Read the story from Genesis.) Do you remember what God substituted for Isaac? It was a ram. To begin the celebration of the Jewish New Year, a ram's horn, called a *shofar*, is sounded to call the people to worship and to celebrate the New Year.

Many years before Christ, the wise men of Israel calculated the years of life for the men of Genesis. They believed that the creation of man took place about fifty-seven hundred years ago. The Jewish calendar dates back to what they believed was the Creation event in the history of mankind.

Descriptions of *Rosh Hashanah* are found in Leviticus 23:23–25 and Numbers 29:1. They tell that a day in the seventh month must be set aside as a holy gathering. This day falls somewhere in September and October. The exact date depends upon the lunar calendar, which is controlled by the phases of the moon. On the day of the New Year gathering, no work is to be performed.

How Jewish People Today Celebrate the New Year

Like the Sabbath, the day begins with the lighting of two candles by the mother and the recitation of the blessing at sundown. People attend synagogue for the blowing of the *shofar*. This is a difficult instrument to play. There is one long note. This is followed by three short notes. Finally, a series of nine short blasts are sounded. These call the people to repent of their sins. Just as Abraham was called upon to sacrifice, or give up, his only son, Isaac, a Jewish person is called upon to give up sin. The Jewish person will also give money to help others. This is a different kind of sacrifice.

Jewish people believe that God opens the Book of Life on this day. The fortune of each person is decided for the next year. God is merciful to those who repent. The prayers for this holiday are directed toward God's mercy for the coming year.

On this day a twisted egg bread is eaten to symbolize the different seasons of the year. It also reminds Jews of God's eternal rule. It is also traditional to eat something sweet. Usually apples and honey are eaten at the beginning of the meal. Jews may also eat special fruit, such as figs, kumquats, and papaya. Cards are exchanged that wish the other person God's blessing for a good year.

After dinner on the first day, the people go to a river. Running water is important. Each person takes bread crumbs and throws them into the river to symbolize their sins. In Hebrew, this is known as *tashlikh*, meaning "You shall cast away." The other activities of the day are repeated during the second day.

What a Christian Can Learn from Rosh Hashanah

Repentance and sorrow for sin are part of the New Year remembrance. There is a desire to make a fresh start. There is also a sense of sacrifice. For the Christian, God has provided a permanent sacrifice in the death of Jesus on the cross for our sins.

We also need to have a time to remember our sins of the past year. Some Christian groups use the forty-day period of Lent before Easter to remember their sins and ask forgiveness. It is less important whether we use Lent than it is that we find a specific time to repent of our sins and seek a new beginning.

Abraham had a significant problem. God promised that He would bless Abraham and bring a whole nation through Isaac. The question for Abraham was, "Can I believe and trust God?" Abraham believed. A ram was caught in the bramble bushes. The ram became the substitute for Isaac. We can trust God too. God provided a substitute for us. We have sinned and deserve the death penalty for sin, but God substituted the death of His Son, Jesus. Believing in Jesus and trusting in God, we can be assured that He will spare us from suffering the penalty for sin—eternal death (see Romans 5:8).

Because of Jesus' death, I can tell God that I have sinned. I can tell Him I am sorry for that sin, repent of my sin, and ask Jesus to come into my

heart and save me from sin. After I die, He will prepare a place for me in Heaven with Him (see John 14:1–4).

Rosh Hashanah not only looks to the past, but it also calls for a new beginning. By trusting God, there is a living hope. One day the *shofar* will sound again from the heavens. Before the Day of Judgment, God will gather all who have put their trust in Jesus Christ. They will be with Him for all eternity (see 1 Thessalonians 4:16–17).

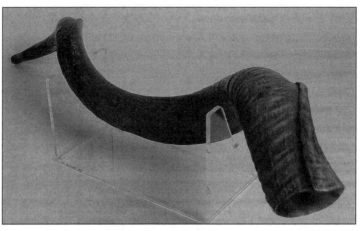

The shofar was an instrument that was made from a ram's horn. It means "hollow." The shofar is a difficult instrument to blow. In Bible times it announced great events. It is still used today by the Jewish people in their synagogue services.

THE DAY OF ATONEMENT

At the end of the Ten Days of Awe comes the holiest day of the Jewish year, the Day of Atonement. It comes five days ahead of the Feast of Tabernacles. In Hebrew this is *Yom Kippur* and occurs in September or October. It begins at sundown and ends the next evening when three stars are visible in the sky. It is a day to atone for one's sins before God.

God is holy. To be *holy*, means to be "set apart." You will recall that God called Moses to take the people from Pharaoh and Egypt for a three-day journey to be set apart and holy before God. God set the standard of what is right and what is wrong. We must live by His laws of right and wrong, not our own. Sin is a violation of God's standard and is punishable by death. God alone can give us holiness.

Under the Old Testament law, God provided the system of sacrifice. When the penalty for sin is death, the person must die or another must die for the accused person. God said that life comes through the blood, and only the blood of another will provide a covering for sin if the sinful person is to live. The sacrificial system was the means for providing the covering for sin. The priests in the Tabernacle in the wilderness and later in the Temple sacrificed the animals so that the people might live.

Celebration in the Old Testament
Leviticus 16 describes in detail the Day of Atonement. The high priest was instructed to wash himself and wear the sacred clothes of the priest. He was then to take a bull and sacrifice the bull for his personal sins and those of his family. A ram was to be sacrificed for an offering to God. Some of the blood of the bull was taken into the Holy of Holies in the Tabernacle or the Temple. No one but the high priest was allowed to enter the Holy of Holies. The ark of the covenant contained the Ten Commandments, a pot of manna from the wilderness journey, and Aaron's rod that budded. The blood was sprinkled between the cherubim (angels) that were on top of the ark.

Two male goats were chosen for a sin offering. One goat would be sacrificed, and the other would be sent off into the wilderness to carry away the sins of the people. The blood of the sacrificed goat was placed upon the ark and other places in the Temple. This provided atonement for the sins of the people for the past year. The second goat, or scapegoat, carried the sins of the people into the wilderness. A red sash was tied around his horns, and he was released. The red sash would become white, showing the people that God accepted their sacrifice for atonement.

The people were required to prepare themselves for this holy day. They were told to fast, that is, not to eat. This was a sign that they were denying themselves. They were to appear in sacred assembly before God. No work was allowed on the Day of Atonement. (This is described in Leviticus 23:26–32).

How Jewish People Today Celebrate the Day of Atonement
When the priestly system ended with the destruction of the Temple in AD 70, the Day of Atonement had to change as well. The essential purpose did not change. It involved turning away from sin and turning to God. It is still a day in which to atone for one's sins and ask forgiveness. Jews believe that on this day, above others, God hears their thoughts and prayers. This day calls for self-denial and self-control by fasting, or not eating, as a sign of the seriousness of this day. Asking for forgiveness applies to sin before God. Asking for forgiveness means that when one has hurt someone else, this is the day on which to make it right.

A meal is eaten before sunset. For some this may include *kreplach*, a soup like Chinese wonton soup. Meat is placed on the inside of the soft dough that covers it. The meat symbolizes the justice of God. The soft dough is like His mercy.

Jewish people also give money to the poor. Fasting helps one better understand the hunger of others. Fasting is required of all persons over age thirteen. It is not required for the sick. The fast lasts for twenty-five hours.

The synagogue service on *Yom Kippur* lasts all day. The greeting for this day is interesting: "May you be sealed in the Book of Life."

The Book of Jonah is read. This book tells of the meaning of repentance and how the great city of Ninevah was saved, and not destroyed, because the people repented. It also shows how an unforgiving heart is not pleasing to God. Remember how Jonah was upset when judgment did not fall on the city. Remember how angry Jonah was when a worm ate the plant that provided shade for him. This is the theme of the Day of Atonement.

There are opportunities for the people to think about their sin and ask God to forgive. There are times for discussion and prayer. For many, a journal or record is kept of their thoughts from the time of *Rosh Hashanah* to *Yom Kippur*. Parents and children may discuss their relationships. Husbands and wives may also talk about their relationship.

The service and holiday end with the last appeal for the mercy of God. The final blast on the *shofar* tells that God's book is closed. The people go home to eat a light meal and end the fast.

What Christians Can Learn from Yom Kippur

The Day of Atonement has special meaning to Christians too. Remember the greeting that Jewish persons give to each other: "May you be sealed in the Book of Life!" For the follower of Jesus, this is assured. We are sealed in the Lamb's Book of Life (see Revelation 20:12).

After the Temple was destroyed in AD 70, the sacrificial system ended. Without this system of sacrifice among Jewish people, atonement has been left to personal prayer and fasting. This was not what the Scripture commanded. Recall the red sash that was tied to the horns of the goat. If God accepted the sacrifice, He would turn the sash white. It is very interesting that one of the ancient Jewish writings, the Talmud (Yoma 39b), tells us that forty years before the destruction of the Temple, the red cord no longer turned white. That would have been about the time of the crucifixion of Jesus, around AD 30. After Jesus' death on the cross, there was no longer any need for sacrificing animals. Hebrews 9:11–14 tells us that Jesus went into the Holy of Holies and took His own blood as a sacrifice for our salvation. His sacrifice was permanent and did not need to be repeated every year. If we accept Jesus' sacrifice on the cross for our sins, we have eternal life, which is life that will last forever. The Temple became only a pile of stones, but the atonement of Jesus lasts forever.

A prayer shawl.

THE FEAST OF TABERNACLES

After the seriousness of *Rosh Hashanah* and *Yom Kippur*, the harvest festival of the Feast of Tabernacles is a joyful celebration. It begins four days after *Yom Kippur* in either September or October. The feast recalls God's protection during the forty years of wandering in the wilderness. Recall the story of the wilderness wanderings from Exodus and Numbers. Remember how God provided food in the wilderness. Remember also how God provided a pillar of cloud by day and a pillar of fire by night to keep the people safe. The Hebrew name for this holiday is *Sukkoth*. It means booths or tabernacles. In the wilderness, the people of Israel constructed booths in which to live. One *sukkah*, or booth, is the symbol of God's peace and care for His people. Each family was to construct a *sukkah*.

Because the Jewish people raised crops in their homeland, this feast was also connected with the harvest. Bringing in the bountiful harvest requires thanksgiving to God for His care. This feast celebrates God's care. It is one of the most joyous holidays of the Jewish year and is similar to Thanksgiving.

Celebration in the Old Testament
Celebrating this holiday for the wilderness wanderings is described in Leviticus 23:42–43. Celebrating the bringing in the crops is described in Deuteronomy 16:13. In Old Testament times the people would go on a journey to Jerusalem. They carried bunches of branches, called the *lulav*. These could be waved as they went on their journey up to Jerusalem. They also carried the fruit, citron, called an *etrog*. They sang as they went. The Psalms of Ascent (Psalms 120–134) were sung. When they got to Jerusalem, they would set up the booths, which were covered with leafy branches similar to the *lulav*. The people lived in the booths for a period of seven days.

During the seven-day period there were special sacrifices in the Temple. One of the most unusual parts of the celebration was pouring water on the altar. The people would watch as the priest poured water on the altar of sacrifice. They would carry their branches and the *etrog*, or citron, and sing praises to God. The Temple trumpets would resound throughout the Temple area.

Evenings in the Temple were also very spectacular. The area was lighted by many candelabras to enlighten the entire Temple. The Levites played their instruments. The men carried torches while they danced and sang.

On the last day of the celebration, the people sang the "great hosanna" from Psalm 118. Children ate the citron that the people had carried. Leaves were spread on the Temple walkways as the people shook the branches of the *lulav*. The whole celebration came to an end at the beginning of the Sabbath.

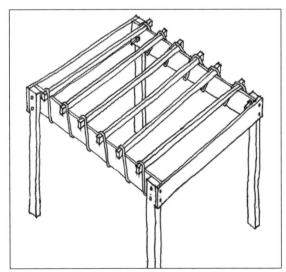

This pictures a sukkah, like the ones in which the Jewish people celebrate the Feast of Tabernacles.

How Jewish People Today Celebrate Sukkoth
After the destruction of the Temple, the people had to find new ways to celebrate the festival. The Sukkot is now usually built outside of the home. It is a three-sided structure and covered with

branches. The walls may be decorated. Coverings for the *sukkah* are usually made of palm, myrtle, or willow branches. The *lulav* is made of the same type of branches. Many families eat their meals in the *sukkah* and may study and relax during the day. Most do not actually live in the *sukkah*, as they did in Bible times. No work is done on this holiday. Children do not attend school.

Synagogue services include the carrying of the *lulav* and the *etrog*, or citron fruit. Instead of marching around the altar, the people will sometimes march around the front of the synagogue. Instead of focusing on the altar of sacrifice, the people march around the scroll of the *Torah*, or the Books of Moses. They wave the *lulav* and the *etrog* east, north, west, and south while they say prayers. In this way, they show their thanks to God for His goodness to them. The elders wash their hands, reminding us that the priest poured water on the altar. In the synagogue service, the Book of Ecclesiastes is read.

The *sukkah* is a place in which to live for a short period of time. It reminds us of the temporary nature of life itself. But looking through the branches at night, one can see the heavens and the eternal home of God.

What Christians Can Learn from Sukkoth

One day we will move from the temporary dwelling place on earth to the eternal dwelling place of God. The *sukkah* points this out. Sometimes we move from place to place and are not sure where we are going. Paul said, "For we know that if our earthly house, a tent, is destroyed, we have a building from God, a house not made with hands, eternal in the heavens" (2 Corinthians 5:1).

THE FESTIVAL OF LIGHTS

In Bible times there was a celebration in midwinter. This celebration marked the shortest day of the year, and it happened at a time just before the days began to get longer. Like sukkoh, it was a happy celebration. It is not one of the celebrations described in the Bible.

The holiday gained new meaning after the Maccabees defeated the Syrians in 167 BC. The Syrians wanted to make Greeks out of all the Jewish peoples, and they wanted the Jewish peoples to worship the Greek gods. They tried to prevent the Jewish people from performing the rite of circumcision. The evil Syrian ruler Antiochus Epiphanes even sacrificed a pig on the high altar in the Temple. The Jewish peoples were no match for the mighty armies of Syria. However, a small band of Jewish fighters, with the help of God, were able to defeat the mighty Syrian army. Their success is celebrated in the Feast of Lights, or *Hanukkah*. The Hebrew word *Hanukkah* means "dedication." It is called the Festival of Lights because of the eight-branched candelabras that are lit in honor of *Hanukkah*. The candelabra is called a *menorah*.

Celebration of Hanukkah

The story is told in the book of 1 Maccabees. While this book is not in the Bible, it is a history of the period between the Old and the New Testaments.

The Maccabeean Revolt

The story of *Hanukkah* begins in a town in northern Palestine. A group of Syrian soldiers were sent by the evil king Antiochus Epiphanes to force the Jewish people to bow down before a golden statue of the god Zeus. The Syrian captain read the order from Antiochus. He was about to force all of the people in the town to bow down to the statue. The old priest Mattathias stepped forward. He refused to bow down before the image. The Syrian captain threatened to hang him. Mattathias took a knife and killed the Syrian captain. Then he and his five sons fled to the hills. The Syrian troops tried to follow, but with no success.

Many more Jews joined Mattathias and his sons. The fighters became known as the Maccabeans. Together they built a little army to fight against the

Syrians. They prayed and asked God to help them. This brave band hid in the caves in the mountains where it was not easy for the Syrians to find them. Mattathias said that one day these men would defeat the army of the Syrians. But as time passed, Mattathias became sick and died. Before he died, he asked the band of followers to follow his son, Judah.

Three years passed before his followers felt strong enough to begin to wage war against the Syrians. One night the Syrian soldiers were sleeping. The Maccabees swooped down out of the mountains. They carried torches, which they used to burn the tents of the Syrians. They chased the sleeping soldiers and won a great victory.

Antiochus was outraged. He sent a larger army to defeat the Maccabees. They were frightened, but Judah encouraged them because they fought for God. The size of the army was not what would determine the outcome. Judah said, "God is on our side, and we will win." That night the band of Maccabees crept down out of the mountains. They sounded trumpets. They sang praises to God. Again, they defeated the Syrian army.

Antiochus could not understand how his troops could be defeated so easily. He raised an even larger army to fight against them. His army had horse-mounted cavalry along with foot soldiers. Judah moved his warriors into the forest. The Syrians tried to follow but could not find the Maccabees. Suddenly, the Maccabees descended upon them and beat them. The war was finally over. With the help of God, the Maccabees had defeated the mighty army of Syria.

This band of brave warriors entered the city of Jerusalem. Instead of receiving shouts of joy, everything was quiet. The city was in ruins. The Syrians had constructed altars to Zeus and to other Greek gods. When they got to the Temple, they found that it had been used for evil purposes. The altar had the remains of a pig that had been sacrificed there. They got to work and repaired the doors to the Temple. They built a new altar and destroyed the images to the Greek gods.

When all was in readiness, they asked the old priest when they should dedicate the Temple. He suggested the date of the mid-winter celebration. They needed holy oil to light the *menorah*. Only one small cruise of oil could be found. They went ahead with the celebration and lit the *menorah*. Instead of burning out, it continued to burn for eight days. This celebration continues today to remember the triumph over the Syrians on that day.

The Hanukkah menorah symbolizes the Festival of Lights in the celebration of Hanukkah.

The Story of Judith and Holofernes

There is also another story associated with the celebration of *Hanukkah*. This is the story of a brave young woman, Judith, and the Syrian general, Holofernes, also found in the Book of Judith in the Apocrypha. The Apocrypha are writings about the period between the Old and New Testaments.

Judith wanted to do her part in helping to defeat the Syrians. She was a beautiful young maiden. The great Syrian general, Holofernes, was struck by her beauty. He invited her to come and visit him.

That evening, Judith gathered together a large basket of food. She brought cheese and wine with her. She told Holofernes to get rid of all of his servants and soldiers. He was very excited and did as she asked. Then Judith spread the table. Holofernes wanted her to eat his food along with him, but she refused. She told him that her people had special rules about eating, and she could not break those rules.

Holofernes ate the salty cheese and the other good things that Judith had brought. Judith filled his cup with wine and continued to refill it as he drank. Soon he was fast asleep. Judith then took his knife and cut off his head. Then she took his head in her food basket to her village. After that, the Syrian army that Holofernes led, was easily defeated. This brave young woman achieved a great victory.

How Jewish People Today Celebrate Hanukkah

The *menorah* is essential to the celebration of *Hanukkah*. The first candle is lit on the first day of the eight-day celebration. The candles are lit from left to right. Each night a new candle is lit and added to the others. As the light increases, it reminds us that the days will soon become longer. The light will increase as spring replaces winter. The *menorah* suggests that the light of freedom may start very small and become very large. This is what happened with the Maccabees.

Cheese is a favorite dish of the Jewish people on *Hanukkah*. It recalls the deed of Judith, killing Holofernes. She fed him cheese to make him thirsty.

Today, the celebration of *Hanukkah* supports a rededication to the Jewish heritage. The services in the synagogue have readings from Zechariah 2:4–7 and from 1 Maccabees. The term *Hanukkah*, or "dedication," refers to the rededication of the Temple.

Since the celebration occurs at the end of November or during December, it competes with the Christian celebration of Christmas. As a result, *Hanukkah* has also become a time for giving gifts. Among the favorite gifts to give on *Hanukkah* is the gift of money.

Dreidel is a popular children's game that is played on *Hanukkah*. The word means "to turn." It is like a top that spins. There are Hebrew letters inscribed on each of the four sides of the top. Children start with an equal number of chocolate coins. They spin the *dreidel*. The meaning of the four letters are:

Noon	נ	Do nothing
GIM-mel	ג	Take all
Heh	ה	Take half
Shin	ש	Add one to the pile

Dreidel is the game children play on Hanukkah.

Each player takes a turn spinning the *dreidel*. When the pile of chocolate coins is gone, each child places one more coin on top of the pile. The game ends when one child wins all the pieces or when the time limit has been reached.

Popular foods eaten at *Hanukkah* are potato pancakes and jelly doughnuts. These are all made with oil, reminding people of the oil that lasted for eight days.

What Christians Can Learn from Hanukkah

The apostle Paul said that "in the fullness of time Christ came." At a point in time when it looked bleak for the Jewish faith to survive, God sent the Maccabees. Their bravery and commitment to God brought a major victory for the Jewish people against the Syrians. God's purpose was carried out.

The Maccabees did not think about their own safety and well-being. They were concerned for God's purposes. Christians need to be just as concerned today about God's purposes. We need to be persons who can stand in the face of danger and trust God as His servants.

THE FEAST OF LOTS

Queen Esther Saves Her People

The Feast of Lots celebrates the faith of Esther in saving her people from the cruel Haman. It is called the Feast of Lots to recall the game of chance that Haman played to determine which day he would kill all the Jews. The Feast of Lots is celebrated with joy. The feast comes at the close of winter and at the beginning of spring. It takes place in either the month of February or March. The Hebrew name for the Feast of Lots is *Purim*. The Hebrew root word *pur* means lot.

Celebration in the Old Testament

Return to the Bible material and read the story of Esther again. You will recall that after seventy years in captivity in Babylon, some Jews returned to Palestine in 536 BC. Later many people came with Ezra. And still later more came with Nehemiah in about 444 BC. The story of Esther took place in Persia, somewhere between 478–473 BC.

Persia had conquered Babylon. Recall the story from the reading of Daniel. King Xerxes had placed Haman in charge of most of his kingdom. Haman plotted to kill the Jews. Mordecai, the uncle of Esther, and Esther herself were responsible for saving the Jews from being killed. Even though the King could not take back his order, he was able to give the Jewish people the right to defend themselves against their attackers. As a result, the Jewish people were saved.

The instructions for celebrating *Purim* were very simple. The day was to be celebrated as a memorial to the bravery of this young woman. Giving gifts to other persons also became a part of this celebration, as well as giving to the poor.

How Jewish People Today Celebrate **Purim**

On the day before the holiday many Jews do not eat. They fast. *Purim* is a day of excitement. Jews must still struggle against enemies that seek to destroy them. Just like Haman, Amalek and Hitler have tried to destroy the Jews. Some synagogues sponsor a carnival just before or after the feast of *Purim*. Many Jews still exchange presents on the Feast of *Purim*. These presents are usually simple things, like baked goods.

The main part of the synagogue service includes the reading of the story of Esther. It is contained in a scroll, known in Hebrew as *megillah*. The scroll is wrapped around one pole, instead of two, as the Scroll of the *Torah*. During the service, whenever the name of Haman is mentioned, the people stomp

Megillah

on the floor to show their displeasure. They also use a noisemaker, known as a *Grogger*. *Groggers* can be made of an empty can and filled with pebbles or rice. Whenever the name of Esther is mentioned, the people clap their hands and shout "Hurray!" They may also throw flowers at hearing the name of Esther. The story is read at the evening service and again in the morning.

Even though God is not mentioned directly in the Book of Esther, it is clear that she did what God wanted her to do. Recall that she said: "If I perish, I perish" (4:16). But God blessed her effort and both she and people of Israel were saved. On the very day that Haman wanted to kill all the Jews, he himself became the victim and was killed. The Jews were spared. In many synagogues the story is acted as a play in the synagogue service. The children often dress in costumes and wear masks representing each of the characters. Jewish people are also expected to give gifts of food or money to help the poor during the celebration of this feast.

In the late afternoon, the Jewish people eat a festive meal. Specialty treats are provided. Among those are the *hamantaschen*. These are three-cornered pastries that represent the hat that the wicked Haman wore.

Purim is also a time to celebrate the escape of Jewish people from other persecutions. Many persecutions have occurred down through history.

THE FEAST OF PASSOVER

When the people of Israel were freed from bondage in Egypt, God instructed them to retell the story of the Passover to their children. Each new generation needs to know how God led the people out of Egypt. This feast is celebrated in the spring, between March and April. At this time of the year the lambs are sheared, and the barley is ripened. In Hebrew, the feast is known as *Pesach.*

Unlike some feasts, this one has a *seder.* The *seder* is a fixed order of events that take place in the celebration of the feast. The historic events are told in a story, known as the *Haggadah.* The *Haggadah* is designed to tell the story and to allow the participants to eat the foods of the *seder* at the appropriate times. The story of the Passover is a miracle that God performed to protect His people and to bring them out of Egypt. The *seder* tells the whole story of the exodus from Egypt. But the specific meaning of Passover is the miracle that the angel passed over the Israelites. The angel killed the firstborn of all humans and animals of the Egyptians. Any home that did not have the blood of the slain lamb on the doorpost became a victim of the angel of death.

Celebration in the Old Testament

The story is told in Exodus 1–14. During the wanderings in the wilderness, the people celebrated Passover to remember the exodus. In keeping with Jewish custom, they ate unleavened bread. Unleavened bread is bread that does not have yeast to make it rise. It is like a cracker. Unleavened bread was a reminder of the haste with which they ate the Passover meal and left Egypt. In both the Old and New Testaments,

leavening symbolizes sin. Like yeast, sin goes through everything (see Leviticus 6:17).

During the Temple years, Passover was a pilgrimage feast. Remember the pilgrimage up to Jerusalem in the Feast of Tabernacles. They sang psalms as they went. The Feast of Pentecost was also a pilgrimage feast.

Central to the feast was the lamb that was slain. When the family arrived in Jerusalem, the father would purchase a lamb for the feast. On the day of the Passover the father would take the lamb to the Temple and slay the lamb in front of the priest. He would take the lamb to the place they were staying. It would be prepared for the Passover celebration. After sunset families would gather for the Passover meal. They would drink a glass of wine and eat the meal of the lamb. They would eat the unleavened bread and bitter herbs. The Passover story would be told as the families drank three other cups of wine. They sang the *Hallel,* or Psalms 113–118. Remember that in the Feast of Tabernacles, the people sang "the great hosanna." It was also taken from Psalm 118.

How Jewish People Today Celebrate Passover

Following the destruction of the temple in AD 70, the celebration of the Feast of Passover no longer used a sacrificial lamb. The most important part of the celebration now centers in the unleavened bread. In preparation for the feast, the family is required to rid the home of any leavening. Any of five grains that have been mixed with water for eighteen minutes or more must be cleaned from the house. These grains include wheat, barley, rye, oats, and spelt. The whole house must be carefully scrubbed. The primary responsibility lies with the mother, but she involves the children in the cleaning as well. No leaven is to be left in the house, nor eaten during this time.

Unleavened bread, or *Matzah,* is made from wheat. But the cooking of *matzah* is done in less than eighteen minutes. Remember, leaven is a reminder of sin. It is also a reminder that we can be puffed up with too much pride. Unleavened bread symbolizes our lack of pride.

Any food that enters the home during Passover must be kosher. Kosher means it is certified by a rabbi to be pure and appropriate for cooking.

On each plate is a copy of the *Haggadah*. The term means "the telling." This is the written story of the Passover. This is used to retell the story completely and in detail. It will guide the conversation during the entire dinner celebration.

The youngest child has the opportunity to ask the questions. The questions are as follows:

1. Why is this night different from other nights? On other nights, we eat either leavened or unleavened bread; why, on this night, do we eat only *matzah*, which is unleavened bread?

2. On all other nights, we eat vegetables and herbs of all kinds; why, on this night, do we eat bitter herbs especially?

3. On all other nights, we never think of dipping herbs in water or anything else; why, on this night, do we dip the parsley in salt water and the bitter herbs in *haroset*?

4. On all other nights, everyone sits up straight at the table; why, on this night, do we recline at the table?

The large *seder* plate is placed in front of the leader of the *seder*. The plate has five sections. Each of those sections has a place for one of the symbols to be used in the *seder*. Each of the symbols plays a part in the retelling of the story of Passover.

The first section of the plate contains *maror*. Remember the hard life of slavery that the people lived in Egypt. The bitter herb *maror* or horse-radish served as a reminder of this painful condition. The second section contains *haroset*. This is a mixture of apples, cinnamon, fruits, nuts, and wine. It is sweet and very good to taste. It reminds the family of the mortar that was used in building the pyramids while the people were in slavery.

The next section contains the shank bone of a lamb. It is called *z'roah*. The shank bone represents the lamb that was eaten in haste as the Hebrew people fled from Egypt. The bone also reminds us that it was the strong hand of the Lord that brought the people out of Egypt.

A roasted egg sits in the next spot on the *seder* plate. It is a symbol of new life that comes after slavery. It also symbolizes the animal sacrifices that were performed in the temple.

Finally, there are fresh greens in the last place. There are known as *karpas*. New life comes after slavery. The *karpas* is dipped in salt to symbolize the tears that were shed when the people were in bondage.

The seder plate is used with the Haggadah, or story of the Passover.

A cup of wine is also placed in the center of the table. It is the cup for Elijah. Remember from your study of the Bible that Elijah did not die. He was taken into heaven in a flaming chariot. Jewish people believe that Elijah will return. He will come to announce the Messiah. The Messiah will bring peace and harmony. The family would welcome the coming of Elijah.

As part of the celebration a half piece of *matzah* is hidden by the leader of the *seder*. It is called the *afikomen*. The word means "dessert." Children hunt for the *afikomen*. When the children find the *afikomen*, the leader wants it returned. The children ask for a treat in exchange for the *afikomen*. At the end of the *seder*, the family group enjoys their fourth cup of wine. The leader voices the hope that they will see the day of the Messiah. Together they pray for the peace of Jerusalem. They say, "Next year in Jerusalem!" The leader of the *seder* closes the meal in prayer.

What Christians Can Learn from Passover

The Passover, more than any other Jewish holiday, has meaning for a follower of Jesus. After the destruction of the Temple in AD 70, the Jews no longer got a lamb without blemish. Remember that the lamb was slain and the blood of the lamb was placed on the door. The angel of death passed over those homes where the blood was over the door. Jesus became our sacrifice. He was a Lamb without blemish. His blood was shed in our place. As a result of His death, we can live eternally.

The *afikomen* has been interpreted differently after the destruction of the Temple. Originally it meant "The Coming One." Jesus used the third cup of wine and the piece of unleavened bread to show His coming death. He was the Lamb of God. This is described in Isaiah 53. At that point it became the bread and cup of the Lord's Supper. This became one of the symbols of the Christian faith.

After the Temple was built, Passover could be celebrated on the anniversary of the departure from Egypt (see Deuteronomy 16:6). Jesus chose to use that occasion to celebrate Passover with His disciples. But notice also that Jesus was crucified on the very day when most other Jews were in the process of sacrificing their Passover lambs. Jesus is our Passover Lamb.

THE FEAST OF PENTECOST

The Feast of Pentecost comes fifty days after Passover. In Hebrew it is called *Shavuot*, which means "weeks." It comes seven weeks after Passover.

The feast celebrates the giving of the *Torah*, or the Books of the Law, to Moses on Mount Sinai. It also celebrates the start of the grain harvest. The *Torah* is read at Pentecost. Some stay up all night to read the Law. The Book of Ruth is also read as part of the Pentecost celebration. For Christians it was during the celebration of Pentecost that the Holy Spirit came upon the band of Christians.

Celebration in the Old Testament

The word *Torah* literally means "instruction." It was exactly fifty days after the exodus from Egypt that God delivered the *Torah* to Moses. You may want to read the giving of the Law and the Ten Commandments in Exodus 19. God's purpose in giving the Law was to set a high standard for living. This was a joyous holiday. Those who love the Law would find this holiday an opportunity to study the Word of God.

But the giving of the Law was not the only purpose for Pentecost. Leviticus 23 describes the Feast of Weeks as a "firstfruits" celebration. It was a time for the farmer to bring in the firstfruits of his

On Pentecost the Jewish people recall the gift of the Torah to Moses. It is the foundation of the Jewish faith today.

grain harvest. It provided an opportunity to express thanks to God for His bountiful goodness. The people were to present to God a wave offering of bread in gratefulness for God's care for them.

How Jewish People Today Celebrate Pentecost

The Firstfruits celebration is no longer celebrated in the Jewish holidays. Counting of the *omer* has survived. An *omer* is a "sheaf." During the fifty days, the benediction (the *omer*) continues to be counted.

On the fiftieth day there are synagogue services to recall the giving of the Law. Some Jews will read the Law all night in advance of Pentecost. The Jewish faith holds that God gave the 613 commandments in the Law. The Ten Commandments are an important part of those commandments. They are read in the synagogue on Pentecost. The feast of Passover reminds us that the Israelites were released from slavery. But on the feast of Pentecost the Hebrew people became a nation.

The synagogue and the people's homes are decorated with greens and fresh flowers for the Pentecost celebration.

It is still the custom to read the Book of Ruth in the synagogue service. Recall the Book of Ruth and read the story from the Bible. It is a good story, telling about the life of a young maiden. She was from the country of Moab. She was a Gentile. After her husband died, she returned to Palestine with her mother-in-law. The story tells about the grain harvest. Ruth married a good Hebrew man, Boaz. He was a farmer. Through their marriage she became an ancestor of King David. (By tradition, David was born and died on Pentecost.) Ruth became an Israelite. She now adopted the Law of the Hebrews as her own. Ruth reminds us of both the Law and harvest celebrations.

Many Jewish families will start the education of their children during this period. Children can also affirm their commitment to the Jewish people at this time.

Fruit, honey, milk, and dairy products are traditional at Pentecost. Some claim that the people were too exhausted after receiving the Law and found this kind of meal easy to prepare. Others hold that this came from the Bible text that held that the people would occupy a land that flowed with milk and honey.

What Christians Can Learn from Pentecost

It is interesting that the Firstfruits celebration ended. There is no reason given by the Jewish leaders. It may be that they ended it because the death of Jesus led to His resurrection on the third day. Paul says, "Christ has been raised from the dead, the firstfruits of those who have fallen asleep" (1 Corinthians 15:20).

Today the *Torah* has become the center of the celebration. The Law is difficult, if not impossible, to keep. For that reason, Jeremiah said that God would one day write the Law on the hearts of His followers (Jeremiah 31:33). With the coming of the Holy Spirit on Pentecost, this became a reality. We cannot keep the Law, because we are not able to live by its commands. But with the Holy Spirit living in us, we can keep God's Law. The connection between the Law and Pentecost becomes clear through the coming of the Holy Spirit.

The harvest theme of the Book of Ruth can be connected through the spiritual harvest that the Holy Spirit brought. The harvest of souls went beyond Israel. More people were brought into the Kingdom of God that day.

Growth and Development of the Church

INTRODUCTION FOR PARENTS AND TEACHERS

After the New Testament, the Church entered upon a very difficult period. For the next two hundred years the Church was persecuted, and many early Christians lost their lives at the hands of cruel Roman rulers. A dramatic change took place when Constantine became emperor of Rome and Christians were given equal rights with other religious groups. The challenges of surviving were now replaced with the new confrontation of living a godly life in the midst of a church becoming secular and worldly. But that has been the story and the challenge of the history of the Church.

In every age, the Church has had to confront threats from the non-Christian world from without and the secularizing influences from within. In each case heroes and heroines have arisen to meet the challenges. In our age there has been a tendency of many people to think of history as boring. If that is your belief, I would challenge you to withhold your judgment. Keep an open mind, read the accounts of the brave men and women who have endured affliction, and in some cases even loss of life, to maintain their faith in Jesus Christ.

The stories that are told in both the Old and New Testaments are accounts of the history of God's revelation of Himself to a lost world. While the historical events of the Church era do not carry the authority of Holy Scripture, they do demonstrate the hand of God in forming and molding the people of God into the Church. Someone has aptly said, "We are a product of our history." Whether we are Baptists, Presbyterians, Methodists, Episcopalians, or Mennonites, we have been shaped by the historical events that have led us to the place where we find ourselves today. Two thousand years

have elapsed since the formation of the Church at Pentecost. If, for example, one is Baptist, the struggles of the early Baptists have played an important part in shaping what contemporary Baptist believers are today. This would be equally true for Presbyterians, Methodists, or other denominational groups in our contemporary culture.

Perhaps the anemic condition of the Church in modern society is in part due to the fact that we have failed to take seriously the lessons that we should have learned from those believers who have gone before us. In their world situations, they had to face difficulties in drawing close to God that may be different because their world was different but similar because many of their ways of facing their crises have similar application in the world in which we live. This is particularly true for our children. They develop heroes or heroines from the sports or music stars of our culture. We need to help them find heroes and heroines among those great saints of the past, who have lived lives to the glory of God rather than for self-gratification.

It is clear that culture has always affected the Church. It is not as clear that the Church has always affected the culture as significantly in every age of history. If we genuinely believe that God has called us to be "salt" and "light" in our generation, then we must help our children to develop an understanding of their faith that will help them to have an impact upon their generation. Understanding the lives of those who have preceded us will help to instill in our children the kind of love for Christ that those early saints had. It will also help them understand the ways by which that love has affected the witness of these saints for Christ in the world.

Many of these saints became martyrs for their faith. The word *martyr* comes from a Greek word that meant "witness." These courageous men and women of faith gave witness to their faith in Christ. They loved God more than they loved themselves or the world. They were willing to give all for their love of Christ. In the early days of the Church, that often meant one who testified to his or her Christian faith, especially by giving his or her life for Christ. That has continued to be true down to the present day. There have been more martyrs in many parts of the world in the twenty-first century than there were in the early days of the Church. While we do not look for death, and most of us will never be called upon to give the ultimate sacrifice, yet our love for God should impel us to love Him more than we love ourselves. Eternal life is a pearl far more valuable than our temporal life here. Many of these saints from the past reflect the kinds of values that demonstrate the significance of their faith. They were willing to affect their culture more than being controlled by their culture. May God help us to have a similar resolve!

Most first and second graders do not have an adequate awareness or understanding of the epochs of history that begin with a fixed point in time. While it is important to place events and people in a time frame, most children do not develop this awareness until at least the third grade. Even then it occurs in a primitive form. Therefore, it would be wise to place the events and persons in the appropriate time sequence but not to insist that first and second graders recall those events in the correct time sequence. To help you as an adult understand the time sequence, however, the following time line will provide a frame of reference for the persons that have been selected to represent each of the eras of the history of the Christian Church. This time frame will also provide a point of reference for the persons from the history of the Church in this section and from missions, the arts, and scientists in coming sections. I will provide a brief explanation for the significant dates in the time line. This is intended for parents and teachers and will appear at the beginning of each section.

CHURCH HISTORY TIME LINE

The Church of the Roman Empire—AD 68 to AD 480
   Polycarp (AD 69 to 155)
   Cecilia (d. AD 230)
   Augustine of Hippo (AD 354 to 430)
The Medieval Church—AD 480 to 1517
   Benedict of Nursia (AD 480 to 547) and Life in a Monastery
   Francis of Assisi (1182 to 1226)
The Reformation—1517 to 1646
   Martin Luther (1483 to 1546)
   *Johannes Kepler (1571 to 1630)_*
   *Robert Boyle (1627 to 1691)_*
   *Sir Isaac Newton (1642 to 1747)_*
The Enlightenment, Revolutions, Revivals, and Missions—1646 to 1900
   John Wesley (1703 to 1791)
   Robert Raikes (1736 to 1811)
   William Carey (1761 to 1834)*
   David Livingstone (1813 to 1873)*
   Lottie Moon (1840 to 1912)*
Modern Period—1900 to the Present
   William Franklin Graham (1918 to the Present)

*Represents persons in the section on Missions
_Represents persons in the section on Science

The Church of the Roman Empire
AD 68 to 590

The Persecuted Church—AD 68 to 313

The first period of Church history is the Church of the Roman Empire. It may be sub-divided into the Persecuted Church from AD 68 to 313 and the Triumph of the Church from AD 313 to 590. From AD 68 to 313, the Church was persecuted by the Roman rulers. Emperor Nero was blamed for the great fire that happened in Rome in AD 68. He did not like being blamed for the fire, so he blamed the Christians who worshiped Jesus. He claimed that they were the cause of the anger of the gods of Rome. From that point until AD 313, persecutions of Christians continued. Many Christians were killed in the arena by the gladiators. Others were killed by wild animals. But the worship of Jesus as Lord continued to grow throughout the Empire.

There were many heroes and heroines for their faith in Jesus Christ. We can learn a lot from two of those courageous Christians who died for their faith. Polycarp was an elderly pastor. He refused to give up his faith, and for that he died. Cecilia was a young woman. She loved God with all of her being and would not give up her faith, even though it meant that she would lose her life for her faith. Both Polycarp and Cecilia gave inspiration and an encouragement to other Christians who came after them.

Polycarp (AD 69 to 155)

Polycarp became a Christian at a young age. He was a disciple of the apostle John. John was punished for being a Christian. He was sent by the Roman Emperor to the island of Patmos. It is likely that John made Polycarp the bishop of Smyrna before John left. Polycarp was well known as a godly bishop. He loved the Lord and refused to have any part in the evil beliefs of some of the people who had left the true gospel.

One of the early Church writers was Irenaeus. Polycarp had been the one who led Irenaeus to the Lord and guided Irenaeus in his Christian life.

Polycarp also wrote a letter to the Philippians. It was circulated among many of the churches near Philippi. There seems to be some support for the fact that Polycarp also made a trip to Rome. Beyond those facts, not a lot is known about the bishop until his death.

Marcus Aurelius was in his sixth year as Roman emperor. Violent persecution broke out in the empire. Many Christians died in the persecution. Each was called an atheist, which is one who does not believe in the gods of Rome. They served the Lord Christ and not the gods of Rome. The Christians also were persecuted because they refused to bow down to the Roman emperor Caesar as a god. The Christians believed that Caesar was only a man. Only Christ was to be worshiped. As the persecution progressed, the evil persecutors began to look for Polycarp. They knew that Polycarp would not bow to the gods of Rome or to Caesar.

The friends of Polycarp insisted that he hide from these evil men. At first, it was fairly easy for him to move from one place to another. He was protected. Not finding him, the persecutors found two boys from Polycarp's home. They threatened to hurt them if they did not tell where Polycarp was. The boys finally told where the pastor was staying.

Soldiers were sent to the place where he was staying. They surrounded the house. Polycarp was upstairs. While upstairs, he had a vision that he would be burned in the fire. Instead of trying to escape, Polycarp came down and surrendered to the soldiers. He invited them into his house for a meal. They were amazed. While they ate, Polycarp prayed for his family and the people that he shepherded as pastor.

They set Polycarp on a donkey and rode with him to town. The Roman ruler of the city of Smyrna was riding in his chariot with his father. When they saw Polycarp, they had him brought to their chariot and asked him to give up his foolishness and bow to Caesar. Polycarp refused. They threw him out of the chariot and made him walk to the arena.

Once inside, both he and those with him heard a voice from heaven. "Be strong and act as a man!" The ruler asked him if he would condemn Christ and hail Caesar. Polycarp again refused. He told them that for more than eighty years he had served Christ and would not betray Christ now. He said, "I am a Christian." The ruler became angry and told Polycarp that he would send the wild beasts upon him. "Call for them!" shouted Polycarp. "If you despise them," said the ruler, "I will have you burned to death." Polycarp told them to burn him. He told the ruler that it would be more bearable for him to be burned with fire here than as the ruler would be burned with eternal fire in the next life.

As they were talking, the crowd grew restless. They began to assemble sticks and wood to burn the elderly pastor. The soldiers took him to the place where the fire would burn him. But when they tried to nail his hands to the wood, he promised that he would not run. They bound his hands behind his back instead. Then they lit the fire. A peace came over the old man. He looked forward to entering his heavenly home with Christ. But the fire would not burn Polycarp. The flames circled his body, but he was not harmed. In anger the ruler had the soldier run a dagger through Polycarp.

Remembering what happened to Jesus, the crowd urged the ruler not to allow his body to be buried by the Christians. It was burned. But the Christians took the bones of the aged pastor and buried them. The story of Polycarp's death was written by the Christians in a letter. It was widely circulated and became a great encouragement to those who were also living through persecution. Polycarp had not died in vain.

Cecilia (d. AD 230)

It is believed that Cecilia was also martyred sometime during the reign of Emperor Marcus Aurelius, during the second century. Like Polycarp, she became a model to encourage other Christians who were in the midst of persecution. Unlike the aged Polycarp, Cecilia was only eighteen years of age. She was the daughter of a Roman senator. She lived in Trastevere, a section of Rome that is across the Tiber River. One can still visit her home today. In her youth she accepted Christ and became a Christian. She was taught well in the Christian faith, as we shall see later.

Her father insisted she marry at age eighteen. He arranged for her to marry a young man named Valerian. He came from a wealthy Roman family. Cecilia told her father that she did not want to marry a pagan young man. But all of her protests did not cause her father to change his mind.

That did not stop Cecilia. She turned away from persuading her father to persuading her new husband to become a Christian believer. He became a Christian. He worked on his brother, Tiburtius, to also become a follower of Christ. They were both baptized. They followed Jesus' command and gave money to the poor people of Rome.

Since they lived near the Tiber River, each night the bodies of those who died for their faith in Christ would come through the sewers and empty into the Tiber River. Valerian and Tiburtius gathered the bodies. They took them to the Catacombs for a Christian burial.

The brothers soon came to the attention of Almachius, a ruler of Rome. Valerian and Tiburtius were summoned to court. The guard, Maxentius, was ordered to take them to the shrine of Jupiter and to sacrifice to Jupiter. On route to the shrine, Valerian and Tiburtius witnessed to Maxentius and led him to faith in Christ.

Maxentius took the brothers to his home. They witnessed to his family, who also became followers of Christ. Maxentius and his family came to Cecilia's home and were baptized. They returned to the shrine to Jupiter. All three men refused to bow down to the image of Jupiter. As a result, Valerian and Tiburtius were beheaded. Cecilia arranged to have their bodies taken to the catacombs for a Christian burial.

Upon hearing that Maxentius had also become a Christian, Almachius was furious. He had

Maxentius beaten to death. His body was taken by Cecilia for Christian burial. He was buried near her husband and his brother.

Cecilia was now put on trial. She was told to sacrifice to Jupiter. Instead, Cecilia witnessed to the people at the shrine. They told her, "We believe that Christ is God because of the witness of His servant." More than four hundred came to faith in Christ and were baptized.

Almachius brought Cecilia to court and demanded to know about what she believed. She answered in riddles. He became angrier. Finally, he asked her if she knew that he had the power of life and death over her. She answered that he was a minister of death, not life. Then Almachius demanded that she sacrifice to the god Jupiter. She responded that this was a mere stone and no god and she would not. His anger grew hotter. But since she was the daughter of a senator, Almachius could not use the same means to have her killed. He told the executioner to take her to her home and have her bath heated seven times its normal temperature. He believed that she would die in the wet heat of her calidarium.

In Rome the people went daily to the Roman baths to cleanse themselves. The baths became social gathering places. Only the wealthiest people were able to have their own bath, or calidarium, in their homes. One can still see the calidarium in the basement of the home of Cecilia. It consists of a stream that is channeled through the basement floor. Under the floor a slave stoked the fire and heated the water for comfortable bathing.

Cecilia was to be placed in the calidarium and left to suffocate. After several hours, the executioner opened the calidarium. Instead of ending Cecilia's life, she was comfortably sitting on the floor and singing hymns.

When Almachius learned that she did not die there, he had the executioner hit her on the neck three times. He used the flat edge of the sword. She did not die right away. Roman law would not allow the executioner to strike a fourth blow. She was left in her calidarium to suffer a slow death. She survived for another three days. Christians cared for her night and day. They sang hymns and read from Scripture together. Many people from the community were present and came to faith in Christ—even as she was close to death.

Finally, the moment of her death came. She turned her face away from the people so they would not see the terrible pain that she was suffering. With her hands stretched out, she continued her witness. Her left hand had the index finger extended. It meant One God. Her right hand had her thumb, index finger, and middle finger extended. They told of Father, Son, and Holy Spirit. In that position she passed into her heavenly home with Christ, whom she loved and served. Years later, Stephano Moderna created a statue of Cecilia that may be seen both in her home and in the crypt in the Catacomb of St. Callixtus.

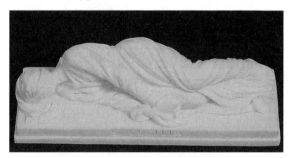

A statue depicting the death of Cecilia.

The Church Triumphant—AD 313 to 590
In AD 313 the persecution of Christians ended with the Edict of Milan that was put forth by the Roman emperor Constantine. Christianity was now able to grow along with the other religions of Rome. While Christians no longer died for their faith, a new set of problems arose. Some groups of Christian believers and other groups of non-Christians had strange ideas about the faith. They tried to attract true believers away from the faith with their false beliefs. It was now necessary to define the beliefs more closely. False beliefs had to be identified and put out of the true Church.

There were several Church Fathers who helped in this process. Perhaps none is greater than Augustine of Hippo. We shall look at his life and ministry.

By AD 480 the Germanic tribes had overrun the Roman Empire. The empire disintegrated, and the papacy emerged to fill the vacuum left by the emperor moving to Constantinople. In AD 590 Benedict of Nursia was born. He brought the era of the monasteries and ushered in the period known as the Middle Ages.

Augustine of Hippo (AD 354 to 430)

Augustine was born in Tagaste in northern Africa on November 13, AD 354. We know a lot about Augustine's life because he wrote about it in his book *Confessions*. His confessions are addressed to God. But we can learn about his life through them. *Confessions* have become a classic in Western literature.

His father, Patricius, wanted his young son to become a scholar. His mother, Monica, became a Christian. She desired that Augustine also become a Christian. To help him, she enrolled him in classes to study the Christian faith. She also taught him to pray. During his boyhood, Augustine became very sick. At that point he wanted to be baptized. But when it came time for baptism, Augustine got better and he wanted to wait at being baptized. Augustine had both a brother and a sister.

School

School days for Augustine were a painful memory. All he wanted to do was to play. He did not like the classroom. His teacher was very strict. When the teacher found Augustine was not working, he was hit across his knuckles with a rod. He remembered many such experiences. His father was not very sympathetic. Augustine hated Greek and did not like to read either Homer's *Iliad* or *Odyssey*. He found reciting his numbers tables boring. "One and one make two. Two and two are four. Four and four are eight." He read with pleasure many of the Latin classics. Unfortunately, as he related later in adulthood, they led him into sin.

From his account, school was not a very happy experience. He recalled that he was more afraid of using improper grammar than he was about showing envy or wanting the praise of other children and youth. He learned to keep bad company. He had friends who did not help him live a good life. As an adult, however, Augustine was thankful to God for his education.

After learning all that he could in the school in his hometown, his father sent Augustine to a nearby city to study grammar, poetry, and rhetoric. Rhetoric means to use language to persuade other persons. At age sixteen his father had him return to Tagaste and prepare to go to Carthage to study further. But Augustine did not go to Carthage for another year. He stayed in Tagaste. His mother, Monica, tried to help him to live a good life, but Augustine was having too much fun. She continued to pray for him.

At seventeen years of age, he went to Carthage to study. He studied at the best school of rhetoric in Carthage. There he had a good learning experience. In AD 370 his father died, but Augustine continued his studies in Carthage. He read all of the works of the great Roman orator Cicero. He had a strong ambition to develop his understanding in wisdom and learning.

In *Confessions*, Augustine admitted that this led to pride and selfish ambition. With his friends he lived a wild life. He also came under the influence of the Manicheans. This was a group that was not Christian. They led him further away from God. Later, Augustine would write his great work, *The City of God*. In that work he wrote about the wrong beliefs of the Manicheans. In spite of all of his problems, Monica continued to pray for her son that God would take hold of him and bring him to Christ.

He returned home from his studies in Carthage and opened a grammar school. This satisfied him for a time. But soon he became restless and returned to Carthage. There he opened a school for rhetoric. He was very successful and able to carry on public debates. This drew him great praise for his ability. In AD 372 he fell in love with a young woman, who bore a son to him, Adeodatus. For nine years he maintained his schools in Tagaste and Carthage.

Conversion

Wanting to go further in his career, he went to Rome. From there he applied for a position to teach rhetoric in Milan. It was in Milan that Augustine was influenced by the great doctor of the Church, Ambrose. Augustine wanted to hear Ambrose for the fame and reputation of the great scholar. He listened to the sermons of Ambrose. He met with Ambrose and gradually began to see the truth of Christianity.

In AD 387 Augustine began to see the error of his ways. He wanted to turn to Christ. He even prayed. Then as he was struggling, he went to the garden to pray. He heard a voice of a child. It said, "Take up and read. Take up and read." He picked up the book of the letters of the apostle Paul. He saw the truth of the passage from Romans 13:13–14. It said, "But put on the Lord Jesus Christ." In tears Augustine turned his life over to Jesus Christ. At thirty-two years of age Augustine gave up his sinful ways and became a Christian. He went and told his mother, Monica. They rejoiced together.

Augustine retired from teaching. He and his friends took residence at the home of a friend. Augustine gave his time to reading God's Word and prayer. Ambrose baptized Augustine at Easter in AD 387. Monica died in November of that year. His son, Adeodatus, died soon thereafter.

Returning to Africa, Augustine lived in his home in Tagaste. For the next three years he studied the Scriptures, prayed, and performed good works. Valerius, bishop of Hippo, had Augustine ordained as a priest in AD 391. After Valerius died in AD 395, Augustine became the bishop of Hippo. He served as bishop for the next thirty-five

years. He was a good pastor and shepherd to the people in his charge.

Augustine wrote extensively. He defended the Church against evil persons who would have changed or destroyed the message of the gospel. His scholarly learning was used by God to further the work of the kingdom of God. God can use whatever skills a person brings and dedicates to Him. Both Catholics and Protestants have benefited from the work of Augustine. A thousand years passed when Martin Luther brought about the Reformation. He depended upon Augustine's work to help him develop his theology.

The Germanic tribe of the Vandals was at the gates of Hippo in May AD 430. The siege continued for many months. But Augustine caught a fever. He knew that his days were numbered and he would soon leave this earth for his heavenly home. On August 28, AD 430, Augustine died.

THE MEDIEVAL CHURCH
AD 480 TO 1517

The Medieval Church lasted for nearly one thousand years to 1517. This period may be roughly subdivided into the Dark Ages from AD 590 to about 1000, and the period of the High Middle Ages from 1000 to 1517. The Dark Ages were a difficult time of life in Europe. Scholasticism brought new learning and the rise of the universities in Europe.

The Dark Ages—AD 480 to 1000

Gradually, the civilization of classical culture and learning began to fade. The great fathers of both the Western churches and the Eastern churches passed on. A new age was dawning. The Germanic tribes overran the Roman Empire. Schools, like the ones that Augustine started, went out of existence. The barbarians would raid communities. They burned the buildings and took many of the people as slaves. Safety was a constant concern. Along the coasts, the Vikings from the north would raid and burn the towns. For the common people, life was dangerous. People just wanted to survive. They lived their lives around farming the land. Life became very difficult as the Dark Ages followed the destruction of the Roman Empire.

The Church suffered along with the rest of life during this time. Local parish priests were poorly educated. Preaching declined and administering the sacraments of baptism, marriage, last rites, etc., became more important. Learning was now almost all confined to the monasteries. There was some safety in the monastic communities. The monks could withdraw from the evil of the world around them. They could spend their time in prayer and study of the Bible. The monks became the missionaries to the communities around the monastery.

There were monastic men and women before Christian monasticism developed. Christian monasticism started with a young man named Antonius. He took seriously the teaching of Jesus for the rich young ruler: "Then, looking at him, Jesus loved him and said to him, 'You lack one thing: Go, sell all that you have and give to the poor, and you will have treasure in heaven. Then come, follow Me'" (Mark 10:21). The term *monastic* means a person who lives a life away from the world. Monastic persons lived a life of prayer and thinking about their Christian faith in meditation. The earliest Christian monastic persons lived alone in the desert. Many lived a monastic life to avoid the persecution of Christians during the time that the Romans tried to destroy the Church. In later years they most often lived in communities and lived by a fixed rule of life.

Benedict of Nursia (AD 480 to 547)
Life in a Monastery
Benedict was born around AD 480 in Italy. He came from a good family. His parents did not believe that he would receive a good education locally. They sent him to Rome to study in the schools there. Benedict was shocked and offended by the immoral behavior of the boys in Rome. He was about fifteen years of age at the time. Benedict went into the lonely desert mountains of Subioco about forty miles east of Rome.

There he met a hermit named Romanus. The hermit gave Benedict monk's clothes and instructions how to live as a monk. Romanus promised to bring Benedict food and water regularly. Romanus would ring a bell and drop the food to Benedict in a basket tied to a rope from above. Romanus promised never to tell anyone where Benedict was located. For three years Benedict lived in this lonely place in prayer and meditation.

Finally, some shepherds were tending their flocks in the area and discovered Benedict. At first they thought that he was a wild animal. He lived among the rocks of a cave where they thought it was not possible for a person to survive. He was dressed in skins and did not appear to be human. But when they discovered that Benedict was a follower of God, they were very impressed with him. They listened as he taught them about the way of God. Now that Benedict had been discovered, many people began to find their way to Benedict's home in the wilderness. They would bring him food and listened to him tell about the spiritual life of poverty and prayer. It was not long before others began to follow Benedict's example, leaving home to engage in a lonely life of poverty and prayer.

The abbot of a monastery in northern Italy died. *Abbot* meant "father." The abbot was the leader of a monastery and demanded complete obedience from each of the monks. The monks asked Benedict to become their abbot. He was not sure that he wanted to do that. But he finally agreed. Many good families sent their sons to become monks in Benedict's monastery. Benedict founded twelve monasteries with twelve monks in each. Benedict remained as leader of all twelve monasteries.

Some time later, Benedict had a problem with Florentius, a local priest from a neighboring village. Apparently, Florentius grew jealous of Benedict. He began to spread false stories about

Benedict. This led to serious problems. Benedict refused to stay in the area. With only a few of his monks, Benedict went south.

He settled in the area of Cassino, a town that is located between Rome and Naples. The people of the area were pagan. They worshiped and sacrificed in a temple that was dedicated to Apollo. Benedict preached to the people, and many became Christians. Then in AD 530 Benedict established a monastery at Monte Cassino at the place where the temple to Apollo had been located. Instead of establishing several monasteries, as he had in northern Italy, Benedict built one large monastery. The monastery attracted many young men. Benedict's sister, Scholasticus, established a nunnery for women nearby.

The Benedictine Rule

Benedict wrote a Rule for the monastery that continues in Benedictine monasteries right up to the present. The Rule gave instructions that all members had to follow strictly throughout their life in the monastery. A new member of the community was on probation for the first year. If the new member failed to obey any of the rules of the monastery, he could be dismissed. The Rule also prescribed poverty, chastity, and obedience. When a person entered the monastery, he had to give up all of his earthly possessions. He could not even keep something that had been given by his parents. He had to be morally pure. Finally, he must give strict obedience to the abbot.

The Rule further prescribed four parts of the monk's day. First, he must work for five hours. The work was usually some form of physical labor, such as farming or baking. This would help him stay physically healthy. Second, he must study the Bible or other spiritual writings for four hours. Third, he must pray and attend services for five hours. These times were prescribed throughout the night and daytime hours.

The life of a monk was regulated. Normally, he did not leave the monastery for any length of time. Many monks lived their entire lives in the monastery. From the time they entered the monastery, they were cared for and even in old age and death. Benedict insisted that monks not eat at other places in the community. He believed that eating and sharing with persons outside the monastery would lead the monks away from their spiritual goal. They were provided with a healthy diet. The main meal was served between 11 a.m. and noon. Before they entered the refectory, monks had to wash his hands in the lavatorium. In the refectory at meals, the monks were not allowed to talk. Someone read from the Scripture or other religious text during the meal.

The clothing was appropriate for the climate. Benedictine monks were known by their distinctive black robes. About every three weeks the monks would gather as a group and shave each other, both the face and head. Baths were rare, since that might give pleasure to the monk and therefore harm him.

The abbot was selected by the monks when the position was vacant. But when the abbot was chosen, he had absolute rule over the monks until his death. He chose the prior, who was next in charge. He also chose persons for the other offices needed to run the monastery. These would include someone to run the refectory, bakery, the farming, etc. The center of life in the monastery was the cloister. This was an arcaded walk around the garden in the center of the monastery. The western part of the cloister was the schoolroom. New members of the monastery and children from the community studied there. Behind that was the library, which was extensive in many of the monasteries in later years. Part of the responsibilities of the monks included copying manuscripts that were borrowed from other monasteries and their own. These were the only libraries during the Dark Ages.

The southern side of the cloister was the darkest and contained the lavatorium, where the monk washed his hands before going to the refectory. Behind the cloister with the lavatorium were kept the linens and eating utensils. On the east side of the cloister was the place where the business of the monastery was carried out.

All of these rules seem strange to us today. But Benedict believed that the monk was engaged in a spiritual warfare. It was necessary to subdue the flesh and allow the Spirit to bring the monk to Christian growth. That could only happen as the monastery practiced strict rules.

In those days the monastery was a very busy place. They served their communities. There were no motels in those days. It was dangerous to travel. The brothers in the monastery provided food and a place to sleep for travelers. There were no hospitals for the sick. The brothers in the monastery took care of the sick. The brothers went into the community and helped to provide for the poor. Most of the brothers were not ordained to the clergy. But clergy were available for the services and sacraments.

High Middle Ages—AD 1000 to 1517

Several movements came together to help Western civilization slowly emerge from its cocoon of the Dark Ages. New life burst forth in education, philosophy, science, economics, theology, and the Church. The period was not without its problems. They came to focus in the Reformation that started the next major church movement that began in 1517. But there was new vitality in every area of life. Universities started during this period. In church life there was growing concern for the laxness of many of the monasteries. One of the concerns that emerged was the desire to get back to the original state of Christianity and to be like Christ. One man stands out in this regard—Francis of Assisi.

Francis of Assisi (1182 to 1226)

Francis was born to Pica and Peter Bernardon in 1182 in Umbria of northern Italy. Peter was a successful cloth merchant and was traveling in France at the birth of his son. Pica seems to have been French. While Francis was named John at his birth,

the nickname "Little Frenchie" seems to have stuck. He even enjoyed learning the French language.

Francis grew up wanting to have fun but was not an evil youth. He never got into serious trouble. One day he passed a poor beggar and did not give him anything. He felt guilty and ran after the poor man to give him some money. He promised from that point on he would never let a poor man go away without help again. That was a promise that he kept to his death.

Francis was a natural leader and became leader of the other youth in Assisi. He dreamed of being a knight. His parents were too busy in their business to provide for his education. But it soon became clear that Francis was not interested in his father's cloth business. That made his father angry. War broke out between the towns of Assisi and Perugia. Francis went to fight for his city but was captured by the men of Perugia. He spent a year in captivity there. When he was allowed to go home, he became very sick. The sickness lasted for a long time. But after it ended, he purchased the best equipment and clothes to go and fight in southern Italy. On the way, he met a poor man and exchanged clothes with him. As he got closer to the battle, he fell ill again. This time he had a vision to fight for the Master, rather than the man.

Returning home, his friends found him very quiet and not like his "old self." They thought that he had fallen in love. He agreed but told them that it was with Lady Poverty. From that point he spent time in prayer and wanted to engage in spiritual warfare. One day he met a leper and not only gave him money, but tried to help with the man's sores. This brought a change in Francis. He now went to the hospitals and tried to help.

One day he was praying in the church of San Damian. He heard a voice from heaven saying, "Go and repair my church." Francis went home and took a supply of his father's cloth to sell. With the money he returned to the church and gave it to the pastor. His father was furious! He got the money back, but he beat Francis and locked him in the basement. When his father left, his mother rescued him.

Upon his return, Peter told Francis that he would take away his inheritance. Francis was brought before the bishop of Assisi. Francis gladly agreed and took off his clothes. He told his father that he would no longer rely on him as father but turn to his heavenly Father. The surprised bishop gave Francis a coat, and Francis went off singing.

Francis returned to the church at San Damian and repaired it himself. He continued to repair two other churches as well. On February 24, 1208, he heard a sermon on Matthew 10:7–10. It provided Francis with a mission. He believed that God was calling him to preach a message of repentance and to go without money or good clothes. He got rid of his shoes and put on an undyed woolen robe that was fastened with a cord. Even though he could have been arrested, he preached to the people of the town. Soon he attracted a little band of followers. He had them wear the same type of robe, and it became the mark of the friars.

Francis wrote a Rule for his followers. It was short and contained mostly Scripture. The Rule required absolute poverty and begging for a living and living a pure life. Poverty was not only in earthly goods. Poverty included giving oneself totally to God and denying oneself. He took the Rule to Rome to receive official license from the Pope. Pope Innocent III was the most powerful Pope in the Catholic Church. He was somewhat disgusted with this poor beggar. According to the story, the Pope told Francis to go and wallow with the pigs, where he belonged. Much to the surprise of the Pope, Francis did just that. He returned and the Pope granted his request.

Francis of Assisi was known for his love of animals.

Francis loved animals. One of the stories about Francis tells of a wolf that he cared for. It was thought to be just a story, but recently, when some digging was done in the basement of his home, wolf bones were discovered. He wrote several verses of poetry to God's nature and His creatures. But Francis cared most for the people for whom Christ died.

Francis tried to go to Palestine to preach the gospel to the Muslims. His ship was wrecked and he had to return home. Next, he tried to go to the Muslims in Spain, but illness forced him to give up that journey. Finally, on his third try, he went to Egypt. The Crusaders were fighting the Muslem sultan, or king. His name was al-Kamil. He went straight to the sultan. The sultan saw in Francis a man who was committed to God. The sultan allowed him to visit some of the holy places in Palestine. This took place around 1217.

Meanwhile, the Franciscan order grew rapidly. That brought problems and Francis had to return home. Francis was suffering from illness. He gave up some of the leadership of the order to engage more fully in prayer, meditation, and ministering to the people. At Christmas in 1223, to honor the Christ Child, he started the first live nativity. That was discussed in an earlier section. During the next year he retired to a little cell in the mountain.

Some time before his death, Francis spoke to his band of followers. He told them to work hard and avoid idleness. He told them to love God, poverty, and the gospel. He blessed them and died on October 3, 1226. Francis loved the Lord and probably was the most like Jesus Christ of persons before or since.

THE REFORMATION
1517 TO 1776

The Renaissance or "Rebirth of Learning" began in Italy with the writer Petrarch in the 1330s. The rise of the universities and the monumental changes in the humanities of literature, art, and music had its effect. There developed a more classical approach from ancient Greece and Rome. Science was also having its effect upon the Renaissance. It should be noted that this was true for the south of Europe.

In the northern parts of Europe, there was a different trend. The Renaissance took a more religious approach and culminated in the Reformation. One invention helped develop literacy in the population. Johannes Gutenberg developed movable type in 1457, which made it possible for the German populace to obtain inexpensive copies of materials and led to more widespread literacy. This helped the Reformation, which shook the Church to its very foundations.

No longer was it possible to have one monolithic church. With a free conscience to study the Bible in one's own language and to believe only what the Bible taught created many new ideas. Many different denominations grew out of the Reformation. The religious changes of the north are also reflected in art, music, and literature. God used one man to change the direction of the Church. That man was Martin Luther.

Martin Luther (1483 to 1546)

In every age, God seeks men and women to do His will. In the early 1500s God chose a man who changed the course of Western civilization. Martin Luther was born in 1483 in Eisleben, Germany, to Hans and Margarethe Luther. At the time, they were a peasant family. But soon after his birth, the Luther family moved to the town of Mansfeld. His father, Hans, started working in the copper mines. Soon he was able to make enough money to become a supervisor. This allowed his family to live comfortably. They were a religious family. As a child, Martin remembered the fear of evil spirits that he dreamed about during the night. He also remembered being beaten for minor misdemeanors by both his mother and father.

His first schooling took place in a strict Latin grammar school. His experience of religion at the school was not pleasant. Next, he went to school in Magdeburg. This was run by the Brethren of the Common Life. He received a good Bible education, and their devotion and personal piety helped Martin in his own Christian life. From there Martin attended the school of St. George in Eisenach. He was taught the languages and made many good friends.

In 1501 he entered the University of Erfurt and completed his study of the liberal arts. He graduated with a bachelor of arts degree in 1502. His studies continued to the master of arts degree. His studies in philosophy, Greek, Hebrew, and Latin were of particular importance for his later work. He received his M.A. degree in 1505. Martin was planning to continue his studies in law. His father was pleased with that decision. God was preparing the young man for all the work that He wanted Martin to do in the years following his education.

Luther Enters the Monastery

Luther began his studies in law in May. He went home to visit his parents in Mansfeld in the summer. On the way back, he was caught in a thunderstorm. Lightning struck the tree and Martin exclaimed, "St. Ann, I will become a monk!"

Martin entered the Augustinian Monastery at Erfurt. When Hans Luther discovered what Martin had done, he was furious. Apparently, Martin had been considering this for some time. He wanted to find some way by which he could receive salvation from a God who seemed to be only an angry judge. He passed his year of probation and was accepted into the order. He tried to atone for his own sin by beating himself and spending more time in prayer than normal. He was trying to suffer to pay for his sin. Nothing seemed to work.

In May 1507 Martin Luther was ordained as a priest. When he thought about the greatness of God, Martin had difficulty getting through the service. Hans came to the service. Martin had hopes that his father would forgive him, but Hans was still angry with his son for leaving law school.

John von Staupitz was Luther's superior. He had great affection for the young monk. Von Staupitz tried to help Martin resolve his problems. He sent Martin to the newly founded University of Wittenberg to teach theology and continue his studies. His order sent him to Rome to discuss the problems that had arisen in the order. Luther was disappointed with the worldliness of the people in Rome. He returned and completed his doctor of theology degree in 1512. Von Staupitz kept Martin very busy by adding to his teaching responsibilities for ten monasteries and preaching in the church.

Luther's studies of the apostle Paul's letter to the Romans in 1515 and 1516 led him to a new understanding of God. He began to see that he could not do good works and achieve God's approval. He had to trust the work of Jesus on the cross that would give him Christ's righteousness in place of his own. It was God's free gift!

The Ninety-Five Theses

Luther posted ninety-five theses in Latin for discussion among the scholars on October 31, 1517. This event started the Reformation that changed Europe. The problem for Luther was the doctrine of penance. From 1215 the Catholic Church required that every Christian had to go to confession. He would be assigned penance to atone for his sin. Going to see relics (objects that were supposed to have Christian importance) was one means. Relics included splinters from the cross

Luther posting the ninety-five theses on the church door.

of Jesus or a gown worn by Mary. Buying an indulgence from the church would help a relative that had died to get out of purgatory. Purgatory was a place where one was cleansed in preparation for going into heaven. Purgatory was a place of punishment. Buying indulgences became very popular. Purgatory is not in the Bible.

The ninety-five theses were translated into German. They were circulated throughout the country. Now that people could read, they were very interested in what was happening with Luther. Duke Frederick the Wise had built the University at Wittenberg. He wanted to protect Luther from the anger of the Catholic Church. Luther wrote several works that explained his position. He was opposed to the wrongs that the Church was doing to the common people. He wanted them to know what the Bible said about forgiveness. With the apostle Paul, Luther exclaimed, "We are justified not by works, but by faith alone!"

The church had Luther's writings burned. Luther responded by burning the canon law of the church and the pope's writing against him. Luther had now completely broken his relationship with the Roman Church. The church wanted to burn Luther at the stake, but Frederick the Wise refused to be part of that. He protected Luther.

The church officials wanted Luther to appear before the Holy Roman Emperor in the city of Worms, Germany. The emperor was Charles V, a Roman Catholic from Spain. Luther appeared on April 17, 1521. As he entered the city of Worms, thousands of people lined the streets to see Luther. The emperor would not allow Luther to discuss his writings.

He demanded that Luther turn his back on his writings or be hunted until he was killed. The next day Luther gave his courageous answer, "My conscience is captive to the Word of God. I will not and I cannot recant. Here I stand! May God help me, Amen."

Charles V placed Luther under the imperial ban. Luther could be hunted and killed, but God did help Luther. Frederick the Wise had Luther kidnapped on the way home. He was taken to an abandoned castle at Wartburg. There he lived under the name of Duke George. Luther did not stop his work of the Reformation. He translated the Bible from Hebrew and Greek into German. Now the people of Germany could read the Bible in their own language.

Even though Luther was not present, the work of the Reformation continued. Many of his former brothers from the monastery left. They were encouraged to continue their Christian ministry. They were encouraged to marry. Many of the nuns left the Convent and married. Things were not going well at the church in Wittenberg. Luther came out of hiding and took up his work as pastor there. He wrote many writings that helped guide the Reformation. He wrote twenty hymns for singing in the church. His most famous is "A Mighty Fortress Is Our God." His fellow theologians at the University of Wittenberg helped. He started the Lutheran Church.

On June 13, 1525, Martin Luther married a former nun, Katharina von Bora. The couple lived in the old monastery. A year later they had their first son, Hans. They had several children. For the rest of his life, Katie was a constant companion and helped Luther through some very discouraging times. Luther was able to preach a shorter catechism and later the longer catechism. These provided children with an understanding of the Christian faith.

It was not easy for Luther in his later years however. The Peasant's Revolt caused trouble between him and the people. It was cruelly put down by the authorities. He suffered sickness. Charles V decided to enforce the Edict of Worms, and two former monks were burned at the stake. But the emperor also wanted to bring peace to the land. The Augsburg Confession was signed by the Protestant leaders, and the warring declined.

On January 23, 1546, Luther and three of his sons set out with a friend for Mansfeld. He ordained two pastors there. Then Luther tried to settle a dispute. On the way home they stopped in Eisleben—the place of his birth. Luther became very ill and died peacefully on February 18.

THE ENLIGHTENMENT, REVOLUTIONS, REVIVALS, AND MISSIONS 1646 TO 1900

The period of revolutions, revivals, and missions started with the American Revolution in 1776. During this period Robert Raikes established the Sunday school movement in 1780. Modern missions came into being with the efforts of William Carey (1761 to 1834) and others.

As Christians, we still struggle today with the problems that the Enlightenment brought. The primary characteristic of the Enlightenment was that reason replaced revelation as the means by which we come to know anything. But in spite of that, the Church continued to grow as John Wesley and the Methodists, for example, came along to revitalize the sagging vitality of the Church of England. By Wesley's time the Church of England was about two hundred years old. The Church of England, or the Anglican Church, had come into existence in England when King Henry VIII decided that he wanted to remarry and the pope forbade it. The church became more evangelical when his daughter, Elizabeth I, became queen.

John Wesley (1703 to 1791)
John Wesley's father, Samuel, and his mother, Susanna, were both very strong-willed persons. They had both been educated in a school for

people who disagreed with the Church of England. But Samuel returned to the Anglican Church and became a pastor in Epworth, England. John was their second son. His mother taught him at home. She had a great influence on her son. Finally, in 1714 John went to Charterhouse School. He showed signs even then of a spiritual life and interest in learning.

In 1720 John entered Christ Church College at Oxford University. Four years later John graduated. He became a deacon in 1725. His father needed help in the church at Epworth and asked John to come and assist him in the ministry. John gained experience and was ordained in 1728. After his brother Charles Wesley went to Oxford, John returned to Oxford, and they became a part of the Holy Club there. Other students called them "Methodists." They studied methodically and engaged in religious devotion together.

John had several opportunities to marry. He was very interested in Sally Kirkham, daughter of the rector of Stanton in Gloucestershire. He corresponded with her regularly, even after she married the Reverend John Chapone in December 1725. Chapone gave his permission for the letter writing. Sally appears to have had an influence on John's growing spiritual awareness. John had difficulty with his own spiritual peace of mind.

During this period the Methodist group at Oxford became concerned about the social needs of the community. They went into the jails and ministered to the prisoners. They distributed food and other necessities to people in the workhouses. At the end of this time in Oxford, John was in love with another young woman, but the relationship ended very unpleasantly.

When the opportunity came to go to Georgia in the New World, both John and Charles accepted. Colonel James Oglethorpe had established a colony in Georgia for prisoners and others to start a new life there. Oglethorpe wanted the Wesley brothers to preach to these people and help reform them from their former life. They also would have opportunity to preach to the Indians in the New World.

There were no planes to carry them across the ocean. They had to take a ship. It took weeks to cross the ocean. While they were on the ship, they met a group of Moravian immigrants. The Moravians were a group of Christian believers who came some years before Luther. They were persecuted back in Germany. Their message of the Gospel was warm and personal. Listening to the Moravians, John felt that they had a spiritual peace that he most desired.

John and Charles arrived in Savannah in February 1736. "The Great Experiment" was the name that John gave their missionary adventure in Georgia. Sadly, the experiment did not go well. Charles left early and returned to England. John met another young woman. But he did not propose to her, and she found another man to become her husband. John was heartbroken and in some legal difficulties. He also did not have the inner spiritual peace that he wanted so badly. As a result, he returned to England after more than two years in Georgia.

Instead of staying in England, he went to the German Moravian village of Herrnhut. On his return to England, he met a Moravian pastor named Peter Böhler. The young pastor was on his way to America. He had a strong influence on both Charles and John. He tried to help John understand that faith is not just reason. Faith is personal between God and the believer. Peace with God comes from a clear understanding of God's love.

Charles had a conversion experience first. Then on May 24, 1738, John attended a Moravian service at Aldersgate in London. The building is no longer there, but there is a marker on the wall of the present building on the spot where John met with the Moravians. Someone was reading Martin Luther's preface to his *Commentary on Romans*. John wrote:

> *In the evening I went very unwillingly to a society in Aldersgate-Street, where one was reading Luther's preface to the Epistle to the Romans. About a quarter before nine, while he was describing the change which God works in the heart through faith in Christ, I felt my heart strangely warmed. I felt I did trust in Christ, Christ alone for salvation: And an assurance was given me, that he had taken away my sins, even mine, and saved me from the law of sin and death.*
>
> John Wesley's journal, May 24, 1738

Even though John Wesley had served as a pastor and missionary, he came to a true understanding of the work of Jesus in taking away his sins. He found help in the writings of the great reformer, Martin Luther. He was thrity-five years of age at this time, and he no longer had doubts. He had peace in his heart. This experience brought an important change in his life.

John and his brother Charles now entered on the Great Methodist Revival. At first John tried to work with the societies from within the Anglican Church. But that brought opposition. George Whitefield, a friend from the Holy Club at Oxford, convinced him to reach the persons who were not Christians. John was himself a powerful preacher, and as his fame grew, his sermons were published.

By 1749 the revival was known throughout England and America. Whitefield became one of the greatest revival preachers, and Wesley established societies and churches across England and Colonial America. Charles wrote more than six thousand hymns to support the movement.

John traveled tirelessly for thousands of miles each year both in England and America to preach and teach the gospel. Since the clergy would not help, John enlisted men from the churches to assist him in the ministry. He instructed the people and wrote rules to protect the newly formed societies. Many of the Anglican clergy were not happy with his work. Shortly after John's death in 1791, it meant a complete break with the Church of England and the establishment of Methodist Church.

God had wonderfully saved John Wesley. He was a man open to God to be used by God. He started a movement that led to the salvation of thousands in England and America. At the end of his life, those who were at his bedside related that John Wesley summed up his work by saying, "The best of all is, God is with us."

MODERN PERIOD
1900 TO THE PRESENT

The modern period of the nineteenth century to the present saw major changes in every area of life. Many of these changes are continuing today. The Industrial Revolution brought people to the cities to find work. They left their religious and altruistic beliefs, that were characteristic of the past generation and the agrarian culture. For many the result was to discover that life had less meaning. The Civil War was a full-scale war in which the whole nation was mobilized. This whole-scale war continued in the two world wars of the twentieth century.

Science has brought many good things to people, but it spurred materialism and the philosophy of naturalism. The philosophy of naturalism suggests that man is nothing more than a group of cells and protoplasm. The naturalists say that man's behavior is nothing more than a product of his environment. Instead of providing hope, naturalism has resulted in hopelessness for many.

In the late nineteenth and early twentieth centuries, many churches and denominations have left their former desire to see men and women and boys and girls come to a saving knowledge of Christ. In the early 1900s the social gospel and equating sin to nothing more than poor upbringing led to a utopian theology. But two world wars brought an end to that kind of theology. It was replaced by a string of theologies—feminist, black, and liberation to name a few. More recently Eastern thought from Buddhism, Islam, and

Taoism have infiltrated theology and on a broader scale our colleges and universities. Groups like the Mormons have also entered the mainstream of American culture.

But in the midst of these changes, God has not been silent to those who will listen. God has raised up His own. They do not see life as hopeless, nor did they succumb to the fads in theology or to the naturalism of our age. Revival is still an important way that God uses to stir His people to a deeper faith, to evangelization of persons outside of Christ, and to strengthen His Church. Billy Graham is an example of a present-day evangelist and leader in the church. His ministry has had an impact both nationally and internationally through his preaching.

William Franklin Graham (1918 to the Present)

Billy Graham was the son of a successful dairy farmer. The family lived near Charlotte, North Carolina, where he went to school. At age sixteen, Graham accepted Christ as his Savior at an evangelistic campaign. The preacher was an old-time evangelist, Mordecai Ham.

Graham went to college in Tennessee, but that did not turn out to be a good experience. He moved to Florida Bible Institute and finished his course of study. He was soon ordained in a Southern Baptist church and began to preach to young people. An opportunity to continue his education allowed Graham to go to Wheaton College in Illinois. There he met and married Ruth Bell. She was the daughter of a Presbyterian missionary to China.

For the next several years he entered into a full-time evangelistic ministry. Torrey Johnson was a pastor in Chicago at the time. Johnson invited Graham to become involved in his radio broadcast, *Songs in the Night*. Through this, Graham met George Beverly Shea, who became a friend and future soloist for the Graham crusades.

When Torrey Johnson founded Youth for Christ, he invited Graham to preach to youth. On one of his trips to England, he met Cliff Barrows. Barrows and his wife accompanied Graham as musicians. Barrows later became a friend and song leader for Graham's evangelistic crusades.

After World War II, Graham began to conduct evangelistic crusades in some American cities. He also became president of Northwestern College. This experience developed his ability to manage an organization.

Through all of these experiences, God prepared Graham for the worldwide evangelistic work that He intended for Graham to conduct. His first major campaign came in 1949, when he and his staff began an evangelistic crusade in Los Angeles. The crusade drew national attention. Graham was invited to the White House by President Harry Truman. Relationships with presidents of the United States continued with succeeding presidents through President George W. Bush.

The Greater London Crusade was followed by the crusade in Scotland. These brought Graham international recognition. He developed a friendship with the Royal family in England. His New York City crusade in Madison Square Garden during the 1950s resulted in many conversions and in national prominence for his ministry.

The Billy Graham Evangelistic Association helped to start the magazine *Christianity Today*. They also produce their own magazine, *Decision*. Each week the association produces the radio program *Hour of Decision*. The organization has produced a number of major Christian films. Graham has been active in his evangelistic ministry for more than fifty years. He has preached in 185 countries to audiences that have exceeded one hundred million persons. The crusades have been televised and have reached many more millions of people. There have been more than two million conversions through his ministries.

As impressive as the numbers are, Graham's success has not been just in speaking to large audiences. He has continued to preach a clear and plain gospel to all people. Through it all, he has maintained his humility. He has remained true to the Bible as the Word of God. He has kept Christ at the center of his ministry. He has maintained a personal love for God that has been at the heart of his ministry. He has been a person open to allow God to use him over the years. As a result God has blessed him greatly.

What We Believe

INTRODUCTION FOR PARENTS AND TEACHERS

What we believe as Christians is one of the most important issues in life. Our beliefs have eternal consequences. In many educational circles, a new philosophy is providing direction for educators to guide and teach American schoolchildren. These educators hold that a child builds his or her own personal and unique view of reality. This is a way for the child to make sense of the world. In this view, the child's personal experience, interaction with other students, and interaction with teachers result in the development of a personal outlook on life and a personal view of the world. Encouraged by secular teachers and peers, a personal view will not likely become a Christian view. For teachers, this personal view is known as Constructivism.

Constructivism provides neither a Christian nor a biblical outlook on life. The biblical worldview begins with God and His creation from the Book of Genesis. The creation of man and the entrance of sin into the world are part of the Christian view. God is in control of His world, and He determines what kind of behavior is right and what behavior is wrong and sinful. The instruction of the child must begin with this reality. God's intent for the instruction of the child must conform to His laws. God's intent for the child's instruction is found in Deuteronomy 6. Moses made it clear that God intended for His people to live in accordance with the instruction that He provided through His servant Moses. The people were told to teach those rules for life that God gave them. Not only were the people of Israel to teach them, but they were required to talk of them in the home. They were instructed to provide constant reminders of the commands of the Lord. There was nothing in this teaching that even remotely suggested that the people could allow their children to form their own view of reality.

The content of what the people were to believe was extremely important. Jesus emphasized this in His response to the Pharisees about the Great Commandment of the Law. Jesus told His listeners that they were to love God with all their heart, with all their soul, and with all their mind (Matthew 22:37). In our current understanding, this would include all the components of our personalities: the affective or emotional component, the volitional or will component, and the cognitive or mind component. Loving God in this manner will result in God's complete control over our lives. To be sure, Christianity is a religion of the heart, but it is also requires a change in both the will and the mind. Anything less is not worthy of the name Christian.

We must not allow our children to construct either their own view of reality or what behaviors are right or wrong. Through His Word, God has provided us with a standard for life, by which we must live. Living according to God's Word is the only way by which we may please Him. Just as Moses instructed Hebrew families, this view must also be taught to our children and our grandchildren. Christian children must learn to live their lives in keeping with God's Word. We must help them to see the world from God's perspective, as provided in His Word.

Modern educational theories have also questioned the value of memorizing anything. It is interesting to note that researchers who study learning have discovered that children have a marvelous facility to memorize. Children lose this ability as they grow older. When we become adults, it becomes much more difficult to memorize. Therefore, children will benefit both now and in the future from time spent in memorization of Scripture texts. You will want to encourage them to do this. Children in grades one to three can learn many texts of Scripture. We have identified some excellent texts for memorization in the sidebars of this section. Learning these texts will greatly assist your children to make learning God's Word a lifelong priority.

Along with memorization a child must develop understanding of the Scripture verses that are learned. Scripture texts often have several levels of meaning. Children may understand the simpler levels of meaning at the time they memorize the text. As they grow older, they may return to the same texts and find deeper meanings that will carry them into the next phase of their growth and understanding.

In this section of the book, children will come to learn and understand some of our most cherished and essential Christian beliefs. We will look first at the necessity for finding a relationship with God through Jesus Christ. He is the only way to God and to heaven. Children have a spiritual sensitivity that is very special. We should not be afraid to recognize and support that sensitivity.

One of the special privileges of parenthood is the process of helping your child to find Jesus Christ as personal Lord and Savior. Do not coerce or push the child to a decision, but do not hold them back either. To assist you, the steps toward salvation are set forth in the text. Be sure that your child understands what he or she is doing. Discourage them from accepting Christ because it will please you or they are merely following their friends. If your child does make a commitment to Christ, you will also want to share that commitment with your pastor and your child's Sunday school teacher.

Our second concern will be to discover that only through a lifelong study of prayer and God's Word can they maintain a relationship with God through Jesus Christ. Third, God has also provided us with rules for behavior. These are the Ten Commandments. Children need to learn the Ten Commandments and to conduct their lives in accordance with them. The Ten Commandments will provide help to resist when they are tempted to live in ways that are not pleasing to God.

"For God loved the world in this way: He gave His One and Only Son, so that everyone who believes in Him will not perish but have eternal life." —John 3:16

JESUS—THE ONLY WAY

In Genesis we discovered that God created the heavens and the earth in the beginning. God created all living things. Adam and Eve, the first man and woman, lived in the Garden of Eden. But Satan came and tempted them to sin against God. They sinned and from that point on, both men and women have had to live with the consequences of sin. Our relationship with God was broken. Our hope for living eternally in heaven with God was destroyed. But God was not willing to leave us in that awful condition. He sent His only Son—Jesus Christ—to earth to become our Savior. God provided us with a Redeemer and a hope for eternal life with Him.

We have studied about Jesus. In the New Testament section of the handbook, the life of Jesus was described from Scripture. In the last two sections, we have described Jesus' birth and His death and resurrection. Jesus was a very special person. He was God, but He was also man through His birth in Bethlehem. Jesus died on the cross to pay the penalty for our sins. God did not leave Jesus in the grave. Jesus rose from the dead on the third day.

Because Jesus rose from the dead, all persons who put their trust in Jesus will find peace with God and be taken to heaven to live with God after death. This is a free gift from God. All we have to do is ask Jesus to forgive our sins and to save us. Just as the early disciples were given the Holy Spirit of God on the day of Pentecost, the new believer is given the gift of the Holy Spirit at the moment he or she trusts in Jesus Christ as Savior. He comes to be with us all the time. He gives us God's guidance and protection through life.

Jesus loves you. He wants you to become part of God's family. God does not force you to follow Him. You must make a decision to become a member of God's family. To become a follower of

Jesus and to find eternal life with God, you need to follow these steps.

Step 1—Admit that you are a sinner. Adam and Eve fell into sin in the beginning of time. We also have sinned. God punishes sin by death.

"For all have sinned and fall short of the glory of God." —Romans 3:23

Step 2—Know that the penalty for sin is death. God's Law requires that the penalty for sin is eternal death. But God loves us so much that He has provided a way for us to escape the penalty of eternal death and eternal separation from God. He sent His own Son, Jesus, to die on the cross and pay the penalty for the sins of all who trust Him.

"For the wages of sin is death, but the gift of God is eternal life in Christ Jesus our Lord." —Romans 6:23

Step 3—Understand that God loves us so much that He was willing for His own Son to die on the cross to open heaven to us who believe and accept His gift by faith and trust.

"But God proves His own love for us in that while we were still sinners Christ died for us!" —Romans 5:8

Step 4—Answer God's love by allowing God's gift to be your salvation from sin and eternal death. Pray and tell God that you know that all have sinned. Tell Him that you have sinned. Ask Jesus to come into your heart and life and save you from sin. Then believe Him at His Word that He has saved you and has sent His Holy Spirit into your heart and life. Thank Him for His love and saving grace.

"If you confess with your mouth, 'Jesus is Lord,' and believe in your heart that God raised Him from the dead, you will be saved." —Romans 10:9

You only need to make this decision one time in life. A new believer becomes part of the family of God. No one can ever take you away from your new life in Jesus Christ. You are eternally safe in Christ. Even though you have been saved, there are still times, however, when you will sin. Each time this happens you must pray to God and ask for His forgiveness. He expects you to admit when you have done wrong. He is willing to forgive you because your sin is covered by Jesus' death on the cross. But you must confess or tell Him what you did wrong and ask for His forgiveness.

Jesus loves you. He wants to be your friend through all of your life. He wants what is best for you. But you will need to allow Him to guide your life. Just as you need to eat the right food and get the proper amount of exercise to grow healthy and strong, so you need to allow Jesus to teach you and to guide you through prayer and following His Word. Ask Jesus each day to have control of your life and to make you what He wants you to be.

PRAYER

Prayer is talking with God. God wants to hear about the things that bother us and the things that delight us. We can pray to God first thing in the morning. We can ask God to care for us during the day ahead. We can pray during the day. When we are in school and problems come, we can ask God to help us face the problems. We can ask Him to help us remember those things we have studied before a test. We can tell God when we are happy. We can talk to God when we are sad. We can pray to God after school, when we are playing with our friends, and ask Him for help when there is a disagreement. At meals we can thank Him for His goodness in giving us enough to eat. We can pray to God before we go to bed at night.

In other words, we can pray anytime. God is always interested in the joys, fears, and tears of His children. You are never alone. God is always just a prayer away. He wants His children to pray about everything. The Bible tells us to "pray constantly."

> *"Pray constantly. Give thanks in everything, for this is God's will for you in Christ Jesus."*
> *—1 Thessalonians 5:17–18*

What Should Be in Our Prayers?

When we read the Bible, there are many examples of prayers in both the Old and New Testaments. The Bible gives us some guidelines that we can use to help us pray more in keeping with His ways. As we learn to pray, we need to remember that we do not need to have a set pattern for prayer. Prayer must grow out of our relationship with God. We must never become careless in our praying. Because of His great love for us, our relationship with God must always be very special. When we come to Jesus, His Holy Spirit comes to live within us. He hears our prayers. Since we have that relationship, God will always answer our prayers. His answers may not always be what we want, but we know that He will always act in doing what is best for us.

Praise

We can always praise God. God is so good! He gives us the rain to make our crops grow. He gives us the sun to keep us warm. He gives us homes where we can find happiness with family. He gives us His love and promises always to be with us, both when we are happy and when we are sad. We can praise Him for always being there for us.

Praise is one of the ways by which we can worship God. Praise means to give honor to God. Praise gives us a way to tell God that we love Him. The Bible gives us many expressions of praise to

God. We need to praise God because He is worthy of our praise!

> *"Shout triumphantly to the LORD, all the earth. Serve the LORD with gladness; come before Him with joyful songs."*
> *—Psalm 100:1–2*

Thanksgiving

Thanksgiving Day has become a time for football games across America, so it may be difficult to think of the first Thanksgiving Day. It took place in Plymouth Colony in 1621. The Pilgrims, who had come to America to worship God as they believed was right, joined together with the Indians for a celebration. They wanted to thank God for protecting them and providing crops and food for them that year. The feast continued in New England for years to come. It occurred after fall harvest. Eventually, it became a national holiday, as it is today. We do not usually think of Thanksgiving as a religious holiday, but that is the way it started. Perhaps we need to get back to the idea of the first Thanksgiving in our day. Along with the traditional holiday feast, we should pause and give God thanks for His care for us during the past year.

That first Thanksgiving captures the idea of thanksgiving in prayer. It expresses to God how we really feel about the good things that God has done for us. Thanksgiving needs to come from an attitude of a thankful heart. Thanksgiving means to tell God that we appreciate His love and care for us. God is good to us each and every day, yet we often forget how good He really is. We do not say thanks to Him for all that He does to care for and protect us. We do not say thanks enough for the provision of food that He provides each day. We need to express our gratitude for the salvation that He provided for us through the life, death, and resurrection of Jesus Christ. Thanksgiving prayer gives us an opportunity to show our thankfulness for these many things that God has given us.

The Bible encourages us to express our thanks to God for His goodness and love for us. No matter how young we may be, we can still say "Thank You" to God. Many Scriptures urge thankfulness.

> "Let us enter His presence with thanksgiving; let us shout triumphantly to Him in song. For the LORD is a great God, a great King above all gods."
>
> —Psalm 95:2–3

Confession

As we get older, there are other forms of prayer that we must pray. Confession is one of those types of prayer. To confess means to tell God what we have done that we should not have done. Sometimes it is embarrassing and very uncomfortable. But God expects that we will tell Him when we have sinned against Him, even if it is uncomfortable. He is willing to forgive us, but we must tell Him about it.

Sometimes we may hurt someone else. On the playground we may become angry and hit another boy or girl. That is not the kind of behavior that God likes us to do. We need to tell the other person that we are sorry. But we also need to tell God that we should not have hit the other person. We need to ask for His forgiveness and try not to do it again.

> "If we confess our sins, He is faithful and righteous to forgive us our sins and to cleanse us from all unrighteousness."
>
> —1 John 1:9

Prayer for Others

Other people need our prayers. In His Word, God has told us to pray for others. It is not difficult to find many persons for whom we can pray. We need to pray for our relatives, who may be experiencing difficulties. We need to remember the people from our church family. There are the boys and girls in our Sunday school class. We need to pray for them, especially when they have special needs. These might include sickness or difficulty in school. We need to pray for our Sunday school teacher and the pastor of the church.

We need to remember to pray for the missionaries, who are in countries far away from home. They are there to teach and preach the gospel to people who have never heard or may never hear the good news that God loves them and wants them to find His Son, Jesus Christ. The missionaries also have children. They may be boys and girls in grades one to three. It is hard enough to grow up here at home, but to live in a foreign country and have to learn a new language and new customs makes it more difficult. They need our prayers.

Sometimes we know about people who have had tragedies in their lives. They may have lost their home and all their possessions in a fire or a flood. We need to pray for these people. You may read about other persons in our country or other countries who have been hurt in some national tragedy. We can pray for these people as well. This kind of prayer pleases God. It is not selfish. It is expressed for the good of other people. Jesus had love and compassion for people He met who were suffering. He is pleased when we do the same for our families and other people.

> "First of all, then, I urge that petitions, prayers, intercessions, and thanksgivings be made for everyone."
>
> —1 Timothy 2:1

Requests for Ourselves

Jesus taught us also to pray for the things that we need. God is not some kind of big Santa Claus in the sky, who will give us anything that we ask for. He loves us too much to give us things that are not good for us. But He does want to provide us with the things that we need. He does want to give us things that are good for us because He loves us and cares for us. Jesus said that God delights in giving us those things that He desires for us.

God does not want us to fret. He does not want us to fear. He will respond when we voice a prayer telling Him we are afraid or have special needs. He wants us to pray for ourselves and for the members of our families. He is there, and He answers our requests in the way that He desires, but it is always in our best interest.

> *"Don't worry about anything, but in every-thing, through prayer and petition with thanksgiving, let your requests be made known to God."*
> —*Philippians 4:6*

How Did Jesus Teach Us to Pray?

There are many prayers in the Bible. We can learn from all of them. But there is one prayer that stands out from the others. It was the prayer that Jesus gave to those who follow Him. Jesus taught the people a model prayer. We can learn a lot about effective prayer by learning the prayer that Jesus taught His followers.

It is one of those prayers in the Bible that even the youngest child can learn to love and appreciate. Yet it is a prayer from which the oldest person can learn as well. You will find it in the sidebar. You will want to memorize Jesus' prayer. Read the prayer and reread it. Become familiar with it. Each time you read the prayer, try to say as much as you can from memory, without looking at it. To help you understand the prayer, return to the text and read the explanation for each part of Jesus' model prayer.

THE LORD'S PRAYER

The Lord's Prayer appears in two places in the Bible. First, Jesus taught the prayer to those who listened to His teaching in the Sermon on the Mount (see Matthew 6:9–15). Second, one of the disciples asked Jesus to teach them to pray as He prayed (see Luke 11:2–4). In the prayer, there are seven requests. The first three are directed to God. They are: "Your name be honored as holy," "Your kingdom come," and "Your will be done." These start with who God is and go toward His kingdom. The next four have to do with us. They are: "Give us today our daily bread," "Forgive us our debts," "Do not bring us into temptation," and "Deliver us from the evil one." They start with our needs and go to God's protective care for us.

> *Our Father in heaven,*
> *Your name be honored as holy.*
> *Your kingdom come.*
> *Your will be done*
> *on earth as it is in heaven.*
> *Give us today our daily bread.*
> *And forgive us our debts,*
> *as we also have forgiven our debtors.*
> *And do not bring us into temptation,*
> *but deliver us from the evil one.*
> *[For Yours is the kingdom*
> *and the power*
> *and the glory forever,*
> *Amen.]*
> —*Matthew 6:9–13*

Honor God (6:9)

We call upon Him as Father. God is Father because He created and rules over the entire world. He is Father in a very unique way to those who put their trust in Him through Jesus Christ. This prayer is intended for those who love God and want Him to rule in their hearts and lives. God is close to us. God loves and cares for us, just as an earthly father would care for his children. God is also removed from us. He is in heaven. But this will change when we go to heaven to live with Him forever.

"Your name be honored as holy." We cannot be careless about the way we use God's name. Often you will hear other people use God's name foolishly. That does not please God. We cannot control what others say, but we must never use God's name uncaringly. Just as God cares for us, we need to respect and love Him. We do not want to dishonor Him. When we treat God with respect and love, we worship Him. Worship means to give honor. No one is worthy of more honor, love, and reverence than our heavenly Father.

Desire God's Rule (6:10)

Because there is sin in the world, God does not rule alone in this world. Jesus brought God's kingdom to earth. God's kingdom comes when those who believe in Him and trust Him allow God to reign in their hearts. They want God to rule not only in their hearts but also in the whole world. One day there will be no question about God's rule. God will rule supreme. In the meantime we have to obey Him and look forward to the time when He will reign alone.

Along with God's kingdom, we also desire that people would be obedient to God's laws. True believers want God's laws to be obeyed. This will happen when we obey God's laws here on earth just as the heavenly creatures obey God's laws in heaven. There will come a day when all people everywhere will come to obey God and live as He commands. Until that day, we need to be sure that we obey Him and look forward to that great day when He will rule the entire world.

We must remember to whom we are praying. Before we come to those things that are important to us, we need to worship God. God wants us to remember who He is. Our thoughts need to be centered in God when we pray. God also wants us to pray for others. God wants us to do the things that are important for His purposes. Then we may ask for the things that are on our minds.

May God Give Us What We Need (6:11)

In the second half of this prayer, Jesus told His followers to ask God for certain things. Jesus used bread as an example. Food is important for life. We cannot live without food. We cannot worship God if we are not cared for with the important things of life. Jesus emphasized the importance of our dependence upon God to provide us with the things that we need to live. Notice that Jesus uses the word *us*. We cannot be selfish. *Us* would certainly include our family. *Us* might also include asking God to care for persons in our church family. *Us* might even extend to those who are poor and needy.

Forgive Us Our Debts (6:12)

Remember when we discussed confession? Jesus said that we should ask God to forgive us our debts. Jesus meant that each day we need to ask for forgiveness. God takes sin very seriously. When we break His law, we need to ask for His forgiveness. Only God can forgive sin. Having our physical needs met is important, but we must have our spiritual needs met as well. That will not happen unless we ask Him for forgiveness.

Along with asking God for His forgiveness, Jesus told us to be sure that we are also forgiving of others. When people do things or say things to us that are mean, we need to forgive them. This is pleasing to God. God wants us to live peacefully with other people. That is part of doing what God commands. Remember that when we do what God commands, we are making His kingdom come on earth. In summary, Jesus said that we should be willing to confess the things that we have done that are wrong. Then we should be willing to forgive others who have done wrong things to us.

Keep Us from Falling into Temptation (6:13a)

Temptation to sin can sometimes seem very desirable. We need God's help not to give in to temptation. God never leads us into sin. Through prayer we can receive God's help not to fall into sin ourselves. We do not know what kinds of things will happen in a day. Temptation can sneak up on us, and soon we are tempted to hit someone or say bad words. But God can help us not to do what does not please God.

Deliver Us from the Evil One (6:13b)

Satan wants us to fall into sin. It pleases him when one who follows God does things that do not please God. Satan wants to hurt and destroy. We cannot deliver ourselves from sin, but God can keep us from falling into sin. That is why we need to pray every day for God's protection and care.

For Yours Is the Kingdom, Power, Glory (6:13c)

God can be trusted and counted upon to care for us. God will meet our needs. God can deliver us from sin. God can protect us from the evil one. The reason is that God rules the kingdom. God has the power. God's glory will shine forth. We can praise God for His love and protective care. Praise honors God and needs to be part of our prayer life. Amen comes at the end of the prayer. It means something like "it is true" or "let it be so." It is an expression of confidence in God. He will do what He has promised.

THE TEN COMMANDMENTS

The Ten Commandments show us that God cares for us. If God did not care for us, He would not care how we lived. God cares for us so much that He will not leave us to live as we please. The Ten Commandments are designed for us to live right. While they were given directly to the Israelites through Moses on Mount Sinai, they apply to all people. They apply all the time. They apply especially to us as followers of Jesus. We do not need to keep the Jewish laws for things like not eating pork. But we are not excused from keeping God's moral law. We must obey the Ten Commandments. In the Sermon on the Mount, Jesus further talked about keeping the commandments. He said that God sees what we do, but God also sees our hearts. He knows when we think mean thoughts about other people and want to hurt them. God wants us to be holy as God is holy. God demands our best.

When we are born into God's family by accepting Jesus as our personal Savior, God's Spirit comes to live within us. God's Spirit will help us to please God by doing those things that are pleasing to God. God expects us to read and learn from His Word—the Bible. The Holy Spirit can take the words of the Bible and guide us through life. This is especially true for the Ten Commandments. We need to memorize the Ten Commandments. The Holy Spirit can use the commandments in our lives to keep us from doing things that displease God.

1. *You shall have no other gods before Me.*

2. *You shall not make for yourself an idol, or any likeness of what is in heaven above or on the earth beneath or in the water under the earth.*

3. *You shall not take the name of the LORD your God in vain, for the LORD will not leave him unpunished who takes His name in vain.*

4. *Remember the sabbath day, to keep it holy.*

5. *Honor your father and your mother, that your days may be prolonged in the land which the LORD your God gives you.*

6. *You shall not murder.*

7. *You shall not commit adultery.*

8. *You shall not steal.*

9. *You shall not bear false witness against your neighbor.*

10. *You shall not covet your neighbor's house; you shall not covet your neighbor's wife or his male servant or his female servant or his ox or his donkey or anything that belongs to your neighbor.*

(see Exodus 20:3–17 NASB)

Like the Lord's Prayer, the Ten Commandments are divided into two parts. The first four commandments tell us how God wants us to relate to Him. Commandments 1 and 2 inform us who God is and how we need to worship Him. Commandment 3 describes the holy reverence we need to have for God's name.

A tablet containing the Ten Commandments.

Commandment 4 tells us how we need to set apart the Lord's Day from the rest of the week.

Commandments 5 through 10 tell us how we are to live in relation to other persons.

Commandment 5 shows us how important the home is to God. Commandment 6 warns us not to take another person's life. Commandment 7 commands us to be true and faithful in marriage. Commandment 8 requires us not to steal another person's property. Commandment 9 tells us not to lie. Commandment 10 does not allow us to envy or wish we had what someone else has.

The Ten Commandments are listed on the previous page. You will want to memorize them. You will want to live your life by obeying them. They will last you a lifetime.

Commandment 1—"You shall have no other gods before Me."

We must have complete loyalty to God! God alone must be worshiped. The Egyptians and other peoples from Bible times worshiped other gods. This displeased our God, Jehovah. Nothing here on earth can take the place of God. Sometimes games, sports, toys, friends, music, or money can become very important to us. We cannot allow other things to become more important to us than God. If those things become more important, then God does not have His right place in our lives.

Commandment 2—"You shall not make for yourself an idol, or any likeness of what is in heaven above or on the earth beneath or in the water under the earth."

God is spirit. God cannot be seen by us. In Bible times, the Egyptians and the Babylonians worshiped the sun, moon, stars, and even crocodiles from the sea. Remember when Moses was in the mountain of God for forty days, and the people made a golden calf to worship. God was very angry, and He sent Moses back to the people. Moses broke the tablets of stone of the Ten Commandments over the golden calf. The people had to repent. God hates idols. Fifty of the 613 laws given to Moses were against idolatry.

We can be guilty of idolatry today. If we joke about God as "the old man upstairs" with a long gray beard, sitting on a throne, we may disobey this command. If we look at the horoscope in the newspaper to guide our lives, we may be guilty of idolatry. To follow a false religion is a form of idolatry. We can become so in love with money or other things that they may become idols in our lives. We cannot do these things and please God.

Commandment 3—"You shall not take the name of the LORD your God in vain, for the LORD will not leave him unpunished who takes His name in vain."

God's name is holy. God's name represents Him. God's name must not be used carelessly or foolishly. It is common today for people to use the name of God when they are surprised or excited. God's name is often used as a swear word. This is wrong! If we love God and worship God, we cannot use His name in any of these ways.

Commandment 4—"Remember the sabbath day, to keep it holy."

Recall our discussion of the Sabbath day in the life of the Jews. The Jews were not allowed to work on the Sabbath. They were to worship God on the Sabbath. Remember also that we looked at the

Lord's Day for Christians. The Lord's Day replaced the Sabbath. It came on the first day of the week in memory of Jesus' resurrection. We are to keep the Lord's Day holy, or set apart to God. We need to worship on the Lord's Day. We need to spend the day thinking about God and His relationship to us.

Commandment 5—"Honor your father and your mother, that your days may be prolonged in the land which the LORD your God gives you."

God provided children with parents. Parents need to love their children and bring them up according to God's direction. This commandment tells us how important the home is to God. Parents are God's representatives to their children. We first learn about God through our relationship with our parents. Children need to love and respect their parents. Children need to obey their parents. He wants us to live together in a peaceful and loving relationship. Children should not allow their friends to make fun of or disrespect their parents. This is not pleasing to the Lord.

Commandment 6—"You shall not murder."

Killing another person is condemned by God. We have been created in God's image. We have no right to take another person's life. Every night on television we can see people killed in the stories that appear there. We can become careless about taking another person's life when we see it staged every day. But God's command prohibits that. We need to be careful not to be caught up in the evil of our culture.

Commandment 7—"You shall not commit adultery."

No man can take another man's wife. No woman can take another woman's husband. God makes it clear that He does not allow people to steal another person's husband or wife. But the meaning of this command goes beyond this. It means that we must be faithful to those we love. Family is important to God. It must be important to us. When we commit ourselves to God, we must also be faithful to Him.

Commandment 8—"You shall not steal."

Stealing is wrong. We cannot take things that belong to other persons. When we get things, they must be obtained in the right way. For example, your friends may want you to go to the store and take something without paying for it. This is wrong. It does not please God.

Commandment 9—"You shall not bear false witness against your neighbor."

In this commandment, God instructs us that we cannot lie. We cannot hurt another person by telling things that are not true. We must not tell things that are not true to damage another person's name. One day, lies will hurt us. Lies lead to mistrust, and they end in unhappiness. All human relationships require honesty and trust.

Commandment 10—"You shall not covet your neighbor's house; you shall not covet your neighbor's wife or his male servant or his female servant or his ox or his donkey or anything that belongs to your neighbor."

American society helps to make people greedy. We want the things that other people have. One only has to look at television commercials, magazines, and advertising. They are always about wanting more and more things. But having more and more things does not satisfy. Our wants only grow. Our wants are never satisfied.

We can learn to love other people. We can replace our selfishness with kindness for persons who do not have as many things as we have. Only as we learn to do this in our homes, can we love others and have compassion on them. God was not selfish. He sent His own Son to earth to be killed in order to save us from our sin. If we follow His example and try to become like Jesus, we will not be selfish and greedy. This is what God wants in us.

Christian Missions

During His ministry on earth, Jesus gave us two commandments. Jesus commanded His followers to respond to the Great Commandment: "He said to them, 'You shall love the Lord your God with all your heart, with all your soul, and with all your mind.' This is the greatest and most important commandment. The second is like it: 'You shall love your neighbor as yourself. All the Law and the Prophets depend on these two commandments'" (Matthew 22:37–40). Loving God, others, and self are foundational to everything else we do. If we do not love God, we cannot do anything else that Jesus taught. Previously, we looked at these verses.

After the Great Commandment, the other commandment Jesus gave His followers was the Great Commission: "Then Jesus came near and said to them, 'All authority has been given to Me in heaven and on earth. Go, therefore, and make disciples of all nations, baptizing them in the name of the Father, and of the Son and of the Holy Spirit, teaching them to observe everything that I have commanded you. And remember, I am with you always, to the end of the age'" (Matthew 28:18–20). In this second commandment, Jesus made it plain that we have a responsibility to be witnesses to everyone about the love of God through Jesus Christ. You will want your children to memorize both of these commandments.

Most of what we have done previously related to the Great Commandment. Now, in this section we will concentrate on the fulfillment of the Great Commission. Before He ascended into heaven, Jesus told the disciples how to carry this out: "But you will receive power when the Holy Spirit has come upon you, and you will be My witnesses in Jerusalem, in all Judea and Samaria, and to the ends of the earth" (Acts 1:8).

What does God desire? He wants us to respond as Jesus did. Matthew tells us, "When Jesus saw the crowds, He felt compassion for them, because they were weary and worn out, like sheep without a shepherd" (Matthew 9:36). God wants us to feel the same compassion that He feels for those who do not know His love as shown through Jesus Christ. The steps to lead another person to saving faith in Jesus Christ were described in the section "What We Believe" of this volume.

"To the ends of the earth" means that we need to go or send missionaries to lands all across the globe. Both we and our children need to be confronted with the insistence and demand that we assume the responsibility for preaching the gospel to persons throughout the world. To be sure, we need to reach people in our local neighborhoods, such as our Jerusalem, and state and nation, such as our Judea and Samaria. But if we would show the compassion of Christ, we must never lose sight of the need to reach the entire world with the gospel message.

The modern missionary movement is a story of heroism and total dedication to Jesus Christ. We will look first at the lives of one missionary family serving Christ today in the country of Guatemala. Then we will look at the lives of three outstanding missionaries of the past who have made a difference for Christ in this world.

We will begin with a missionary family, Roger and Vicki Grossmann, who are missionaries to Guatemala. The Grossmanns have three children. They work among Hispanic peoples in Guatemala. Roger is responsible for evangelization and church planting. Vicki is a nurse practitioner and works toward helping persons with health needs, which often leads to opportunities for evangelism.

Next, we will go back to three missionary pioneers of the nineteenth century who paved the way for today's missionary movement. The modern missionary movement started with the British Baptist William Carey in 1792. He founded of the Baptist Missionary Society. He has been called the "Father of Modern Missions." Throughout the nineteenth century, Christian missionaries from

Great Britain and America traveled around the world to bring the gospel to people who needed their Savior.

David Livingstone was another nineteenth-century missionary pioneer. He sailed for Africa and began his missionary ministry in 1840. He explored the continent of Africa and made possible missionary expansion across Africa for generations after his death. The Christian church is strong in the parts of Africa today where Livingstone explored and opened Africa to the gospel.

Lottie Moon was a missionary to China toward the end of the nineteenth century. Her life continues to inspire young people toward missions. The first offering for her was taken in a church in Georgia in 1881. Today the Lottie Moon Christmas Offering continues to provide for missionaries to serve around the globe.

Currently, the needs for developing Christian faith in other parts of the world are overwhelming. At the present time, this is more than six and a half billion. Of these, about 32 percent are considered some form of Christian, 29 percent are Muslim, 15 percent are nonreligious, 13 percent are Hindu, and 6 percent are Buddhist. The remainder of the population is composed of a variety of other religions.

Viewed from the perspective of North America, the money spent for foreign missions among all churches in the United States amounts to only 5 percent of the total giving. That means that we spend 95 percent of all ministry money on ourselves in North America. Of the 5 percent, only half of 1 percent of the money goes for frontier missions, such as unreached people groups.

Another way to view this problem is that 93 percent of all graduates of Christian colleges and seminaries in North America minister to only 5 percent of the world's population from North America. In the United States and Canada there are 401,000 churches. This amounts to one church for every 687 people. As you know, the needs in North America are great. But the needs in the rest of the world are staggering!

MISSIONARY MOVEMENT

The modern missionary movement has made an impact upon the rest of the world. Other religions have attempted to follow the Christian approach in seeking to evangelize peoples for their false beliefs. As the world population grows, the need for missionaries grows. Christians are not keeping up with the growth of the world population today. As Christians, we need to be sensitive to the Great Commission that Jesus gave to His disciples. We are to go into all the world and make followers of Jesus.

In the past, missionaries had to go to a foreign country for a lifetime. Going by ship took them many months to get to the field. Today, though it is still not easy to be a missionary, with jet planes the length of time to travel takes only hours instead of months. God still calls men and women to serve Him in different places around the world. Everyone who loves the God of the Bible needs to consider the role that he or she will play in missions. This means going to express God's love to someone who does not know Him. Today there are many opportunities to see firsthand the missionaries at work and to minister for Christ. Short-term mission projects are one means that have been especially helpful.

Roger and Vicki Grossmann

Let us begin our adventure in missions by looking at missionaries Roger and Vicki Grossmann, who, with their three children, are serving God today in Guatemala.

Perhaps you have wondered what a missionary is and what a missionary does. Below, missionary Vicki Grossmann tells us about some of her experiences. In a later section, we will look further at their family.

"It was Sunday, December 19, 1994, when we were in Santa Rita to work with a group of

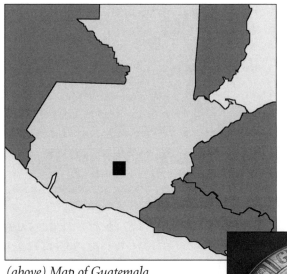

(above) Map of Guatemala
(right) Plate from Guatemala

children. About forty children were going door-to-door singing Christmas carols. This was something that they had not done before. The children memorized nine traditional carols in Spanish and went through the village singing and passing out tracts. Afterward, we had hot dogs, chips, Cokes, and Christmas cookies at the home of one of our Christian families.

"We were getting ready to climb into our cars for the drive home. After caroling, it was about 7:00 in the evening. Someone came around to our car and said, 'Vicki, there is someone looking for you!' I was tired and wanted to get home. But I got out of the car and saw a young man standing in the shadows. He was thin and his head was covered with a hat and scarf. All I could see were his eyes staring at me.

"He looked at me and asked me if I would help him. I asked him what the problem was. He promptly took off the hat and scarf and showed me his face. It was shocking! He had open sores all over his face. The sores were a mixture of blisters and a rash that covered every inch of skin, including his neck. I asked him if there were any more. He then took off his shirt, revealing that every inch of his body was also covered with a similar rash and blisters. They ran together. Many had broken. They

caused his shirt to stick to his chest and back, as if stuck with glue. Again, I asked if there were more. He began to remove his pants. It was chilly and dark, and I quickly told him that I now understood his problem. He told me that not an inch of his skin was free from these awful sores.

"His sad eyes quietly looked at me, and then he finally said, 'If you tell me the name of the medication I need, I will buy it from the pharmacy.' I told him that I could not do that. I was not sure what the root of his problem was. I asked him several questions, including how long he had been ill. He told me he had had these sores for the past nine months. I then asked what he had done to attempt to stop the sores. He told me that he had gone to the hospital for six weeks. The doctors and nurses said that they did not know what to do for him. They released him and told him they could not help him.

"As we stood there, I talked with the Lord and told Him that I had no idea of how to help Adam. Adam's problem was far too great for me to handle alone. I then told Adam I was not sure what was wrong or how to help him. I also told him that I knew an excellent physician who I felt could possibly help him. I gave him Dr. Cifuentes' address, along with directions on how to travel to her office. I told him to go there at 11:00 the next day. He was to ask the secretary to call me, and I would come and meet him there.

"The next day, promptly at 11:00, the secretary called me and informed me that the doctor was in surgery. She was not expected at the office until 3:30 p.m. I told the secretary that Adam was extremely ill. He would require medical attention in order to stay alive. I asked her to talk with Adam. She needed to convince him that we could see him at 3:30. Dr. Cifuentes would be there.

"Shortly after 3:30 the doctor called me. Her first words were: 'Sometimes you scare me too much. I am a doctor who repairs broken bones, not a skin doctor. Adam is really sick! I am wearing gloves as I examine him. Come quickly!'

"I immediately left and went to her office. As we examined Adam, it was more obvious that his condition was very serious. After we examined him, we sat down together. Dr. Cifuentes asked me, 'What do you think?' We were worried about his immune system. We decided to order a lot of tests at the laboratory. Then we started him on an antibiotic to stop the infection. We also gave him medicine for the sores on his face and neck.

"Then, I felt compelled to sit with Adam and tell him, 'Adam, you may not be aware of this, but we are not the most qualified persons to treat you. Dr. Cifuentes is a bone surgeon and I am a nurse. You really should have a skin specialist, who can better treat your condition. But we will do our best. Whatever medications we have at our disposal, we will give to you free of charge. Whatever money has been donated to help needy people in Guatemala by Christian people, we will also use for your care. We will not charge you for any help we offer. You need to know that we are not sure what the disease is that you are suffering from. Two thousand years ago, a Man came to earth who was the Son of God. His name was Jesus, and we celebrate His birth during this time. He loves you and wants to save you. If you are ever healed physically, it will be because He wanted to heal you. It will be through His intervention, not through any skill of ours. We just want you to know that before we even start.'

"Adam was thankful and told us that he had nowhere else to go. We asked him about anything he might have done to cause these sores. He could not think of anything. Nonetheless, we educated him on prevention in order to not expose his wife or son to his possibly infectious condition.

"We saw him on Christmas Day six days later. We reviewed the lab work that had been done, but he was not any better. We continued with his care. We gave him more medication. Dr. Cifuentes decided to try cortisone. Then, another strong medicine was added to the medicines he was already taking. He improved with both of these, but his condition did not completely clear up.

"A veterinarian came to visit us. He offered to take a biopsy of Adam's sores back to the United States. He believed that a good laboratory might help us better diagnose his illness. We stood in the office with the patient on the examining table. We selected sites to biopsy. I was struck with the uniqueness of this situation. Here, a nurse, bone surgeon, and a veterinarian were deciding where the best places to take samples of his sores were located. I thought how ridiculous this would look back home in the United States. We joked about this, but we seriously knew that we were Adam's only hope.

"Dr. Rasche, the veterinarian, took the samples back to the United States. Then he sent us the report. It told us exactly what he had and how serious his condition was. We were then to put together a treatment plan, which included long-term cortisone. There was a concern about continuing cortisone for a long length of time. We knew that we had no other choice for Adam. Adam rapidly improved with this therapy. When we saw him the next time, we saw how handsome a man he truly was. He was able to arrive without a scarf or hat, and his skin was totally clear.

"Finally, one day I arrived at the office, and Adam was in the waiting room. Adam was visibly excited, and told me, 'I have done what you said.' Surprised, I said, 'What have you done, Adam?' He told me, 'I have accepted the Lord, and I am now a brother in Christ.' He then told me that he had gone to an evangelical church in the village of Santa Rita. He had asked the pastor to lead him to the Lord. He was now experiencing great joy and peace, and it was a delight to talk with him.

"Shortly after that, we lost him to therapy. We worried about his prognosis and outcome. We did not have a current address and could not locate him. Dr. Cifuentes waited patiently in her office for him to reappear, but months went by, and he did not come to visit us. We wondered if he had found a new physician. We wondered if he was worse or had died. Perhaps he was just continuing with the medication, without our help. It is possible to purchase cortisone over the counter in Guatemala. Or perhaps he had left the country.

"A year later, I was visiting another patient in the public hospital. I heard my name being called vigorously. 'Hermana Vicki, Hermana Vicki!' I turned and at first did not recognize the person who was calling so urgently. With a shock, I realized it was Adam. I was so happy to see him. I was anxious to know who his physician was. I told him that we had missed seeing him but were so happy to see he was obviously now in good health. I asked who his new doctor was. Adam looked confused and said, 'Doctor! I don't have a doctor now.'

"Well then, where are you getting your medication?' I asked.

"He answered, 'I'm not taking any medication now. I'm well. I don't need medication.' At the surprised look in my face, he then said, 'You said God could heal me. Didn't you believe He would?'

"Out of the blue, one day, Adam appeared in Dr. Cifuentes' office to see us. We were so excited to see him because it had been a couple of years. Adam related his gratefulness to God for healing him. He was also thankful for our help. He said, 'You know when I came to see you, everyone was afraid of me. They ran from me when I came near. Now I sometimes see my mother crying when she sees me because she is so happy that I am cured.'"

Situations like this cause people who love the Lord to go to far-off lands to serve Christ. People in other countries do not have the kind of medical help that we have here in the United States. Like Jesus, the missionaries bring help to those who are suffering with physical needs. More important, many do not have the message of eternal life that the missionaries also bring.

Missionary Service in Guatemala

How did Roger and Vicki Grossmann enter missionary service in Guatemala? Let us look more closely at the path on which God led them into missionary service. Roger Grossmann was born in St. Louis, while Vicki came from South Carolina. At age eleven, Vicki moved to St. Louis. Both Roger and Vicki were raised in Christian homes. As a child, Roger remembers his father reading from the Bible and acting out the stories as he read. Vicki recalls the impact that both her parents and grandparents had upon her as they prayed for her. In high school, Vicki had a strong sense that God was calling her into His service.

They were both involved in a local church. During their teenage years, Roger was involved in a city mission's project. Roger remembered killing roaches in his basement apartment that were ever present as they sought to present the gospel of Jesus Christ to inner-city youth. One of the converts was a former gang leader. He was very rough. But he was truly saved from his former life.

Both Roger and Vicki entered the University of Missouri at St. Louis. At the end of their freshman year, they went on a short-term mission trip to Haiti. They spent most of their time in the city of Port au Prince. They ministered in the lives of children. The children lived in poverty and misery. Their diet was very poor. They lived on only two meals a day. It seemed as if the children had no hope. But these were Christian children, and they sang, "No problems, we have Jesus."

Roger and Vicki had to eat bread that had ants crawling on it. It was not pleasant, but it was necessary if they were to be a witness for Christ to these precious children. These experiences for nine days in Haiti had a profound effect on both Roger and Vicki. During this time they discovered that they cared for each other. They both felt the call of God on their lives to follow Christ in missionary service. They both committed themselves to Christ, wherever He would lead them.

Roger finished college and took a job in the area of his major, chemistry. Vicki felt the need to continue her education through nursing. They were married during this time. A couple of years passed, and Roger entered Southwestern Baptist Theological Seminary. Vicki worked on the nursing staff at the seminary. She also completed a family nurse practitioner program at the University of Texas. Finally, Roger graduated in July 1983. Their first son, Joshua, was born while they were in Texas.

Roger became an associate pastor at Cresset Baptist Church in Durham, North Carolina. Vicki took a job with the Durham County health department. This gave her opportunity to work with the poor of Durham County. God was preparing them both for the tasks He had in store for them. Roger also taught chemistry and Bible at the Christian school, along with the work that he did at the church. Their daughter Melanie was born at this time.

Harry and Jean Byrd were missionaries to Guatemala under the International Mission Board. They came to speak at the school. As they talked, it became evident that there was a need for Roger in church planting and for Vicki in nursing in Guatemala.

In October 1987, Roger and Vicki set out with their two children for language school in Costa Rica. God guided them through language preparation. They returned home to North Carolina briefly, before entering their service in Guatemala.

During the first term on the field, they were called to start new churches. They started a Bible study in their home. They would go into the community and knock on doors and pass out tracts. In addition they would hold medical clinics every four to six weeks. In the town of Santa Rita, Vicki worked with the women and children. It was difficult to get the men involved in the work of the church.

Traveling home with two of her children from a clinic in the mountains one day, Vicki's car was hit by a drunk driver. This was almost more than she could take. Four months earlier she had been hit by a bus. Four months before that she had been chased by a bad man. Vicki felt that she just wanted to get the car fixed and drive north through Mexico and back home to the United States. But God was there. Some very kind people helped her and cared for her and the children. They found Roger and brought him to the place where they had taken Vicki and the children. The fear Vicki had was taken away by God's protective care. Their family was in the place where God wanted to use them. He sheltered them with His protective love and care. When you know that you are pleasing God, this makes the sacrifice worthwhile.

Since going to Guatemala, they have also had another son, Nathanael.

Mission to Huehuetenango

Roger was called to plant churches. In 1997 he and Efrain Juárez went to Huehuetenango to scout the possibilities of starting a Baptist church in the area. There was only one man with a very small church of six people in the entire city. They conducted a city-wide campaign, but it brought almost no results.

Next, they brought a medical team to conduct a clinic and a Vacation Bible School. More than five hundred people a day came to receive medical treatment and free medicine for their bodies. But fewer than fifty came at night in search of eternal medicine for the souls. That seemed to have much less appeal.

"One day Douglas came to the clinic complaining of a skin rash that was 'driving him crazy.' He was so upset, I asked him if something else was bothering him. He told me that maybe it was cocaine and marijuana and that he had tried to quit many times. He just could not stop. I was shocked and concerned for Douglas, knowing how hard it was to quit cocaine. I told him that only God could help him. I went through a tract with him. Douglas showed a lot of interest. I called Efrain Juárez over, and together we explained the plan of salvation. Then Douglas helped with the Vacation Bible School for the rest of the week. But nobody thought his life would really change. Everyone was discouraged. One of the doctors from the United States said at the end of this crusade that he thought the whole effort during the evangelistic week had been very disappointing. But Douglas became a Christian that day and continues even today.

"Another night Rudy came down the aisle at the invitation to accept Jesus. Rudy was the town drunk. He had not shaved. His clothes were dirty. He smelled of alcohol. With all of his alcohol, Roger had difficulty talking with him. Roger prayed and told him that if he wanted to be saved, to come back the next night. Rudy returned the next night with his wife. This time Rudy was clean, sober, and well dressed. When the invitation was given, they both came forward.

"For the next two months, Efrain and Roger worked with Douglas and Rudy. The people of the city knew Rudy as the town drunk. Rudy had been just like his father. He would be away for several weeks at a time. Then he would be found drunk alongside the street in a ditch. The people also knew that Douglas took drugs. They asked what happened. Their lives were so different! Others wanted what they had. Both Rudy and Douglas would tell about what Jesus Christ had done in their lives. Seventy people came to Christ as a result of their testimonies. Every day, it seemed, Efrain would call with the news of people accepting the Lord. This church divided and became two churches. Roger suggested they divide since there were really some differences between the two groups. One was formed in Huehuetenango and the other in Aguacatillos. Both men became involved in the church.

"A year went by and Douglas came to another medical clinic. Douglas had another rash. Roger asked Douglas if the rash had not been the reason why he had come to the clinic a year earlier. He said, 'Yes! Vicki did very well with my soul, but she can't do anything with my feet.'"

"The church continued to grow. Church planting is difficult and discouraging work. But when God is involved, the changes do come. The church grew to one hundred fifty people. It is still a growing church today."

One of the greatest problems for the missionary helping Christians grow is that most of the people from the country cannot read or write. As Christians, we know that it is very important to read the Bible. But people cannot do that if they cannot read. Roger developed a simplified Bible that tells the main stories of the Bible through pictures. It only has a few words. It is called the *Understandable Bible*. The writing is in Spanish and is called *La Bibliá Para Todos* or *The Bible for Everyone*. Thousands of copies of the *Understandable Bible* were passed out in Huehuetenango by youth from America and Guatemala. The *Understandable Bible* looks like the following cartoon description of the Grossmann's ministry to help the people of Guatemala read the Bible.

The Grossmann family serves Christ in Guatemala. During the past year while on furlough, they continue to work hard. Josh is now in college. Roger is pursuing a doctor's degree at Southeastern Seminary. Vicki is working to strengthen her skills in nursing at the University of North Carolina in a post master's program. Melanie and Nathanael are attending a Christian school. God has blessed this special family. Their commitment and dedication to Christ and their love for the people of Guatemala are evident.

Now let us look back to the early missionaries of the nineteenth century who have pioneered the way to missions today.

William Carey, Missionary to India, 1761–1834

William Carey was a giant in the Christian faith. Carey was born in 1761. As a boy, his father would fire his imagination with stories of far-off lands. Carey was excited about someday traveling to those far-off lands.  At age fourteen he was apprenticed to a cobbler, a person who repairs shoes. Carey did not have the benefit of a good education, like many other boys his age. One of the other apprentices, John Warr, was a Christian. He witnessed to Carey. Carey recognized that he was a sinner and needed to be saved. Warr led Carey to faith in Jesus Christ.

In 1781 William Carey married Dorothy Plackett. She was six years older than William. Carey also began to preach in a local church. He was not a good speaker. In fact, he was so bad that the church refused to ordain him to the gospel ministry. But Carey did not give up easily. He worked as a cobbler and studied Greek as he worked. He also became the pastor of the church at Olney. For ten years he worked in the shoe repair business during the week and served as pastor on the weekends. He also helped his income by opening a school.

During this time Carey was becoming more concerned about ministering to people who did not know Christ elsewhere in the world. He addressed the Baptist Association about missions. He was told by one of the leaders of the association, that if God wanted to save the heathen, He would do it without Carey. He told Carey to sit down and be quiet. Carey was not discouraged. He wrote a book on converting the heathen in 1792. This book became the battle cry to go to foreign mission fields for those who came after Carey. In the same year, Carey preached his famous sermon "Expect Great Things from God, Attempt Great Things for God." This encouraged Andrew Fuller, another leader in the association, to form a Baptist Society for teaching the gospel to the heathen.

The Baptist Mission Society began seeking candidates to go to the mission field in India. A medical doctor, John Thomas, and his family volunteered. Carey was moved to volunteer also. Carey's wife, Dorothy, was going to have another child. She was not excited about going to far-off India. The trip was delayed because John Thomas had to settle his finances with some people to whom he owed money. Meanwhile, Dorothy had her baby and the whole family set sail for India. The voyage took five months. Dorothy was sick for most of the trip.

Arrival in India was no better. The Thomas family was able to go to suburbs of Calcutta and settle in a good area. To help provide enough money for his family, Carey managed an indigo plantation. Indigo comes from a plant and is used to dye cloth with a blue color. The area was filled with malaria. Malaria is a disease that is carried by the mosquito. Malaria is still dangerous in many parts of the world. This area was jungle and dangerous with tigers, snakes, and other wild animals.

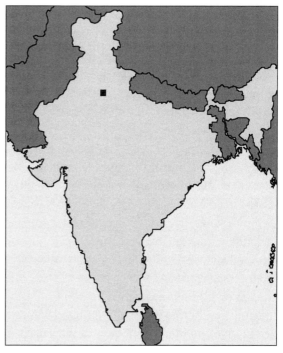

Map of India

The entire family suffered from tropical diseases during this time. Peter Carey, their son, died of one of the diseases. Dorothy was never the same after that. She was very sick. She never fully recovered. There were no converts during those early years. A person less committed to Christ would have left and returned home.

Carey stayed and began to learn the language. He translated the entire New Testament in Bengali. Then in 1800 the Careys moved to Serampore. Three years later Carey baptized twenty-five converts. His Bible translation work continued. But his preaching turned from criticism of Hinduism to the death and resurrection of Jesus Christ. His message was now more powerful and he began to have results. During these years Carey translated the complete Bible into six Indian languages. He also made portions of the Bible available in an additional thirty languages. Dorothy died after a long illness. Carey soon married Charlotte. Carey opened more than one hundred schools to teach more than seven thousand students.

Carey established the church so that it was not dependent upon the missionary. He wanted the Indian church to grow. God blessed Carey's work. By 1821 he baptized 1,400 converts. The years that Carey spent with his second wife were very happy years. Sadly, she died in 1821. In 1822 he married his third wife, Grace. They remained together for the rest of their lives.

William Carey died in 1834 at the age of 73. He never returned home to England. What he had started in the missionary movement continued. Carey asked that the words of a hymn be placed on his gravestone. They read, "A wretched, poor, and helpless worm, On Thy kind arms I fall."

His dedication and commitment have inspired many missionaries to follow his example. Carey and his family suffered for their love for Christ and the Indian people to whom they ministered. Carey left his mark on India. The people of India had two very evil practices. Carey worked hard to write papers and make speeches against these two evil

practices. Before he died, the government ended both of them. Even though his life was not always happy, William Carey left his mark on India and the Indian church in the cause of Christ. He also strongly influenced all of the modern mission movement.

David Livingstone, Missionary to Africa, 1813–1873

If India was wild and dangerous, the continent of Africa was even a more frightening place. It was known as the "Dark Continent" and the graveyard for the white man. Opening Africa to the gospel of Jesus Christ was due largely to the efforts of one man, David Livingstone. Livingstone was born in Scotland. He came from a hardworking family. As a young man he had to work long hours in the cotton mills. Along with his work, he was able to obtain his college degree. During this time he became interested in missions. He wanted to go to China. To prepare, Livingstone went to the University of Glasgow and graduated with a degree in medicine. But there was a war going on in China over the drug opium. Livingstone had to look elsewhere. Robert Moffat was a missionary from southern Africa. Moffat helped Livingstone see that there was a place for him back in Africa. Livingstone left Scotland and sailed for Africa.

During his early days in Africa, Livingstone tried to serve on a mission station. Livingstone settled into mission life by teaching school and gardening among the Tswana people from 1843 to 1853. During that time Livingstone married Robert Moffat's daughter, Mary Moffat. Livingstone did not experience great success in reaching the people with the gospel. He had only one convert. But when the one convert returned to his former life, Livingstone was very upset. He was restless and wanted to do something else. He believed that God was leading him to explore some of the most dangerous country of Africa to the north. He wanted to open "God's Highway" across the interior of Africa. He believed that by opening this area, the raw materials taken from the interior could be sent to Europe for manufacture. This new opportunity for Europeans, he hoped, would end the slave trade and open Africa to the gospel.

Livingstone reached the coast in 1854. He did not accomplish what he wanted on his journey. He then retraced his long journey back along the Zambezi River to its origin at the Indian Ocean. The trip covered twenty-five hundred miles and he arrived in 1856. He returned to England and was given the welcome of a hero for his explorations. The London Missionary Society, which had sent Livingstone to Africa, was not happy with his exploration. They wanted him to win converts to Christ. While in England, Livingstone arranged to return with help from the British government.

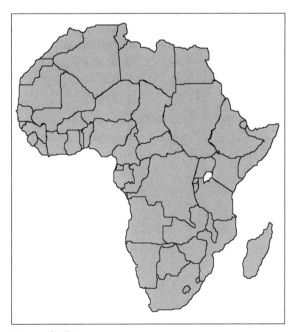

Map of Africa

This allowed him to continue his work without interference from the London Missionary Society. Livingstone continued to explore the Zambezi River. He did not realize that there were rapids on the river, however. He could not take his boat along the long course of the river. His dream was not realized. He then turned to another river, but the British government decided that they did not want to continue to pay for his exploration. He had problems with both his wife and the men that went with him. After the birth of their sixth child, his wife died in 1862.

Livingstone returned home to Britain in 1864. He did not receive a hero's welcome this time. With a heavy heart, Livingstone went back to Africa in 1866. He received financial help from the Royal Geographical Society to continue his exploration of this great continent. For the next two years Livingstone became very sick and almost died. He said later that during that time he read the Bible through four times. With his sickness, he disappeared from the outside world.

The public in England and America were both interested in what happened to this brave explorer and missionary. Henry Morton Stanley was a journalist. He saw a good story in Livingstone's adventures. Stanley took a rescue party to find Livingstone. Finally, they arrived and Stanley saluted Livingstone with those now famous words, "Dr. Livingstone, I presume?" Livingstone convinced Stanley that he did not need to be rescued. Livingstone was doing what he wanted to do. Together, they explored the region around Lake Tanganyika. Then Stanley left for home to write a book about his adventures in Africa.

Livingstone was interested in finding the source of the Nile River. He was also intent on showing that the roots of Judaism and Christianity were to be found in Africa. Livingstone became very sick with dysentery, a disease that affects the intestines. He was kneeling in prayer. He never got up off his knees and died there in 1873. He died in what is the present-day country of Zambia. Livingstone's exploration papers, his medical instruments, and his body were carried from the place of his death to the island of Zanzibar on the Indian Ocean. The trip took nine months. In 1874 the body of David Livingstone was returned to his homeland in England. There he was buried as a hero in London's Westminster Abbey. His journal was published after his death.

Many complained that it was often difficult to work with David Livingstone. He caused, or at least contributed, to some of the problems for his wife and family. But David Livingstone was a man called by God to serve in the vast continent of Africa. He went places where no white man had ever been before. He opened the interior to the gospel of Jesus Christ. Few people would have had the ability to travel for long periods in very difficult circumstances to do what Livingstone was able to do. His life inspired new missionaries to take up the cause. The churches in central Africa are strong today. That is a credit to the life and work of David Livingstone.

Lottie Moon, Missionary to China, 1840–1912

Charlotte Diggs "Lottie" Moon was born in Viewmont, Virginia, on December 17, 1840. She was given the nickname Lottie. Her family was very wealthy. Her  father had been a Presbyterian who later became Baptist. Although her family was very religious, Lottie chose not to be religious. As Lottie grew older, she was known for being very mischievous.

At fourteen years of age, Lottie attended the Virginia Female Institute. She studied the French and Latin languages. She also took courses in algebra, English composition, and natural science. One year, on the day before April Fool's Day, Lottie climbed into the bell tower and stuffed the bell with towels and sheets to prevent the bell from ringing the next morning. Everyone in the school overslept. The headmaster of the school was very angry, and Lottie was disciplined for her prank.

Lottie was a good student. Her effort prepared her to continue her education at the Albemarle Female Institute in Charlottesville, Virginia. There she studied more languages, as well as other subjects. She was among the first women to receive the master of arts degree during that time in the South.

While she attended Albemarle, Dr. John Broadus spoke in a revival service at the school. Dr. Broadus was a very famous Southern Baptist preacher. He met Lottie and saw great potential in her. He and many on the campus began to pray that God would touch the life of Lottie Moon.

Lottie was persuaded to go to the evening service. She wanted to make fun of the service and the people who attended. Instead, she found Christ and spent the rest of the night praying. On the next day, she told Dr. Broadus about giving her life to Christ. Dr. Broadus baptized Lottie Moon.

Through the Civil War, Lottie was needed at home to help with the farm. She served as a teacher for her younger sister, Edmonia. Her experience with her sister helped her to find a position tutoring for families in Alabama and later in Kentucky. Not finding those positions satisfying, she went to teach at the Cartersville Female Academy in June 1871. While in Georgia, Lottie was concerned for the poor people. She would provide clothing, even if she had to pay for the clothing from her own savings.

Crawford Toy was a professor at the Southern Baptist Theological Seminary. He had fallen in love with Lottie Moon. He asked her to marry him, but Lottie was not sure that God wanted her to marry at that time. She graciously rejected his proposal.

Meanwhile, her sister, Edmonia, felt the call of God to volunteer as a missionary to China. Her older sister had gone to medical school and then went to the Middle East as a missionary doctor. Lottie attended a church service in February 1873. That night the text came from Jesus' words in John 4:35b: "Open your eyes and look at the fields, for they are ready for harvest." Lottie committed herself to missionary service in China.

Lottie Moon was appointed by the Foreign Mission Board of the Southern Baptist Convention to missionary service in China in July 1873. She traveled by train to San Francisco and boarded a ship for Shanghai, China. She journeyed over land from Shanghai to Tengchow for several days. Tengchow became her home for many of her years in China. By 1877 Edmonia became ill. Lottie Moon returned home to Virginia to help her sister recover.

Lottie Moon went back to Tengchow, China, on Christmas Eve that year. Recall that Lottie had learned several languages while gaining her education. She now gave herself to master Chinese, a very difficult language. She adopted the dress of the Chinese. Lottie Moon wanted to identify with the Chinese people so that she could minister to them. She wanted them to find Jesus as their Savior. At first, the people of China called her the "Devil Woman." But that did not stop Lottie Moon. She loved the people.

For fourteen years she worked among the Chinese people before she returned to America. She did not receive the help she needed from the Foreign Mission Board. When the Mission Board suffered financially, she loaned them money from her own inheritance.

Lottie Moon returned to the United States in the early 1880s. The leader of the Foreign Mission Board said that she planned to marry Crawford Toy. Toy had been fired by Southern Seminary for false and dangerous teaching about the Bible. He

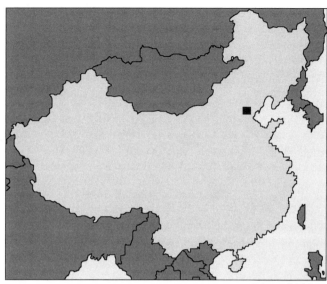

Map of China

went to teach at Harvard University. Lottie Moon was very disappointed and knew that she could not marry him. She returned to China for the last time with a very heavy heart.

At first she worked only among women. The needs were great. Later, she began to teach in the area of Pingtu and became involved in planting churches. She was now in an area where few missionaries were able to check on her safety and provide protection. The area around Pingtu became one of the most effective areas for evangelism and the planting of churches. The Chinese pastor in Pingtu baptized more than one thousand converts during the next twenty years. Even after her ministry on earth ended, she was effective among the churches.

On Christmas Day, 1881, her church in Georgia took the first Lottie Moon Christmas Offering. The offering was very small, but that event started a precedent that has continued to the present day among Baptists in the Southern Baptist Convention. Contributions now exceed one hundred twenty million annually at the Christmas offering for world missions. The Lottie Moon Christmas Offering for Missions has become a heritage that has lived long after Lottie Moon. It has made possible the sending of thousands of missionaries to carry the gospel to all parts of the world.

Lottie Moon loved the people of China. She was no longer called the "Devil Woman." Instead, they called her "The Heavenly Book Visitor." She sacrificed her life for winning the lost people of China to Jesus Christ. Her sister, Edmonia, died. This hurt Lottie very much. She wrote, "I hope no missionary will be as lonely as I have been."

For many Christians, the Boxer Rebellion war in China caused great hardship and suffering. Famine hit China and many Christians starved. Lottie Moon identified with the Christians. She gave what little food she had. Then she stopped eating herself. In 1911 a missionary doctor visited her. She was very weak. He sent her back to the United States. A missionary nurse was sent to accompany her for the long journey. The ship was docked in Kobe, Japan, on Christmas Eve 1912. After thirty-nine years as a missionary in China, Lottie Moon died on the way home to America. She went to her new home in heaven with Jesus. Her body was cremated, in keeping with Japanese law. Her ashes were returned to the United States.

Concluding Thoughts

These early missionaries of the nineteenth century all suffered for their faith and their love for Jesus Christ. Their pioneering efforts opened the door for many missionaries who followed them. India, Africa, and China have all benefited from their early efforts. The missionary enterprise would not have been possible without their dedication and commitment. The Lord still calls men and women to leave all and follow Him. It may be to serve as a member of a local church, to give, and to pray. It may be to work in the ministry of a local church. Or it may be to go to another country to minister to the needs of the people and to bring the good news of the gospel. Whatever God calls us to do for Him, we all need to share our faith with those around us. Whenever God calls, we must obey and answer Him.

Christianity and the Fine Arts

Christian fine arts are composed of both the visual arts and the musical arts. The visual arts include Christian symbols, painting, sculpture, architecture, and stained glass. The musical arts take in many forms of sacred music, such as hymns, oratorios, spirituals, anthems, and Christian songs. There is a long history of sacred art and music, which dates back to the early Church in Rome. From the first century at each successive stage of history, art forms have played a significant role in describing the beliefs and dream of the artist. To be sure, the artwork has a connection to its age, but the composite picture produced by art and music give us an understanding of the Christian faith of believers in every age. The art that we shall examine represents the highest Christian ideals of each era in which it was produced.

In the midst of all of the ugliness and problems in our world, God has provided us with beauty. He has endowed us with both the ability to see and hear. In the Book of Leviticus, God instructed the Hebrews to construct a Tabernacle for worship that had appeal to three of the five senses: visual or seeing; aural or hearing; and olfactory or smell. Although God prohibited the making of images of Himself, He did not exclude beauty from our worship or everyday life. At various times the prohibition has been interpreted very differently among Christian believers, who are equally serious about their faith. In many quarters, this has produced great misunderstanding about art from the past. Most Christians today would accept the use of sacred art, as long as it does not become an object of worship that takes the place of the living God. Nevertheless, over the centuries, Christians have produced a wealth of artistic expression that can draw us into the worship of God and foster our appreciation for beauty in the church and in God's wider universe. These artistic creations reach the highest ideals and aspirations of the artist that produced them.

Perhaps we need to raise the question, why is it important to teach your children about Christian art and music? First, we have a long history of Christian art and music. Today's secular art and music are totally new phenomena. Christian art and music are some of the finest examples of art and music that the world has ever known. The vast majority of art from the past has contributed to the aesthetic beauty of the church and its place in the world. We are not interested in art for its own sake. Rather, we view art as a lens through which Christian artists and composers have viewed their world from a Christian perspective. We look at art and listen to great Christian music as they have affected their culture. Perhaps we can gain some clues from the past that was more Christian on ways that will help us to deal with our visually and aurally oriented culture in this century. Note that both the art and music sections are presented chronologically. For the first and second grader, this time sequence may be less important. You will want to use your judgment about identifying the time sequence.

Second, regarding the visual culture of today, much of this present approach is through the media of television and film. The great art of the past was still media. Nevertheless, we have our own still images in our political symbols, our business symbols, and our social symbols. The composite of these symbols will tend to lead us deeper into the contemporary secular culture. Christian art was symbolic from its very beginning. It helped the Christians of the second and third centuries to deal with the possibility of persecution and even death. During the middle ages, much of the entire society had become Christian.

Great cathedrals were built to magnify the glory of God. Both the Reformation and Counter-Reformation used art to express Christian ideals. Christian art is a factor in helping us understand how Christians of different ages have responded to their understanding of God in a secular world. Christian art can help us in this quest. We need to develop contemporary visual expressions.

Third, as noted, music has become a very dominant part of our culture. Much of today's music is very bad music. The ancient philosopher Plato pointed out that music is one of the most important factors in the moral education of children and youth. As a parent, it is important to listen to the lyrics of the songs that your children listen to regularly. Some of those lyrics are evil or pornographic. Help your children develop good taste in music. Good Christian music can help children to develop better taste in music as well. While it is beyond the scope of this book to discuss classical music, it would be helpful to expose your children to good music.

In the brief space allotted, only the basics of good Christian art and music can be included. Don't skip this section, but try to understand it and use it to help your child develop his or her sensitivity to good art and music. There are several specific things that you can do to help your children in this area. In art, be sure to read all that is included here. Then take your children to an art museum. Help them understand what they are seeing. There are many books available that will help you interpret the paintings or artifacts. Many museums conduct tours of the highlights of the museum. Such tours can help you interpret the paintings or other art pieces. Help your children understand and appreciate good Christian art.

This book will help you find some quality hymns. In your church, try to encourage choirs, use of musical instruments, and understanding of church music. Avoid duplicating what the school is doing for your children in this area. But learn what they are doing and when it will be done. Then have your children participate with you in these various areas of music that are healthy and educational.

Christian Works of Art

What is Christian art? A very simple answer is, art that includes Christian symbols, paintings, sculptures, and even buildings that are used for Christian purposes. These art works also tell stories that have Christian themes. Many of these artworks are among the greatest works of art that the world has ever seen. We have a vast treasure of Christian art that can lead us closer to God if we are willing to spend some time and become familiar with the wealth that is available to us. Today, our world is much less interested in the Christian ideas expressed in art. Students of art are more interested in the art itself than in the Christian themes that are behind those works. As followers of Christ, we need to reclaim Christian art. We need to return to the great Christian themes of art and allow them to enrich our love for Christ, worship in the church, and our relationship to God.

To illustrate what has happened to Christian art, recall the story of Jesus' baptism. The dove, who was the Holy Spirit, descended on Jesus to indicate to all that Jesus came from God. There was a picture of the baptism of Jesus in an art museum. A guide was leading his group of visitors past the painting when one of the persons asked, "Why is that bird on the person in the painting?"

Christians from past centuries illustrated their Christian faith in works of art. For the earliest Christians, the art was very simple. The art included paintings or etchings of Christian subjects on the walls. Many of them were symbols. But these symbols or pictures helped many Christians face the trials and persecutions that happened in Rome in the first three hundred years. We will examine some of these symbols and their meaning.

When Christianity became more established as the religion of Europe, the builders of the Middle Ages constructed great cathedrals "to the glory of God." Architectural beauty was brought into the service of God. Unlike the buildings constructed today, these great worship centers have lasted. Their building techniques seem simple to us, but the buildings continue to stand today, even hundreds of years later. Inside these great buildings the artists decorated the great cathedrals. Carvings, paintings, sculptures, and stained glass help us to better understand the meaning of Christian faith to these people from the medieval period. Our study will take us to examine a great cathedral and a beautiful little stained-glass window from another cathedral.

Architecture was not the only form of art. Paintings and wall etchings were done in the early Church. Perhaps the greatest paintings of all time were done by Christian painters in the 1500s in Europe, close to the time of Martin Luther. Remember that we studied the life of Luther in the "Growth of the Church." Two of the paintings and a sculpture we will study came from this period. Some artists used different media to produce great works of art. Etching with an ink pen was one media for teaching Christian faith. We will look at one etching. Then we will return and complete our study with two additional paintings.

Christian Symbolism Found in the Catacombs

Recall the brave young woman, Cecilia, who was martyred in Rome in the third century. Her husband and his brother lost their lives because they helped to give a Christian burial to Christians who were killed in the persecutions. They were buried in the catacombs. Some of the earliest Christian art can still be found today in the catacombs.

In order to better understand the symbols of early Christian art, it may be helpful to take a closer look at the catacombs. They are burial places below the ground that were made from lava of volcanoes that no longer erupt. The lava rock, called tuffa, allowed the grave diggers to make passageways under the ground. They did not need to provide additional supports to the walls or ceilings.

Along the walls, grave diggers would cut holes in the rock in places for the bodies. When one set of graves was filled, they would dig a new passage with more burial places. At the ends of the passageways, they would carve out a larger room and might even open the room to the outside for light and air. This room became a chapel for worship. Family members could come here and remember their relatives who had died. In the burial places and in these chapels, the early Christians carved and painted symbols on the walls.

Catacombs

Catacomb, the name for these burial places meant "near the hollow." Above ground there were hollows in the ground near the Old Appian Way. Recall that the Old Appian Way was the road on which the apostle Paul traveled on his way to Rome. Christians were not the first to discover the lava rock. For many years, Roman citizens had been buried in graves cut out from the lava rock as well. They called the burial place by a term that meant "the place of the dead." By Christian times, however, most Romans who died were cremated. But the Christians believed that the body needed to be preserved for the resurrection. The Christians used the term *cemetery* to mean "the place of sleep." In the cemetery the Christians buried their dead. The catacombs became a good cemetery.

The Roman emperors knew that the Christians buried their dead there. Romans had respect for any person who was dead, even Christians, so the

Romans did not disapprove of burial in the catacombs. Perhaps for very short periods of time the Christians may have hidden in the catacombs from the persecution, but that was not a common practice. After the persecutions ended many Christians went to the catacombs to remember the martyrs who were buried there. This continued for the next four hundred years. After the ninth century, people forgot about the catacombs until the seventeenth century. Even then, little was done. But in the nineteenth century the archaeologists began to uncover the secrets of the catacombs. There are more than two dozen catacombs, but only three of them may be visited today. We can still see the remains of the artwork that appears on the walls of the catacombs.

The Chi Rho

One of the often-used symbols in the catacombs was the symbol of the first two letters for the name of Christ. These were *chi* and *rho*. The *X* stands for the Greek letter *chi* and the *P* stands for the Greek letter *rho*.

The Dove and the Olive Branch

In the Old Testament when Noah was in the ark after the rain stopped, he sent a dove out of the ark.

The dove returned with an olive branch. The meaning is both forgiveness and eternal peace. For the Christian believer this is a beautiful picture of the peace that Christ brings to his or her life. The dove is loving and tender. It also reminds the Christian that the dove is a symbol of the Holy Spirit. When Mary came to sacrifice in the temple after the birth of Jesus, she brought two doves.

The Fish

The Greek word *ichthus* means fish. Fish became a common symbol for Christians. The first letters of the Greek word stand for *ichthus*, "Jesus Christ, God's Son, Savior." The fish also carried the idea of baptism. You will remember that when Jesus called Peter and the other disciples, He said to them, "Come, follow me and I will make you fishers of

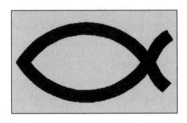

men." After Jesus rose from the dead, Peter went fishing, and Jesus came and met with the disciples alongside the Sea of Galilee.

The Anchor

The anchor symbolizes hope. A Christian needs to stand firm in the midst of trials. It was taken from Hebrews 6:19: "We have this [hope]—like a sure

and firm anchor of the soul—that enters the inner sanctuary behind the curtain." The anchor holds the ship in place when it is in the harbor. For the Christian the anchor suggests the cross. The cross made eternity possible for the follower of Jesus. Then the anchor keeps the believer safe in the harbor of eternity. Death is not the end but only the beginning for all of eternity.

The Good Shepherd

The good shepherd was an image that came from the ancient Romans. It was quickly adopted by the early Christians to represent Christ. Jesus used the idea of the good shepherd many times to describe Himself. In John 10:11–18 Jesus said, "I am the good shepherd." Remember from the occupations in Bible times that the shepherd sleeps with his body in front of the door to the sheepfold. No animal or robber can come and take the sheep. Jesus does that for those who follow Him. In Matthew 18:10–14, Jesus told the parable of the "Ninety and Nine." The one sheep was lost, but

Jesus went out and sought the one that was lost. The good shepherd was pictured on the walls of the catacombs, and the good shepherd also appeared as a statue. This was one of the most popular themes for early Christian art.

When the early Christians came to the catacombs to remember their family members and friends who died in the persecution, they encouraged by the hope and encouragement these images brought to the early Church. The images were carved or painted on the walls of the burial places and the walls of the small worship centers. Even today we see the symbol of the fish on our cars. The symbol of the cross also appears in our churches and on our jewelry. Both the fish and the cross remind us of Jesus, just as it did the early Christians. We are not suffering for our faith as the early Christians did, but the symbols of the fish and the cross give us hope as we think of Jesus and His death on the cross to save us.

Medieval Building to the "Glory of God"

During the Middle Ages the populations in the European countries grew rapidly. To protect from fire and the raiding parties of the Vikings, new military and government buildings were built of stone rather than wood. The medieval church also began to construct its buildings of stone. In most cases the largest of the church buildings was built in the center of the town. They were much more glorious than the military or government buildings. Millions of tons of stone were cut and shaped at quarries and shipped to the building sites. The builders constructed the outside of the buildings. Others were employed to decorate the inside of the buildings as well. Stained glass windows were prepared for the churches. The stained glass allowed the sunlight to enter the building and give a variety of colors to the inside of the church. Stone images were also used to adorn the buildings. Paintings were created for the churches and cathedrals. They were hung on the walls of the cathedral. Many stonemasons worked for their entire lifetime to create these magnificent church buildings. There were also small parish churches. Others were large churches. But the largest were the cathedrals.

Why did the medieval builders construct these great church structures? The people of the medieval world wanted to serve God. They built the cathedrals to the "glory of God." In the large spaces within the cathedrals, one could get a feeling for the majesty and greatness of God. The stained-glass windows allowed the colored sunlight to shine on the walls and the floors and increase the sense of wonder at the greatness of God. When the sunlight was not present, candles lit the inside of the building. These would flicker and also add to the sense of the glorious majesty of God. The statues, paintings, carvings, and stained glass were not just for decoration. At a time when most people could not read, these art pieces told the story of the gospel of Jesus

Christ. For example, a person could look at the stone figures around the main door to the church. They usually told the story of the Last Judgment. Jesus sat on a throne and was judging the people. Those who were saved went to heaven, while those who were lost and did not believe in God were sent to eternal punishment. We will look at some examples of different kinds of decoration that told the story of Christ and salvation.

The word *cathedral* comes from a word that means "the bishop's chair." Most cathedrals represented the place where the bishop's chair was located. Usually, the cathedral was a very beautiful church for Christian worship. It usually had many stained-glass windows. It was a center for worship and learning about the Christian faith. People came from far away to visit the cathedral, and they still do today.

The Cathedral of York, England

York is a city in the northeast section of England. (See the map below.) The city was built during Roman times. Recall Constantine, the Roman emperor who became a Christian and ended the persecution of Christians in AD 313. Constantius Chlorus became the emperor for the Western part of the empire in AD 296. In AD 306 Constantius Chlorus died in York. His son Constantine was crowned emperor in that year. It is probable that the crowning took place at the same location where the present cathedral stands in York. Constantine returned to Rome and conquered the emperor of the East at the Battle of the Milvian Bridge. Constantine conquered Rome in the name of Christ. The *Chi Rho* symbol that we observed in the last section was placed on the banners of Constantine's troops.

Rome was overrun with the Germanic tribes. Rome was forced to leave England in the fifth century. The Germanic tribe of the Anglo-Saxons conquered the native Celtic tribes in England. In AD 625 a missionary, Paulinus, brought Christianity back to York. Ethelburga was a Christian princess from Kent. To the north in Northumbria, Edwin was the most powerful king in England at the time. He wanted to marry the princess. She refused unless Edwin would allow Paulinus to preach Christ in Northumbria. Finally, Edwin agreed. Two years later he became a Christian and was baptized at or near the location of the present cathedral. The wooden building was replaced by a stone building. But that was destroyed in 1069 when the Norman king from France, William the Conqueror, was moving north to bring all of England under his rule.

A Norman cathedral was constructed to replace the Anglo-Saxon church that was destroyed. It was completed by 1100. Remains of the ancient church are still present in the basement of the present cathedral. Work on a new York Minster Cathedral was begun in 1220. The builders tried whenever possible to build over the old cathedral. The new cathedral was dedicated in the year 1472. That was more than 250 years after the work on the cathedral began. This is the present York Minster Cathedral. During the nineteenth century there were two major fires in the church. In 1967 the foundations were beginning to crumble. Major work had to be done to assure the safety of the cathedral. Another great fire swept through a portion of the cathedral in 1984. Both volunteers and employed persons preserve and maintain the cathedral today.

Map of Great Britain

Today the York Minster Cathedral belongs to the Church of England, known as the Anglican Church. After the Revolutionary War in the United States, the Anglican Church in America separated from the Anglican Church in England. In the United States, that denomination is known as the Episcopal Church.

BUILDING A GREAT CATHEDRAL

Building a cathedral was no easy task. When the building projects began to use stone instead of wood, the architects used the barrel vault. They had learned this technique from the Romans. Recall that the Romans built large buildings. The pressure of the building pushed down from the center of the vault to the ground. It was not possible to open the

York Minster Cathedral

vault very far to place windows to the outside. The buildings had to be lighted from within. Without electricity, they were usually dark inside. Because the model used was Roman, this type of architecture was called Romanesque. There are some good examples of Romanesque cathedrals in both Germany and France.

By the twelfth century, the medieval builders started to construct cathedrals on a different principle. The builders began to use a rib vault. (See the illustration.) The pressure of the weight of the roof and the upper part of the building pushed down the ribs or pillars that came from the center of the vault.

Now the architect could force the pressure of the weight of the roof down along the ribs, or pillars, of the vault into the ground. That meant that it was possible to partly open the sides of the vault. The master builder could place windows in the openings of the vault and allow light to flow into the building. To further strengthen the walls, the builder would place additional pillars along the outer wall of the church. These pillars became known as flying buttresses. (See the illustration of the flying buttresses from York Minster Cathedral.) This kind of construction became known as Gothic architecture.

Romanesque architecture had thick stone walls with rounded barrel vaults. The decoration was simple.

Gothic architecture was a medieval style with pointed arches, rib vaulting, and flying buttresses. The decoration included painting, sculpture, and stained glass.

Master Builder

The master builder had to be employed to oversee the entire project. The master builder had to be an architect. The master builder had to be more than an architect. He had knowledge of geometry and mathematics. He understood the qualities of different types of building material. The master builder was able to sketch his ideas. From these sketches, he was also able to construct models of the building and technical drawings of what he wanted to build. Architects do these same things for buildings today. As the building projects became bigger and more difficult, master builders specialized in a particular kind of construction, such as bridges, castles, or cathedrals.

York Minster Cathedral flying buttresses

The master builder was responsible to hire all of the persons who worked on the cathedral. The master builder was responsible for the money that was spent on the building project. He was responsible for the quality of the building. He served as foreman, who directed all the workers on the project. In other words, the master builder was the most important person in the planning, design, and the building of the cathedral. He carried a lot of power.

Masons

Masons were very specialized. In a building project like York Cathedral, they were also very important to the success of the building. To become a mason, a young man had to become apprenticed to someone who worked in the trade. After a long apprenticeship, he became a mason. He had to know how to work with the different kinds of stone that were necessary for different purposes. One type involved the large piers that would hold up the building. Then there were more delicate and attractive kinds of building stone that would allow openings for the stained glass and the doors. The stones had to be cut properly in order to fit perfectly into place. Limestone was often used, since it was easy to cut and place. Limestone was not as hard as marble and would easily be worn away by the weather. In England, marble had to be imported and was very expensive. Marble was very strong but difficult to cut and place.

> ### Apprentice
> *An apprentice is a learner who is legally bound to work for someone already in the trade in order to learn the trade. A mason, metalworker, or carpenter may each have an apprentice.*

Metalworkers

Metal was used for the roofs. Often lead was used for this purpose. Lead was also used between the panes of stained glass. Metalworkers had to be skilled in their trade also. Metalworkers usually worked with one type of metal and became very skilled in working with that metal. Metalworkers were also apprenticed to someone already skilled in working with a particular kind of metal. Other types of metal were used. Brass was used a lot because it was less expensive than gold and provided a good substitute. Chandeliers, candlestick holders, and other furnishings in the inside of the church were often made of brass. Iron was used for some things but was very heavy. For some things gold was used. It was very pliable and easy to work but very expensive.

Carpenters

The carpenter was very much in demand. Like the other specialized occupations, the carpenter learned his trade through an apprenticeship to another master carpenter. Wood was used as scaffolding for the building of the towers in the cathedral. Oak was often used in the cathedral because it is a hard wood that lasts. Pine was a softer wood and was readily available. Pine was used for many purposes in construction. Mahogany was expensive and had to be imported. The color and lasting durability of mahogany made it a good choice for many of the fur-

Pulpitum of York Cathedral

nishings. Like the masons and metalworkers, the carpenters specialized in the kind of work they did. The pulpit in York Cathedral is a good example of the craftsmanship of the carpenter.

Glaziers

With the development of the Gothic cathedral, the glazier was very much in demand. The glazier was the worker with glass, who created the beautiful stained glass for the cathedral. Making glass is an ancient art that came from places like Egypt. Glass was very important to a cathedral, as it would allow light into the building. Glass did not change much, as other materials, when the temperature outside became warmer or colder. Glass was also important because the Bible taught that light was important. In the Old Testament, God is described as the One who created light. In the New Testament, Jesus is identified as the light of the world. In the Letters of John, light is identified with goodness.

Glass is made from silica. Silica is found in sand. Sand was heated to a very high temperature. For some glass this meant almost 3,000°F. Potash was added to the sand to lower the temperature at which the sand melted. Lime was also added to the mixture. Glass is colored by adding other ingredients. Cobalt was used to color glass blue. One way to shape glass was to pour the liquid glass into a mold or cast. Another way was to blow the glass into a shape while the glass was still at very high temperatures. It can also be pressed, rolled, or drawn. Designs may be etched into the glass or painted on the glass. We will examine one piece of stained glass from the cathedral in Ulm, Germany.

Other Craftsmen

Building a cathedral required the services of many other craftsmen. The demand for craftsmen is illustrated in the great cathedral in Chartres, France. There are nearly two hundred stained-glass windows. Some are single panels, but many have thirty or more different scenes in one window. The individual stone sculptures in the cathedral number several thousands. In each section, both on the outside of the cathedral and on the inside, they are clustered together to tell a story from the Bible and even some stories that went beyond the Bible stories.

In addition to these, many cathedrals, like York, have paintings that adorn the walls. Cloth is used for decoration on the inside of the cathedral. The benches often have seat cushions. Kneeling cushions for prayer are often used and decorated with Christian symbols. Persons skilled in making cushions and doing needlework were also required.

The floors of the cathedral were either marble or required tile. Another occupation for many cathedrals was the person who could lay the tile. Tilers were needed for placing tile on the floors of the cathedral.

Bells are an important feature of the cathedral also. There was a special art to making bells. Normally, a clay form was molded in the shape of the bell. This was lined with a coating of wax that would be about the same width as the bell. Another layer of clay was inserted into the mold over the wax. When the clay was hard, the wax was melted. The mold was ready for the hot metal to be poured into the clay mold. When the metal hardened, the clay was broken away, and the bell was ready to be tuned. When the tune was right, it was hung with the other bells in the church.

Day Laborers

There were persons who moved the stones. This was very heavy labor. Others mixed the mortar to hold the stones in place. A host of other persons were needed to work on a building project that large. For many of these people, their entire adult work life was devoted to the construction of one cathedral. While their names will never appear in its history, they contributed to building the beautiful cathedral. It was constructed for the glory of God.

DESIGN OF A GREAT CATHEDRAL

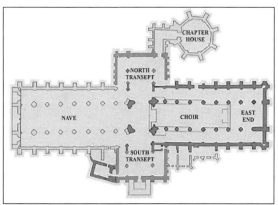

Floor plan of York Minster Cathedral

Interior of York Minster Cathedral

INTERIOR OF THE CATHEDRAL

Ambulatory is the aisle that goes around the choir.

Arcade is the aisle between the outer wall and the piers on either side of the nave.

Baptismal font is a large stone basin that is used for infant baptism.

Cathedra is the bishop's chair.

Chapterhouse is the building from which the clergy administer the business of the church.

Clerestory (clear story) are the windows that allow light into the cathedral above the arcade.

Crossing is in the middle section, where the transepts, or arms, cross the nave at the center of the cathedral.

Choir is the section of the church that is at the top section of the church and contains the fixed pews for the choir, organ, cathedra, and the high altar.

Flying buttresses are piers outside the church that exert pressure to support the walls.

Lectern is the brass stand that is used for reading the Scripture.

Nave is the main part of the church, where the congregation stands or sits.

Piers are solid blocks that support the arches and ceiling of the cathedral.

Pulpit is the platform from which the preacher delivers his sermon.

Transept is the section of the cathedral that contains the north and south arms of the cross.

Vault is an arched structure that supports the ceiling or roof. (See diagram at left.)

Most Christian cathedrals are laid out in a similar fashion. They are in the shape of a cross. The east end of the church contains the high altar. The worshipers enter through the doors at the west end of the church. The main part of the church is called the nave. The nave is the place where the people sit or stand during the worship service. On either side of the nave, the arcade provides a walkway between the outer wall and the piers that support the building. The arms of the cross are known as the north and south transepts. Where the transepts cross the nave, this is known as the crossing. In some cathedrals, like York, the central tower rises over the crossing. At the front end of the church is the choir. It contains the fixed pews for the choir, organ, cathedra, and the high altar. Between the wall and the choir on either side of the church is a walkway, known as the ambulatory. At various points along the outside wall, there may be smaller chapels. For many worship needs, small weddings, or funerals in the church, the small chapel serves well. Notice that there is a chapterhouse at the cathedral in York. It is located off the north transept. The chapterhouse was a place for monks who were associated with the cathedral to meet and conduct the business of the cathedral.

As you look up toward the ceiling of the cathedral, several things are visible. Notice the large piers that line the nave. These are the structures that support the weight of the roof and upper part of the church. They carried the force of the weight deep into the earth. The windows that are above the arcade are known as clerestory windows. In the picture of the interior of the cathedral, you can just barely see the crossing and the tower that extends upward above the roof over the nave. Notice that the ceiling is composed of vaulted arches. Observe how the ribs of these arches carry the weight of the cathedral down the large piers. You can see that in the picture of the vaulted ceiling.

Vaulted ceiling

Furniture of the Cathedral

Inside the cathedral are several different types of furniture. At the front is the altar. It is normally covered with a white cloth. On the table are placed a cross and a candle, one at each end. The high altar is used for the Christian service of communion.

The pulpit of the church is raised and stands on the left side of the nave. (Look at the picture of the pulpitum of York.) The wooden cover was placed over the pulpit to help the congregation hear the preacher since it was built before we used public-address systems with microphones and loudspeakers. On the right side of the nave is a brass lectern. This is used for reading from the Scripture. The baptismal font is a stone basin that is used for infant baptism. It is located near the front door of the church.

The cathedra is located in the choir. (See the diagram of the church floor plan on the previous page.) You will recall that the cathedra is the chair of the bishop. It is usually very well decorated. The cathedra is a symbol of the power of the bishop.

Purpose of the Cathedral

In Exodus and Leviticus, God told Moses how to build the Tabernacle. God intended for the Tabernacle to reflect His glory and beauty. Craftsmen, similar to those who built York Minster Cathedral, were employed to construct the Tabernacle and later the Temple in Jerusalem. In the New Testament there is no similar command to build a Tabernacle or Temple. After the temple was destroyed, the Jews have worshiped and studied since that time in the synagogue. Cathedrals were medieval man's attempt to bring Christians closer to God.

As we have seen, much of medieval culture was spiritual. In every age a culture has those things that it holds dear. Those are the

East end of York Minster Cathedral

things that make one culture special and different from others. In the Middle Ages, the triumph of Christianity was powerful. The cathedral was in the shape of the cross. This has always been the symbol of Christianity and very important to all Christians. The immense size of the cathedral shows forth the glory and majesty of God. The cathedral was built to last for hundreds of years. That carries the idea of eternity. The beauty of the cathedral symbolizes how God created everything beautiful. In a world that is often ugly, the beauty of the cathedral stands out from the drab culture that surrounds it.

Stained-Glass Window— Noah's Ark

In keeping with the spiritual purpose of the medieval cathedral is a beautiful little stained-glass panel from the Cathedral at Ulm, Germany. The panel is not in a prominent place in the cathedral. It is hidden in one of the smaller chapels. The panel illustrates the beauty and simplicity of the faith of many Christian believers from the medieval period. The panel is called *Noah's Ark*. The ark is the ark of safety that protected Noah and his family from the floodwaters that rose as God destroyed the world for its

Hans Acker's Noah's Ark

sinfulness. The ark floats on the foaming sea. The storm has ended and the white clouds and blue sky appear above the ark. Noah's son is looking out from the window in the upper story of the ark. The bright colors and simple shapes of the stained glass highlight the importance of the quiet scene.

Noah extends out from the large chimney at the top of the ark. His hands are clasped in prayer. He has sent the dove from the ark to discover whether the waters have gone down. The white dove flies to Noah with a branch in its beak. Remember from the catacombs that the dove with a branch spoke of peace and hope. Here Noah waits in the middle of the swirling floodwaters with a hope that God has promised to renew the earth after the flood has passed. But all is not peace. On the rock that juts out of the waters in the front of the ark is a large black raven that has already killed a rabbit.

If that were all that this stained-glass window showed, it would still be a special window. There is more for the Christian believer. Notice that the shape of the ark is in a triangle. The ark symbolizes the ark of safety for a believer in Jesus Christ. The triune God is represented in the triangle— Father, Son, and Holy Spirit. In case you missed that, the Father is at the peak of the triangle in the chimney. Jesus is pictured in the window at the front of the ark. The Holy Spirit is pictured as the dove above the ark. The devil is portrayed as the raven that is out to devour the believer. On the stormy sea of life, the ark is a place of safety and shelter to all who put their trust in God's protective care. This is a marvelous expression of the ark of salvation.

Christian Painting and Sculpture

Paintings and sculptures are expressions of the artist's ability to see beyond the ordinary. He uses the painter's canvas or the material for sculpting to tell a story. When an author writes a novel, he tells a story in words. The artist tells his story by using shapes, colors, and paint on flat surfaces in two dimensions: height and width. Along with paintings are etchings, which use lines with a pen to create the picture. The sculptor takes the metal, clay, marble, or other material to create an image that has three dimensions: height, width, and depth.

In this section we will explore several paintings, an etching, and a sculpture. Each of these is a masterpiece of the artist who created it. The first painting, *Enthroned Madonna and Child,* came from an Italian from Sicily in the thirteenth century. *Merode Altarpiece* is believed to have been painted by Robert Campin in Flanders about 1426. Michelangelo is the Italian sculptor for *Pietà,* was completed about 1498 or 1499. The third painting was painted by another Italian, Raphael. It is *Alba Madonna* and was painted about 1510. The Dutch painter Rembrandt etched *The Hundred Guilder Print,* which was completed about 1648 or 1649. *Forest Scene* was painted by the Dutch painter, Jacob van Ruisdael about 1660. The last painting is American, *Peaceable Kingdom,* painted by Edward Hicks in 1834.

The artist tells his story in the painting by giving you clues about what he is trying to say. Looking at the picture, you may miss what he wants to tell you unless you look very closely. To see what the artist wants you to see, let's make this like a treasure hunt. I want you to look very closely at each of the paintings. Try to see everything that you can see. Then take a pencil and paper and write down what you see before you read the things that I will tell you. Then, only after you have tried on your own, read the questions that I have given. This will help you further to find out what you might want to look for. After you have done all that you can do by yourself, then read the answers. These will guide you to see what the artist wanted you to discover. The first time you look, you may not see the things the artist intended right away. Don't become discouraged. With a little help, you will begin to find things that go beyond even my suggestions. This exercise can be fun, and you can learn something at the same time. At the end of each description, I will tell you some things about the painting that you may not know.

Enthroned Madonna and Child

What is the first thing that catches your eye about this painting? Do you know who the two main persons are in the painting? What are they doing? What are the expressions on the faces of the two main persons in the painting? What are the figures doing with their hands? Are there other figures in the painting? Do you notice anything about the colors of the painting? What else do you see in this painting?

Enthroned Madonna and Child, *Unknown artist, c. AD 1280*

Probably, you noticed that the painting has a lot of gold in the background, the throne, and Mary's robe. If you said that this is a painting of Mary and the baby Jesus, you were correct. Mary is seated on a throne. On her lap she is holding Jesus. Mary looks peaceful. Her robe is dark blue and gold. Remember that Mary came from the royal line of King David. This painting probably hung on the wall of a church. Mary is looking down at you from her throne. With her left hand she supports Jesus on her knee. With her right hand she is pointing to Jesus the Savior. Notice that the bodies of both Mary and Jesus are flat. But the heads of both are rounded to give an idea of depth to the figures.

Jesus does not look like a little baby. He is a miniature man. He is shown that way in many pictures like this one. The artist did not want you to think that the Savior of the world was merely a baby. Notice that His robe is red. The color red means that Jesus is God and that He will shed His blood on the cross for our salvation. In His left hand, Jesus is holding the scroll of the Word of God. His right hand is extended above the person who is looking up at Him. He holds out two fingers. Even though He is not looking down as Mary is, Jesus is blessing the person below Him. In this case you are the one being blessed. Above Jesus' head is a halo. It is made up of three red parts that suggest the Trinity of God—Father, Son, and Holy Spirit. The red and gold of the halo allow the God nature of Jesus to shine forth.

At the top of the painting are two angels. You can tell that they are angels by their wings. They each hold a globe and a scepter. The globe is symbolic of the earth. The scepter is the sign of power. The angels suggest the power of the Lord of salvation over the earth in this painting. This divine power is also seen in the throne on which Mary sits with Jesus. The throne is also made of gold and holds a red cushion. There is nothing in the background except the gold.

This painting, like the others that we will examine, tells a story. There is nothing in the Scripture that would suggest that Mary sat upon a gold throne with Jesus on her lap. The only likely place where that might have happened would have been when the wise men came to Bethlehem. But Mary and Joseph were too poor to have a gold throne. This is a devotional painting by the artist. It is not an event from the Bible. It is intended to lead the viewer to a closer relationship to Christ and Mary.

The painting has value in the persons that it shows. It also has value in the gold that is all over the surface of the painting. The gold would also serve to show the spiritual nature of the painting. Remember that this would have hung in a medieval church. Churches were lit by candles, and there were lighted candles in racks below the painting. These candles flickered and cast shadows on the gold of the painting. This would add to the spiritual quality of the painting. It is similar to the stained glass in the cathedral, with the sunlight shining through the varied colored glass in the church. This painting came from a church in Spain. The shape of the painting is rectangular. This was typical of the paintings of this type that came from that time period in history.

> ### SPIRITUAL
> *Spiritual means having qualities of the spirit. These would relate to the sacredness of God. It is the opposite of the physical, or body.*

Mérode Altarpiece

As you look at *Mérode Altarpiece,* what stands out? What is different about the frame of this picture? Who are the people in this painting? What do you think that the people are doing? What story do the colors tell? What are the objects in the picture? What do the objects tell that will help you understand the painting? What do you notice about the detail of the houses and street scenes? What is different from *Enthroned Madonna and Child?*

This beautiful painting is different from all of the other works of art that we will view. It has three

Mérode Altarpiece, *Robert Campin (the Master of Flémalle), c. 1426*

different panels. Because it has three panels, it is called a triptych. The center panel shows the annunciation by the angel Gabriel to Mary that she will bear a son, who will become the Savior of the world. This story is told in Luke 1:26–38. Joseph was not present when the angel of Lord came to Mary. The artist painted Joseph in his carpenter's shop in the panel at the right. But who are the people in the left panel? An artist can do things that a photographer cannot do. The artist can take persons from a very different period of time and put them in the scene. That is what Robert Campin did here. The person for whom Campin painted this picture was probably a merchant. He and his wife are painted by the artist and placed in the left panel. He and his wife are kneeling, and he is holding his hat, as they have the privilege of looking at this holy scene. There is also a knight standing behind the couple. Who do you think the artist intended that person to be?

Let's look at the center panel first. Your eye travels first to Mary. She is seated humbly on the floor rather than on the bench. She is reading a book. She looks very much like many Flemish girls would have appeared at the time the artist painted. Her dress is red. That symbolized the purity of Mary as one chosen by God to carry God's Son. The bench behind Mary is covered with purple cushions, the color of royalty. On both ends of the bench is a lion. They represent Christ, the Lion

of Judah. The angel Gabriel is to the left. He has his right hand raised as he is about to tell Mary this great news. Mary is not yet aware of the presence of the angel. Notice the little round windows above the angel. Through the left window comes a shaft of sunlight. If you look closely, on the beam of sunlight you can see a cherub or the baby Jesus carrying a cross to Mary. As the angel told her, Mary would become the mother of the Son of God. The birth of Jesus is clearly set forth in this panel, as well as Jesus' death for our salvation.

There are several objects in the room. There is a table in the center. On the table are three important objects. Each object is symbolic of this holy scene. On the front of the table is a book that is open. If you were to look closely, you would see the prophecy from Isaiah: "Therefore the LORD himself shall give you a sign; Behold, a virgin shall conceive, and bear a son, and shall call his name Immanuel" (Isaiah 7:14 KJV). That prophecy has a connection to the knight standing in the back of the left panel. Does that give you an idea who the knight might be?

Also on the table is a candle that has just been snuffed out. That tells the viewer that the life of Jesus will be brought to an early end by the cross that the cherub is carrying on the shaft of sunlight. At the rear of the table is a vase from the East that holds a lily. The lily is a symbol of the innocent beauty of Mary. It also speaks of Easter and the triumph of Jesus in His resurrection from the dead. On the wall hangs a brass pot, or laver. The laver was used in the Old Testament by the priests for cleansing. The blood of Jesus that He shed on the cross provides cleansing for the believer from his sin. On the towel rack hangs a towel, which reminds us of the washing of the disciples' feet that Jesus performed before His crucifixion.

On the right panel Joseph sits in his carpenter's shop. He is drilling a piece of wood, which may have been from a winepress. Both drilling the holes in the wood and the winepress are symbolic of the nails that were put through Jesus' hands and feet and his shed blood on the cross. Notice the detail of the town scene that you can see outside the window. It must have looked like the town in which the artist painted this beautiful picture. There is a mousetrap on the workbench. In case you miss the one on the carpenter's table, there is another on the ledge outside the window. In one of Augustine's writings, he said that the cross of Christ was the mousetrap of the devil. The artist wants you to see the connection between the cross and the crucifixion and Jesus' birth from the main panel and this panel.

On the left panel, the merchant and his wife are quietly kneeling. Notice the expressions on their faces. He is clearly amazed at what he is witnessing. She quietly looks at the scene also and perhaps is trying to think how she would feel if the angel Gabriel had come to tell her such news. Did you discover who the knight is? He is probably Isaiah. Remember that the artist, unlike the photographer, can bring persons from different times into his painting. Isaiah is the prophet who many years before foretold that Jesus would be born of a virgin. Now it is actually about to happen, and the artist makes Isaiah a witness to this great event.

Remember that it is a triptych or painting in three panels. They were hinged together. The two side panels could be closed across the main panel. The main purpose for this painting was a devotional reminder of God's love in the birth, death, and resurrection of Christ for our salvation. The triptych would help the merchant and his wife when they stopped during the day to engage in prayer. At that point, they could open the triptych, and it would cause them to remember and worship God. When they were not using the triptych for worship, they could close it and prevent it from being scratched or collecting dust.

Mérode Altarpiece was painted in the city of Tournai, Belgium. Robert Campin was most likely the artist for this devotional masterpiece. The Metropolitan Museum of Art in New York City purchased the painting. It now hangs in the Campin Room in the Cloisters. The Cloisters is the only museum in the United States devoted completely to medieval art and architecture.

Pietà

Who are the main figures in this sculpture? What is the meaning of the expression on the face of the woman? Why is the man on her lap limp as a lifeless form? Is there a spiritual meaning to this sculpture? What are the feelings caused by the sculpture? How do you feel about the sculpture? What kind of material do you suppose Michelangelo used to create this sculpture?

If you said that the two figures in the sculpture were Mary and Jesus, you are correct. All of the works with Mary as one of the main characters that we have looked at so far have come from Jesus'

Pietà, *Michelangelo, 1498–1499*

childhood. This sculpture comes from the death of Christ. The word *pietà* means an artwork that shows Mary holding the dead body of her Son, Jesus. The Gospel of John tells us that Mary, Jesus' mother, was at the foot of the cross (John 19:25). At that moment Jesus turned to the apostle John and asked him to care for Mary. Even though we do not know if this scene ever actually happened, this scene of Michelangelo's sculpture certainly might have happened. There is no way to be sure since the Bible does not give us any more description of how Jesus was taken from the cross.

Continuing in the same chapter of John, the writer tells us that the next day was the Sabbath. Neither Pilate nor the priests wanted any bodies left on the cross for the Sabbath. The soldiers were instructed to hasten the death of the persons on the cross. When they came to Jesus, He was already dead. They pierced his side with a sword (John 19:31–37).

Michelangelo's *Pietá* statue happens after Jesus has just been taken down from the cross. In many pictures, the artist shows both John and Mary Magdalene. Michelangelo does not include these other figures in his sculpture. Mary is seated alone on a stone bench. She takes the dead form of Jesus in her arms and holds Him in her grief. Michelangelo does not show Mary as one who is frightened or wailing. She has resigned herself to the death of her Son. Sadly, the sorrow does not come any easier

As she sat there, Mary must have remembered the words of the prophet Simeon when Mary and Joseph took the baby Jesus to the temple as a very young child. After Simeon had blessed Jesus, he said to Mary, "Indeed, this child is destined to cause the fall and rise of many in Israel, and to be a sign that will be opposed—and a sword will pierce your own soul—that the thoughts of many hearts may be revealed" (Luke 2:34–35). Now that had come to pass.

As she continued to sit there with His limp body close to her, she must have remembered many times holding Him as a child. Those were happy times. He had been a good son to her. Now with deep sorrow, Mary holds Him in her arms for the last time.

In the statue, the wounds of the nail holes in Jesus' hands and feet, along with the spear cut in His side, are very small. Michelangelo believed that the inner beauty of Jesus would minimize these evil signs on His body. Look closely at the wrists of Jesus. They show even the detail of His veins.

Be sure to look at the face of Mary. Her grace and inner beauty show through in the clear lines of her face—from her eyes, nose, and lips. This is not the face of an older woman but a young and beautiful woman. Michelangelo answered those who complained by saying that her purity kept her beautiful and young. She shows that beauty even in this time of her greatest grief.

This statue was created out of a single block of marble. Michelangelo was the greatest sculptor and painter that ever lived. Most of his art was dedicated to the church. This sculpture is the only one of all of his creations that carries his signature. He created this magnificent statue when he was only twenty-three years of age. It is recognized as the greatest Christian religious sculpture in the world today. *Pietá* was placed in two churches before it was moved to its present location in St. Peter's Basilica in Rome. In spite of that, Michelangelo was not entirely satisfied with *Pietá*. He produced two other sculptures of the same subject later in his life. So concerned was the sculptor with perfection, that he was working on another *Pietá* just a few days before he died.

Alba Madonna

Who are the main figures in this painting? What are the expressions on the faces of each of the figures? What do you notice about the clothing of each of the persons in the painting? What is the focus of the painting? What other things are included in the painting? Do the colors mean

Alba Madonna, *Raphael, c. 1510*

anything? What are the shapes within the painting? What do the shapes add to the painting? How do the shapes contribute to the painting? What do you notice about the background of this painting? (Remember *Enthroned Madonna and Child* and *Alba Madonna* painted the same subject and a similar scene). How would you compare *Alba Madonna* with the picture that you just observed, *Enthroned Madonna and Child*?

There are three persons in this painting. Mary is the largest figure. To her right is Jesus, and beyond him is John the Baptist. She is sitting on the ground rather than on a throne. Mary is looking toward her right. With her left hand she holds her finger in the book on her lap. Notice that her right hand supports Jesus, who is on her lap. Her right hand reaches behind Jesus to John the Baptist. This unites the three figures. Remember that John was the cousin of Jesus. We do not know what book Mary was reading, but it could have been the Bible and the prophecies about Jesus in the Old Testament. Her dress is blue. Blue tells of Mary's purity. The red of her inner garment would also suggest the blood of Jesus at the cross. Notice that Mary is very beautiful. Her mood is

not happy, however. She seems sad as she thinks about the cross that Jesus will have to bear.

Jesus is seated on Mary's right knee. Jesus looks like a chubby little boy, not like a miniature man, as we saw in the previous painting. The focus of Jesus is on the cross that He is taking from John the Baptist. Recall the Scripture that led to Jesus' baptism by John the Baptist in Matthew 3. As a small boy, Jesus is not clothed in this picture. He does not have a halo around His head as He would have had in the medieval painting.

John the Baptist is looking up to Jesus. Remember from the Gospel of John their first meeting as adults. John the Baptist told the people, "Here is the Lamb of God, who takes away the sin of the world!" (John 1:29). In the painting, John is giving the cross to Jesus. The cross is the focus of Mary, John, and Jesus. John the Baptist is clothed in the camel's hair that was described in Matthew 3. Recall that John was the older of the two cousins. He is pictured as larger than Jesus.

The background of the picture is a quiet countryside. The painter made the background of hills and plains, blue sky and wispy clouds. The background does not take away from the figures in the picture. The figures are very clear. They stand out from the hazy background.

Notice the circle in which the figures are painted. For many artists it was difficult to paint within a circle. Before you read further, try to think why this might be so. The danger is that the circle may seem to appear to roll over. To prevent this from appearing to roll over, the artist composed the picture in the shape of a pyramid. Mary's head forms the top point of the pyramid. Her left arm forms the base and side of the pyramid. Remember that her arm also unites all three figures. John the Baptist forms the right side of the pyramid. As a result, the painting appears to be solid.

In *Enthroned Madonna and Child*, the picture is rectangular. *Alba Madonna* is a circle. The figures in the first painting are placed on a throne, while the figures in the second painting are seated on the ground. The setting for Raphael's work is more natural. The first painting was designed for a church. The second could be used in a person's home as well as a church. In Raphael's painting Mary looks more like a woman that you might see in your neighborhood. Jesus is presented as a little boy in the second painting, rather than a miniature man. But the theme of the cross and the salvation offered by Jesus is true for both paintings.

You may have wondered why this painting by Raphael is called *Alba Madonna*. Raphael went to Rome to paint in 1508. He painted this Madonna in 1510. The picture was taken to Spain during the seventeenth century. It was brought into the home of the Duchess of Alba. It stayed there for about one hundred years and took the name of its owner. Eventually, it was sold and went to the Hermitage Museum in St. Petersburg, Russia. From there it was purchased for the National Gallery of Art in Washington, DC, where it can be seen today.

The Hundred Guilder Print

What do you see in this print? Who are the many characters? Who is the main character? Why are so many people pictured in this print? How do the people on the left side differ from the people on the right side? What do the facial expressions tell you about the people? Can you find the donkey in this print? Why do you suppose that the artist used the etching technique to create a print instead of painting to carry his message?

Jesus is the main character in this etching. This picture is based on Matthew 19. Jesus commands your attention immediately as you look at the print. Jesus appears just slightly to the left of the center of the etching. He is easily identified by the way He stands and the light that surrounds His head. Notice the expression on Jesus' face. His face shows kindness, concern, pity, tenderness, and love. Look closely at the faces of the other people in the picture. We will come back to the facial expressions later.

Notice the people on the right of Jesus. They all have something in common. They are all sick

persons. They have come to Jesus to be healed. Matthew said, "Large crowds followed Him, and He healed them there" (Matthew 19:2). Some have been able to walk by themselves, but others had to be carried or wheeled on a cart. Look closely at their faces. Some express their sadness at the length of time that they have been sick or unable to walk. Others are begging Jesus to heal them, such as the two women with their hands clasped in front of the Master, begging for His mercy. Behind the ladies, a man stands with outstretched hand to bring the lame man with the cane or the person on the cart to Jesus for healing.

On the left side of the picture, next to Jesus, stands Peter. Look first at the three Pharisees who stand to the right of Peter and slightly behind him. Look at the expressions on their faces. They show self-satisfaction. They have a mean, mocking look on their faces. They are going to try to make fun of Jesus so the people will turn away from Him. That is the meaning of the Bible text that states,

The Hundred Guilder Print, *Rembrandt van Rijn, c. 1648–1650*

111

"Some Pharisees approached Him to test Him" (Matthew 19:3a). Their attempt to hurt Jesus' ministry of love for the people continued through Matthew 19:3–12. When they were not able to do what they wanted, they stood by and watched, hoping to trap Jesus in some other way.

The apostle Peter is standing to the right side of Jesus. He is trying to prevent the women from bringing their children to Jesus. But Jesus put out His right hand to stop Peter from holding the children back. Notice the two women in the front. They are each carrying a child. The one is coming to Jesus. The other is not sure that Jesus wants to see the child. But a little boy is in front of her and trying to encourage her to bring the baby to Jesus. This is described by Matthew: "Then children were brought to Him so He might put His hands on them and pray. But the disciples rebuked them. Then Jesus said, 'Leave the children alone, and don't try to keep them from coming to Me, because the kingdom of heaven is made up of people like this'" (Matthew 19:13–14).

Behind the women with the children and in front of the Pharisees sits a young man. This is the rich young ruler. Matthew tells us, "Just then someone came up and asked Him, 'Teacher, what good must I do to have eternal life'" (Matthew 19:16). Jesus asked the young man if he had kept the Ten Commandments. The man told Jesus that he had obeyed those commands since he was a child. He asked Jesus what he still needed. Jesus answered, "If you want to be perfect, . . . go, sell your belongings and give to the poor, and you will have treasure in heaven. Then come, follow Me" (Matthew 19:21). Matthew tells us that the young man went away sorrowful. He had a lot of things. He did not want to give them up. Rembrandt shows the young man sitting there with his hand on his chin. He is thinking about what Jesus told him. He does not yet seem ready to give up all of the things that he had.

Jesus turned to His disciples and told them that it would be easier for the camel to go through the needle's eye gate than for a wealthy person to come to the kingdom of God. In New Testament times, the gates of the city were closed to prevent thieves or soldiers from entering the city while all the people slept. But in one corner of the wall was located a very small gate. Travelers from far away might arrive late in the night. To allow them to enter the city, there was the needle's eye gate. The merchant would have to unload the camel and push all of the packages through the gate. If a camel were to get through the gate, it would have to kneel down and squeeze through the gate. Finally, the merchant would go through the gate himself. Jesus was telling the disciples that this was easier than for a wealthy man to come to the kingdom. Jesus is not saying that a rich person cannot come into the kingdom of God. It is usually more difficult for the same reason this young man was unwilling to give up his wealth.

Although the gate is much larger, Rembrandt has included the camel with the merchant and his packages. Look closely at the gate on Jesus' left side. The camel is carrying his burden and bringing it through the gate. Do you also see the donkey to the far side of the picture? That was an addition of Rembrandt's. On the other side of the print, you can also see a number of people gathered beyond the Pharisees. One is even lying down on the large rock. These figures can be seen, but they apparently are bystanders and are not subjects of the story from Matthew 19.

This is a very beautiful example of a Bible story that is effectively retold by the artist. Rembrandt was a master at the use of light and shadow in painting and also etching, as you see in this example. He used light and shadow to help tell his stories. Notice the large dark areas on the right side of the etching. These increase our ability to see Jesus. The etching technique was done with an etching tool that had a metal needle. The artist also had other tools that would cut into the metal and cause wider or narrower lines. The artist then prepared a metal plate with wax. He would etch a groove into the plate through the wax. When the etching was completed, the artist would put the plate in an acid bath. The acid would eat at the metal, deepening the grooves that the artist made. Then the plate could be inked and printed. This print was called *The Hundred Guilder Print* because Rembrandt tells us that once he had to pay one hundred guilders to get a copy of his own print. This etching is found in Amsterdam at the Rijksprentenkabinet.

Forest Scene

Is this a Christian religious painting? Is this painting simply a beautiful country forest scene? Is there a deeper meaning to this painting? How does this painting differ from all of the other works of art that we have seen so far? What are the main elements of this painting? Are there any people in this painting? If there are people, what are they doing and why? What story do you think the artist is trying to tell in this painting?

When you first look at this painting, it appears to be a peaceful scene from a walk in the woods. In the front of the painting is a very large broken birch tree. It has fallen into the stream that runs through the center of the painting. There is a waterfall just behind the fallen birch tree. Also, behind the birch tree is a large solid oak tree that seems to merge with the clouds in the sky. On the left side of the painting are some sheep grazing alongside the stream. A path is next to the place where the sheep graze. Along the path are a man and woman walking. The man and woman seem small inside this huge dark forest. The path goes off into the distance. In the sky there are threatening storm clouds. If the two people walk too far from home, they may run into a storm.

In the seventeenth century some of the Dutch artists, such as Jacob van Ruisdae, were influenced by theology. These artists were fearful that they would disobey the Second Commandment. Their problem was to find out how they could give glory to God and not paint scenes from the Bible. For them, one solution was to paint God's nature. The only problem with this solution in the history of art is that artists today are ignorant of the original meaning, or else they purposely ignore its Christian meaning. As followers of Christ, we can also benefit today from their discovery. By painting nature, they could show the work of God in creation. They could also use the elements of that painting to tell a story that would remind people that life is short. Their message is that we need to be careful how we live our lives. God will judge us one day for the way we have lived our lives.

You will remember from reading Genesis 3 that the Tree of Knowledge of Good and Evil stood in the middle of the Garden of Eden. Adam and Eve were told by God not to eat of the fruit of this tree. But the serpent tempted Eve and she ate. Then she gave to Adam and he ate also. God expelled them from the Garden of Eden. During the Middle Ages, the Tree of Life was shown as a tree that was healthy and growing. The Tree of Life also became identified with the cross on which Jesus died. Therefore, the Tree of Life became a symbol of eternal life in heaven with God. The Tree of Death was broken and not healthy.

Forest Scene, *Jacob van Ruisdael, 1660–1665*

The artist was also well aware of the Christian symbolism of the tree. He was able to use this symbolism to tell his story. The person who purchased this painting from the artist would be reminded every day when they got up in the morning that they had to make choices that day. The choices could either be good choices or bad choices. The Tree of Life suggested that they needed to make good choices that would please God. The temptation to make bad choices was also there and was symbolized by the broken dead birch tree of death. We live in a world that can seem overwhelming. But when we choose to follow God, we can have His strength to help us make the right choices. In this way the artist believed that he did not disobey the Second Commandment and still was able to tell a moral story to the people who purchased his paintings.

All of these elements were combined in *Forest Scene* by Jacob van Ruisdael. The painting hangs today in the National Gallery, Washington, DC Other Dutch painters painted with a similar intention. They did not want to use Bible scenes but used nature to carry their content. Some painted flowers, fruit, and other forms of still life to carry similar messages that life must be lived with care and in keeping with what God desires.

Peaceable Kingdom

How does this painting differ from all the paintings that we have examined so far? What are the most important parts of this painting? Why are there several groups of people? Who are these people? Can you name each of the animals that are included? What are the most important animals? How do you know that they are most important? Who are the little people?

The painter of this work of art is Edward Hicks. His first painting of the peaceable kingdom was done between 1816 and 1818. It is believed that he painted more than one hundred of the peaceable

kingdom paintings until his death in 1849. Only sixty-two are known to exist today. He gave the paintings to his friends and neighbors. There is something very appealing about this kind of painting.

This painting is very different from any that we have examined so far. This is American folk art. Folk art in America was created by persons who did not have any formal training in painting or the other arts. In this case the painting is done on a flat surface. The figure of the child is placed between the tiger and the lion. The child appears to be standing in space.

Perhaps the largest animal in the painting is the water buffalo. Next to the water buffalo are a lion and a tiger. In the front are two leopards. On this side of the leopard is a black bear and an ox. There is a gray wolf under the tiger and a bear cub. There are goats and a lamb. There is also a cow in the picture. There appears to be a bison toward the top of the painting. Some of these animals are from the farm. Some of the other animals in this painting cannot be trusted, like the lion, leopard, bear, and wolf. Why would the artist put these different animals together? Let's look at the prophecy from Isaiah. Isaiah wrote in 11:6–9:

Peaceable Kingdom, *Edward Hicks, 1834*

The wolf also shall dwell with the lamb, and the leopard shall lie down with the kid; and the calf and the young lion and the fatling together; and a little child shall lead them. And the cow and the bear shall feed; their young ones shall lie down together: and the lion shall eat straw like the ox. And the sucking child shall play on the hole of the asp, and the weaned child shall put his hand on the cockatrice' den. They shall not hurt nor destroy in all my holy mountain: for the earth shall be full of the knowledge of the LORD, as the waters cover the sea. (KJV)

The children are at play with the different animals. There is no fear. God has taken the fear from the children. He has made the animals safe to be together.

Look at the left side of the painting. There are groups of people talking together. These were included in most of Hicks' paintings of *Peaceable Kingdom*. The groups of people are Quakers, led by William Penn. In 1682 Penn brought a group of Quakers, who were being persecuted in England, to America. This was a very important event to Edward Hicks. It was the foundation of the Quakers in America. For him *Peaceable Kingdom* represented the establishment of the Quaker colony in Pennsylvania. Penn also established Philadelphia as a city of brotherly love.

From things he said and wrote, Hicks always believed that one had to be careful of the lion and the leopard. The lion was often used to represent England. Hicks did not trust the English Quakers. Therefore, one had to be careful in dealing with them. The girl in the front of the painting may represent liberty. Again, it is important to be watchful to protect the freedoms that we enjoy in America. Anyone can enjoy this painting. It can speak to all of us. We look forward to the time when the lion will be able to lie down with the lamb and the leop-

ard, and the child will be safe. It will happen one day when God's kingdom comes, as the prophecy in Isaiah tells us.

To understand this painting a little better, you may need to have a little background about the artist. Edward Hicks was born in 1780 in Pennsylvania. He became an apprentice to makers of horse-drawn coaches in the Pennsylvania town of Langhorne. There he learned how to paint and decorate the coaches. In 1800 his apprenticeship ended, and he made a living by painting. Three years later he became a member of the Quaker Meeting in Middletown. He also married in 1803. By 1811 he set up shop in Newtown, Pennsylvania. In the same year he became a Quaker minister. Even though he had many problems both in his business and the ministry, Edward Hicks started to paint for his own enjoyment. He painted a number of scenes from the local American countryside. He also painted some scenes from the Revolutionary War. But the theme that interested him most was the *Peaceable Kingdom*.

Christian Hymns and Spiritual Songs

Music has a long heritage in all cultures. The earliest mention of musicians in the Bible comes from a passage in Genesis 4:21: "His brother was named Jubal; he was the father of all who play the lyre and the flute." The Canaanites used musicians. The Egyptians also had music as part of their cultural heritage.

Among the ancient Israelites, music played an important part in both the national and the spiritual life of the nation. Even though music was played before David's reign as king, it is with David that we see professional musicians employed to play in the religious life of the Hebrew people. Many of the Psalms were written by David. Others were written by his choirmaster and for specific musical instruments. First Chronicles 6:31 states, "These are the men David put in charge of the music in the LORD's temple after the ark came to rest there." David himself was a skilled musician. Remember that he played for King Saul to calm him at times when the king was upset.

During the Middle Ages the monks developed the Gregorian chant as one musical means for worship. The cathedrals had great organs, which filled the large churches with music for worship. Martin Luther wrote many hymns during the Reformation. Later, when Methodism developed, Charles Wesley wrote many hymns. The evangelistic rallies of the nineteenth century used hymns to stir the congregation. Today, Billy Graham uses music at his evangelistic rallies for stirring people's emotions and encouraging them to come to Christ.

In recent years there has been a new emphasis upon writing praise choruses for worship. The danger that we face is that we may lose the great heritage of hymns that have come down to us from the past. Many of these great hymns provide us with good theology that can help us make sense of life and strengthen our faith. We should be happy for the new songs that can help us worship today, but we do not want to lose the great hymns of the Christian faith that come from past generations.

Music has the power to affect our emotions. Music can calm, excite, praise, and help us celebrate. It is needed in the worship of God. Music can help us go to sleep at night and can be there when we awaken in the morning. Music can help fill our day. In this section we want to examine a hymn and a Christmas Carol. We will look first at John Newton's hymn "Amazing Grace." Then, we will examine Franz Gruber's Christmas Carol "Silent Night."

"Amazing Grace"
John Newton, London, 1779

The hymn "Amazing Grace" was written in 1779 by John Newton. Newton wrote six verses of the hymn that we now sing, though our hymnals usually include four verses. "Amazing Grace" is based on 1 Chronicles 17:16–17: "And David the king came and sat before the LORD, and said, Who am I, O LORD God, and what is mine house, that thou hast brought me hitherto? And yet this was a small thing in thine eyes, O God; for thou hast also spoken of thy servant's house for a great while to come, and hast regarded me according to the estate of a man of high degree, O LORD God" (KJV). In these verses Newton described his life story. He always thanked God that he was a sinner who had been saved by God's grace. From the story of his life we can learn why he was so grateful to God for saving him.

John Newton was born in London, England, in 1725. His mother was a strong Christian, and she taught John the way of faith. Sadly, his mother died when he was almost seven years of age. John's father was not a Christian. He was a ship's captain, and young John learned to live a life of sin from his father. At age eleven he left home and joined his father at sea. To improve his own situation, John joined the British Navy and was assigned to a man-of-war ship. Life in the navy was difficult. He was beaten and had to learn to stand up for himself.

AMAZING GRACE

Amazing grace! how sweet the sound,
That saved a wretch like me!
I once was lost, but now am found,
Was blind, but now I see.

Twas grace that taught my heart to fear,
And grace my fears relieved;
How precious did that grace appear
The hour I first believed!

Thro' many dangers, toils and snares,
I have already come;
Tis grace hath bro't me safe thus far,
And grace will lead me home.

When we've been there ten thousand years,
Bright shining as the sun,
We've no less days to sing God's praise
Than when we first begun.

Soon he sought his fortune elsewhere. He became very greedy and sinful. John moved from the navy to slave trading. He worked hard and soon became the captain of his own slave-trading vessel. His ship went to Africa and picked up slaves that he brought to America. He then would sail to the West Indies and pick up molasses and take it back to New England to make rum to be traded for slaves in Africa. The slave trade was very profitable. He said later that he often wished that he could have believed in the God that his mother worshiped. But he loved his sin too much.

One day he became so drunk that he slipped and fell into the sea. His men did not respect him, even though he was the captain. They did not throw him a line. Instead, they shot a harpoon into his hip. He was rescued, but it left him with a disjointed leg for the rest of his life. From that time on he walked with a limp.

In 1748 his ship almost sank as he was coming home to England. Newton prayed for the first time in many years. He remembered what his saintly mother had taught him years before. During the rest of the voyage he began reading Thomas á Kempis's *Imitation of Christ*. His life changed. He still wanted to continue to run his slave ship. He tried to hold services on the ship for the crew and the slaves. As time went on, he realized that he could not live that kind of life and still please God.

He gave up the slave trading and his ship. In 1750 Newton married Mary Catlett. She had been waiting for him to change his way of life. Now he took a job as a clerk in Liverpool. He worked there for the next several years, until he came under the influence of George Whitefield as well as John and Charles Wesley. He began to feel that God was calling him to the ministry.

Now almost forty, Newton responded to the call and was ordained. He chose to stay in the established church, the Anglican Church, rather than become a Methodist. He became pastor of the Anglican Church at Olney. This town was very near Cambridge. Newton preached whenever he could. He would tell how God had gloriously saved this wicked captain of a slave-trading ship. People responded and came to Christ. He also became an outspoken critic of the evils of slavery. Newton wanted Parliament to act to stop the inhuman practice of slavery.

William Cowper was already a well-published author. Newton joined with his friend, William Cowper, and together they wrote hymns. They produced a hymnal, *The Olney Hymns*. Cowper wrote 67 hymns; Newton wrote 282 hymns. It was published in 1779. The purpose of the hymnal was to assist believers to deepen their faith and trust in Christ.

Newton retired from the church at Olney and moved to St. Mary's Woolnoth Church, London. This was an important church in London. There he served for the next twenty-eight years of his life. Mary, Newton's wife, died of cancer in 1790. Newton was heartbroken but continued to preach.

Among the hymns that Newton wrote was the hymn that best described his life story, "Amazing Grace." Before he died at age eighty-two, he had written the inscription he wanted on his tombstone. He is buried with his wife in the cemetery at St. Mary's Woolnoth Church in London. The tombstone reads, "John Newton, Clerk, once an infidel and libertine, A servant of slaves in Africa: Was by the rich mercy of our Lord and Savior, Jesus Christ, Preserved, restored, pardoned, And appointed to preach the Faith, He had labored so long to destroy. Near sixteen years at Olney in Bucks; and twenty-seven years in this church." It is perhaps especially fitting that in the year of his death, 1807, Parliament outlawed the slave trade. You will want to go back and read again the words of this great old hymn. Think about John Newton, who gave this as a personal testimony to the grace of a loving God.

"Silent Night! Holy Night!"
Joseph Mohr, Oberndorf, Austria, 1818
One of the great traditions associated with Christmas is the singing of Christmas carols. Perhaps the most beloved of all Christmas carols is "Silent Night! Holy Night!" There are several stories about the way in which "Silent Night! Holy Night!" came to be written. On one point all of the stories seem to agree. Joseph Mohr and Franz Grüber combined their talents to create this special Christmas song. Some years later, the carol was sung at the Leipzig Fair in Germany. Its popularity grew quickly. Soon it was translated into English and made its way to America in a Methodist hymnal. It is now sung in churches and Christmas celebrations in countries around the world. How did it come to be written? How did it spread so quickly to other languages and cultures throughout the world?

Joseph Mohr was a Catholic priest in the small village of Oberndorf in the Austrian Alps. He was a pastor of St. Nicholas Church. He and his friend Franz Grüber talked about finding the perfect Christmas hymn that would honor the birth of the Christ child. Neither Mohr nor Grüber thought much more about it until Christmas Eve in 1818. It was a snowy evening as Mohr made his way to the home of one of his parishioners, a woodcutter and his wife. Arriving at the home, he found that the woodcutter's wife had just delivered a baby boy. Mohr found the baby in a rough cradle that the woodcutter had made. The baby was sleeping peacefully. The new mother was very peaceful and happy. Mohr spent time on this pastoral call with the woodcutter and his wife.

SILENT NIGHT, HOLY NIGHT

Silent night, holy night,
All is calm, all is bright
Round yon Virgin Mother and Child,
Holy Infant so tender and mild,
Sleep in heavenly peace,
Sleep in heavenly peace.

Silent night, holy night,
Darkness flies, all is light;
Shepherds hear the angels sing,
"Alleluia! hail the King!
Christ the Saviour is born,
Christ the Saviour is born.

Silent night, holy night,
Guiding Star, lend thy light;
See the eastern wise men bring
Gifts and homage to our King!
Christ the Saviour is born,
Christ the Saviour is born.

Silent night, holy night,
Wondrous Star, lend thy light;
With the angels let us sing
Alleluia to our King!
Christ the Saviour is born,
Christ the Saviour is born.

As he left the home of this little family, Mohr had to walk on foot to a home of another parishioner in the village. His only transportation on that snowy evening was by foot. He trudged along through the snow, thinking about what he had just witnessed. The evening was very still as he came over the rise and looked down on the twinkling lights in the village below. The only sound he could hear, the sound of the stream gurgling below. The snow had stopped, and he could see the beauty of the heavens as the stars shown in all their beauty that night. He stood for a moment gazing at this beautiful and peaceful scene before going on to his destination. The party had already started when he arrived. Mohr stayed for a while but left as soon as he could to go home.

In his study he thought about the events of the afternoon and evening. He thought about the new mother and the little baby in the rough cradle. He recalled the stillness of the night, only interrupted by the sounds of the bubbling stream. He remembered the stars that shown in the darkness after the snow had passed. He thought about the twinkling lights in the village below. Mohr was not in a mood to party. He wanted to write about what he had seen.

Those beautiful words began to flow from his pen. "Silent night! Holy night! all is calm, all is bright. . . ." Mohr worked late through the night. It was four o'clock in the morning when he finally stopped writing. He did not know how to put his words to music. So he thought that early the next day he would ask his friend Franz Grüber to come and put the words to music.

Mohr was so excited that he did not sleep much that night. He awoke early and called on his friend from Arnsdorf. Arnsdorf was in a town nearby to Oberndorf. Franz Grüber was the town schoolmaster and a musician, who played the organ. Grüber was excited about the work of his friend. He took the words and put them to music. Together that Christmas night, Mohr and Grüber sang their new song to the little congregation at Oberndorf. This was their Christmas present to the little church family. Everyone loved the beautiful Christmas song.

A year passed and it was November when the organ broke down. They called Fritz Mauracher from Zillerthal, another local mountain village. After working on the old organ for several days, he asked Grüber to test out the organ. Since it was near Christmas, Grüber played "Silent Night! Holy Night!" Mauracher was thrilled by the piece and pleaded with Grüber to give him a copy of the words and the music.

Mauracher gave the music to a women's singing group, the Strasser Quartet. They sang the song for the next several years. In 1831 they sang "Silent Night! Holy Night!" at the Leipzig fair. It took a few more years before the emperor finally heard the song. From that time on, it became a popular Christmas song throughout Germany. It slowly made its way from Germany to the United States. After World War I, it became very popular among American service veterans, who had heard it in Germany. Since that time that beautiful carol has become the most popular Christmas song among Christians around the world.

Science and Christian Faith

Science has contributed a lot to our lives. We have benefited from the improvements in medicine. Outer space has proven to be a place that we can explore. Only a few years ago, it would have been impossible to put a man into space. Although the understanding of many of the systems of celestial physics necessary has been with us since before the time of Columbus, however, we have not always had the technology to attempt such a mission. Today, with the advances in science and technology, it has been possible to place a man on the moon. It has been possible also to explore deep space with our unmanned space probes. Our telescopes have improved significantly from the simple ground-glass variety. Giant observatories can track clusters of stars in a galaxy. Earth-orbiting satellites have improved our vision of outer space, without the interference that comes from the atmosphere that surrounds the earth.

Until the advent of the computer, it was not possible to accomplish all of the mathematical calculations necessary in real time to safely send a man into space. This aspect of technology could not have happened without the electronic digital computer. The first such machine was built as recently as 1945 at the University of Pennsylvania. It was called the Electronic Numeral Integrator and Computer, or ENIAC for short. The machine weighed sixty thousand pounds and consisted of eighteen thousand vacuum tubes, which burned out at the rate of two thousand per month. ENIAC did not store programs, but had to be reprogrammed for each new task. Its uses were primarily military.

The success of ENIAC led to miniaturization with the development of the transistor. Programs could now be stored, and the age of the personal computer (PC) was born. As a result, home computers today have more capability than ENIAC did

at the middle of the twentieth century. Measuring all of the systems necessary to allow manned space travel would not be possible without the computer. Millions of checks must be run in a very short time to assure that all systems are in readiness for the rocket launch of a space vehicle. Computers are a vital part of any launch and the continuation of the mission. But computers are also very much part of everyday life in America today.

Turning to another area of science, the science of medicine, it has only been within the last century that we now have the tools to cope with disease. Life expectancy in the United States has risen from about forty-seven in 1900 to seventy-six at the turn of the twenty-first century. Cardiovascular disease and cancer are the two leading killers in America. Yet even they can be controlled in ways that were not possible as recently as two decades ago. Coping with disease and providing for good health has come with a very high price tag, however. Health care costs in the United States in 1998 reached $1.1 trillion. Costs continue to escalate annually.

Space, computers, and greatly improved medical care are only three of many areas in which science has brought about significant change in our lifestyle and life expectancy. Without doubt, science has ushered in a new era. We are all affected by scientific advances in our culture. There are those who believe that science is our new god. This poses a problem for many children in school. Many educators, who are the purveyors of this new form of idolatry, espouse the system of thought called naturalism. Naturalism assumes that there is a natural cause or law for everything that exists. There are no theological, moral, or spiritual reasons behind any phenomena or event. Naturalism is rife within our culture. Our children are exposed to naturalism, in its many forms, very early in their education. Our problem is not whether science is good or bad. When it helps humanity, it is good; when it provides for mass destruction, it is bad! It is the philosophy of naturalism that is at fault. Christians have nothing to fear from science. It is the philosophy of naturalism that poses a threat, similar to idolatry found in the Old Testament.

Charles Colson and Nancy Pearcey point out in their book *How Now Shall We Live?* that in his very popular television series and book *Cosmos,* the late astronomer Carl Sagan pushed the idea that the cosmos is "all that is, all that ever was, or all that ever will be." This has been popularized in one of the Berenstain Bear books for young children entitled *The Berenstain Bears' Nature Guide* where the bears go on a nature walk. Sagan's phrase about the cosmos is pictured in the sky on the first rays of the morning sun for a new day.

A year ago, my wife and I were looking for some books to comfort children at the loss of a loved one. What we found in a bookstore were two paperback books that clearly mirror the message of naturalism. One was Lifetimes: *The Beautiful Way to Explain Death to Children.* This one tells the child that insects, plants, and people die. "That's how things are ... EVERYWHERE!" I cannot imagine that comforting a child who has lost a parent or grandparent. The other book is *Someone Special Died.* It recommends that the child make a scrapbook of the lost loved one. That way the child will have continuing memory of the loved one. There is nothing else. It may be a good idea to make a scrapbook, but that is not all there is to life and death.

That brings us to the crux of the issue. Science has its proper place toward making life better. But science is not a god. It does not and cannot answer the crucial questions of life: Where did I come from? Where did evil originate? Why do I do evil? What is the answer to the human dilemma of evil? Where are we headed? Theism can answer these critical questions. God created the universe. Man chose to morally reject God and His laws, creating our sin problem. The gospel of Jesus Christ can provide a solution to the human sin dilemma.

At the end of time, God will judge us. There is hope for life after death in eternity with God, provided that we find new life in Jesus Christ.

There have been, and are still, very reputable scientists who believe in theism. For children in grades one to three, there is no need to provide extensive objections to naturalism. That can come in later years. But we do want children to know that there are many scientists and mathematicians who worship and love God. Many of these have provided the background for today's scientific discoveries about God's great universe. We shall look at the lives and accomplishments of three of these men. Johannes Kepler was a German astronomer who was a believer and wanted to substantiate God's rule in life. Sir Isaac Newton was a strong Christian believer and brilliant British mathematician who prepared the way for modern astrophysics with his mathematical principles. Robert Boyle was a Christian believer and contemporary of Newton. Boyle is the father of modern chemistry.

Science and Christian Faith

You are growing up in a world that is strongly influenced by science. Many of the things that come from the laboratory of the scientist can help us toward a better life. Science has been very successful in many areas of life. It has done a lot to prevent and cure many of our diseases. It has allowed us to go into outer space. Science deals with many of the problems that we face. But science cannot do everything. As you go through school, science will play an ever more important role in your studies in the upper grades.

In this section we will look at the lives of three great scientists, who have made a difference in our world. Each of these scientists was committed to Jesus Christ. Johannes Kepler was an astronomer and mathematician. Kepler made some important discoveries about the world we live in. Sir Isaac Newton improved our understanding of the universe further. Newton's work has brought us to a better understanding of mathematical principles that are used in our scientific discoveries even today. Newton was a strong believer in Christ and the Bible. Robert Boyle has been called the father of modern chemistry. Boyle was also a strong believer in the Christian way of life.

Johannes Kepler, 1571–1630

Did you ever look up at the heavens on a clear starlit night and wonder how the stars and planets move through space? Did you ever wonder what keeps them together in such predictable patterns? Johannes Kepler was a scientist who helped us to understand the way the planets move. Kepler believed that our understanding of that helped us to see the way God constructed His universe.

Kepler was a German astronomer. He is known best for his three laws of movement of the planets. Kepler was a Lutheran Christian. He intended to go to school and prepare for the gospel ministry. One of his teachers convinced him that there were other ways by which he could minister. He continued his education in science, showing how God has provided the vast universe for us to understand Him better.

Kepler was born in a small town, Weil der Stadt, Germany. His father was a soldier. His father left home when Johannes was five. His father went to war. He never came back. It is believed that the elder Kepler died in battle in Holland. His mother grew up in the home of an innkeeper. After the death of his father, Johannes and his mother returned to her home at the inn. For elementary education, Kepler went to school locally. Then he went to the University of Tübigen, which was Lutheran. After his general education was completed, he intended to continue his education for the ministry.

One of his professors, Michael Maestlin, taught astronomy. He saw great potential in the young Kepler. While Kepler studied the ancient Ptolemaic system of astronomy from the ancient Egyptians, Maestlin wanted Kepler to learn of the new system of Copernicus. In the Ptolemaic system it was believed that the moon, sun, and planets moved around the earth. Copernicus tried to show mathematically and astronomically that the moon revolved around the earth. The earth and the other planets moved around the sun. That agrees with what scientists believe today.

About that time, young Kepler had difficulties with the Lutherans. He did not agree with one of the issues that was decided in the Augsburg Confession for Lutherans. As a result, it is not surprising that Maestlin convinced Kepler to take a teaching position at the University of Graz. Kepler taught at Graz from 1594 to 1600. In spite of his differences with the Lutheran Church, he was still a Protestant. That caused him some problems at Graz.

Fortunately, he received an invitation to go to the observatory of the Danish astronomer Tycho Brahe near Prague. Brahe was brought up in a home of wealth. Kepler was not. They had many problems in their relationship. But when Brahe died in 1601, Kepler gained all that Brahe had done and became court astronomer to the Holy Roman Emperor, Rudolf II. In this position, Kepler gained prestige. At first he thought incorrectly that the planets move around the sun in the orbit of a circle. He changed that view as he wrote his several important scientific writings. In one of these, he calculated the exact orbit of the planet Mars. He discovered his first law, that planets move around the sun in an elliptical pattern. An ellipse is roughly egg shaped, as opposed to circular. His second law tells us that planets move more quickly in their orbit as they come closer to the sun.

Think about that for a moment. If the orbit is an ellipse, the ends of the ellipse are further away from the sun. On the sides of the ellipse the planet is closer to the sun. The sun exercises a force that keeps the planet in its orbit. Why would the sides of the ellipse cause the planet to move faster?

Sir Isaac Newton used Kepler's discoveries to build his own understanding of the laws of gravity. After Newton, we now know it is gravity that keeps the moon in an orbit around the earth. How would that relate to planets going around the sun?

Kepler formed a third law as well. Kepler said that the size of the orbit of the planet is related to the time that it takes for the planet to make a full orbit. Kepler helped to develop the basic principles for calculus, which is an advanced mathematical system. You are not likely to study calculus until college. The mathematics of calculus were advanced by Sir Isaac Newton. Kepler also wrote a major work on lenses and optics. He had a wide understanding and interest in many mathematical subjects and made very important contributions.

Some scientists today try to tell us that he had some elements of his thought that were not important to his contributions to science. Kepler believed in the Creator God of the Bible. Kepler believed that all of his mathematical calculations were a product of what God had done already when He created the universe. Kepler believed that he merely rediscovered what God had already done. Far from being a false view of science, Kepler was right in his understanding that God created this vast universe. We only rediscover what God has already set forth in the universe.

Sir Isaac Newton, 1642–1727

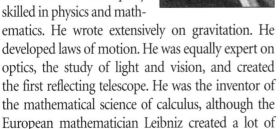

Sir Isaac Newton is probably the greatest scientist that ever lived. He was equally skilled in physics and mathematics. He wrote extensively on gravitation. He developed laws of motion. He was equally expert on optics, the study of light and vision, and created the first reflecting telescope. He was the inventor of the mathematical science of calculus, although the European mathematician Leibniz created a lot of trouble for Newton because Leibniz claimed to be the founder of calculus. Newton was a believer. He believed that the God we worship was the Creator of the universe and, like Kepler, we discover the laws that God has already put into the universe. He read the Bible every day as a guide for his life.

As a lad, Isaac Newton was quiet. He was born in 1642 after his father had already died. His family was poor. His mother wanted her son to become a farmer. While he should have been plowing, Newton was found studying something that interested him. It is said that he got his first idea about gravitation as he sat under an apple tree reading. An apple fell on his head, and that caused him to think about the gravitational pull that would cause the apple to fall down, rather than up. Newton had no interest in farming. As a lad he had a talent for constructing things and was very interested in how they worked. He said later in life that he did not have much interest in school during these elementary school years. He also had problems with his mother and especially with his stepfather. He developed a lot of anger toward them, and this caused him problems later in life.

One of his teachers did see great potential in young Isaac. The teacher convinced Isaac's mother that he should go to Cambridge University. As a result of his delayed start at the university, he was older than most of the students. Nevertheless, in 1661 Isaac Newton was admitted to Trinity College at Cambridge University. He had to clean rooms and do other chores in order to pay for his education. Isaac soon found a place at the University. He studied mathematics and theology. His mathematics professor was Isaac Barrows, a very famous mathematician. Newton earned his bachelor's degree in 1665. He wanted to continue his studies, but an outbreak of the bubonic plague forced the university to close for the next two years. Isaac Newton went home. These two years were important to the young college graduate. He expanded his studies of optics, mathematics, and motion. These studies would have an impact upon his continued studies and papers that he would write later in life.

Isaac Newton returned to Trinity College at Cambridge in 1667. This time he received a fellowship that would pay his way for his graduate course of study. He received his master's degree at the university. His interest at this time was focused on optics. In 1668 he constructed the first reflecting telescope. He could magnify the stars, planets, and moons in the sky many more times than just looking directly through the lens of the telescope at those objects. The next year he presented his professor with a mathematics paper that he had written. It was the foundation for the mathematics of calculus. An unfortunate dispute with the European mathematician Leibniz concerning who founded calculus followed.

In 1669 his teacher and professor, Isaac Barrows, retired from Trinity College at Cambridge. Barrows named Newton to take his place. Newton's first lectures were about the subject that he had just been studying, optics. In 1672 Newton was named a Fellow in the Royal Society. He was now appreciated for the scientific discoveries that he had made. Several years later, in 1679, he returned to his study of the orbits of the planets. He built upon the work of Kepler. Probably, his most important work was *The Principia*, which appeared in 1687.

The course of his career changed when King James II wanted to return England to the Roman Catholic Church. The king asked the university to give special treatment to a Benedictine monk who would come to the university. Isaac Newton was asked to defend the university against such action. Newton won the case. James II was soon overthrown in the Glorious Revolution of 1688. Now Newton served in the university senate. By 1705 Queen Anne was on the throne of England. She knighted Newton as Sir Isaac Newton. He was at that time the most important person in European science. After the peace in Europe, Newton began to affect science on all of the continent of Europe, as well as in England.

In his later years, Sir Isaac Newton moved to London and left his post at the university. He was given a post at the royal mint. There he developed ways to prevent people from counterfeiting coins. He was involved there until his death in 1727. Sir Isaac Newton will be remembered for his contributions to science and mathematics. His writings on gravitation, optics, motion, and calculus have never been equaled. In recent years Einstein's laws of relativity have modified some of Newton's ideas about the universe. But his other motion studies still stand as valid as the day he wrote them. Sir Isaac Newton will also be remembered for his insistence that God created and rules the universe.

Robert Boyle, 1627–1691

Robert Boyle was a very interesting person. He was born into vast wealth. He chose to live a simple life. He founded the Royal Society, which was intended to foster British science. He developed Boyle's Law, which shows the relationship between pressure and  volume in gases. He carefully used the scientific method to conduct his experiments and helped to bring the scientific method into general use among scientists. His friends included some of the most important people of his day: Sir Christopher Wren, the architect; Samuel Pepys, writer; Sir Isaac Newton; and John Milton, writer. These are only a few of his long list of friends. He was a devout Protestant believer, who was as interested in theology as he was in chemistry.

Robert Boyle was born in Lismore County Waterford, Ireland, in 1622. He was the fourteenth child to Richard Boyle, who was in his sixties at the time of Robert's birth. His mother, Catherine, was the second wife of Richard and was in her fourties at the time. The Boyles believed that their children should go away to school. In 1635 Robert entered Eton College. He soon left there, and from 1639 to 1644 he traveled throughout Europe. He was educated by a tutor. When he was in Venice, he learned Italian. Upon his return he had to visit his estates in Ireland, but he did not stay in Ireland. There was very little chemistry equipment available in Ireland. He could not continue his experiments there. Also there were struggles between Protestants and Catholics that did not make Ireland a good place. He settled in England.

Boyle moved to Oxford. These years at Oxford were among his most productive. There he worked together with the inventor Robert Hooke. Hooke helped Boyle construct a compressor that would build pressure for gases. This equipment helped Boyle carry out his experiments in chemistry and led to Boyle's Law. His law states that the pressure of gases is related to the volume, or amount, of gas in the tank. In 1660 he published this in his work *The Spring of Air*. He described what he had learned about gases in that book. His scientific work involved experimentation. He wanted to take the guesswork out of scientific investigation. He is remembered for his careful use of the scientific method. During the same year, he studied combustion, or how fires burn in air. We know now that oxygen is the part of air that allows fire to burn, but that discovery did not come until many years later. He also was the first to use litmus paper. Litmus paper is still used today to determine whether a liquid is an acid or alkaline.

In 1661 he published *The Sceptical Chymist*. This book helped chemistry to become a science. Previously, chemistry had been tied up with alchemy. Alchemy was a medieval idea that cheap metals, such as iron, could be turned to precious metals, such as silver or gold. While he was in Oxford, Boyle became part of the Invisible College. Their aim was to develop the new sciences. The Invisible College later became the Royal Society. It was chartered by King Charles II in 1663. Boyle became a member of its council. In 1665 Boyle created the first hydrometer. This instrument is still used to measure the density of a liquid.

His sister, Katherine, Lady Ranelagh, lived in London. Robert went to live in her home for the remainder of his life. Many of his friends came and visited him in London. It became necessary to limit the time of the visits, since he wanted to save some time to continue to conduct his experiments. Some of his friends tried to convince him to get married, but this was not something that Robert Boyle was interested in doing. In 1670 he had a stroke that left him partially paralyzed. As he regained his health, he continued hosting his friends and conducting experiments.

He continued to do some experiments. One of these experiments led to the invention of the match in 1680. It consisted of a thin piece of wood that was coated with sulpher. The sulpher tip was struck on a base of phosphorus. This created a spark and lit the match.

Robert Boyle was a strong defender of Christianity. He was an Anglican, a member of the Church of England. He was influenced strongly by his sister toward Puritanism as well. He studied the Greek and Hebrew languages, as well as Syriac. These would help him study the Scriptures in their original languages. He spent his own money on having the New Testament translated into other languages, such as Turkish and Irish. He believed that the study of nature was a very important responsibility for Christians because that was God's creation. After his death, Robert Boyle left a sum of money to provide for the continuation of a lecture series "for proving the Christian Religion against notorious Infidels." The lecture series continues today.

CONCLUDING THOUGHTS

We have looked at these men who were pioneers in science and were also Christians. There are also scientists today who believe the Bible and continue to seek God's truth. We need to be careful to maintain our allegiance to the God of the Bible while still doing good science. It is exciting to see the world that God has created. We need to give Him thanks for His goodness to us.

Lesson Plans

INTRODUCTION TO LESSON PLANS FOR PARENTS AND TEACHERS

The most important book that we have is the Bible. But as R. A. Torrey once observed, "He who knows only the Bible does not really know the Bible." There is a wide culture out there that can capture the imagination and develop the interests of our children. But it needs guidance. We send our children to school to learn things that will help them prepare for adulthood and finding an occupation and to discover this wide range of culture.

The enjoyment of good art, music, and literature are necessary components of that wider culture. For example, children need to develop good judgment about music. If they are exposed only to the taste in music provided by the secular culture, they will never learn to appreciate God's gift of good music for their enjoyment. The same is true for art and literature. It also applies to science. Not all scientists are atheistic and secular. In this volume, your children will be exposed to some good examples in each of these areas. These will need to be developed further as the children grow if they are to develop good sense of taste in each of these areas. But the background they will gain here will give them a start along that road.

Programs like the Core Knowledge Foundation series have clearly shown that children are capable of learning good comprehensive material. This material will provide them with a solid foundation for their future. If we do not develop this foundation in the elementary schoolyears, they are unlikely to learn it during the teenage years. Their interests turn elsewhere during adolescence.

Significant advances have been made in the last two decades in the science of learning and how the mind works. It is clear from what we know about the mind today that prior knowledge is essential to further learning. This prior knowledge base must be built during these elementary schoolyears. Their exposure to good material will affect what they attend to in the future.

This handbook is designed to introduce children to God's redemptive relationship to mankind and toward a Christian world- and life view. It is important to help your children gain this understanding and appreciation early in life. This book and its activities may be used for several years. There are a variety of activities that can be used with children at different age levels.

As children get beyond second grade, they can begin to deal with the concepts of time and place more easily. Before that time, you will need to help them to see the specific relationships to their life in this time and place. The world in which we live is secular and postmodern. We must run against the tide and cannot capitulate to the postmodern worldview. If we do not help our children, we will lose their generation.

Children need to learn basic content. The content that they learn in this series will have an added benefit to what they are learning in their school subjects. There is material on geography, history, science, art, music, and moral development that will inform and assist them to develop a Christian view of life. With a solid foundation, they will be able to progress. Their minds are being stimulated with knowledge that will last them for a lifetime.

COURSE OVERVIEW

We have tried to provide all that you will need to teach your children about their Christian heritage.

The course is divided into fifteen lessons. Lessons 1–5 guide you through background material for the Old Testament. In addition to studying occupations in Palestine, the religious practices of

Jews and Christians are presented. Understanding Jewish practices is a particularly exciting and rewarding discovery for children.

Lessons 6–8 lead you through the growth of the church from the New Testament times to the present. Lesson 9 leads a child to know how to find a relationship with God through Jesus Christ and how to maintain that relationship through prayer and following God's moral law. Lessons 10–11 introduces the mission of the church to the world. Lessons 12–14 introduce the child to Christian art and music. Lesson 15 introduces scientists who have been believers and viewed their science as a support to faith.

For each lesson there are a variety of learning activities. (Activity sheets are after each lesson and may be enlarged and duplicated. The answers are found in the back of the book.) You will need to pick and choose activities that will stretch every child you teach. Remember that if the children are going to go deeper later, they will need to learn good content now. The curriculum should spiral back on itself as the child grows older. It is not a problem to return to the material in this volume as the child moves a year ahead. You will want to recycle through this material again as your child continues to grow. Just remember to choose activities that will appeal to the child advancing in age.

It is important to allow children to memorize Scripture. Each lesson provides at least one verse for memorization. Research has shown that children have an amazing facility to memorize. We lose that ability as we grow older. Children can certainly understand what they are memorizing at their level, even if the full import of the Scripture is not gained until later. But if they have not memorized the Scripture now, they will be unlikely to more fully appreciate the meaning later.

SUGGESTIONS FOR PREPARATION

1. Study the handbook in advance. Read the material from the handbook that you need to cover with your child. Read the passages of Scripture from a modern translation, such as the Holman Christian Standard Bible.

2. Read the objectives for the lesson you plan to teach. Examine the identifications so that you will be able to help your child understand new concepts, persons, or geographical locations.

3. With the objectives in mind, read through the learning activities. Think about what activities will best suit your child at his or her level of learning. Star those activities that you plan to include in each lesson. Prepare a simple lesson plan, which will include objectives, Scripture to be studied, identifications, content, and the particular activities that you plan to use. You need only a sentence or phrase to identify what you will do. Most of the work is already done for you. The lesson plan is important, as it becomes a road map for where you plan to take your children and later shows where you have been with them.

4. Locate any additional resources that you might use. Let me emphasize that you do not need to go beyond the materials that are available at a stationary store or that you may already have at home. But you may want to look at your church library, public library, or Web sites and supplement what is suggested. A word of caution is in order concerning videos and other media. Make sure that the content maintains fidelity with your Christian objectives. Some videos take liberties with Christian ideals. Be careful.

5. Do background studies as appropriate. Study background for Egypt, Babylonia, Palestine, Persia, Rome, and Greece. Your child will benefit in his or her studies at school as well. Take field trips. Expose your children to as many good experiences as possible.

6. You will want to keep records of what you have covered. Test the children periodically. Suggested activities have test-related items, such as crossword puzzles, fill-in the blanks, etc. Find out what they are learning and emphasize or reteach concepts, persons, or places as necessary. Keep records of progress. You will also want to

keep samples of the work of your children, particularly good examples.

7. Help children to see and understand that Christian faith has for centuries been part of the cultural context in which we live. Christianity has stimulated more good art and music than any other topic. Our children need to be exposed to good examples in each of these areas.

8. Try to select activities that are age appropriate. For first and second graders, you should do some work with time and place. They will not fully understand, but they can see time and place as related to the place where they are today. By third grade they have basic understanding of time and place, so time lines and maps become even more important.

9. Have fun with your children! Learning should be fun. It somewhat depends upon your attitude. You can inspire your children to enjoy their learning experiences.

To Parents

In today's world the temptation is to believe erroneously that the only experiences in culture are secular ones. This is far from the truth. Some of the best music, art, literature, and science have come from Christian believers. Do not deprive your children of the exposure to good culture. They will benefit from this preparation for the rest of their lives.

Use opportunities to expose your children to good culture. Take them to a concert or to a museum. Because you "will never pass this way again," make the most of your opportunities. There are suggestions for good field trips that will enrich both you and your children. Take advantage of these times together.

Read to your child. Treasure the opportunities, when you may hold your child on your lap and read aloud to him or her. Talk about your faith in Christ and how it affects what you listen to, watch on television, and the life you lead. Learn along with your child. Select learning activities that you can do by simply modifying them to use with your child. If you are homeschooling, you might want to invite other children who are being homeschooled to join you and your family for the study of these subjects as well as the Bible.

We are praying for you!

To Teachers

You have a God-given opportunity to make a difference in the lives of the children that God has entrusted to your care. It is essential to teach the school subjects. But you have a particular opportunity to teach them that Christianity is not isolated from other areas of life. Their Christian faith can integrate all of their other learning.

They can memorize large portions of Scripture. Jesus, Himself, went through this kind of preparation. It is not surprising that He was prepared by age twelve to talk with the religious teachers in the Temple. He amazed them! When we next see Jesus in the Gospels, He is baptized and moves directly to the wilderness and the temptation experiences. Remember how He responded to Satan. In each case, Jesus quoted from the Word of God. Can we do any less for our children?

We have a marvelous Christian heritage from which to draw. Our secular world would have us believe that we are isolated from learning and good art, music, literature, and science. That is not true. We need to prevent this attitude from becoming part of the understanding of our children. They need to see the vast wealth of culture that is based upon Christian ideals.

There are a number of activities in each lesson from which to choose. You should find enough in order to teach effective lessons.

May God grant you wisdom and guidance as you minister to the precious lives of your children.

We are praying for you.

Religious Practices—Lessons 1–5

UNIT SUMMARY
This set of lessons will provide the learner with background information about Jewish and Christian religious practices. The learner will gain a rich understanding of the background that affected biblical practice. The learner will also be encouraged to develop a lifelong love for God and His Word.

OVERVIEW
Objectives
By the end of this unit, the learner should be able to:
- understand religious and nonreligious occupations from Bible times,
- understand Jewish religious worship during Bible times, and
- understand and appreciate the Jewish calendar and the weekly and annual observances of the calendar in its feasts and celebrations.

Content Summary and Rationale
The content of this unit is varied. Learning about Jewish religious and secular occupations will help the learner understand many of the parables and other discussions that lead to deeper understanding of biblical material.

This is followed by a study of religious worship for Jews. The Jewish year and the Christian church year are also part of this study. As boys and girls grow in their understanding of the background of Jewish practices, they can better understand the Christian practices, many of which grew out of Jewish practice. This knowledge will help the children develop a better understanding that will lead to greater interest as they grow older.

Key Concept
It is important for children to develop their understanding of worship and the background of worship in order to engage in worship themselves. We have for too long allowed children to develop very meager understanding of that to which they are committing the rest of their lives.

Prior Knowledge Needed
In most cases, children have some understanding of God and Jesus. The stories that they have heard in Sunday school have helped them to develop some small understanding of the Christian faith. Their knowledge is very limited. It is during their early years that they are developing their understanding that will affect their future lives.

You can use the limited knowledge that they currently have to enlarge their understanding. Help them develop a more comprehensive view of the fact that Christianity is not just a religion but a "way of life." That was the concept of the early church. They were known as "the people of the Way." Help your children integrate their understanding of Judaism and Christian faith. The Bible presents a history of the drama of redemption. Children and older persons need to have this understanding if they are going to grow in their faith and understanding.

RESOURCES FOR TEACHERS AND STUDENTS
- Buchanan, Edward, *Parent/Teacher Handbook: Their Christian Heritage, Vol. 2* (Nashville, Tenn.: Broadman & Holman, 2003).
- Butler, Trent, ed., *Holman Illustrated Bible Dictionary* (Nashville, Tenn.: Holman Bible Publishers, 2003).
- Dockery, David, ed., *Holman Bible Handbook* (Nashville, Tenn.: Holman Bible Publishers, 1992).
- An encyclopedia—*World Book, Funk and Wagnalls, Britannica*, etc. (may use CD-ROM)

LESSON 1: BIBLE CUSTOMS

Readings from the Parent/Teacher Handbook: Their Christian Heritage, Vol. 2: "Bible Customs"

OBJECTIVES

By the end of lesson, the learner should be able to

- demonstrate understanding of life in Bible times in the following occupations:

    shepherding for boys and men

    farming for boys and men

    fishing for boys and men

    family roles for girls and women

- describe the occupations of craftsmen in the following areas: clay potters, metalworkers, carpenters, stonemasons, and

- explore ways in which these occupations affected life in Bible times and were employed in the Scripture, e.g., Jesus' parable of the sower, or Jeremiah's use of the clay potter.

IDENTIFICATIONS

Concepts

Sheep herdsman—one who tends and herds sheep and goats

Farmer—one who plants and harvests grain, plants and tends grape vines, tends and harvests olive trees to make olive oil

Fisherman—one who engaged in the fish industry; important only in New Testament times

Family roles—cooking, cleaning, washing, and weaving, usually done by girls and women

Potter—craftsman who works with clay to make pottery

Carpenter—one who works with wood and other building products in building projects

Stonemasons—one who makes bricks and uses stone in building projects

Weavers—one who makes cloth, wool, or linen products

Tanners—one who prepares leather products

Metalworker—tradesman who works mines and smelts metal products

MATERIALS NEEDED

Parent/Teacher Handbook: Their Christian Heritage, Vol. 2

Activity Sheets for Lesson 1

Crayons and markers

White drawing paper, lined paper for writing

Modeling clay or a dough recipe

Tempera paints

Mixing bowl

Construction paper

Small metal looms (from a craft store)

Weaving material (from a craft store)

Dowels to use for fishing poles

Decoupage, decoupage finish paint (from a craft store)

String

Grape juice, Grape Kool-Aid

Crackers

Baking materials, cookie sheet, sieve

Flour, salt, sugar, eggs, margarine, baking powder, vanilla

Wooden plaques

Sponge brushes

Acrylic paint

Old Christmas cards

LEARNING ACTIVITIES FOR LESSON 1

Activity 1—Matching Occupations from Bible Times

Review the "Bible Customs" section from the handbook. Make copies of Activity Sheet 1.

Read and talk with your children about the different occupations from Bible times. When your students are thoroughly familiar with all of the occupations, have them complete the matching exercise on Activity Sheet 1.

Discuss the answers in light of your teaching on the different occupations.

Activity 2—Make a Clay Dish

Read carefully "The Clay Potter" in the handbook. Discuss this occupation with your class.

Before this session, obtain modeling clay at a craft store or use the following recipe:

Assemble the following items: flour, salt, alum, and vegetable oil.

Pour 2 cups of water into a saucepan and bring to a boil on the stove. Add food coloring to make a dough the color of either a light brown or gray.

In a mixing bowl, mix 2 cups of flour with $1/2$ cup of salt. Pour in 1 tablespoon of powdered alum and 3 tablespoons of vegetable oil.

Add the colored water to the other ingredients in the mixing bowl. Knead the dough until it is soft and pliable. Place the dough in an plastic bag that will keep out the air until you are ready to use the dough.

Prepare tables with a plastic covering or oilcloth. Have a bowl of water available for each student. Provide paper towels. Place a piece of waxed paper on the table at each child's work area.

Roll the dough. Have each child fashion a clay vessel from the dough as follows: Make a round bottom for the vessel. Then form ropes of the dough to wrap around and make the sides. Pack them tightly together. When the sides of the vessel are at a good height, use the water to smooth the bottom and sides of the vessel and fashion into a bowl.

Allow the bowls to dry overnight. Decorate the bowls, using a toothpick to etch symbols on the bowl. Paint the bowl.

Activity 3—Weaving a Pot Holder

Read carefully "The Weavers and Tanners" in the handbook. Discuss this with the class.

To give children a sense of what the weaver did, have your students weave pot holders. In preparation for this session, purchase simple metal looms and weaving supplies at a local craft store. If you are unfamiliar with this type of weaving, there are usually directions provided with the looms.

Teach the children how to weave on the looms. Carry out the projects and have the children take the finished products home.

Activity 4—Domestic Responsibilities—Cooking

Read carefully the "Family Roles for Girls and Women" in the handbook.

The major occupation for girls and women in Bible times was cooking, cleaning, and weaving. A good activity to illustrate this is to bake a batch of sugar cookies.

Recipe for Sugar Cookies
$2^3/4$ cups of sifted flour
1 teaspoon of baking powder
$1/2$ teaspoon of salt
$3/4$ cup of soft butter or margarine
1 cup of sugar
1 teaspoon of vanilla
2 eggs

Beat the butter, sugar, eggs, and vanilla together. Beat in flour mixture. Chill for one hour. Roll out dough to $1/8$ inch thick on a floured cookie sheet. Cut dough in desired shapes.
Bake at 375° for 8 to 10 minutes. Ice cookies, if desired.

Talk about cooking and baking in Bible times. The flour was not milled but had to be ground. The butter had to be churned. There were many tasks to be performed to do one cooking or baking operation. It was not as easy as it is today.

Activity 5—Vineyard Dresser—Grape Kool-Aid

In preparation for discussing the grape vineyard, read carefully the subsection, "Farming in Palestine" in the handbook. The vineyard dresser was another occupation that was prevalent in New Testament times. Discuss this occupation with your class.

Prepare grape Kool-Aid to simulate the use of grape juice. Have this with the sugar cookies from the activity above.

Activity 6—Fishing for Characteristics of a Christian

Before this session read "Fishing in Palestine" in the handbook. Fishing did not become an important occupation in Palestine until the New Testament era. On the Sea of Galilee, it became a very important source of food and continues to be important even today.

Use the fish pattern on Activity Sheet 6. Duplicate the fish pattern on card stock and punch a hole in the nose of the fish. (An alternative to punching a hole in the nose of the fish would be to purchase small magnets at a craft store to glue the magnets to the nose of the fish.) On each fish write one characteristic of a Christian from the list of Christian virtues in Galatians 5:22–23. They are "love, joy, peace, patience, kindness, goodness, faith, gentleness, self-control." Prepare fishing poles for each of your class members. Use a dowel and attach a 9-inch string to the end of the dowel. At the end of the string, fasten a paper clip. If you punched the nose of the fish, you will need to pull out the end of the clip to form a hook. (Leave closed if using magnets.)

Place the fish in an aquarium or box with a smooth bottom. If you have a large class, you may need to have several of these available. Have the children dangle their lines in the container and hook the fish.

When you have finished this activity, glue the fish to a sheet of posterboard. Title the poster, "The Fruit of the Spirit." Discuss with the children the occupation of fishing, and note that several of Jesus' disciples were fishermen—Peter, James, and John. Then talk about the fruit of the Spirit. What does each term mean? How can we more effectively live by the Spirit and please God?

Activity 7—Decoupage for Woodworking

Read carefully "The Carpenter" in the handbook. Discuss woodworking in Bible times.

In advance of your session, obtain wooden plaques for class members from a craft store. You will also need fine sandpaper, sponge brushes, a base coat acrylic paint, and decoupage finish. Use old Christmas cards for the prints to place on the plaque.

Have the children sand the wood smooth. Apply several coats of acrylic paint, lightly sanding between each coat. Cut pictures from old Christmas cards. Carefully cut around the picture. Apply a coat of decoupage finish to the back of the picture. Then place the picture on the plaque and apply decoupage to the front of the picture and plaque. Let dry overnight.

Activity 8— Field Trip to Watch a Carpenter and Stonemason at Work

Read carefully "The Carpenter" and "Stonemasons and Bricklayers" in the handbook. Talk about these occupations.

In advance of this session, prearrange with a local contractor who builds homes in the community to bring your class to watch the building trade in operation. Indicate that you are studying a unit that involves the building trades. Take your children to the home-building site. Have the carpenter and the stonemasons explain to the children what they do. Watch them in operation.

Activity 9—Writing to a Pen Pal
Have the children discuss what life for a boy or girl would have been like in Bible times. Consider the many occupations that we have examined. There would be many chores to be done. Write to an imaginary pen pal, telling about a day in your life as a boy or girl.

Activity 10—Field Trip to a Craft Museum or History Museum
Take the class on a field trip to a craft museum or history museum in your community. Craft museums and many history museums have exhibits that are relevant to building trades and domestic activities in time periods of the past and present. Many provide hands-on activities for children. Many of the activities from these occupations in the nineteenth century and before were done in a primitive manner, similar to Bible times. Note similarities and differences. This can provide an excellent learning experience for children.

Activity 11— Memorize Psalm 23
To help your children understand what the shepherd life was like, have them memorize Psalm 23. For younger children, you may want them to memorize only verses 1–4. Have the children write this psalm in their Bible Verse Memory Books and illustrate it.

> *The Lord is my shepherd;*
> *there is nothing I lack.*
> *He lets me lie down in green pastures;*
> *he leads me beside quiet waters.*
> *He renews my life;*
> *He leads me along the right path for His name's sake.*
> *Even when I go through the darkest valley,*
> *I am not afraid of any danger,*
> *for You are with me;*
> *Your rod and Your staff—they give me comfort.*
> *You prepare a table before me in full view of my enemies;*
> *You anoint my head with oil;*
> *my cup is full.*
> *On goodness and faithful love will pursue me all the days of my life,*
> *and I will dwell in the house of the Lord as long as I live.*

ACTIVITY SHEET 1: MATCHING OCCUPATIONS FROM BIBLE TIMES

Directions: Match the description of the occupation on the right with the occupation on the left by placing the correct letter in the space provided.

___ 1. Tanner	a.	Tends and herds sheep and goats
___ 2. Domestic	b.	Plants and harvests grain, plants and tends grape vines, worker tends and harvests olive trees to make olive oil
___ 3. Stonemason	c.	Engaged in the fish industry, important in New Testament times
___ 4. Shepherd	d.	Responsible for cooking, cleaning, washing, and weaving, usually done by girls and women
___ 5. Metalworker	e.	Craftsman who works with clay to make pottery
___ 6. Farmer	f.	Works with wood and other building products in building projects
___ 7. Fisherman	g.	Makes bricks and uses stone in building projects
___ 8. Carpenter	h.	Makes cloth, wool, or linen products
___ 9. Potter	i.	Prepares leather products
___ 10. Weaver	j.	Tradesman who works mines and smelts metal products

ACTIVITY SHEET 6: FISHING FOR CHARACTERISTICS OF A CHRISTIAN

LESSON 2: JEWISH RELIGIOUS OCCUPATIONS

Readings from the Parent/Teacher Handbook: Their Christian Heritage, Vol. 2: "Religious Occupations"

OBJECTIVES

By the end of lesson, the learner should be able to

- explain the various religious occupations and religious groups of first-century Judaism, including: priests, levites, prophets, scribes, pharisees, sadducees, zealots, and
- explore the effects that these groups had on first-century Judaism.

IDENTIFICATIONS

Concepts

Priests—from the tribe of Levi; chosen to teach the Law and conduct sacrifice

Levites—helped with the sacrifices and assisted the priests

Prophets—persons who told forth the message of God

Scribes—office began in the Kingdom period; later became the legal experts

Pharisees—conservative religious group who were very careful not to defile themselves

Sadducees—more liberal religiously, but represented the ruling class in Judea

Zealots—group who opposed Rome

Places

Jerusalem: center of Jewish worship

MATERIALS NEEDED

Parent/Teacher Handbook: Their Christian Heritage, Vol. 2

Activity Sheets for Lesson 2

Crayons and markers

Blank sheets of white paper for drawing

Masking tape and plastic tape

3x5-inch index cards

Lined paper for writing

Posterboard

Construction paper

Various props for Activity 6

LEARNING ACTIVITIES FOR LESSON 2

Activity 1—"I am . . ." Descriptions of the Jewish Religious Leaders

In the handbook sudy carefully the "Religious Occupations." Talk about the various religious leaders and their role in Jewish society around the time of Jesus. Note that the occupations that were studied in the last lesson affected physical survival, but the religious occupations studied in this lesson changed history.

Duplicate copies of Activity Sheet 1. Have the members of your class complete the statements.

Conclude the activity with a discussion of the various tasks.

Activity 2—Who Were the Essenes?

For this activity carefully read "Other Religious Groups" and the subsection, "The Essenes" in the handbook.

Using the description in the book, help the children to understand this group of devout Jewish persons, who loved God and followed Him. Then have them answer the questions on Activity Sheet 2.

Activity 3—The Zealots Defend the Land

For this activity carefully read "The Zealots" in the handbook.

Make copies of Activity Sheet 3, a true/false quiz. Describe the Zealots from the material in your handbook. Then have students complete the quiz.

Activity 4—Venn Diagram of the Pharisees and the Sadducees

In the handbook study carefully "Religious Occupations." Talk with your students about the Pharisees and Sadducees and their role in Jewish society around the time of Jesus.

Compare the parties of the Pharisees and the Sadducees. Both groups were powerful. The Pharisees were very conservative and very religious. The common people admired the Pharisees. The Sadducees were more liberal. They did not believe in the Oral Law and did not believe in the resurrection from the dead, as did the Pharisees.

Duplicate copies of the Venn diagram on Activity Sheet 4. Have the students work in pairs to complete the exercise. Place the numbers of the characteristics for the Pharisees in the left circle. Do the same for the Sadducees in the right circle. Write the numbers of the characteristics that apply to both in the middle.

Activity 5—Decode the Message

Some of the Pharisees were godly men. One of those was Nicodemus. Nicodemus was the one who went to Jesus by night and sought to discover how to be born again. From that conversation came John 3:16. Probably, Nicodemus followed Jesus at other times as well. We again see him at the cross. Nicodemus participated in the burial of Jesus' body.

Copy enough Activity Sheet 5 so each student has a copy. Tell them to decode the secret message, using the secret code at the bottom of the page. The message states, "Rabbi, we know that you have come from God as a teacher, for no one could perform these signs you do unless God were with Him" (John 3:2).

Activity 6—Scribal Message

Divide your class into two teams. Have members of each team serve as scribes. Each team will compete until all members of the group have written the Scripture passage on a new blank copy of a scroll. The first member will have the printed text of Daniel 7:26–27: "But the judgment shall sit, and they shall take away his dominion, to consume and to destroy it unto the end. And the kingdom and dominion, and the greatness of the kingdom under the whole heaven, shall be given to the people of the saints of the most High, whose kingdom is an everlasting kingdom, and all dominions shall serve and obey him." (KJV) He/she will write the text on another scroll. The other members of the group are not allowed to see what is written. The second scribe will copy what the first scribe has copied. (This person will not see the original printed version.) Remind the team members that they are being timed. This will continue until each of the members of the group has written the text. The winning team is the one that is the fastest to complete the task and has the least number of mistakes.

When all of the groups have completed the exercise, announce the winning team. Use this occasion to talk about the work of the scribe. Hand copying from one person to another can lead to errors. This was a major problem before printing.

Activity 7—Charades for Identifying Different Groups

For this activity, divide the class into nine groups. Each of the groups needs to work on its project in a manner that the others will not know what they are doing. Have each group act out, without talking, a scene that will illustrate one of the following groups. Let the other groups guess what role the group is portraying. Keep track of the time that it takes for the other groups to guess. You may suggest that they make simple props with construction paper.

Group 1—the priest: The priest is in the process of making a sacrifice on the altar. A prop might be a head turban for the high priest.

Group 2—the prophet: For this group, they might select one of their members to tell God's Word. They might use a Bible as a prop.

Group 3—the Levite: Since the Levites helped in the Temple, you might have one clean with a broom. The broom would serve as a prop.

Group 4—the scribe: The scribe should be writing a manuscript. The manuscript might serve as a prop.

Group 5—the Zealot: This group could portray a Zealot coming behind a Roman and stabbing him. A prop might be a dagger made from construction paper. A headdress for the Roman might be helpful as well.

Group 6—the Essene: Showing hospitality was characteristic of this group. Entertaining for dinner and waiting on the tables would be a good scene for the Essenes. Props might include paper plates.

Group 7—the Pharisees: This group was perceived by the rest of the populace as very holy. You might have one person praying, "Lord, I thank you that I am not as other men." Jesus condemned them for their pride.

Group 8—the Sadducees: These were the rulers and the high priest came from this group. One might wear the headdress of the high priest. Another might stand with arms crossed in an authoritarian manner.

Group 9—the rabbi: The rabbi continued to teach the Word of God both inside and outside Jerusalem. He was one who knew and taught the Scriptures. You might have him holding the Bible and teaching it.

Your students may want to become more involved in this activity by researching each of these groups further in a Bible dictionary or other resource.

When they have finished their dramatic episodes, move directly to the next activity.

Activity 8—Effects of Religious Groups on the First Century

This is a very important activity toward showing the significance of each of these groups to the entire history of both Jews and Christians. While the occupations of the people we examined in the previous lesson were important to the everyday life in Palestine, the people in this lesson not only changed the course of history of Palestine but also of the entire world. We are still experiencing the effects even today in the twenty-first century with the events in the Middle East.

Keep the groups from the previous activity together, or if you start this activity on another day, designate each of the eight groups with a sign. Then go stand by each group as you give a few sentences about the importance of that particular group in the first century and in history.

Group 1—the priests: The priests carried on the rituals in the Temple. Their work of Temple sacrifice and teaching the Law continued until the Roman General Titus came into Jerusalem and destroyed the Temple. Because Jesus came, the need for Temple sacrifice was no longer necessary. By His death on the cross, Jesus became our sacrifice once and for all. We can enter into the Holy Place in the Temple without a priest if we have been cleansed from our sin by believing in Jesus Christ.

Group 2—the prophets: The prophets were men who were called by God to deliver His Word. In the first century, John the Baptist was the last of the prophets. He proclaimed the coming of the Messiah in Jesus Christ. Prophecy was a gift of God that became part of the church in the new age with the coming of the Holy Spirit on believers. For example, John's prophecies in the Book of the Revelation replaced the Old Testament form of prophecy. God gives the ability to speak His Word to more people by the Holy Spirit living within persons who come to Jesus Christ as Savior and Lord.

Group 3—the Levites: The Levites were a group who were responsible to assist the priests in the service of worship in the Temple. With the destruction of the Temple in AD 70, their responsibilities ended, like that of the priest.

Group 4—the scribes: The scribe was the one who was literate. He could read and write. His work for many years involved copying manuscripts. During the first century the scribe copied and recopied the Word of God. Preservation of the Word of God was an important role that they played. We would not have the Word of God as accurate as we have it today if it were not for the work of the scribes. They also interpreted the Law of the Lord. That is how they became legal experts in Judaism during that period. After the destruction of the Temple, they disappeared.

Group 5—the Zealots: The Zealots were very militant patriots. They wanted to overthrow the domination of Rome in Palestine. Whenever they could, they stirred up rebellion against the Romans. They killed Romans if the opportunity presented itself. They played a large role in the destruction of Jerusalem in AD 70. They were the last to hold out against the Romans at the Masada. The Masada was a fortress on top of a mountain. It was difficult to get to the fortress because the Romans could not climb to the top of the mountain. The Tenth Roman Legion built a ramp to the top of the Masada. It took months to build. When they got to the top of Masada and took the fortress, they found that all of the nine hundred men, women, and children had killed themselves rather than be taken by the Romans. The Zealots changed history.

Group 6—the Essenes: The Essenes were a group of Jewish persons, who sold all that they had to join the Essene community. They were very godly. They looked for the coming of the Messiah. They had a large community along the Dead Sea at Masada. They were responsible for the Dead Sea Scrolls, which were found in 1947. Many scholars believe that after Jerusalem was destroyed, many of these people turned to Christ and became part of the early church. They brought clean living and love for God to the church.

Group 7—the Pharisees: This group was the most powerful of the religious group in Palestine in the first century. The people believed that these were holy men. The Pharisees scrupulously kept the Law of Moses, including the Oral Law. They believed in the resurrection from the dead and in heaven and hell. Some served on the Sanhedrin, the court of the Jews, that met in an area of the Temple. Some were involved in the death of Jesus. Others, like Nicodemus, were godly and followed Jesus. They kept away from Gentiles and even from other Jews to remain ritually pure.

Group 8—the Sadducees: These were the rulers, and the high priest came from this group. The Sadducees came into being during the period between the Old and New Testaments. They became the most powerful political group in Palestine. They were liberal in their ideas and only held to the written Law. They did not follow the oral Law. They did not believe in resurrection or heaven or hell. The high priest came from the party of the Sadducees. Many of them participated in the death of Jesus, like the high priest Caiaphas.

Group 9—the rabbis: The term *rabbi* means "my master." These were men who were well educated in the Law of Moses. After the fall of Jerusalem in AD 70, the rabbis became the spiritual teachers among the Jews. They continued to protect and study the Word of God. Their discussions have become part of Jewish literature. They continue today to serve in doing the same kinds of things that a minister does in a Baptist church.

Conclude this presentation by pointing out to the children that these groups of people played an important role in Judaism and have even affected Christianity. Use the next activity as a review of what you have discussed.

Activity 9—Wordfind with the Names of the Groups from This Lesson

Give each child a copy of Activity Sheet 9. Have your students complete the activity as a review of the lesson.

Activity 10—Memorize Psalm 119:33–36

To help your children understand the importance of the Bible and what it means to us, have your children memorize Psalm 119:33–36. For younger children, you may want them to memorize only verse 33.

Teach me, O LORD, the meaning of Your statutes, and I will always keep them. Help me understand Your instruction, and I will obey it and follow it with all my heart. Help me stay on the path of Your commands, for I take pleasure in it. Turn my heart to Your decrees and not to material gain.

Have the children write this Scripture in their Bible Verse Memory Books, memorize, and illustrate it.

WORKSHEETS FOR LESSON 2

ACTIVITY SHEET 1: "I AM . . ." STATEMENTS

_____ 1. I AM one who came from the tribe of Levi and led worship in the Tabernacle and later in the Temple. I conducted sacrifices and taught the people about God.

_____ 2. I AM also from the tribe of Levi and assisted the leaders of worship in the Temple.

_____ 3. I AM one who was not paid but spoke the Word of the Lord to kings and the people.

_____ 4. I AM a person who came on the scene during the time of the kings to write documents for the kings and later became an interpreter of the Law.

_____ 5. I AM a member of a very strict and conservative religious group, who came into conflict with Jesus during His ministry.

_____ 6. I AM a member of the ruling group in Judea during the New Testament times. My group does not believe in the resurrection.

_____ 7. I AM a member of a group of persons who lived along the shores of the Dead Sea in the Quamran community. We looked forward to the coming of the Messiah.

_____ 8. I AM a member of a group who wanted to rid Palestine of the Romans, and I fought vigorously against them.

ACTIVITY SHEET 2: THE ESSENES

1. Who were the Essenes? _____
2. What did a person have to do to become a member of the Essene community?

   _____
3. What were the Essenes known for? _____
4. What was the Book of Discipline? _____
5. Where and when was the Book of Discipline found? _____
6. How was it found? _____
7. What are the Dead Sea Scrolls? _____

ACTIVITY SHEET 3: TRUE/FALSE QUIZ ON THE ZEALOTS

____ 1. The Zealots were a peace-loving people.

____ 2. The Zealots wanted to get rid of all foreign armies from the land.

____ 3. Matthew, one of Jesus' apostles was a Zealot.

____ 4. The Zealots were willing to give their lives to defend the House of the Lord.

____ 5. The Zealots opposed the use of force to rid their land of the evil Romans.

____ 6. The Zealots were afraid of the Romans.

____ 7. The Zealots kept the Law of God.

____ 8. The Zealots took every opportunity to kill Roman soldiers.

ACTIVITY SHEET 4: COMPARISON BETWEEN PHARISEES AND SADDUCEES

Directions: A Venn diagram will help you compare the Pharisees and Sadducees. From the characteristics below the Venn diagram, select those characteristics that are only present in the Pharisees and write those numbers in the left side of the circle. Do the same for Sadducees on the right. Write the numbers of the characteristics that are true for both in the ellipse that intersects both circles.

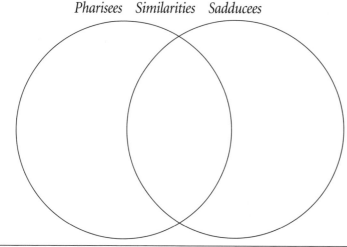

Pharisees   Similarities   Sadducees

Characteristics
1. Religious leaders
2. Did not believe in the resurrection
3. Strictly followed the oral law
4. Conducted trial of Jesus before the high priest
5. Opposed Jesus
6. Kept every letter of the Law of God given by Moses
7. Had political power
8. Best-known religious group
9. Did not believe in heaven or hell

Not all Pharisees opposed Jesus. There was a Pharisee named Nicodemus who came to Jesus at night and asked the following question. Can you decipher the secret message?

Directions: Use the secret code below to find the meaning of the message.

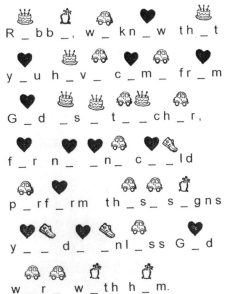

R _ b b _ , w _ kn _ w th _ t

y _ u h _ v _ c _ m _ fr _ m

G _ d _ s _ t _ _ ch _ r,

f _ r n _ _ n _ c _ _ ld

p _ rf _ rm th _ s _ s _ gns

y _ _ _ d _ _ nl _ ss G _ d

w _ r _ w _ th h _ m.

Secret Code:

a	e	i	o	u

Directions: As a review, complete the wordfind by finding the nine names of the groups that were discussed in the lesson.

```
U Q K W G S M H S M M B Q A O
N W Q T A W N G E G O J Z W S
I O S Q P R O P H E T P Q T A
L Z E A L O T E K C H T J V I
S G G H Q E A E D A F S A F T
A D J S H L V S R B X E Y X M
D H D G Q H H I E B O I E M L
D Y A N C T S R T B M R L M K
U V A W A E R A S E I P L L S
C I X B E Z N H U S Y R A G M
E F B C F I T P Y S S J C A I
E A D X N P H Q D E I H O S V
S E I R H K T K V N A M L W V
X G V W O H S Y M E H L G M A
L H J B M E D V O J Z R M M F
```

LESSON 3: JEWISH RELIGIOUS WORSHIP

Readings from the Parent/Teacher Handbook: Their Christian Heritage, Vol. 2: "Religious Practices of Jews and Christians"

OBJECTIVES
By the end of lesson, the learner should be able to
- describe worship,
- define the Sabbath,
- describe the Tabernacle in the worship of God,
- explain the role of the Temple in Jewish worship,
- explain what happened to worship in the synagogue, especially after the destruction of the Temple, and
- demonstrate understanding of the rabbi as the worship leader.

IDENTIFICATIONS

Concepts
Sabbath—seventh day of the week; set aside for worship
Tabernacle—a tent designed for worship before the building of the Temple
Temple—the place for national worship for the Jews in Jerusalem

Synagogue—local meeting place for Jews to worship and study
Rabbi—educated clergy who lead Jewish worship
Cantor—like a worship leader in our churches; he assisted the rabbi

Places
Jerusalem: center of Jewish worship in the Temple

MATERIALS NEEDED
Parent/Teacher Handbook: Their Christian Heritage, Vol. 2
Activity Sheets for Lesson 3
Crayons and markers
White drawing paper
Lined paper for writing
Masking tape and plastic tape
4x6-inch index cards
Glue
Scissors
Posterboard

LEARNING ACTIVITIES FOR LESSON 3

Activity 1—Worship (1 Chronicles 16:23–29; Psalm 100, 150; John 4:24; Romans 12:1)

Ask the children what the word *worship* means. Write their definitions on the chalkboard. When you have exhausted their ideas, talk about the meaning of *worship*. In our English language, the word refers to "reverence, honor, respect, awe that we give to God." One of the earliest uses in the English language appeared in one of the early English manuscripts, the *Lindisfarne Gospels,* around AD 950. It had reference to worship given to God.

The Bible uses the term to mean adoration that human subjects give to God. The Bible never clearly defines worship, but we can learn a lot about worship from what Scripture does tell us. Try to find at least one characteristic for each of the passages listed above.

Here are some examples. In 1 Chronicles 16:23–29 we are exhorted to magnify the Lord. He is worthy of our praise. He is to be feared with an awesome respect. From Psalm 100 we are to express joyous songs to God. We are to go into the gates of the Lord's Temple with praise and thanksgiving. From Psalm 150 we are to express thanksgiving and praise with musical instruments joyfully. From John 4:24 God is not like us. God is Spirit. God must be worshiped in truth and honesty. Finally, in Romans 12:1 we learn that we are to be a temple for God and our bodies are to be pleasing and holy to Him.

Write the characteristics that you discover on the chalkboard. Emphasize that we need to worship God not only in church or on Sunday but also in our everyday lives all week. Worship must express our respect, love, and fear of God. His Son Jesus brought us to the point where we can be part of God's family. Tell the children that while this lesson is about Jewish practices of the Sabbath, the Tabernacle, and the Temple, all of these are about worship of God.

Provide the children with a sheet of construction paper. Have them write the meaning of worship to them personally. Have them draw a picture of one way they can worship God.

Activity 2—Study of the Sabbath Day from the Old Testament

You will want to summarize the history of the Sabbath day, *Shabbat*, observance for your students. Below is an outline, with Scripture references of the material that you may wish to cover. Recall the essential time periods from biblical history. You will find a time line for God's redemptive action in the Old Testament and the New Testament on Activity Sheet 2-A. You may want to list your main points on the chalkboard or an overhead transparency. Review the history of redemption and relate to the celebration of the Sabbath.

1. *Where and why did the Sabbath originate?*
   The Sabbath originated with God at Creation; God rested on the seventh day of the week—
      Genesis 2:2–3
   The Sabbath day was commanded at Mount Sinai—Exodus 20:8–11
   After the Exile to Babylon, the Sabbath was also encouraged—Nehemiah 10:31
   It is the observance of a perpetual covenant—Exodus 31:16–17
   Sabbath was made for the good of man—Mark 2:27
   Christ is Lord over the Sabbath—Luke 6:5
2. *What does God require on the Sabbath?*
   The Third Commandment says to keep the Sabbath holy—Exodus 20:8–11
   Work is prohibited on the Sabbath—Leviticus 23:3
   Business is forbidden on the Sabbath—Jeremiah 17:21–22
   Worship is required on the Sabbath—Ezekiel 46:3
   Do good works of mercy on the Sabbath—Matthew 12:12
3. *Why did the followers of Christ change it to the first day of the week?*
   Day of Christ's resurrection—Mark 16:9; John 20:1, 19
   Day after the Sabbath—Mark 16:1–2
   Day of worship for Christians—Acts 20:7; 1 Corinthians 16:1–2
   Called "the Lord's Day"—Revelation 1:10

Find the true/false quiz on Activity Sheet 2-B. Duplicate copies and have the children complete the exercise as a review of the information that you have covered.

Activity 3—The Tabernacle (Exodus 33:7–10)

Carefully read "The Tabernacle" in the handbook.

The Tabernacle was the place where God chose to live among His people, Israel. It was sometimes called the Tent of Meeting. God instructed Moses and the people of Israel how to construct the Tabernacle and what furniture to place inside it.

After the people sinned by making the golden calf while Moses was on Mount Sinai, God chose not to live with the people. A second Tabernacle was constructed outside the camp. After David conquered Jerusalem, a third Tabernacle was constructed in Jerusalem. It provided a more permanent place for the people to worship God. The Tabernacle contained particular furniture that God instructed Moses to place within its walls. Although it was much more elaborate, the Temple also had the same essential furniture.

In this activity your class members will make flash cards out of 4x6-inch index cards. The flash cards will have a picture of the furniture on one side of the card, and they will paste the meaning of the piece of furniture on the lined side of the card. Then they will work in pairs to show the picture while the other person tells what the piece of furniture was and what it meant. Help the children understand that God provides for our aesthetic nature by making things that are beautiful and appeal to our senses.

Turn to Activity Sheet 3-A, 3-B, and 3-C. Duplicate copies of the Tabernacle and the furniture that was placed inside the Tabernacle. Have the students cut out the pieces of furniture. Give them each a 4x6-inch index card and ask them to paste the picture on the blank side of the card and the description on the other side of the card. Then have them try to identify and describe the Tabernacle and each piece of furniture that was in the Tabernacle.

On Activity Sheet 3-D, you will also find the floor plan of the Tabernacle and the furniture. Duplicate this sheet and have the children match the furniture to the position where they were placed in the Tabernacle. They may draw a line from the piece of furniture to the approximate location in the Tabernacle.

Activity 4—The Temple
In the handbook, read "The Temple."

In class, talk with the students about the role of the Temple in Jewish life. It played a critical role and was the center of Jewish life. You will find adequate information in the handbook, but you may wish to supplement that information by exploring a Bible dictionary. You may wish to note the significant points on the chalkboard or on an overhead transparency.

When the children are familiar with the Temple, have them complete the learning exercise on Activity Sheet 4.

Activity 5—The Synagogue
The synagogue became the center of Jewish worship after the fall of Jerusalem. Read "The Synagogue" section in the handbook.

Talk about the three major topics: the house of prayer, the house of study, and the house of gathering. List those topics on the chalkboard and have the children divided into three listening groups. As the teacher reads the section on "The Synagogue," group one listens to the reading to find out why it is called a house of prayer. The second group will listen for things related to the house of study. The third group will listen for things related to the house of gathering.

After you have finished discussing the synagogue, ask each group to tell you what they heard. List their contributions on the chalkboard under the appropriate topic. Tell the children that the synagogue is the place of worship for Jewish people today and is used for similar purposes as their church.

Activity 6—Visit a Synagogue
An excellent learning experience for your class would be to make arrangements with a rabbi in your community to take your class to a synagogue. Preferably, look for an orthodox or conservative synagogue. Ask the rabbi to talk about worship in the synagogue. Help the children to be observant and look at the differences between their church and the synagogue. Be sure that you have prepared the

children to behave well in the synagogue and with the rabbi. After you have returned, write a letter of appreciation for the visit.

Activity 7—Field Trip to the Mennonite Information Center and Biblical Tabernacle Reproduction

The Biblical Tabernacle Reproduction is an interesting educational experience. Located in the heart of Amish and Mennonite country, the center provides a life-size model of the Tabernacle and its furniture. A lecture tour, which tells about the construction and spiritual significance of the Tabernacle, is provided. A life-size wax figure of the high priest is also presented at the center. The center is located at 2209 Millstream Road, Lancaster, PA 17602 and may be reached online at www.mennoniteinfoctr.com. Additional educational resources about the Tabernacle may be obtained from the bookstore at the center.

Activity 8—Field Trip to the Holy Land Experience™

It would be ideal to take your children across the ocean to the Holy Land. Assuming that is not possible, there is an alternative in the United States. It is the Holy Land Experience in Orlando, Florida. The Holy Land Experience™ is a Christ-honoring experience of the Holy Land covering three thousand miles and as much as seven thousand years ago. It is an educational experience with reproductions of the Tabernacle and Herod's Temple that we studied in this lesson. It also has reproductions of the tomb of Jesus, a bazaar, and the Quamran caves where the Dead Sea Scrolls were discovered that were discussed in lesson 2.

One of the best exhibits is the authentic reproduction of Jerusalem in the first century. The prominence of the Temple is very evident. This is the largest indoor facility of its kind in the world. A little further along is the Scriptorium: Center for Biblical Antiquities. Housed in this unique eighteen thousand square foot museum are copies of many of the rarest manuscripts from biblical times. They are presented in a way that will excite even the dourest museum visitor. In addition, there are many dramatizations during a typical day at the Holy Land Experience.™

This would be an excellent means for summarizing many of the studies in which your children have been engaged through the volumes in this series. You may learn more about the Holy Land Experience™ by visiting their Web site at www.holylandexperience.com.

Activity 9—Crossword Puzzle Review of Lesson

Duplicate copies of the crossword puzzle. You will find the puzzle on Activity Sheet 9. Use this activity as a review of this lesson. Discuss the answers.

Activity 10—Memorize Psalm 100

The purpose of using the Tabernacle, the Temple, or a church today is to worship God. God loves His people. We are called to worship Him. This psalm helps us to understand our responsibility before God. Have your students memorize this psalm.

> Shout triumphantly to the LORD, all the earth. Serve the LORD with gladness; come before Him with joyful songs. Acknowledge that the LORD is God. He made us, and we are His—His people, the sheep of His pasture. Enter His gates with thanksgiving and His courts with praise. Give thanks to Him and praise His name. For the LORD is good, and His love is eternal; His faithfulness endures through all generations.

Have your students draw a picture in their Bible Verse Memory Book that will illustrate this passage and write the verse, as they have done in previous lessons.

ACTIVITY SHEET 2-A: REVIEW OF THE HISTORY OF REDEMPTION

Review of God's Redeeming Grace

1. God **creates** the heavens, the world, seas and fish, animal kingdom, and man.
2. Adam and Eve—the first parents—sinned against God; **sin** entered the world.
3. The world grows more **evil**—Cain murders Abel, Noah is saved from the flood, and the building of the Tower of Babel.
4. God calls out Abraham and redeems a new people through the **Covenant** and makes a **Promise** to Abraham.
5. Isaac is heir to **God's Promise.**
6. Jacob is heir to **God's Promise** and Jacob's sons become the fathers of the twelve Tribes of Israel.
5. Joseph becomes vice regent of Egypt and the family of Israel goes to Egypt. This ends the **Period of the Patriarchs.**
6. The Israelites spend four hundred years in Egypt; they grow as a people but suffer during the reigns of new Pharaohs.
7. Moses is born and grows up in the household of Pharaoh; this begins the **Period of the Exodus.**
8. God **redeems** Israel from slavery through Moses.
9. Moses leads the people of Israel into the wilderness to worship God.
10. God makes a new **Covenant** with the people of Israel at Mount Sinai and gives the Law and Ten Commandments.
11. Forty years the people wander in the wilderness; God leads them with a cloud by day and a pillar of fire by night.
12. Moses dies; God calls Joshua to lead the people into the **Promised Land**; this is the fulfillment of **God's Promise.**
13. The people live in the **Promised Land** and are ruled by the **Judges.**
14. The Judges fail to unify the people as in the case of Samson.
15. **Samuel** is both a **Prophet** and a Judge; God told him to anoint Saul king and the **Period of the Judges** ends; later Samuel anointed David to replace Saul.
16. Saul begins the **Period of the Monarchy** or kings of Israel; Saul did not obey God and his family was removed from power and replaced by David.
17. **David** reigns as King of Israel about 1000 BC; David conquers **Jerusalem; Worship** is now centered in Jerusalem—The City of David.
18. **Solomon** becomes king at David's death; Solomon builds the **Temple** in Jerusalem.
19. **Sacrifices** in the Temple show God's demand of death for the **Redemption** of man.
20. After Solomon, the northern ten tribes of Israel break away from the two tribes to the south in Judah—The country is divided between **Israel** to the north and **Judah** to the south.
21. Israel's kings did evil in God's sight; Israel was taken into captivity by **Assyria** as God's **punishment** in 722 BC.
22. God raised up **Prophets** to proclaim His Word in Israel and called the people to **Repentance**—like Jeremiah; but the people would not listen.
23. Judah had good kings and bad kings; they survived as a nation until God brought punishment on them by having them taken into captivity by **Babylonia** in 587 BC; Captivity ended the **Period of the Monarchy.**
24. Captivity in Babylonia, under the Babylonian king Nebuchadnezzar; beginning the **Period of Exile.**
25. In the **Period of the Exile**, the people of Judah remained true to God; they repented; God gave them prophets in Captivity—like Daniel to keep them true to God.
26. In captivity, **Esther** became queen of Persia and helped to keep the Israelites from being destroyed by the wicked Haman.
27. Under Ezra and Nehemiah, many of the people returned to the land of Judah—this was the **Return to the Promised Land.**
28. The **Temple** was rebuilt and completed in 515 BC; **Worship of God** is restored in Jerusalem.
29. The **Old Testament** ends with the Prophet Malachi

ACTIVITY SHEET 2-A: TIME LINE FOR NEW TESTAMENT EVENTS

	(dates are approximate)
400–4 BC	Period between Old and New Testaments—Malachi to Matthew
4 BC	Birth of Jesus* *(Note: During the Middle Ages there was a mistake in calculating the date for the birth of Jesus)*
AD 24	Baptism of Jesus
AD 25–27	Ministry of Jesus
1st year	Early Ministry and relative obscurity
2nd year	Year of popularity
3rd year	Year of conflict and opposition
AD 27	Crucifixion of Jesus
AD 33	Conversion of Paul
AD 47–48	Paul's first missionary journey
AD 49–52	Paul's second missionary journey
AD 52–56	Paul's third missionary journey
AD 56	Arrest of Paul in Jerusalem
AD 56–58	Appearances of Paul before Felix and Festus
AD 58-61	Paul travels to Rome
AD 62	Release from prison
AD 64	Burning of Rome; Emperor Nero blames Christians
AD 67	Paul'second imprisonment in Rome
AD 67	Paul is executed by Emperor Nero
AD 70	Destruction of Jerusalem under the Roman general Titus (later Emperor)
AD 100	Death of John the apostle

ACTIVITY SHEET 2-B: TRUE/FALSE QUIZ REVIEW OF THE SABBATH

Directions: Read the sentences and circle T if you think the sentence is true or F if you think the sentence is false.

T   F   1. God created Sabbath at the time of Creation.

T   F   2. Followers of Jesus worship on the Sabbath or seventh day of the week.

T   F   3. Work was allowed on the Sabbath under the Law of Moses.

T   F   4. God made the Sabbath for the good of mankind.

T   F   5. Acts of mercy were permitted on the Sabbath.

T   F   6. The Lord's Day is the day of worship for followers of Jesus.

T   F   7. The Sabbath in the Old Testament was a day of rest, not a day of worship.

T   F   8. Jesus' resurrection took place on the Sabbath.

T   F   9. Jesus taught on the Sabbath

T   F   10. Throughout their history, the Jews have kept the Sabbath.

Directions: Cut out the descriptions of the furniture and glue them to 4x6-inch index cards.

The Altar of Incense provided a sweet-smelling perfume. This represents the prayers of God's people that ascend to God. A person who is humble and prays acts like a sweet-smelling aroma before God (Exodus 30:1–10).

The Table of Showbread held twelve loaves of bread. This meant that God provided adequately for each of the twelve tribes of Israel. Bread provided food for the priests and symbolized the dependence of the people on God (Exodus 25:23–30).

The Golden Lampstand, or *Menorah,* had seven candles placed in holders. They showed God's care for His people and their dependence upon Him (Exodus 25:31–40).

The Altar of Burnt Offering is a large altar that stood outside the Tabernacle. On the altar the animals were sacrificed. People had to bring animals that did not have any blemishes. These were sacrificed, and their blood was shed for the sins of the people (Exodus 27:1–8).

The Bronze Laver was used for the purification of the priests before they went into the presence of the Lord. The priest had to wash his hands before he sacrificed the animals. Priests were offering sacrifice on behalf of the people and had to observe all of the regulations that God gave them (Exodus 30:17–21).

The Ark of the Covenant was the most important structure in the Tabernacle. This was the place where God dwelt. A priest entered the Holy of Holies only once a year to place the blood of the goat on the mercy seat between the cherubim. The priest was tied with a golden cord so that he could be removed if he died while inside the Holy Place (Exodus 25:10–22).

ACTIVITY SHEET 3-C: THE TABERNACLE

Directions: Glue the Tabernacle and the description to a 4x6-inch index card for study.

The Tabernacle was a tent where God dwelt among His people during the wilderness wandering in the desert. It was a temporary house of worship and was moved from place to place. The Tabernacle housed the furniture that God commanded.

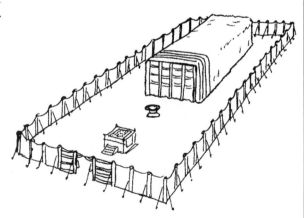

ACTIVITY SHEET 3-B: FURNITURE OF THE TABERNACLE

Directions: Cut out the pieces of furniture and glue them to 4x6-inch index cards.

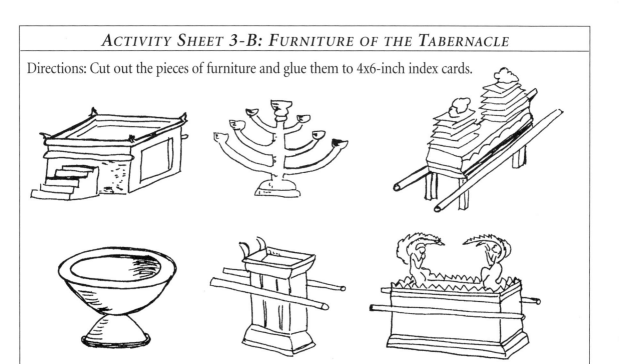

ACTIVITY SHEET 3-D: FURNITURE OF THE TABERNACLE

Directions: Draw lines from each piece of furniture to the place it was found in the Tabernacle.

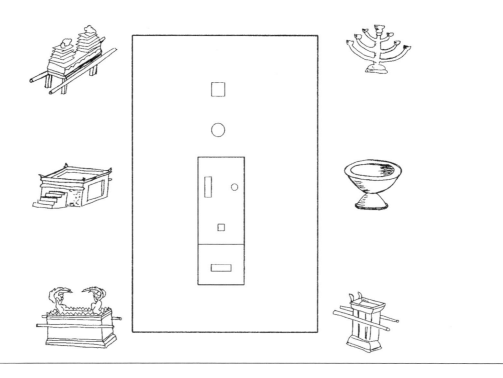

ACTIVITY SHEET 4: FILL IN THE BLANKS—THE TEMPLE

Directions: Select the word from the list below that best completes each sentence.

1. The first Temple was built by _____.
2. The differed from the Tabernacle in that it was a _____ dwelling place for God.
3. The _____ in the Temple was similar to what was found in the Tabernacle.
4. The size of the Temple was much _____ than the Tabernacle.
5. The Temple was a symbol of _____ dwelling with His people.
6. God allowed the Temple to be destroyed by _____, the king of Babylon.
7. The Babylonians stole the _____ from the Temple and took it back to Babylon.
8. Cyrus, king of Persia, provided _____ and _____ for the rebuilding of the Temple.
9. The second Temple lasted for _____ years.
10. Herod the Great made improvements on the _____.
11. The Temple was destroyed by the _____ in AD 70.
12. The only trace of the Temple that remains today is the _____.

Words: money	permanent	Solomon	larger	materials	Temple
Nebuchadnezzar	Wailing Wall	gold	furniture	God	
five hundred	Romans				

ACTIVITY SHEET 9: CROSSWORD PUZZLE REVIEW

Directions: Use the answers to the statements below to complete the puzzle.

Across:

2 This tent of worship was moveable as the people moved
4 Altar for good smell
6 God is _____
7 Furniture in the Temple—the Table of
_____
8 The _____ conducted sacrifice in the Temple
9 Worship took place on which day of the week?

Down:

1 Holds candles in the Temple
3 Basin in which the priest washed
5 Angels in the Holy of Holies
10 Worship in Jerusalem took place

LESSON 4: FEAST DAYS IN THE JEWISH CALENDAR—PART 1

Readings from the Parent/Teacher Handbook: Their Christian Heritage, Vol. 2: "The Jewish Year"

OBJECTIVES

By the end of this lesson, the learner should be able to

- identify and explain the major feast days in the Jewish calendar, and
- provide a detailed description of each of the major feast days.

IDENTIFICATIONS

Concepts

Jewish New Year—Rosh Hashanah a solemn festival, where Jewish people look back over the past year and ahead to the new year in September or October

Day of Atonement—Yom Kippur is the holiest day of the year, where atonement is made for sins past, one week after the New Year

Feast of Tabernacles—Sukkot is a harvest festival that signifies the bountiful protection of God, celebrated outdoors in booths, five days after *Yom Kippur*

Shofar—a ram's horn to recall that a ram was sacrificed in place of Isaac, and it is blown to remind Jews that sacrifice to God is necessary

Atonement—propitiation of God by the expiation of sin, bringing reconciliation between God and man

Confession—acknowledging one's sin or sinful condition

Scapegoat—goat that was sent into the wilderness to carry the sins of the people on the Day of Atonement

Places

Jerusalem—center of Jewish festivals until the fall of Jerusalem in 70 AD

MATERIALS NEEDED

Parent/Teacher Handbook: Their Christian Heritage, Vol. 2

Activity Sheets for Lesson 4
Crayons and markers
White drawing paper
Lined paper for writing
Masking tape and plastic tape
3x5-inch index cards
Dowels
Posterboard
Construction paper
Glue
Scissors
Citrus fruit
Grocery bags
Party horn—4 to 6 inches
Paper plates or coffee cans
Paper cups
Grape juice

LEARNING ACTIVITIES FOR LESSON 4

Activity 1—Calendar of Jewish Feasts

Jewish feasts tell a great deal about Jewish history and culture. They are inextricably tied up with both the Old and New Testaments of the Bible. This lesson will help your students become more familiar with the festivals of the Bible and better understand how God used the festivals as a reminder to His people of the obligations and relationship to Him.

You will want the students to develop a booklet of each of the Jewish feasts described in this series. Activity Sheet 1 is a form that the children can complete for each of the different feasts in this lesson. Duplicate enough copies for the members of your class to have one for each of the seven annual feasts. In addition, include the Sabbath, *Shabbat,* the weekly feast we studied in the last lesson. Along with each of the charts, the children can illustrate the feast with a picture of their own creation on plain construction paper. Together, these will comprise their Jewish Holidays booklet.

You will find coloring pages and lengthier descriptions of the different Jewish holidays online. Use a keyword search of "Jewish holidays" or the specific holiday name. (Optional)—Additional help in curricula for Jewish holidays can be obtained from Lederer Messianic Publications, 6204 Park Heights Avenue, Baltimore, MD 21215.

Activity 2—Rosh Hashanah *or Jewish New Year (Leviticus 23:23–25; Numbers 29:1)*

Rosh Hashanah is the Jewish New Year. It is not celebrated with fireworks and jubilation as we celebrate the New Year on January 1. Of all the festivals, *Rosh Hashanah* does not have a biblical historical base, even though it was celebrated generations ago as mentioned in the passages above. It celebrates the birthday of the world. God recalls the deeds of persons—good or bad. Hence, the serious purpose of this holiday. It is also associated with Abraham's sacrifice of Isaac, which accounts for the origin of the shofar, or ram's horn. A ram was sacrificed in place of Isaac.

After you have discussed the holiday from the section in the handbook "The Jewish New Year," have the children complete the chart for this holiday on Activity Sheet 1. Add it to the Jewish Holidays booklet. Read the story of Abraham's obedience to God in sacrifice in Genesis 22:1–19. Tell the students about the connection to the shofar, or ram's horn.

You may also want the children to make a ram's horn or shofar. It is traditional to blow the shofar on the Jewish New Year, except when it falls on Sabbath. Obtain party horns with a large end away from the mouthpiece. Cut coarse brown paper from a grocery bag to completely cover the horn. Paint glueon the brown paper. Wrap the party horn completely. Bend the horn about two-thirds of the way from the mouthpiece to give it the appearance of the bend in a ram's horn. Allow to dry overnight. It should hold its shape when dry. Attach string to the horn so that it may be slung over the shoulder. The shofar is designed to call people to repentance. Three sounds are made by the shofar. One involves a long note. The second is a series of three short broken notes. The third consists of a series of nine short notes.

Emphasize the Christian significance of the Jewish New Year. Read "What Christians Can Learn from *Rosh Hashanah*" in the handbook.

Activity 3—Rosh Hashanah *Greeting Cards*

A custom for *Rosh Hashanah* that originated in the nineteenth century is that of sending New Year cards. In many ways these greeting cards are similiar to Christmas cards that are sent by Christians to their family and friends.

Provide each child with construction paper and markers. Have them create his or her own greeting card. They may use symbols from the Jewish community, such as the star of David, the *menorah*, etc. They may use the inside of the card to tell about their home and family. Encourage the children to be creative.

Activity 4—Celebration of Rosh Hashanah

One of the customs of *Rosh Hashanah* is the provision of apples dipped in honey. The idea behind this custom is wishing the members of your family a sweet New Year. Usually, the honey is placed in a very attractive, decorated jar. There are a variety of apples that may be used for this purpose. They may include Courtland, Jonathan, Red Delicious, Winesap, or McIntosh.

You may want the children to experience this tradition. In advance prepare a decrated jar, like a mason jar, for the honey. A good choice for the honey would be a cinnamon honey. Then slice different types of apples from the list above to dip into the honey. Allow the children to experience this tradition and explain its purpose.

Activity 5—New Year Blessing

In many Jewish homes it is customary to offer a blessing to each person. This tradition has its origin in the Bible with the blessing of the sons of Issac. At *Rosh Hashanah* it is possible for the members of the group to go around the table and offer a blessing for each member. You might combine this with the previous activity, as the children are dipping their apple slices in the honey.

Have the first child ask the child to his or her left, "With what would you like to be blessed?" After the second child has answered, have the first child respond, "May you be blessed with . . ." Then continue the blessings around the entire group.

Activity 6—Yom Kippur *or the Day of Atonement (Leviticus 23:26–32)*

The Day of Atonement comes at the end of the Ten Days of Awe. It is the holiest day on the Jewish calendar. On the Day of Atonement the two rams were killed. By lot, one was selected for sacrifice. The priest would take the blood of the sacrificed ram into the Holy of Holies in the Tabernacle or the Temple. He would place the blood on the mercy seat between the cherubim on the ark of the covenant. The other ram became the scapegoat. It was tied around the horns with a red cord, representing the sins of the people. The scapegoat was sent off into the wilderness to carry the sins of the people away. This was no longer necessary after the death of Jesus.

Read "The Day of Atonement" in the handbook. Review this material with the members of your class.

Have your students complete the ATONEMENT puzzle on Activity Sheet 6. They may color a picture as well for their Jewish Holidays booklet.

Read and emphasize "What Christians Can Learn from *Yom Kippur*" in the handbook.

Activity 7—Read the Book of Jonah

It is customary to read the Book of Jonah on *Yom Kippur*. Jonah is the story of a prophet who did not want to go and tell the people about a loving God. Jonah was afraid that God would forgive the sins of the people of Assyria. They were an evil and cruel group of people. The Hebrew people feared Assyria. So Jonah took a ship toward what is present-day Spain. He thought he could run away from God.

The men on the boat finally had no choice but to throw Jonah into the sea. God had prepared a great fish to swallow Jonah and bring him safely to land three days later. Jonah obeyed God this time and went to the people of Ninevah in Assyria. He preached and they repented. God spared the people of Ninevah. God does the same for us, if we repend and turn to Him.

This is a great book to read on the Day of Atonement. Find a children's version of the story of Jonah and read it to your class. Talk about God's love and forgiveness.

Activity 8—Sukkot *or The Feast of Tabernacles (Leviticus 23:42–43)*

The Feast of Tabernacles was a fall grape harvest festival. Celebrated in September or October, this festival celebration commemorated the long and arduous journey through the desert after the Israelites were free from Egypt. The people built small tabernacles that were called *sukkah*. When they encamped in the burning desert by day, the *sukkah* protected them from the hot sun. At night the sukkot provided protection as well.

Read "The Feast of Tabernacles" in the handbook.

Before you talk about the feast, you may want to have tables set up in a manner that will stimulate the *sukkah*. Take tables that are eight feet long and have them set on their sides. Drape a sheet or covering over the table. Place branches on top of the coverings to make it seem like the children are sitting in a booth covered with branches. Allow the children to sit in small groups under the protection of the simulated *sukkah*.

Tell the story of the Feast of Tabernacles. Then tell them the story of the people wandering in the wilderness. You will find the story in volume 1 of *The Parent/Teacher Handbook*. Conclude their activity under the simulated *sukkah* with the children eating a snack of citrus fruit. They can also drink grape juice to commemorate the grape harvest. In the actual Jewish celebration, they eat citron, called *etrog*. This is similar to a lemon.

After you have cleaned up the room, have the children add this holiday to their Jewish Holidays booklet. You will also want to stress the Christian significance of *Sukkot* by reading "What Christians Can Learn from *Sukkot*" in the handbook.

Activity 9—Harvest of Fruit for the Feast of Tabernacles
The Feast of Tabernacles is done at the time of harvest. You will want to bring a large basket of fresh fruits and vegetables. Give one item to each child and have them fill the basket with the fruits and vegetables. When all have been contributed, have the children recite together the verse for memorization— Psalm 118: 29. Conclude with a prayer of thanksgiving to God for His love and provision for us.

Activity 10—Memorize Psalm 118:29
Consider the activities of this lesson. God is good! He is willing to forgive our sin. He has provided a way for us. He gives us good things to enjoy, such as the Feast of Tabernacles. This verse reminds us to be thankful.

Give thanks to the LORD, for He is good; His faithful love endures forever.

Have the students draw a picture and add the verse to their Bible Verse Memory Books.

ACTIVITY SHEET 1: CHART FOR JEWISH FEAST DAYS

Celebration of the Feast of _____

In what month is it celebrated? _____

How many days are involved? _____

Why do the Jews celebrate this feast? _____

In what ways was this feast celebrated? _____

How has this feast changed since the past? _____

What can we, as Christians, learn from this feast? _____

_____

ACTIVITY SHEET 6: ATONEMENT PUZZLE

Directions: Complete the puzzle from the sentences below.

The ____A_____ was sent into the wilderness, carrying the sins of the people. On this day Jewish people F_____; they do not eat. This day is __O_____ to the Lord. Normally, the Book of ____N____ is read on this day. This is a day on which the people want to R_____ themselves to God. They must look for God's M_____. The penalty for sin is __E_____. The blood applied to the Mercy Seat in the Holy of Holies covers ____N. God wants His people to be ____T apart to be holy.

```
__ __A_____ _____
____T
__ O____
____N____
_____E_____
M_____
_____E_____
____N
____-__T
```

Readings from the Parent/Teacher Handbook: Their Christian Heritage, Vol. 2: "The Jewish Year"

OBJECTIVES

By the end of this lesson, the learner should be able to

- show how the Jewish feast days were important to Jews and later to Christians, and
- describe what Christians can learn from the feast days of the Jewish calendar.

IDENTIFICATIONS

Concepts

Festival of Lights—Hanukkah commemorates the rededication of the Temple after being freed through the Maccabees; occurs in December

Feast of Lots—Purim is the feast to celebrate Esther's protection of the people against the wicked Haman; usually in February or March

Feast of Passover—Pesach, or the commemoration of the exodus from Egypt, occurs in March or April

Feast of Pentecost—Shauvot, or a spring harvest festival, that occurs fifty days after Pesach

Megillah—handwritten scroll of the Book of Esther

Grogger—rattle or noisemaker that is used whenever the name of Haman is said in reading from the Megillah

Dreidel—a four-sided spinning top used to play a game at Hanukkah

Seder—means "order" and is used at the Passover meal

Haggadah—story of Passover

Afikomen—matzah given at the end of the Passover

MATERIALS NEEDED

Parent/Teacher Handbook: Their Christian Heritage, Vol. 2

Activity Sheets for Lesson 5

Crayons, markers, and pencils

White drawing paper

Lined paper for writing

Masking tape and plastic tape

Dowels

Posterboard

Construction paper

Glue

Scissors

Apples

Honey

Jar

Card stock paper

Chocolate candies

Ingredients for dough

String

Brush

Party horn—4 to 6 inches

Tongue depressors

Beans

Decoupage

Felt

Matzah, vegetables, lamb shank bone, etc. (see Activity 3)

LEARNING ACTIVITIES FOR LESSON 5

Activity 1—Hanukkah *or The Festival of Lights (1 Maccabees [from the Apocrypha])*

One of the joyous feasts of the Jewish year is *Hanukkah*. It comes near the time of the Christian celebration of Christmas. The term *Hanukkah* means "dedication." This is the time when the Maccabees were successful in ridding the land of the Syrians to the north. The Syrian Antiochus had sacrificed a pig on the altar in the Temple. The brave band of Maccabees fought valiantly to reclaim the land and the Temple. The dedication of the Temple took place, lighted by the *menorah*, or the seven candlesticks. The feast was marked with bright lights in the Temple and in Jewish homes.

Read "The Festival of Lights" in the handbook. Tell the story to the members of your class. You may also want to tell the interesting story of Judith and Holofernes, found in this section. You might use one of the many artworks about the story to help you retell it to your class.

One of the games that is played at Hanukkah is dreidel. Either purchase the dreidel top or make your own by copying the pattern on Activity Sheet 1 on card stock.

You can have a number of children playing the game, probably between five and eight children, at one time. The game "Spin the Dreidel" is played by spinning the dreidel. There is one Hebrew letter on each of four sides of the spinner. They are Nun (נ), Gimel (ג), Hey (ה), and Shin (שׁ). It is believed that the letters stand for a Hebrew acrostic that means, "A great miracle happened there."

Chocolate wrapped in gold foil is used when the game is played. But you might use those little packages of Hersheys milk chocolate or some other small candies. All players put a piece of chocolate in the center to start the game. The first player spins the dreidel. If the letter comes up Nun (נ), then the player does not win or lose anything. If it falls on Gimel (ג), then the person who spun gets all of the chocolate. If it comes up Hey (ה), then the person gets half of the chocolates in the center. If it comes up Shin (שׁ), that means the person spinning gets one chocolate from the center. After each player takes a turn, then everyone puts another candy in the center. Continue to play as many rounds as there are candies. Then the one who has the most candy at the end wins the game.

Activity 2—Purim *or The Feast of Lots (Esther)*

The Feast of Lots, or *Purim*, is the feast given in honor of Esther. Esther became queen of Persia. When the wicked Haman wanted to destroy all Jews, Esther did a brave thing. She went to the king on behalf of her people. King Xerxes was kind to her and listened to her. Eventually, Haman was killed. The king could not retract his law, but he did provide the Jews with protection. Esther saved her people from being killed. This story is told in the Megillah, which is a scroll of the Book of Esther. The rabbis use the Megillah to retell the story of Esther, so that her bravery will not be forgotten.

Become thoroughly familiar with the story of Esther from the handbook or from the biblical account. Have the children in your class make masks to play the parts of Xerxes, Esther, Mordecai, Haman, and the others in the story. You will find a pattern for the mask on Activity Sheet 2. Duplicate the mask on card stock paper and provide string to tie the mask around the head. Then you may want the children to play the roles of each of these characters and retell the story of Esther.

Along with the masks, make groggers to make noise at the sound of Haman's name in the story. To make the groggers, use paper plates, stapler, tongue depressors, tape, and beans. Fold the paper plates in half. Staple the tongue depressor at the crease in the paper plate. Then put beans in the plate and fasten the edges with tape. Decorate with crayons or markers. Perhaps an easier way to make a grogger involves the use of a can, with a plastic sealable lid. Place beans in the can, cover, and shake. Every time the name of Haman is mentioned in the story, have the children shake the groggers.

Finally, make *hamantaschen*. These are pastries for the children to eat. The pastries are food that are eaten at the Feast of Purim. Use the same recipe for sugar cookies found in Lesson 1 on Activity Sheet 4. If needed, increase the recipe. Roll out the dough. Cut into circles. Place pastry filling, such as peach or apricot, in the middle. Fold the edges into a triangle position and bake until lightly browned. These represent the tri-cornered hat that Haman wore while he served the king.

Activity 3—Pesach *or Passover (Exodus 1–12; Leviticus 23:5–8; John 1:29; 1 Corinthians 5:7; 1 Peter 1:18–19)*

Recall the last plague on the Egyptians. It involved the angel of death passing over all of the Hebrew homes that had the blood of the sacrificial lamb on the lintel of the doorpost. On the Egyptian homes, the angel of death killed the firstborn of humans and animals. From that event the people of Israel were freed from bondage in Egypt and were allowed to begin the journey to the Promised Land. Through the Feast of Passover, Jewish families are reminded of this great event. The *seder* or "order" guides the celebration for the family. To make ready for the celebration, every bit of *hametz*, or leaven, must be removed from the house. Then the seder table is set. At each place the *Haggadah* is placed on each plate. *Haggadah* means "to tell" and is the specific order of events to tell the story of Passover.

Familiarize yourself with the story of Passover from the handbook and from the biblical account, Exodus 1–12. You can find the seder on the Internet or from Lederer Messianic Publications (see the address under Activity 1). Search with a key word, "Jewish holidays" or "Passover."

You can conduct a simplified version of the Passover to help your children appreciate the significance of the Passover celebration. Set tables with a place mat. These can be made from construction paper. Have your children decorate the place mats with a variety of Jewish images, which may be found online. Laminate clear plastic to the place mat.

Make your own seder plates. Use a paper plate. From old magazines, cut the symbols of the items to be placed on the plate. If you cannot find these pictured items, write the words symmetrically around the plate. These include a lamb shank bone, *haroset*, parsley, horseradish, and egg. Draw a star of David in the center of the plate. Use decoupage or clear acrylic spray to coat the plate. Allow the plate to dry overnight. On the plate, place paper cups that have been cut down to about an inch from the bottom. In the cups, place the various items used in the seder.

Make an afikomen bag of felt. Glue 3 sides together. Decorate the bag with markers, glue and glitter, or other means.

Prepare cups of grape juice in advance. Have the children drink a small quantity of grape juice and give thanks to God for His protection. Then have one child ask each of the following four questions. You may answer each of these questions:

1. Why is this night different from other nights?
2. Why do we eat only bitter herbs?
3. Why do we dip the vegetables twice?
4. Why do we eat reclining?

In the cups on the plate, begin with *maror*, which is horseradish. This is bitter to remind Jews about the bitterness of slavery. Next comes *haroset*, which is a mixture of about 2 apples, 1 teaspoon of cinnamon, 1 cup of nuts, dates, or raisins, 2 teaspoons of honey, and 2 tablespoons of grape jujce for about ten persons. Haroset is good to taste and a reminder of the mortar used to build the pyramids of Egypt. Bitter herbs are a reminder of the bitter life in Egypt. The shank bone of the lamb may be obtained at the grocery store in the meat department. A hard-boiled egg is a symbol of the new life for the Hebrew people after slavery. It also symbolizes the animal sacrifices in the Temple. *Karpas*, or parsley, is dipped in salt to remind Jews of the tears that were shed when the people were in bondage in Egypt.

An empty place is set at the table with a glass of grape juice. This empty place is set for the prophet Elijah. They believe that he will come back one day. The empty place looks forward to that day.

Have the afikomen hidden in the afikomen bag, previously made. It consists of a piece of matzah. It is hidden, and the child that finds it receives a reward to give it back, usually wrapped chocolate. Read the great *Hallel* psalm. *Hallel* means "praise." "The Great Hallel" is Psalm 136. Finally, drink another cup of grape juice and indicate "next year in Jerusalem." The goal of every pious Jew is to go to the Holy Land to celebrate the holidays, particularly the Passover.

After you have completed the basic structure of the Passover, consider what the Passover means to Christians. Read "What Christians Can Learn from Passover" in the handbook. Examine the following

New Testament Scriptures: John 1:29; 1 Corinthians 5:7; 1 Peter 1:18–19. Emphasize the importance of the sacrificial lamb. Jesus became our sacrificial lamb. No further sacrifice is needed, only faith and trust in Jesus, the Messiah.

Activity 4—Shavuot *or Pentecost (Leviticus 23:10–22; Ruth; Acts 1:4–8; Acts 2)*

The Feast of Pentecost, as the name implies, comes fifty days after Passover. Originally, it was to celebrate the good gifts of God in the grain harvest. It is celebrated with milk and honey, since the Promised Land was a land flowing with milk and honey. As the people came to the Temple in Jerusalem, they would bring loaves of bread, the flowers of spring, and firstfruits of the grain harvest.

This agricultural tradition is kept alive today through the reading of the Book of Ruth. Ruth is first and foremost a story of the harvest festival. By tradition, David was born on Pentecost and died on Pentecost. Ruth was an ancestor of David. You will recall that Ruth came from the country of Moab and accepted the Law of Moses and Israel's God.

In later years Pentecost also took on greater significance for the giving of the *Torah*, since Moses received the Law on Mount Sinai fifty days after the exodus took place. Today, many Jews stay up all night and read the *Torah*. Others start the education of their children on Pentecost.

After the resurrection, Jesus promised that the Comforter would come. When the pilgrims were in Jerusalem for the Feast of Pentecost after the resurrection, the Holy Spirit came upon the Christian believers. Many of the pilgrims had come to Jerusalem to celebrate the holiday. The disciples spoke in their languages. Many Jewish persons became followers of Jesus on that day.

Read about the Feast of Pentecost in the handbook. Along with the material presented in this activity, retell the story of Pentecost.

Have the children work in small groups to make a scroll of the Ten Commandments. Provide large lined paper. Have each group copy one or more of the commandments found on Activity Sheet 4. Tape the pages together. Tape a dowel to each end of the extended paper and roll the paper around the dowels to make a scroll.

You may also want to obtain cheese blintzes at the grocery store. This is traditional food at the Feast of Shavuot.

Activity 5—Summary Chart of Jewish Feasts

As a summary activity for this unit, have your class members fill in the Summary Chart of Jewish Feasts on Activity Sheet 5. After the children have completed the exercise, you will want to review the feasts with them. Talk about the interesting things that the children did during this lesson.

Activity 6—A Christian Perspective on the Jewish Feasts (Leviticus 23)

Let us take a fresh look at the Jewish feasts from the perspective of the coming of Christ as the Messiah. Read Leviticus 23. Note that the more recent feasts of Purim and Hannukah are not present in this list. In place of those feasts are the Feast of Unleavened Bread and the Feast of Firstfruits. Instead of starting with *Rosh Hashanah*, as the beginning of the New Year, the first feast is Passover. There are four feasts in the spring and three feasts in the fall of the year.

Passover—14th of Nissan

Passover occurs on the 14th day of the Jewish month of Nissan. Included in the Passover is the hiding of the afikomen. This is a part of the Passover seder for which the rabbis have no explanation, except that it is tradition. It is believed that the use of the afikomen occurred before the destruction of the Temple in

AD 70. The father places three pieces of matzah in a cover with three pockets. The second piece of matzah is broken and placed in a separate bag for the afikomen. This bag is hidden. At the appropriate time in the seder, the children search for the afikomen. The one who finds the afikomen is rewarded. Then each member of the family partakes of the broken afikomen.

The rabbis do not know when this part of the Passover ceremony came into the seder. Their explanation is that it may refer to priests, Levites, and Israelites or to Abraham, Isaac, and Jacob. Recall that Isaac was to be sacrificed, and that accounts for the broken matzah. Even in Jewish sources there is a Messianic reference to the broken matzah.

Jewish believers in Jesus have a different perspective on the afikomen. The matzah bag holds three pieces of matzah that represent the One God in Israel with a Tri-unity—the Father, (middle and broken piece of matzah) the Son, and the Holy Spirit. The child who finds the afikomen receives a gift. The Son was broken, and we partake of Him to receive the gift of eternal life.

Finally, the word *afikomen* itself is interesting in origin. It apparently comes from a Greek word, *aphikomenos*. This word means "He has come." This part of the seder is described in Isaiah 53. Jesus can be the only one who fulfills this role.

Feast of Unleavened Bread—15th of Nissan
This feast speaks of the deliverance of the children of Israel from Egypt. There was no time for the Israelites to bake bread. But there is another significance to unleavened bread. Sin is often pictured as leaven in the Bible.

Note that when Jesus was crucified, along with two common thieves, Jesus' body was not thrown with the garbage outside the walls of the city. Rather, it was prepared for burial in a new tomb. In the Messianic Psalm 16, David wrote:

> For You will not abandon me to Sheol;
> You will not allow Your Faithful One to see the Pit. (Psalm 16:10)

Jesus did not decay as every other person who has died throughout history. Rather, Jesus was resurrected on the third day. He was sinless and pure. He carried our sins away. Jesus represents us, and He calls us not to sin.

Feast of Firstfruits—16th day of Nissan
The observance of this feast meant that the firstborn was sacred to the Lord. This was an early grain harvest. Barley would have ripened in time for this feast in the early spring. A sheaf of barley was brought to the Lord on this feast day.

It is not surprising that Paul used the illustration of the firstfruits to identify the resurrection of Jesus from the dead. He wrote:

> But now Christ has been raised from the dead, the firstfruits of those who have fallen asleep. For since death came through a man, the resurrection of the dead also comes through a man. For just as in Adam all die, so also in Christ all will be made alive. But each in his own order: Christ, the firstfruits; afterward, at His coming, the people of Christ. (1 Corinthians 15:20–23)

This is also applied to believers, who are set apart to God. They become the firstfruits to God as a result of Jesus' death and resurrection. James wrote:

> By His own choice, He gave us a new birth by the message of truth so that we would be the firstfruits of His creatures. (James 1:18)

Feast of Pentecost—seven weeks and one day from Passover, or the fiftieth day
This feast, you will recall, was a feast of early summer harvest. The firstfruits of the summer crop were brought to the Lord. It also marked the end of the Passover celebration. After the fall of the Temple in AD 70, the celebration of the giving of the Law had become an important part of the Pentecost celebration.

In the New Testament it has a new meaning. Pentecost is the fulfillment of the prophecy of Jeremiah 31:31. This is the new covenant that God has made with His people. There was the sound of the rushing wind. The Jews, who were in Jerusalem for the celebration of this festival, must have wondered if this was the fulfillment of the prophecy of Ezekiel:

I looked and there was a whirlwind coming from the north, a great cloud with five flashing back and forth and brilliant light all around it. In the center of the fire, there was a gleam like amber. The form of four living creatures can from it. And this was their appearance: They had human form, but each of them had four faces and four wings. (Ezekiel 1:4–6)

And again in Ezekiel 3:12, the prophet wrote:

The Spirit then lifted me up, and I heard a great rumbling sound behind me—praise the glory of the LORD in His dwelling place!

The men who had come at the sound of the wind must have wondered whether the Shekinah glory of God was again descending upon Israel. It was indeed the glory of God descending upon the New Israel. The Holy Spirit had come to the hearts of all who believed in Jesus Christ. Peter proclaimed this message in Acts 2. Many came to the church as a result.

Rosh Hashanah—fifth holy day in the fall season and described in the Leviticus 23 listing

The feast of *Rosh Hashanah* was not known as the New Year or "Head of the Year" festival until after the second century AD. Prior to the second century AD, this feast was known as the Feast of Trumpets. Since the sacrificial system ceased with the destruction of the Temple, this feast naturally assumed a new role in Jewish life.

The four spring feasts were fully realized in the coming of Jesus. The fall festivals will fulfill their purpose in the future at the second coming of Jesus. Interestingly, the rabbis described the feasts in with a Messianic fulfillment. They believed that their ancestors had been redeemed from Egypt in the month of Nissan, as shown above. They believed that the three fall feasts spoke of redemption in a future time.

The prophets talked about the Day of the Lord as a day of judgment (see Amos 5:18–20). Zephaniah also spoke of the day of judgment:

The great Day of the LORD is near,
near and rapidly approaching.
Listen, the Day of the LORD—
there the warrior's cry is bitter.
That day is a day of wrath,
a day of trouble and distress,
a day of destruction and desolation,
a day of darkness and gloom,
a day of clouds and blackness,
a day of trumpet and battle cry
against the fortified cities,
and against the high corner towers. (Zephaniah 1:14–16)

Notice the sound of the trumpet. It is not surprising that Jewish people today see this holiday as one of solemnity. They look back over the past year and ask forgiveness for their sins. But the day will come when Israel will repent at the Messiah's return. It will be as Jesus said of His second coming with the sound of the trumpet:

Then the sign of the Son of Man will appear in the sky, and then all the tribes of the land will mourn; and they will see the Son of Man coming on the clouds of heaven with power and great glory. He will send out His angels with a loud trumpet, and they will gather His elect from the four winds, from one end of the sky to the other. (Matthew 24:30–31)

The Day of Atonement—sixth of the holidays from Leviticus 23

Recall that this day is the most solemn and holy of all the days of the Jewish year. During the Temple years, on this day one ram was sacrificed and the blood placed on the mercy seat between the cherubim in the Holy of Holies, first in the Tabernacle and later in the Temple. The other ram became the scapegoat and carried the sins of the people into the wilderness. Remember that without the shedding of blood, there is no remission of sins. This is further supported in the New Testament:

> According to the law almost everything is purified with blood, and without the shedding of blood there is no forgiveness. (Hebrews 9:22)

There is no forgiveness today, without trusting in the death of Jesus. He was God's perfect sacrifice for sin. To all who put their trust in Christ, God says, I will no longer remember your sin (see Jeremiah 31:34). For Israel the day will come when they too will acknowledge the sacrifice of Jesus for sin and find in Him their long-awaited Messiah.

The Feast of Tabernacles—seventh and last holiday from Leviticus 23

Remember that this is the feast of booths. It is a joyous celebration. The people, even today, build a hut or booth, in which they live temporarily during the week of celebration. It is called the feast of Ingathering (see Exodus 23:16). Recall that it is a joyous celebration.

Often the Bible refers to the Day of Judgment as a harvest (see Hosea 6:11; Matthew 13:39; Revelation 14:15). There is a particularly poignant passage in Malachi:

> "For indeed the day is coming, burning like a furnace, when all the arrogant and everyone who commits wickedness will become stubble. The coming day will consume them," says the LORD of Hosts, "not leaving them roots or branches. But for you who fear My name, the sun of righteousness will rise with healing in its wings, and you will go out and playfully jump like calves from the stall. You will trample the wicked, for they will be ashes under the soles of your feet on the day I am preparing," says the LORD of Hosts. (Malachi 4:1–3)

This speaks of the millennial reign of Christ in His kingdom. He will gather in the remnant from both Israel and the Gentiles. That will be a glorious day!

Talk to your children about the prophetic significance of each of these holidays from a Christian perspective. Chart each of these holidays from Leviticus 23. List the feast in the first column. In the second column, give the reference from Leviticus 23. Describe the feast with a word or phrase and place the description in the third column. In the fourth column, write the Christian significance of the feast in its past fulfillment for the spring feasts. Then consider the future fulfillment in the fall feasts.

Activity 7—*View the Video* The Prince of Egypt

Rent or purchase the video, *The Prince of Egypt*. Show the video to your class. Be sure to discuss the video when finished. Even though there are some differences with the biblical text, the video is a good introduction to the events that took place before and during the Passover.

Activity 8—Memorize Exodus 5:1b

In honor of Passover, have the children memorize the verse from Exodus 5:1b. Remind the children that God protected His people from the Egyptians. Review the story of the Passover as the children write and illustrate the verse in their Bible Verse Memory Books.

This is what the Lord, the God of Israel, says: Let My people go, so that they may hold a festival for Me in the wilderness.

WORKSHEETS FOR LESSON 5

ACTIVITY SHEET 1: DREIDEL PATTERN

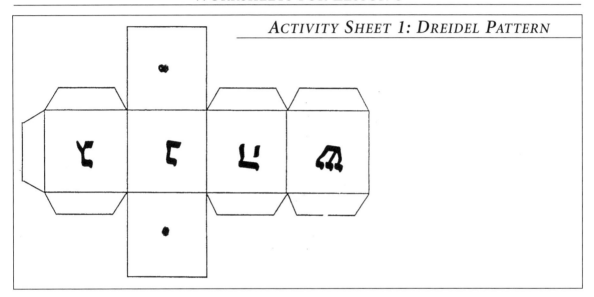

ACTIVITY SHEET 2: MASK PATTERN

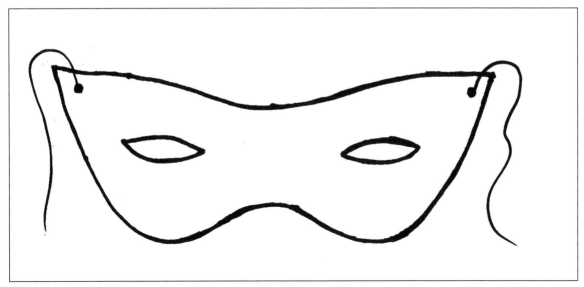

ACTIVITY SHEET 4: TEN COMMANDMENTS (TO BE COPIED)

The Ten Commandments

"I am the Lord your God who brought you at of Egypt, where you were slaves."

"You shall not have any other gods before me."

"You shall not make any statute to serve or worship. If you serve false gods, you and your children will suffer. But if you keep my Commandments, you will experience my love."

"You shall not take the name of the Lord carelessly, but with reverence."

"You shall keep the Sabbath day holy. You may work during six days, but the seventh day is holy to Lord. The Sabbath day is a holy day."

"Show respect for your mother and father that you may live long on the earth."

"You shall not kill."

"You shall not be unfaithful to your husband or wife."

"You shall not steal."

"You shall not speak falsely against her neighbor."

"You must not envy any other person's possessions."

ACTIVITY SHEET 5: SUMMARY CHART OF JEWISH FEASTS

Name of Feast	*Directions:* Fill in the blanks concerning the Jewish Feasts. *Purpose of Feast*	Date Feast Held
	Marks the beginning of the _____ year	September or October
	Marks a time of national repentance, _____, and atonement	October
	Commemorates the wilderness wanderings and the completion of the _____ harvest. This is a joyous and popular feast	October
	Marks the rededication of the temple by Judas Maccabeus, with _____ in the temple and at home	December
	Notes the deliverance of Israel in the time of _____	March
	Marks the Exodus from Egypt and the beginning of the _____ harvest	April 14, 15–21
	Marks the completion of the grain harvest and the commemoration of the giving of the _____	May or June

Adapted from Thomas D. Lea, *The New Testament: Its Background and Message* (Nashville, Tenn.: Broadman & Holman Publishers, 1996), 58.

Christian Faith and Practice—Lessons 6–11

UNIT SUMMARY

This set of lessons will provide the learner with background in the development of the Church through the years since the New Testament. This unit will also focus upon what we believe and will explore the Great Commission in today's world.

OVERVIEW

Objectives

By the end of this unit, the learner should be able to

- review the religious practices from the previous five weeks,
- understand the persons who are significant to the history of the Christian church and be able to describe their contribution to the fulfillment of God's purposes,
- understand and appreciate what we believe as Christian believers, and
- understand how God is still moving in His world through Christian missions.

Content Summary and Rationale

The church did not simply stop growing and becoming at the end of the New Testament era. Very important changes have occurred over the past centuries in the growth and development of the church. We will explore some of the most important persons who have affected the development of the church in the past and some contemporary persons. We will examine some of these more important changes that have brought the Church to the place it is today.

As a Christian believer today, it matters what one believes. We maintain the beliefs of the historic Christian faith. We hold to the authority of the Bible in all matters of faith and practice. It is important for children to be exposed to the historic truths of Christianity. This section affirms those beliefs and provides instruction for children on the ways by which they can strengthen their belief in the Triune God, the authority of the Bible, prayer, and salvation in Jesus Christ.

To complete this unit, we examine the role of the Great Commission in the life and ministry of the Church today. We observe typical contemporary missionaries in their work and ministry on a foreign mission field. Then we look back at the development of modern missions as well as significant missionaries who have brought modern missions to its place today.

Key Concept

There are three key concepts in this set of lessons. First, how has the church become what it is today? In the early centuries, as today, people may die for their faith. These heroes and heroines of the faith are some of God's choicest saints. Two thousand years have passed since the New Testament. There have been dramatic changes in the culture and in the Church since that time. Today, we try to move as close to the New Testament church as we can. This is a dramatic and fascinating story.

Second, our beliefs are firmly planted on the Word of God. We examine what it means to be a Christian, and we explore ways by which children can strengthen their foundational beliefs.

Third, Christian missions is not a "nice" thing to do. God has commanded us in the Great Commission to go and teach the gospel througout the world. We will explore missions in the past and today.

Prior Knowledge Needed

Most children have not been exposed to the history of the Church. For younger children, the past is a difficult concept. But even they can be introduced to the persons who have been significant in the history of the Church. The following lessons will expose them to significant information that may be enlarged in the future.

Christian beliefs are vitally important, making the difference between eternal life and its alternative. Children usually do not have a consistent understanding of beliefs. This section will help them develop the relationship between beliefs and the everyday life they live. It will build a foundation.

The subject of Christian missions is another topic children know little about. This section will provide a foundation for deeper understanding.

RESOURCES FOR TEACHERS AND STUDENTS
• Buchanan, Edward, *Parent/Teacher Handbook: Their Christian Heritage, Vol.* 2 (Nashville, Tenn.: Broadman & Holman, 2003).

• Butler, Trent, ed., *Holman Illustrated Bible Dictionary* (Nashville, Tenn.: Holman Bible Publishers, 2003).
• Dockery, David, ed., *Holman Bible Handbook* (Nashville, Tenn.: Holman Bible Publishers, 1992).
• An encyclopedia—*World Book, Funk and Wagnalls, Britannica,* etc. (may use CD-ROM)

ADDITIONAL SUPPLEMENTARY RESOURCES FOR TEACHERS
• Sims, Lesley, *A Visitor's Guide to Ancient Rome* (London, England: Usborne Publishing, 1999). Available at major bookstores and online.

LESSON 6: THE CHURCH OF THE ROMAN EMPIRE AND THE MEDIEVAL CHURCH

Readings from the Parent/Teacher Handbook: Their Christian Heritage, Vol. 2: "Growth and Develpment of the Church," "The Church of the Roman Empire," and "The Medieval Church"

OBJECTIVES

By the end of this lesson, the learner should be able to
• demonstrate understanding of the role of martyrdom in the history of the early church,
• identify and describe several selected Christian martyrs of the early Church,
• explain why the early church was important in the history of the Church,
• understand the role of the early Church in setting the direction for all that followed,
• identify and describe the role of the monks and monasteries in the Middle Ages,
• differentiate between the Dark Ages and the High Middle Ages, and
• identify scholasticism of the High Middle Ages.

IDENTIFICATIONS

Concepts

Martyr—one who voluntarily suffers death for his or her Christian faith

Caldarium—a Roman hot bath

Edict of Milan—Edict of Emperor Constantine, which provided that the Christian faith was legal in the Roman Empire in AD 313

Dark Ages—period from AD 600 to AD 1000 in which learning declined

High Middle Ages—period from about 1200 to 1500 in which learning increased

Scholasticism—movement to place faith and philosophy into a logical system

Monks—persons who gave up their worldly possessions to join a monastery

Benedictine Rule—rule established by Benedict of Nursia for communal living of monks in a monastery

Refectory—place where the monks ate dinner

Friars—preaching monks, who usually begged for their living

Crusades—wars against the Moslems to free the Holy Land

People

Polycarp: Christian martyr, AD 69–155

Cecilia: Christian martyr, died AD 230

Sebastian: Christian martyr, died AD 288

Constantine: Roman emperor who converted and legalized Christianity in the Roman Empire with the Edict of Milan, AD 313

Augustine: early Church father

Vikings: seafaring men from Scandanavia

Benedict of Nursia: founder of the Benedictine Rule for monasteries; died c. AD 547

Francis of Assisi: celebrated as an imitator of Christ; founded the Franciscan friars; died in 1228

Places

Rome, Italy: center of the Roman Empire and later home of the Roman Catholic pope

Nursia, Italy: place where Benedict founded his monastery for communal living of the monks

Assisi, Italy: place where Francis started his band of friars

MATERIALS NEEDED

Parent/Teacher Handbook: Their Christian Heritage, Vol. 2

Activity Sheets for Lesson 6

Crayons and markers

Construction paper

Posterboard

Blank sheets of white paper for drawing

Roll of shelf paper or butcher paper

Masking tape and plastic tape

Reusable adhesive

3x5-index cards

Lined paper for writing

Tempera paints

Brass paper fasteners

Card stock paper for duplication

Scissors

LEARNING ACTIVITIES FOR LESSON 6

Activity 1—Time Line for the Growth and Development of the Church

Read "Growth and Development of the Church" in the handbook. Pay particular attention to the time line. This will provide an overview for the first two lessons in this unit.

Turn to Activity Sheets 1-A and 1-B. This expanded time line and map of the Roman Empire shows when and where things happened in the early Church and beyond.

Have your students make a booklet containing the important persons, places, and events from this time period and beyond. Without a foundational understanding of the development of the Church, a student will have difficulty understanding how denominations began or why they are from a particular denomination. This is an important unit. Contrary to popular opinion, it is also an exciting unit. Younger children will need a lot of help with this exercise, but they do need to be exposed to the names of these people.

Activity 2—Polycarp: Early Martyr

Study the subsection "The Persecuted Church—AD 68 to 313," including "Polycarp," in the handbook.

To be a Christian in those early days of the Church meant that you could be persecuted and even killed. Remember that Jesus said, "If anyone wants to be My follower, he must deny himself, take up his cross, and follow Me" (Mark 8:34). For the early Christians, that meant that they could be tortured, put in a den of lions, or sent to die at the hands of the gladiators. Why would they take that risk? They listened to Jesus Christ and loved Him more than they even loved life itself. They believed that eternal life was more to be cherished and valued than their own lives. Not everyone is called upon to be a martyr, but it does happen, even today.

One of those early believers who was martyred was Polycarp. He was the bishop of Smyrna. During the reign of Marcus Aurelius, a violent persecution broke out. The pagans insisted that the Christians give up their faith in Jesus Christ. The pagans thought that if they could punish the believers severely enough, the

Christians would turn away from Jesus and become pagan again. But the Christians had found something better than life itself. They had found peace with God through Jesus. They would not give that up for any amount of torture, nor would they bow to Caesar as a god.

The pagan proconsul arrested Polycarp. Polycarp was hidden, until one of the boys in his home was threatened and told where Polycarp was hiding. He was upstairs in a room in someone else's home. He had a vision of being burned. The soldiers came and surrounded the home. Polycarp surrendered and invited the soldiers to dine before they took him away. They set him on a donkey and rode him into town. The proconsul took him into his chariot. He ordered Polycarp to bow to Caesar. Polycarp refused. They threw him out of the chariot and forced him to walk into the arena.

In the arena a voice was heard from heaven: "Be strong and act as a man." He was again told by the pagans to forsake his foolishness and bow to Caesar as a god. Polycarp refused and said that for eighty years he had served Christ and would not stop now. The proconsul became angry and told him that he would set the wild beasts on him. "Call for them," said Polycarp. "If you despise them, then I will have you burned to death," said the ruler. Polycarp told the proconsul to burn him. Polycarp told the ruler that "it will be more bearable for me to be burned with fire here than it will be for the ruler to be burned with eternal fire in the next life." He was not burned up in the fire, so the ruler had him killed with a dagger.

Select several children to play the parts of the characters in this story. You may want to make some props to make the story more realistic.

When you have finished, talk about how important it is to stand up for what you believe.

Activity 3—Story Spin Wheel

Read the story of Cecilia in the handbook. Tell the story of this brave young woman to your class. Discuss what she did.

In advance of this session, duplicate copies of Activity Sheets 3-A and 3-B onto sheets of card stock paper. Have the children cut out the two parts. Then fasten the top sheet to the bottom with a brass paper fastener.

Have the children turn the top sheet so that the line from the first third of the opening is vertical. Use masking tape to hold the sheets on the desk in place. In the first third, write:

Cecilia—
    She was the daughter of a Roman senator.
    In her youth she became a Christian.
    Her father arranged her marriage to Valerian.

Move the top sheet spin wheel to the second area and write:
    Cecilia married Valerian against her wishes.
    Cecilia led Valerian and his brother to faith in Jesus.
    Valerian and his brother buried Christians in the catacombs.

Move the top sheet spin wheel to the third area and write:
    Cecilia's husband and brother were killed for their faith.
    Cecilia was put on trial.
    Cecilia's faith and virtue led many others to trust Christ.

Talk about the story in review. God does not call all of us to die for our faith, but He does want us to be faithful to Him. Look at our memory verse for this lesson:

Blessed are those who are persecuted for righteousness, because the kingdom of heaven is theirs. (Matthew 5:10)

Activity 4—Emperor Constantine Allows Christian Faith

The persecution of Christians came to an end when Emperor Constantine became the ruler of the Roman Empire. It happened like this. At the Milvian Bridge to the west of Rome, there was a decisive battle between Constantine and Maxentius. Maxentius ruled part of the Empire, while Licinius and Constantine ruled other parts.

On the night of the battle, Constantine had a vision. He saw the *chi rho* symbol in the sky and took that to mean that Christ would be victorious. (Recall the symbol from the last lesson.) Constantine had the monogram *chi rho* emblazoned on the shields of his troops. Constantine won a stunning victory. In AD 313 Constantine passed the Edict of Milan, which allowed Christianity as a legitimate religion in the Empire. Persecution of Christians came to an end.

Licinius still posed a threat to Constantine. The final showdown came in AD 324, when Licinius believed that some of his troops were Christians and loyal to Constantine. Licinius took action against the men, who he thought were traitors to his cause. That was a miscalculation on his part. Constantine raised a large army and naval fleet. The two forces met at Hadrianopolis. Constantine won another great victory and eventually Licinius surrendered.

The defeat of Licinius made it possible for Constantine to promote Christianity. Constantine forbade pagan worship. He built churches. He restored property to Christians that had been confiscated by the pagan emperors. He got involved in theological controversies. Constantine convened the Council of Nicea in AD 325 and established Christian orthodoxy.

Interestingly, however, he remained as a catechumen until he was on his deathbed in AD 337. Catechumens were persons who expressed the desire to become a Christian. They were appointed sponsors or a godfather or godmother. The godparent was responsible for the Christian instruction of the catechumen. The godparent was also responsible to observe the moral life of the new convert. The entire process usually took two to three years and culminated in baptism on either Easter or Pentecost. But Constantine did not receive baptism until twenty-five years after his conversion to Christianity.

With the exception of a brief period when Julian became emperor, the peace with Christians was secure. Julian was a pagan and tried to restore paganism and stop the Christians. He was unsuccessful and ruled for only a brief period of time. Christianity was secure. It became the religion of Rome.

On Activity Sheet 4 you will find a shield. Enlarge and duplicate copies of the shield for your students. After you have told the story about the end of persecution to Christians with the rise of Constantine, have the children make a shield with the *chi rho* symbol emblazoned upon it. Use colored markers or crayons to make the symbol.

Activity 5—Augustine: Doctor of the Church

With the struggle for survival now behind, the church had to pay attention to developing its doctrine becoming God's "called out ones." In the Western Church three leaders came forward. They were Jerome (AD 331–420), Ambrose (AD 339–397), and Augustine (AD 354–430). They are all very interesting men and were influential in the Church.

Jerome was a gifted scholar. He studied and understood great classical literature, such as Virgil and Cicero. As a young man, he felt called to become a hermit monk. After several years Jerome had a vision.

In the vision, he was accused of being more a "follower of Cicero than Christ." From that point on, Jerome put his classical learning behind. He became a Bible scholar. He taught himself Greek and later Hebrew. He was commissioned to translate the Bible into Latin. He translated it from the Greek Septuagint version and the Greek New Testament. After he learned Hebrew, Jerome returned to his work and corrected parts of the Old Testament. His version became the official Latin Vulgate version of the Bible for the Roman Catholic Church. For the rest of his life, Jerome wrote commentaries on the Scripture.

Ambrose was a theologian. At the death of the heretical bishop of Milan, Ambrose was chosen by the people to become the bishop there. He was a good administrator. He worked with politicians, like Emperor Theodosius. He was the first theologian to coerce a ruler of the state. He opposed the heresy of Arianism. He introduced hymn singing in church. He wrote extensively on living a practical Christian life. One of his most important roles was that of helping Augustine come to know Christ and grow as a Christian.

The names of these doctors of the Western Church should become recognized by your students. You will want to spend some time in advance of this session to study the life of Augustine. You will find a short biographical passage "Augustine of Hippo (AD 354–430)" in the handbook. Talk with your students about each of these men but focus most upon Augustine.

At the conclusion, have copies of the questions about Augustine ready for the students to answer (see Activity Sheet 5). Summarize the importance of Augustine. He was important for the Catholic Church, but he was also very influential on the Protestant theologians Luther and Calvin.

Activity 6—Structuring the Monk's Day

The Vandals and the other Germanic tribes overran the Roman Empire. It lingered for a while, but finally law and order broke down and the Roman Empire came to an end. The Dark Ages followed. Learning declined to almost nothing. Life for the common person was a matter of survival. To protect themselves from others who would harm them, people banded together on a manor or plantation around the lord of the manor, their protector. They would work the land for the lord in exchange for protection. Each manor had its own parish church, with a priest to perform weddings and funerals. The priests did not even have an eighth-grade education.

Outside of the manor, the only other place of safety was the monastery. The monastery provided education for those who could afford it. It also kept boys who were homeless or desired to become monks. The monastery was the only hospital. In short, the monastery was a haven in a very difficult world. Discipline in the monastery was very rigid.

Activity Sheet 6-A shows the structure of the monk's day. Talk about Benedict of Nursia and the monastery after reading "The Dark Ages" in the handbook. Then pass out Activity Sheet 6-B. Have the students complete this sheet. At the conclusion, discuss the harshness of life in the monastery. Help the learners to see that devotion to God was an essential part of life in the monastery. People renounced the world voluntarily in order to find salvation and new life in Christ.

Activity 7—Benedictine Rule

If your children are in third grade or above, you may want them to go to the library, view a CD encyclopedia, or go online to research the topic of medieval monks and monasteries.

Have them look at the Benedictine Rule. As an example, it includes the following sections:

1. Concerning the Kinds of Monks and Their Manner of Living
22. How the Monks Shall Sleep

39 Concerning the Amount of Food

40. Concerning the Amount of Drink

55. Concerning Clothes and Shoes

The life of the monk was very regulated because it was necessary for them to live together harmoniously. Ask the children to think about their life in the classroom. What rules do you need in the classroom to live harmoniously. Brainstorm ideas. Record those ideas on the chalkboard. Then summarize and reduce the number of rules. Students may want to write these on a sheet of posterboard and hang the poster in the classroom.

Activity 8—Wordfind on the Monastery

To complete the study of the monks and monasteries, duplicate the wordfind for the Monastery on Activity Sheet 8. Have children find the words in the sentences. Then have them complete the wordfind. Discuss the wordfind with them.

Activity 9—Francis of Assisi Story Cube

Read the section entitled "High Middle Ages," and the subsection "Francis of Assisi (1182 to 1226)" from the handbook. Talk to the students about Francis of Assisi. If your children are old enough, you may want them to research about the life of Francis of Assisi. They may find help online, in the library, or in a CD- ROM encyclopedia.

In advance of your session, duplicate the cube for Activity Sheet 9. Have the children answer the five Ws by using simple drawings and one- or two-word descriptions for each of the five squares. The five Ws include: *who* he was, *when* he was born and when he died, *where* he lived and ministered, *what* he did and what happened to him, and *why* he chose to live and act as he did. Note the fact that Francis wanted to be like Jesus. He is revered by Protestants and Catholics alike for his devotion to Christ.

Activity 10—Memorize Matthew 5:10

Think back over the activities for this lesson. The verse for memorization relates particularly to the martyrs. Tell the children that we may not be asked to give our lives for our faith in Jesus Christ, but there will be times in life when you may be ridiculed for your faith or criticized. In those times this verse should help.

Blessed are those who are persecuted for righteousness, because the kingdom of heaven is theirs.

Have students draw a picture and add this verse to their Bible Verse Memory Books.

Activity Sheet 1-A: Time Line for the Growth and Development of the Church

The Church of the Roman Empire (AD 68–480)

The Persecuted Church (AD 68–313)

1. Polycarp (AD 69–155)—early Christian martyr

2. Cecilia (died AD 230)—early Christian martyr

3. Sebastian (died AD 288)—early Christian martyr

The Church Fathers (AD 313–480)

1. Emperor Constantine (c. AD 272–337)

2. Jerome (AD 331–420)—translator of the Latin Vulgate and doctor of the church

3. Ambrose (AD 339–397)—bishop of Milan and doctor of the church

4. Augustine of Hippo (AD 354–430)

The Medieval Church (AD 480–1517)

1. Benedict of Nursia (AD 480–547)—founded monastic group living

2. Francis of Assisi (1182–1226)—imitator of Christ; founder of order of Franciscans

The Reformation (1517–1776)

1. Martin Luther (1483–1546)—reformer and founder of Lutheranism

2. John Calvin (1509–1564)—protestant theologian

3. John Knox (c. 1514–1572)—founder of Presbyterianism

4. Johannes Kepler (1571–1630)—astronomer after Copernicus

5. Robert Boyle (1627–1691)—developed modern laws of chemistry

6. Sir Isaac Newton (1642–1747)—physicist and mathematician

The Enlightenment, Revolutions, Revivals, Missions (1776–1900)

1. John Wesley (1703–1791)—founder of the Methodist Church

2. Robert Raikes (1736–1811)—founder of the Sunday school

3. William Carey (1761–1834)—father of modern missions, specifically India

4. David Livingstone (1813–1873)—missionary to Africa

5. Lottie Moon (1840–1912)—missionary to China

Modern Period (1900 to the Present)

1. William Franklin Graham (1918 to the Present)—evangelist of the twentieth century

ACTIVITY SHEET 1-B: MAP OF THE ROMAN EMPIRE

ACTIVITY SHEET 3-A: TOP SHEET OF STORY SPIN WHEEL

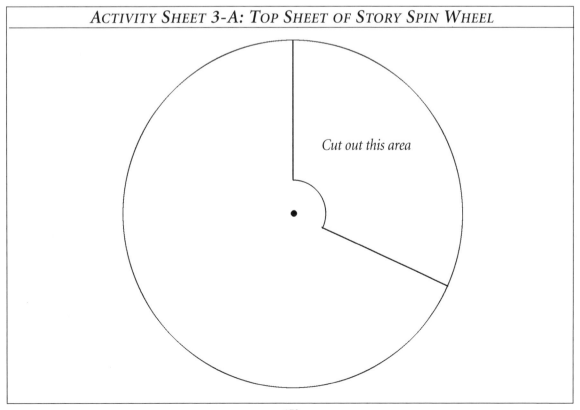

ACTIVITY SHEET 3-B: BASE OF STORY SPIN WHEEL

Directions: Cut out the top circle and remove the marked area. Then cut out this circle. Place a paper fastener through the center of both. Write text in each of the three areas, as you move the top sheet around to the three areas.

ACTIVITY SHEET 4: SHIELD FOR CONSTANTINE'S VICTORY AT THE BATTLE OF MILVIAN BRIDGE

Chi Rho symbol to be drawn on the shield:

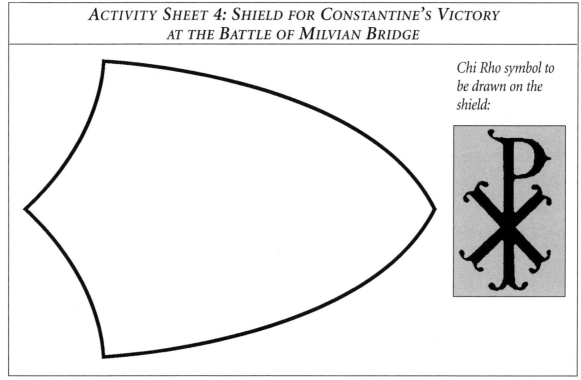

ACTIVITY SHEET 5: QUESTIONS ON THE LIFE OF AUGUSTINE

1. What was the title of the book that told about the life of Augustine? _____

2. Augustine's memory of his schooldays was painful. He remembered that the teacher would strike his _____ when the teacher found him not working.

3. He studied grammar, poetry, and _____, which is the subject of persuading others to your point of view.

4. His mother, _____, wanted Augustine to become a Christian. She was influential in his life.

5. Augustine taught _____ for a period of time.

6. In a garden, he heard the voice of a child say, "Take up and read." Augustine was struggling over whether to become a Christian. He read from Romans 13:13–14. In tears he turned his life to

   _____.

7. For the next thirty-five years, Augustine served as the bishop of _____ on the northern coast of Africa.

8. He used his great scholarship and learning to further the kingdom of _____. He died as the Vandals were at the gates.

ACTIVITY SHEET 6-A: STRUCTURE OF THE DAY IN THE LIFE OF A MONK

Sundown to about 6 a.m.
Sleep from sundown to about 2 a.m.
Private reading and meditation
Church service—Nocturns
Sleep (about 1 hour)
Church service—Lauds
Private reading and meditation to 6 a.m.

6 a.m. to Noon
Church service—Prime
Work
Church service—Terce and Mass
Work
Church service—Sext

Noon to 6 p.m.
Work
Sleep
Church service—None
Work—copying manuscripts

6 p.m. to Sundown
Church service—Vespers
Private reading and meditation
Church service—Compline

Four Parts in a Day of a Monk
1. Work for five hours—farming, baking, etc.
2. Study the Bible or copy manuscripts
3. Pray and attend church services, five hours a day
4. Eat and sleep

ACTIVITY SHEET 6-B: WHAT MIGHT LIFE BE LIKE AS A MONK?

If you had lived in those days, what things did the monk do that you would have liked and what things would you not have liked?

Directions: Write an L in front of the things you would have liked. Write an N in front of those things you would not have liked.

_____	1. Absolutely no talking during meals
_____	2. Caring for cows and sheep
_____	3. Wearing black robes
_____	4. Studying in the classroom
_____	5. Reading books
_____	6. Never leaving the monastery
_____	7. Copying the Bible and other books
_____	8. Caring for the sick
_____	9. Helping people in need
_____	10. Never taking a bath
_____	11. Praying regularly to God
_____	12. Having head and face shaved
_____	13. Frequently washing hands
_____	14. No personal life
_____	15. No social life
_____	16. Being protected from evil people

ACTIVITY SHEET 8: WORDFIND FOR MONASTIC MOVEMENT

Words to Find

1. B_____ was the founder of the commu nal monasticism.
2. Four hours each day were spent in C_____ manuscripts like the B_____.
3. In the center of the monastery was a quiet G_____, known as the C_____.
4. A man in the monastery was known as a M_____ and he lived by the Benedictine R_____.
5. Each monastery had a R_____ where the members ate their meals in S_____.
6. Each monastery had a S_____ where the monks educated boys from both inside and outside the monastery.
7. Monks were asked to S _____ their evil desires, _____ personal feelings, and personal wishes in order to live holy lives.
8. Each monk had to W_____ in the fields or doing other jobs at least five hours each day.

```
L A S P C L U J Z Y J C O U S
J W W S I L E N C E S H L W A
B L W E H L B N F C S G R L K
O C L U H I O I H X T Q R Z R
Z L U D F Z X O B I E T Y E O
H M N B C C O R U L E C F D W
W Q H U K L U M M S E E N V N
H C Q S R O K M H P C B U L J
U R U O J I O G O T E R S Z B
Q M O P K S M A O N O A Z Z E
E M Y P G T F R E D K J O J H
W N Y X J E Y D F O O M N C O
Q G P Z Z R I E G Q L V X L U
Y R R N E C G N I Y P O C S F
M I B M T O Q A Z U C K R D U
```

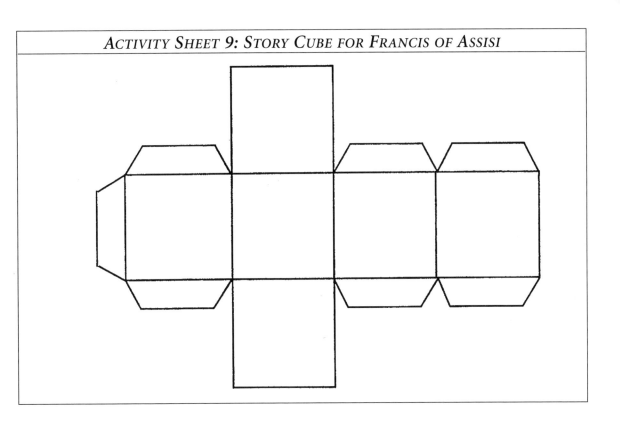

LESSON 7: THE REFORMATION

Readings from the Parent/Teacher Handbook: Their Christian Heritage, Vol. 2:
"*The Reformation—1517 to 1646*"

OBJECTIVES

By the end of this lesson, the learner should be able to

- identify the events of the Reformation, and
- explain the significant persons of the Reformation, particularly Martin Luther.

IDENTIFICATIONS

Concepts

Reformation—an attempt to reform or correct the abuses of the Church

Printing—invention of moveable type that made it possible to reproduce many copies of a manuscript

Relics—things that had spiritual significance that were venerated by the people

Ninety-five theses—sentences of Martin Luther that identified the abuses in the Church

People

Martin Luther: leader of the Reformation, who nailed his ninety-five theses to the church door at Wittenberg on October 31, 1517

Johannes Gutenberg: inventor of moveable type; Reformation would not have likely happened without printing to disseminate the literature on abuses in the Church

Frederick the Wise: Duke of Saxony who was responsible for Luther's protection

Charles V: Holy Roman Emperor from Spain who condemned Luther

Katherina von Bora: former nun and wife of Martin Luther

Places

Wittenberg, Germany: town in which Luther was teaching and the parish church where Luther nailed the ninety-five theses on the church door

Worms, Germany: town where Luther was tried before the court of the Holy Roman Emperor, Charles V

MATERIALS NEEDED

Parent/Teacher Handbook: Their Christian Heritage, Vol. 2

Activity Sheets for Lesson 7

Crayons and markers

Posterboard

Blank sheets of white paper for drawing

Masking tape and plastic tape

Reusable adhesive

Lined paper for writing

Pictures from magazines

Tape recorder or CD player

LEARNING ACTIVITIES FOR LESSON 7

Activity 1—Johannes Gutenberg and Moveable Type

It may seem strange to discuss moveable type when we are dealing with the Reformation. The Reformation would not likely have occurred as it did were it not for this invention of Johannes Gutenberg.

Johannes Gutenberg was born about 1395 in an aristocratic family. He probably learned metallurgy from his uncle, who was a master at the mint. What Gutenberg did that was so unique was to create a mold in which letters could be cast of equal size and quality. This made possible the creation of typefaces that could be set by hand in a large frame or form. Wedges were used to hold the type in place.

Gutenberg also developed ink for his printing from the tempera colors of the Flemish artists. He experimented until he found ink that would create the effects that he desired. Some presses still work similarly to those of Gutenberg, although the process for setting type is very different today. Type is machine set, not set by hand.

Gutenberg created very beautiful manuscript books. Some of his Bibles are still extant in Germany, the United States, and other countries of the world.

Without the invention of the press, it would not have been possible to communicate the writings of Luther so generally throughout Germany. The people became very interested in the theological issues as a result of the printed material that they received. This helped to bring popular support to the work of the Reformation that Luther started in 1517.

Tell the students about the work of Gutenberg. You can search the British Library Web site for digitized images of the Gutenberg Bible. You may want to show this to your students. It is found at http://prodigi.bl.uk/gutenbg/default.asp.

Activity 2—Letter and Design Poster

Have the children work in small groups and letter a poster with the great verse of the Reformation from Romans 1:17b, "The righteous will live by faith."

Ask them to decorate the poster with pictures that represent the Reformation. Martin Luther, the Bible, the ninety-five theses, the cross, etc. may be used. The students may find additional suggestions in a CD-ROM encyclopedia, under the "Reformation."

Discuss the meaning of this great verse and its meaning to Martin Luther.

Activity 3—Printing and a Manuscript: Luther's Great Hymn "A Mighty Fortress Is Our God"

You may wish to try your hand at some manuscript printing. If you have access to a computer with different font types and a color ink-jet printer, you can create a manuscript in a matter of minutes that will demonstrate some of the beauty and significance of printing in today's world. You will find the words for Luther's great hymn "A Mighty Fortress Is Our God" on Activity Sheet 3.

You might choose a type, such as Script MT Bold, or experiment with other fonts. They are available at the top of the screen in your word processor. You can also change the size of the font in the little window to the right of the font style. You may find a border from computer images or find a border at a craft store to cut out and place the manuscript behind it as a frame. A color ink-jet printer will produce the manuscript and the border (if you have access to borders on your computer). This would be a good project for your students to complete and take home.

You will want to talk about the origin of Luther's hymn from the Reformation. Luther composed the hymn in 1529. It is based upon Psalm 46. This hymn became the hymn of the Reformation. The music was also written by Luther and is believed to have been an adaptation of a Gregorian melody.

Activity 4 —"A Mighty Fortress Is Our God"

Listen to the great hymn of the Reformation. Have the children sing the words to the music. You can find the music on the following Web site: www.cyberhymnal.org/htm/m/i/mightyfo.htm.

Discuss the meaning of the words of this great hymn. Tie the meaning of the words to the Reformation. Why was this great hymn the battle cry of the Reformation?

Activity 5—The Ninety-five Theses of Luther

Why was the Reformation necessary? There were many problems in the Roman Catholic Church. We will not go into all of the reasons. They are too complex. But we can examine some of the more obvious theological reasons.

During this time the Church was in the process of beautifying Rome. This cost money. Clerics from Rome were dispatched by the pope to other countries to sell indulgences. An indulgence promised that if you had sinned, you could simply pay for an indulgence and you would be forgiven. The money would then go to Rome and help pay for the expenses of the artists who were working in Rome.

Be sure to read "Martin Luther (1483–1546)" in the handbook.

Martin Luther was teaching at the University of Wittenberg at the time. He read Paul's Letter to the Romans and was outraged by the attempts of the Church to sell God's forgiveness. To respond, Luther nailed his ninety-five theses to the church door at Wittenberg. You may obtain a copy of the ninety-five theses from the Web site for Project Wittenberg at http://www.iclnet.org/pub/resources/text/wittenberg/luther/web/ninetyfive.html.

Read several of the theses, such as the following: 6, 45, 50, 51, 53, 62, 82, and 86. Talk about their meaning. It is not possible for a man to forgive sins. Only God can forgive sins. God does this freely by His grace. Grace is a free gift of God, not given because of our works of righteousness. Look at the passage of Scripture from the apostle Paul, Ephesians 2:8–9:

> For by grace you are saved through faith, and this is not from yourselves; it is God's gift—not from works, so that no one can boast.

Have your students work in small groups, using posterboard to write several of the theses of Martin Luther. Use Ephesians 2:8–9 and the memory verse for today, Romans 1:16–17. Write these Scriptures on the posterboard along with the theses. How did the world react to Luther's bold assault on the Church at Rome?

Activity 6—Aftermath of Luther's Assault on Rome Through the Ninety-five Theses

On Activity Sheet 6 you will find a list of possible responses to Luther. Duplicate the list and have the children guess what things happened as a result of the ninety-five theses.

Talk about this with the children.

Activity 7—Time Line of Luther's Life

Martin Luther stands out as one of those rare persons who changed the course of the history of the Western world. Cut sheets of posterboard in half. Have the children work in small groups. Each of the groups may take two or three of the events in Luther's life and make a poster with the date, the event, and a picture of that event. Show a connection among the events by running a string of yarn the length of all of the posters. Your reading and several additional items will provide material for the time line. You do not need to include all of these items. Include only those items that you think need to be included from the following:

1483 Born in Eisleben, Germany, to Hans and Margarethe Luther
1502 Graduated from the University of Erfurt with a Bachelor of Arts degree
1505 Graduated with a master of arts degree
   Was caught under a tree that was struck by lightning; promised, "St. Ann, I will become a monk!"
   Entered the Augustinian Monastery
1507 Was ordained a priest
1512 Earned his doctor of theology degree

1515–1516 Read Romans and found "justification by faith!" Taught at the University of Wittenberg

1517 Nailed the 95 Theses to the Wittenberg church door (October 31, All Saints' Day)

1520 Luther publicly burned the "Bull of Excommunication" from the pope

1521 Was tried before the Holy Roman Emperor, Charles V. Told the court about his writings, stating "Here I stand!"

1521–1522 Was sent to Wartburg Castle for his safety by Frederick the Wise
Translation of the New Testament was completed

1525 Married Katharina von Bora

1529 Wrote the Large Catechism and his great hymn, "A Mighty Fortress Is Our God"

1534 Completed the German Bible

1546 Died on the way home from Mansfeld, Germany

Activity 8—Results of the Reformation

Martin Luther left his mark on history. A variety of changes happened in the world. All of these changes may not be directly attributable to the work of Martin Luther in the Reformation, but he did affect all of them.

Below is a list of some of the changes. Provide construction paper for drawing. Ask different children to illustrate each of these changes. You may want the children to go to the library or use a CD-ROM encyclopedia to help with the illustrations.

1. Luther advocated public education and wrote extensively to have the civil government assume responsibility for educating children.

2. Dutch artists, such as Jan Vermeer, avoided painting pictures of the Holy Family, which were so popular with Catholic artists. Instead, he painted scenes that were moral scenes but did not violate the commandment against making graven images.

3. Science made strides and could not be held back by the authority of the Catholic Church. Previously, Galileo was censured by the church for his scientific discoveries. Now scientists did not have to fear the inquisition of the church.

4. Hymnology in churches improved through singing hymns such as "A Mighty Fortress Is Our God." This was further improved by composers like Johann Sebastian Bach.

5. The Roman Catholic Church brought reform to itself through the Council of Trent. Some of the abuses of the church were corrected.

Activity 9—Memorize Romans 1:16–17

Martin Luther made a difference in his world. He came to understand that God provides His grace freely for all. There is no charge for grace. God loves us. He wants us to find salvation in His Son, Jesus Christ. Then we must live by faith. Memorize the following great verses. They are verses that you will want to stay with you as you grow older.

For I am not ashamed of the gospel, because it is God's power for salvation to everyone who believes, first to the Jew, and also to the Greek. For in it God's righteousness is revealed from faith to faith, just as it is written: "The righteous will live by faith."

You will definitely want the children to add these verses to their Bible Verse Memory Books and illustrate these great truths.

ACTIVITY SHEET 3: "A MIGHTY FORTRESS IS OUR GOD"

. *A mighty fortress is our God,*
A bulwark never failing;
Protecting us with staff and rod,
And power all prevailing.
   What if the nations rage
And surging seas rampage;

What though the mountains fall,
The Lord is God of all;
The Lord of hosts is with us.
(Public Domain)

ACTIVITY SHEET 6: RESULTS OF LUTHER'S WRITINGS

Directions: Check the items that you think happened as a result of Luther's ninety-five theses.

___1. People went to confession as a result of Luther's writings.

___2. People said that the sale of indulgences should not continue.

___3. The ninety-five theses were translated from Latin to German.

___4. The Catholic Church was angry with Luther.

___5. The Catholic Church forgave Luther.

___6. The Church had Luther's writings burned.

___7. The church leaders wanted to burn Luther at the stake.

___8. Later in his life, Luther recanted or turned back to the Church of Rome.

LESSON 8: THE MODERN CHURCH

Readings from the Parent/Teacher Handbook: Their Christian Heritage, Vol. 2: "The Enlightenment, Revolutions, Revivals and Missions—1646 to 1900," and "The Modern Period—1900 to the Present"

OBJECTIVES
By the end of this lesson, the learner should be able to
- identify and explain the significance and ministry of John Wesley,
- explore the modern period from the 19th and 20th centuries, and
- identify events and facts from the life of Billy Graham.

IDENTIFICATIONS
Concepts
Revival—an important way that God uses to stir His people to a deeper faith

Naturalism—making science a god and has greatly influenced our culture

People
John Wesley: student of the Word of God, preacher and founder of Methodism

George Whitefield: evangelist and preacher, contemporary with Wesley

Billy Graham: 20th century evangelist, who holds crusades, calling people to repentance

Places
Georgia, USA: where Wesley came to the New World to evangelize and start churches

Charlotte, NC: birthplace of Billy Graham

MATERIALS NEEDED
Parent/Teacher Handbook: Their Christian Heritage, Vol. 2
Activity Sheets for Lesson 8
Crayons and markers
Posterboard
Pencils
Blank sheets of white paper for drawing
Masking tape and plastic tape
Lined paper for writing
Construction paper
Pictures from magazines

LEARNING ACTIVITIES FOR LESSON 8

Activity 1—John Wesley: Founder of Methodism
Read "John Wesley (1703 to 1791)" in the handbook. Talk about the life of this great saint of God who started the denomination of Methodism and evangelized both in England and America.

Have copies of the crossword puzzle ready to pass out as a review for the study of Wesley. You will find the puzzle on Activity Sheet 1. After the children have finished and you have checked their answers, summarize what they have discovered.

Activity 2—Questions About the Wesley Brothers and Whitefield
Duplicate the sheet with the set of questions on Activity Sheet 2. After you have thoroughly discussed the material on John Wesley from "The Enlightenment, Revolutions, Revivals, and Missions" in the handbook, ask the students to respond to the questions. Go over the answers with your children and discuss them.

Activity 3—Adoration to God
Adoration means "to give honor to God." There are many examples in the Bible of different acts of adoration. Have your children match the acts listed below with the Bible references. (There may be more than one reference to the description.)

Taking off your shoes:_____

Bowing down:_____

Kiss on the feet:_____

Covering your mouth:_____

Bowing the knee:_____

References: Genesis 41: 43   Job 21:5   Luke 7:38   Genesis 43:26   Exodus 3:5
            Psalm 39:9   Daniel 2:46   Joshua 5:15   Job 29:9

Activity 4—Hymn, "O for a Thousand Tongues to Sing"

One of the best known of the six thousand hymns of Charles Wesley is the hymn, "O for a Thousand Tongues to Sing." Recall from the last activity that adoration means to give honor to God. Charles Wesley's hymn was a song of adoration. The words of verses 1–3 are as follows:

O for a thousand tongues to sing
My great Redeemer's praise,
The glories of my God and King,
The triumphs of His grace!

My gracious Master and my God,
Assist me to proclaim,
To spread through all the earth abroad
The honors of Thy name.

Jesus! the name that charms my fears,
That bids our sorrow cease;
Tis music in the sinner's ear,
Tis life, and health, and peace.

Divide the class into three groups. Have each group take one of the verses and write the words of verse on large paper. Allow space below the words for the children to illustrate the significant words. Here are just a couple of exampes: *many persons singing* from verse one, *the earth* from verse two, and *good health and peace* from verse three.

After completing the exercise, have each group share their posters. Talk about the meaning of the words for each verse.

Activity 5—Robert Raikes

Robert Raikes was mentioned in the introduction to the section "The Enlightenment, Revolutions, Revivals, and Missions—1646 to 1900" in the handbook. He is a person who has been beloved by children for several centuries. He started the Sunday school. Here is his story.

Raikes was born in 1702. He was the editor of the *Gloucester Journal,* which was the newspaper for the English town of Gloucester. Raikes was concerned for the many children whom he found playing on the streets of Gloucester only on Sunday. He learned that many of these children were chimney sweeps, coal mine workers, and factory workers. Factories kept these children chained to their jobs. They were as young as six to twelve years of age. They were forced to do heavy work. On Sunday they were on the streets, where they were swearing and fighting.

Raikes was very concerned for prison reform. As he studied the situation, he found that many of these children ended up in prison. He decided to take some preventive action. He hired four women to serve as teachers in his Sunday school. Some of the children were afraid to come to Sunday school. They did not have fancy clothes. But Raikes told them that all they needed was a clean face and combed hair.

The purpose of the Sunday school was to teach the children to read and write. He used the Bible and three other textbooks to accomplish this. The result was that the children were transformed by their study, moral teaching, and church attendance. Several of the factory owners observed that the children's behavior had greatly improved as a result of their involvement in church, Sunday school, and moral guidance.

The Sunday school grew rapidly. It spread throughout England and then to America. By the time of his death in 1811, the Sunday school in England had more than 400,000 students in attendance each week. By 1931 in England, it had grown to 1.25 million children.

In America it took a slightly different direction. The Sunday school was not focused on prison reform. It was aimed at teaching the Bible. Public schools took over most of the teaching of reading. There is still a very important place for Sunday school to teach the Bible and Christian principles. There is also a desperate need to teach moral character education as well.

On the average Sunday morning there are four million volunteer teachers ready to teach God's Word in the Sunday school. There are more people in attendance than at all of the NFL games in America. Sunday school still has a significant role to play in our churches.

After you have talked with your children about Robert Raikes and the Sunday school, give them each a copy of Activity Sheet 5. Have them complete the activity. Conclude the study by singing the old favorite Sunday school hymn "Jesus Loves Me."

Activity 6—*Your Experience in Sunday School*

Have each child answer the following questions:

1. How long have you been coming to Sunday school?
2. What do you like best about Sunday school?
3. What is your favorite Bible story from Sunday school?
4. How does Sunday school help you at school?
5. How does Sunday school help you at home?
6. What is your favorite memory verse from Sunday school?
7. What would you miss if you did not have Sunday school?
8. Who is your favorite Sunday school teacher? Why?

Perhaps not everyone in the group can respond to every question, but have several children share their answers with the whole group. Talk about the reasons why Sunday school is so important. Consider things like learning about Jesus and knowing God, how to become a child of God, etc.

Activity 7—"Katy's Metaphysical Adventure" *(Older Children)*

Naturalism is a very difficult concept for children. However, on television, in school, and even at an amusement park, children will be exposed to naturalism. Naturalism has come to dominate our world today. It is very insidious. Science has brought us many good things, but when science becomes a god, it is wrong. God has given us an eternal soul. After death, we continue to live in a different state.

For older children, the video *Katy's Metaphysical Adventure* is an excellent introduction to the evils of naturalism. It may be found in the Leader Kit for *How Now Shall We Live?* by Charles Colson. Set in the theme park at Disney Land, it shows how naturalism is so subtle that it can fool even persons who love

God. You will want to show the video and talk about the importance of knowing that God has given us His Word to help us understand that life is more than cells and protoplasm. We cannot succumb to the evils of naturalism.

Activity 8—Billy Graham—Ladder Graphic Organizer

In this activity, your students will fill in a ladder with facts about the life of America's foremost evangelist, Billy Graham. There is a ladder graphic organizer and a list of facts to fill in the ladder. The material comes from the reading "William Franklin Graham (1918 to the Present)" in the handbook. You will find these materials on Activity Sheets 8-A and 8-B.

Activity 9—Memorize Romans 10:9

Evangelists, like Billy Graham, have made a difference in our world. Consider the following verse for your children to memorize. It tells of the importance of believing on Christ for salvation.

If you confess with your mouth, "Jesus is Lord," and believe in your heart that God raised Him from the dead, you will be saved.

Be sure to have the children add this verse to their Bible Verse Memory Books and illustrate its great truth.

ACTIVITY SHEET 2: QUESTIONS ABOUT THE WESLEY BROTHERS AND GEORGE WHITEFIELD

(Activity Sheet 1 on next page)

Directions: Place the appropriate letter or letters for the person or persons described on the line at the left of the statement.

a—John Wesley
b—Charles Wesley
c—George Whitefield

_____ 1. Between my brother and me, I had the earliest conversion.

_____ 2. I stayed the longest, between my brother and me, in Savannah, Georgia.

_____ 3. Of the three men, which was the greatest revival preacher?

_____ 4. I wrote more than six thousand hymns during my ministry.

_____ 5. I graduated from Christ Church College at Oxford University in 1724.

_____ 6. I had a lot of difficulty with the girls I dated.

_____ 7. On the way to Georgia, I met some Moravians. After returning to Europe, I went to the German Moravian village of Herrnhut.

_____ 8. I was thirty-five years old when I had a true conversion experience.

_____ 9. I was a friend from the Holy Club at Oxford University and preached revival in Europe and America.

_____ 10. My father was a pastor at Epworth, England.

ACTIVITY SHEET 1: JOHN WESLEY CROSSWORD PUZZLE

Across

2 When Wesley returned from America, he went to the M_____ village of Herrnhut.

4 His brother, C_____ wrote six thou sand hymns.

6 After Herrnhut, John had a conversion at A_____, London

7 John went to O_____ University.

8 Wesley wanted R_____ to take place in America.

Down

1 Wesley was O_____ in 1728.

2 He founded the M_____ Denomination.

3 His mother's name was S_____.

5 He was persuaded to minister among the people of G_____.

ACTIVITY SHEET 5: REVIEW OF THE WORK OF ROBERT RAIKES

Directions: From the list below, fill in the blanks to review the work of Robert Raikes.

Words—

Sunday	Dlean	Prison	Women	Bible	Hair
Gloucester	America	Raikes	Jail	School	Died
Children	Ragged				

Robert R_____ was the editor for the G_____ Journal. He was concerned with

P_____ reforms. One day while walking in the slum section of the city, he saw ragged, rowdy

C_____ playing in the street. S_____ was their only day off from working

in the factories. They did not go to S_____, so they had no education. He wanted to help

them, so they would not end up in J_____. He hired four W_____ in the neighborhood

to teach the children. Some children were afraid to come because they had R_____ clothes.

But Raikes told them all that they needed was a C_____ face and combed H_____.

The children were taught to read the B_____ for their main textbook. This was the beginning of

the first Sunday school. By the time he D_____ in 1811, there were 400,000 children in Sunday

school. The Sunday school also came to A_____.

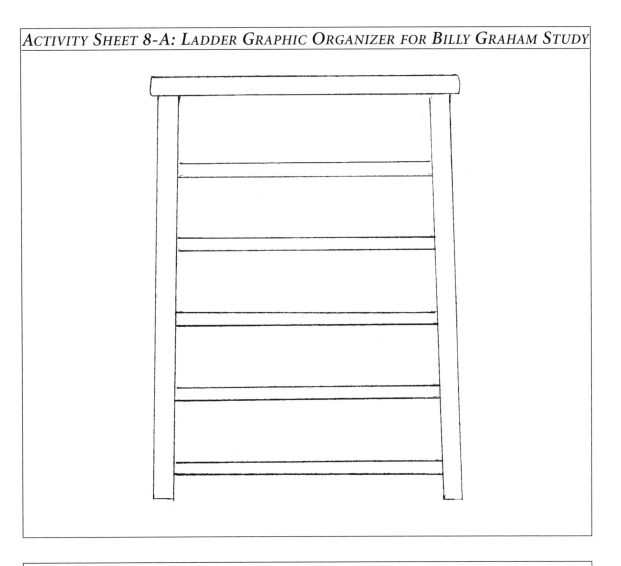

ACTIVITY SHEET 8-B: FACTS ABOUT BILLY GRAHAM FOR THE LADDER GRAPHIC ORGANIZER

Directions: Use the facts below to help you complete the Ladder Graphic Organizer.

1. He accepted Christ as his Savior at the age of sixteen.

2. During college years, Billy Graham began to preach to young people.

3. At Wheaton College, Billy Graham met Ruth Bell, who later became his wife.

4. Graham entered full-time evangelistic ministry.

5. He met George Beverly Shea and Cliff Barrows and they became the musicians for his evangelistic crusades.

6. Mr. Graham has conducted evangelistic crusades all over the world for more than fifty years.

LESSON 9: WHAT WE BELIEVE

Readings from the Parent/Teacher Handbook: Their Christian Heritage, Vol. 2: "What We Believe"

OBJECTIVES

By the end of this lesson, the learner should be able to
- identify and explain the way of salvation,
- understand the importance of prayer and the practice of praying,
- develop the ability to talk with God through prayer,
- understand and act on Jesus' model prayer, and
- develop an understanding of God's expectations in our lives and learn to live our lives in accordance with the Ten Commandments.

IDENTIFICATIONS

Concepts

Sinner—we are all sinners and in rebellion against God

Salvation—God's provision for establishing a relationship with Himself through Jesus' death on the cross

Praise—to glorify and to adore God

Confession—when we tell God what we have done wrong and ask His forgiveness

Thanksgiving—expression of gratitude and thanks

Petition—asking God to supply and meet our needs

Intercession—asking God to help other persons

God's rule—where God reigns supreme

Forgiveness—pardon and remission of a debt

Debts—that which is owed to another

Evil one—Satan

Kingdom—God's realm

Power—God has almighty power

Glory—the splendor and bliss of God and His dwelling

Other gods—idols that detract from our honor to God

Taking God's name in vain—swearing using the name of God

Holy—set apart for God; consecrated to God

Honor—high respect; reverence

Murder—to take the life of another

Adultery—violation of the marriage covenant

Stealing—taking what does not belong to a person

False witness—lying about something

Covetousness—strong desire to possess something that belongs to another

MATERIALS NEEDED

Parent/Teacher Handbook: Their Christian Heritage, Vol. 2

Activity Sheets for Lesson 9

Crayons and markers

White paper for drawing

Lined paper for writing

Card stock paper

Masking tape and plastic tape

3x5-index cards

Posterboard

Tempera paints

Construction paper of assorted colors

Slate (can be obtained at a craft store)

Old magazines to be cut up

Scissors

Paste or rubber cement

LEARNING ACTIVITIES FOR LESSON 9

Activity 1—Define Salvation and the Steps of Salvation

Read "Jesus—the Only Way" in the handbook. While it is important to know *about* Jesus, it is much more important *to know* Jesus. In this lesson, we want to help parents and teachers lead a child to Jesus Christ as Savior and Lord. It has been said that 80 percent of people who find Christ as Savior do so by age eighteen. It is imperative that we introduce children to Jesus.

You will want to help children know and understand what salvation is and how they can find salvation. Salvation is God's free gift to a fallen humanity, who through sin are not able to establish a relationship with God. An unrepentant and unsaved sinner will spend eternity apart from God in hell.

Salvation means that God has provided a way for a sinner to receive God's forgiveness for his or her sin. This way provides that a person may live eternally with God. Salvation begins right now. After the relationship with God is established, a person can experience a new life in Christ. Things that had appeal previously no longer are important. New desires and goals replace the old ideals.

Salvation may be defined from the perspective of Christ. Salvation may also be described from the vantage of the believer. Each has a past, present, and future component.

From the perspective of Christ, our Lord paid the penalty for sin by dying on the cross and shedding His blood. His death purchased our salvation. This happened in the past at the cross. Remember the Old Testament sacrifices; that was preparation for the one true sacrifice of Jesus in His death. Remember the Day of Atonement, when the scapegoat carried the sins of the people into the wilderness; it is no longer necessary.

When I accept Christ and that atonement for my sin, God no longer sees me as a sinner, for my sin has been covered by the precious blood of Jesus. Jesus atoned for my sin once and for all. I now am a member of the family of God. Jesus continues to intercede and care for me. This is the present.

One day, when my life here on earth is over, I will spend all eternity with God. I will experience the joy of God's presence forever. There will be no more sin or sorrow. God will reign in His kingdom, and I will be a part of that kingdom. This is the future.

From the vantage of the believer, the past comes in the form of seeing my life for what it really is. Watch a small child. The child wants his way. He is selfish and self-centered. If we do not become Christians, that selfishness grows in adulthood and becomes much worse. Recognizing my sinful past, I throw myself on the mercy of God and ask for His forgiveness. I ask God to give me the free gift of His grace. That gift of grace involves the shed blood of Jesus. It covers my sin and brings me into the family of God. This is the past.

After accepting forgiveness, salvation provides the Holy Spirit. The Holy Spirit lives within me. He gives me the power to keep from sin. He teaches me about Jesus Christ. He gives me an understanding that I am a member of the family of God. He helps me to live life as a follower of Christ. It is the picture of One who walks with me, with His arm around me, as I go through life. It does not mean that I am removed from pain and sorrow. But it does mean that the One who walks beside me helps me not to become overwhelmed by life. Rather, I can be victorious in life if I allow the Holy Spirit to guide me. That is the present.

One day I will go to live with God for all eternity. That is a promise from God Himself. I do not have to fear death. That is why the martyrs were not afraid to die for their faith in Christ. God's love is worth it all. That is the future.

Tell the children about salvation. Bring all that they have studied about the sacrifices of the Old Testament and the atonement to bear on your discussion. You may want to have your children make a poster on posterboard of SALVATION. Have them work in small groups. Tell them that you are looking for the best poster. Keep it simple. You might have a cross in the middle and a Scripture across the bottom. Tell them not to be limited by that suggestion but to use their creativity. You may want to circulate through the class and have them tell you what they plan to place on the poster. Give them some suggestions if they do not have any ideas or their ideas are unworkable.

Activity 2—Wordless Book

A excellent but simple way to explain the way of salvation to children is through the use of the wordless book. You can purchase a wordless book at a Christian bookstore or you can make a wordless book. You can use the wordless book to tell the story of salvation to your class members. This would be a good project for your students. It would give them a simple tool to help them to witness to their classmates.

The wordless book consists of a green cover and four colored pages. You might make it three inches wide and four inches tall. It should be a size that will permit it to be put in a pocket. From front to back, the first page is gold. The second page is a dark page of black. The third page is red. The fourth page is white. A simple way to complete the wordless book would be to staple the outside edge near the fold of the green cover.

Gold is a precious metal. It has intrinsic worth. The gold page speaks to us of the holiness of God. Isaiah 6:3 identifies that aspect,

> And one called to another:
> "Holy, holy, holy is the LORD of Hosts;
> His glory fills the whole earth."

This gold page also suggests the the holy city in Revelation 21:18:

> The building material of its wall was jasper, and the city was pure gold like clear glass.

Next comes the dark page. God is not willing that any should perish. But God is also just. He cannot allow sin. He punishes all sin. The apostle Paul wrote:

> For all have sinned and fall short of the glory of God. (Romans 3:23)

Then comes the red page. God cannot abide sin. That is a problem, except that God provided a way for us to experience both His mercy and His grace. (Mercy is not receiving death, which we deserve, while grace is receiving eternal life with God, which we do not deserve). God is love. He reaches out to us, even in our sinful condition, to save us. Paul wrote:

> But God proves His own love for us in that while we were still sinners Christ died for us! (Romans 5:8)

Next comes the white page. This page tells us that God wants to take away our sin because of Christ's death on the cross. His conditions are met, and the darkness of sin is covered by Jesus. That brings us to our memory verse for this lesson. It is Isaiah 1:18:

> "Come, let us discuss this," says the LORD.
> "Though your sins are like scarlet,
> they will be as white as snow;
> though they are as red as crimson,
> they will be like wool."

The green cover tells us of spiritual growth and salvation. It indicates that we need to grow in Christ. The apostle Peter stated it this way: "Like newborn infants, desire the unadulterated spiritual milk, so that you may grow by it in [your] salvation" (1 Peter 2:2). We do that by the following:

- Reading and studying the Word of God, the Bible
- Talking to God in prayer and allowing Him to talk to us
- Witnessing to other persons about the salvation that God has given us and is available to them
- Attending worship, study, and fellowship with God's people in church

You may use the wordless book with your children to help them to grasp the meaning of salvation. They can use the wordless book with their friends.

Activity 3—Prayer: Talking to God

Read the section "What We Believe" and the subsection "Prayer" in the handbook. This section deals with five types of prayer. Help your children understand that all five types of prayer need to be included in our praying to God each day. Stress the importance of prayer for our relationship with God. We would be very sad if our mothers or fathers did not talk to us each day. The same is true for God. When we do not talk with Him, we miss a great opportunity to grow close to Him, just as with our parents.

You can begin this lesson by asking the children what prayer is. Write their contributions on the chalkboard. Point out what Philippians 4:6 says about prayer: "Don't worry about anything, but in everything through prayer and petition with thanksgiving, let your requests be made known to God."

God wants us to come to Him in prayer and tell Him the things that make us happy, as well as the things that make us sad. He cares about us. The more that we talk with Him in prayer, the more we get to know Him and how He wants us to behave and act.

Tell the children that there are five types of prayer. Write these on the chalkboard as you discuss each type.

The first is PRAISE. Ask: "What is praise?" (Have the children contribute, and write their responses on the board). Be sure to include these ideas: praise means to glorify and to adore God; God has created us; God loves us and deserves our honor.

The second type of prayer is CONFESSION. Ask: "What is confession?" Include these ideas: confession occurs when we tell God what we have done wrong and ask His forgiveness; I need to ask God to forgive me for hitting my brother; I need to confess when I take my sister's doll from her.

The third type of prayer is THANKSGIVING. Ask: "What is thanksgiving?" Include these ideas: thanksgiving gives us the opportunity to express gratitude and thanks to God for the good things that He gives us and does for us; thank You Lord for our families; thank You Lord for our teachers; thank You for brothers and sisters.

The fourth type of prayer is PETITION. Note that this is a big word. Ask the children what it means? It means to ask God to supply and meet our needs. When we have studied, we can ask God to help us do our best on a test. We can ask God to help us live for Him. We can ask Him to help us obey our parents.

The fifth type of prayer is INTERCESSION. Note that this is another big word. Ask what it mean? Intercession means asking God to help other persons. We can ask God to heal our brother's cold. We can pray for our missionaries in far-off countries, that God will protect them and that they will win boys and girls to Jesus. We can pray for our President, that God will give him wisdom.

Did the people in the Bible pray? Let us look at some of their prayers. Perhaps they can help us to better know how to pray.

Duplicate Activity Sheet 3. Distribute the sheets to the children. If you are working with younger children, you may need to read the verses to them and have them guess what type of prayer is represented. Have them match the type of prayer at the right of the sheet with the prayers by placing the correct letter in the space provided.

Activity 4—Prayer Calendar

Now that the children know the different types of prayer, they can make a prayer calendar to help them organize their prayers and give examples of prayers of each type. Distribute five 3x5-inch cards to each child. Place the cards in a vertical position, then have the children label each card with a different type of prayer—Praise, Thanksgiving, Confession, Petition, and Intercession. Punch two holes at the top of each of the cards. Tie the cards together with a short piece of string. Cut off the excess string.

Have the children work on this project in small groups. On the Praise card, you may help them write an example of a prayer of praise. Some of the psalms are excellent for this purpose. For example Psalm 9:1–2:

I will thank the LORD with all my heart;
I will declare all Your wonderful works.
I will rejoice and boast about You;
I will sing about Your name, Most High.

For Thanksgiving, the psalms again provide some of the best expressions of thanksgiving. For example, Psalm 100:4–5:

Enter His gates with thanksgiving and His courts with praise.
Give thanks to Him and praise His name.
For the LORD is good, and His love is eternal;
His faithfulness endures through all generations.

For Confession, there are several good examples:

If . . . My people who are called by My name humble themselves, pray and seek My face, and turn from their evil ways, then I will hear from heaven, forgive their sin, and heal their land. (2 Chronicle 7:14)

Be gracious to me, God, according to Your faithful love;
according to Your abundant compassion, blot out my rebellion.
Wash away my guilt, and cleanse me from my sin. (Psalm 51:1–2)

On the Petition card ask the children what they want to pray for. Good health, help with their studies, obedience to parents, and growing close to Jesus might be some of the things that they would like to pray for. Probably, they can list things that are similar for their own situation. Parents can help them name those things that are special to them.

On the Intercession card ask for persons who are close to them; for example, parents, brothers and sisters, their minister, their teacher, and their friends.

After they have finished, have them decorate their calendars.

Activity 5—Durer's Praying Hands

A Hungarian family lived in a suburb of Nuremberg. Albrecht Durer and his wife had eighteen children. He was a goldsmith and had all that he could do to make ends meet. Two of their sons, the young Albrecht, and his brother, Albert, were interested in going to the academy in Nuremberg to study art. But there was not enough money to fulfill this dream.

One night as they were talking, they decided on a plan. They would flip a coin, and the one who won would go to the art academy while the other brother would work in a local mine to earn enough money to support his brother. The young Albrecht won and went off to the academy. His brother toiled long and hard in the mines to support Albrecht.

The young artist exceeded even some of his professors' abilities. His etchings, woodcuts, and paintings began to earn some handsome fees. He returned to his hometown, and the family held a feast in his honor. As the dinner progressed, Albrecht toasted his brother for all of the help that he had provided, making it possible for Albrecht to come to this point in his life. He told Albert that it was time for him to go to Nuremburg and Albrecht could support him.

The people at the feast turned to Albert. Instead of showing happiness, Albert was crying. He said, "No . . . No . . . I cannot go!" When he regained his composure, he told Albrecht that it was too late. He had ruined his hands in the mine and could no longer make the delicate brush strokes that would be necessary to paint or etch. He was suffering from a severe case of arthritis, and it was too late.

Some time later Albrecht did a drawing as a tribute to his brother. Albrecht drew his brother's gnarled hands raised in prayer to express his gratitude for all that his brother had suffered in order for Albrecht to go to art school. Albrecht entitled the drawing *Hands*, but the world has renamed it *The Praying Hands*.

Ask the children to put themselves in the place of each of the brothers. How would they have felt if they had been the artist Albrecht Durer? How would they have felt if they had been the brother Albert? If you have access to a copy of *The Praying Hands*, you may want to display it in front of the class. You can find the drawing on the Internet. Ask the children to try to draw their own version of the Durer drawing.

Activity 6—The Lord's Prayer

You may wish to try your hand at some manuscript printing. The Lord's Prayer provides an excellent opportunity to prepare a printed manuscript that can be hung in the child's room. If you have access to a computer with different font types and a color ink-jet printer, you can create this manuscript in a matter of minutes. The words for the Lord's Prayer are in the text of "The Lord's Prayer" in the handbook.

You can choose a type, such as Script MT Bold, or experiment with other fonts. These are available at the top of the screen in your word processor. You can also change the size of the font in the little window to the right of the font style. Use a color ink-jet printer to produce the manuscript. This would be a good project for your students to complete and take home.

Suggest that the parents purchase a simple frame in which to place the Lord's Prayer for their child as a reminder to pray. Hang it on the wall.

Activity 7—The Ten Commandments

Read the section "The Ten Commandments," in the handbook. This is God's moral law to be obeyed. When we sin, we violate God's moral law. We do not have to keep all the ceremonial laws of the Old Testament, but we must keep God's moral law—the Ten Commandments.

As a reminder of the Ten Commandments, provide each child with a piece of slate. (The slate can be purchased at a craft store). Using tempera paints, write each of the Ten Commandments on the piece of slate. It is not necessary to repeat "You shall not. . . ." Write that once and then write the one word or short phrase as you list the other commandments. Encourage parents to purchase a picture stand that will hold the slate on a dresser or desk. This too can serve as a reminder of our obligation to God to keep His moral law.

Activity 8—Picturing the Ten Commandments

Have the students work in small groups of not more than four students to a group. Provide them with posterboard, scissors, paste or rubber cement, and markers. Depending on how many groups you have, assign one, two, or three commandments to a group.

Tell them that they are to find pictures that will illustrate the commandments when they are being obeyed. For example, obeying the commandment not to commit adultery might be pictured as a married couple or family together, caring for each other. Tell the students to use their creativity and picture the positive side of the commandments.

Hang the posters around the classroom or out along the hallway.

Activity 9—Complete the Word Puzzle

In advance of this session provide your students with copies of the word puzzle on the Ten Commandments on Activity Sheet 9. This puzzle can serve as a review. Ask the children to read the sentences below the puzzle and find the word that is needed. Then write the letters in the spaces provided to complete the word *Commandments*.

Activity 10—Memorize Isaiah 1:18

God provides a way for us to have fellowship with God. He has provided His Son, Jesus. Jesus' death on the cross provides for us new life. Though our sins are keep us from knowing and loving God, God wants us to discover His love for us. Memorize this verse. It tells us of the forgiveness that we can have:

"Come, let us discuss this," says the LORD.
"Though your sins are like scarlet, they will be as white as snow;
though they are as red as crimson, they will be like wool."

Have the children write this verse in their Bible Verse Memory Books and illustrate it.

ACTIVITY SHEET 3: WHAT TYPE OF PRAYER?

Directions: Read the following verses and match the type of prayer to the prayer.

___1. Jesus asked God to forgive the soldiers for what they did. (Luke 23:34)

___2. Paul thanked God for the believers at Philippi. (Philippians 1:3)

___3. David sang praises to God. (Psalm 63:3)

___4. The Church prayed for Peter in prison. (Acts 12:5)

___5. Hannah prayed for a child. (1 Samuel 1:1–10)

___6. David prayed for forgiveness. (Psalm 51:1–2)

___7. Jesus prayed in the Garden of Gethsemane. (Matthew 26:36)

___8. Paul prayed and sang hymns to God after being thrown in jail. (Acts 16:22–25)

___9. Jesus gave thanks for the bread and fish. (Matthew 14:19)

Types of Prayers
A. Praise
B. Thanksgiving
C. Confession
D. Petition
E. Intercession

ACTIVITY SHEET 9: WORD PUZZLE ON THE TEN COMMANDMENTS

Directions: Use the sentences below to find the words to complete the puzzle.

```
        C __ __ __ __ __ __ __ __ __
        __ O __
    __ __ M
    __ . __ M
        __ A __
    __ __ N __ __
__ __ __ D __ __
        __ M __ __ __ __ __ __
    __ __ E __ __
        __ N __ __ __ __ __ __ __ __
__ __ __ __ T
    __ __ __ S __ __ __ __
```

Sentences about the Ten Commandments: (Sentences contain the words to be found)

As C_____ of God, we must obey His commands. We need to learn what

G_____ wants us to do. We first must worship H_____. We need to have reverence for

God's N_____. We need to set apart the Lord's D_____. We must

H_____ our fathers and mothers. We must not M_____ or kill.

We must be faithful in our M_____. We must not S_____.

We must not lie about our N_____. We must not C_____ or

desire what our neighbor has. God alone must be W_____.

LESSON 10: CHRISTIAN MISSIONS IN THE MODERN WORLD

Readings from the Parent/Teacher Handbook: Their Christian Heritage, Vol. 2: "Christian Missions"

OBJECTIVES
By the end of this lesson, the learner should be able to
- understand why missionaries go to faraway countries to tell other people about Jesus, and
- relate to missionaries, who are preaching the gospel in the country of Guatemala today.

IDENTIFICATIONS
Concepts
Family nurse practitioner missionary—missionary who attends to the health needs of people as part of the work

Church planter—missionary who is responsible to start new churches on the mission field

People
Roger Grossmann: church planter missionary to the Quiche Indians in Guatemala

Vicki Grossmann: wife of Roger and family nurse practitioner missionary in Guatemala

Places
Guatemala: country in Central America; immediately south of Mexico

MATERIALS NEEDED
Parent/Teacher Handbook: Their Christian Heritage, Vol. 2

Activity Sheets for Lesson 10

Crayons and markers

White paper for drawing

Lined paper for writing

Roll of shelf paper or butcher paper

Masking tape and plastic tape

Reusable adhesive

3x5-inch index cards

Tempera paints

Construction paper

Scissors

Card stock paper for duplication

LEARNING ACTIVITIES FOR LESSON 10

Activity 1—What Is a Missionary?

Read the section "Christian Missions" and subsection, "Missionary Movement" in the handbook.

Mission work has always been part of the work of the church. Today the church is very concerned about evangelizing persons across the globe. But what is a missionary? For our purposes, let us define a missionary in the following way: A missionary is a person who has been called by God to cross the world to reach people with the gospel of Jesus Christ.

Remind the children that God calls everyone to be a witness for Him, but He does not call everyone to be a missionary to a foreign country. But if God calls us, we must be ready to go. Remember Jonah and his unwillingness to go.

Turn to the list of statements on Activity Sheet 1. Duplicate them in advance of this session. Have the children check all the statements with which they agree. Also put a star next to the statement that is most important.

When they have finished, discuss the statements with them.

Activity 2—Missionary Quotations

Turn to the list of missionary quotations on Activity Sheet 2-A. You will find a list of quotations from missionaries and missionary statesmen. Duplicate the list of quotations. Select from that list quotations that seem appropriate to your class situation. Provide the students with lined paper and have them write the quotations that you have selected. Mount the quotations on construction paper. Decorate the room with the quotations around the room.

Also include maps of countries of the world. A map of the world is included on Activity Sheet 2-B. You may find help with maps and current pertinent missions information on the following Web site: www.worldmap.org.

Activity 3—Map of the World

You will want to decorate your room with maps from the various countries of the world as you proceed with this unit on world mission. You will find help with current maps of the countries of the world and other pertinent missions information on the following Web site: www: worldmap.org. Create awareness on the part of your children for peoples who live elsewhere in the world. Many of these people do not worship Jesus. Many have not even heard the name of Jesus. But they need to know our Jesus also. They will not hear unless we send missionaries to tell them about Jesus.

You will also want to have a map of the world for the children to see. There is a map of the world located on Activity Sheet 2-B. You may make a copy of the map. Then make a transparency and with an overhead projector, enlarge the map on a sheet of posterboard on the wall. Trace the map and place it in a prominent location for the children to see. For older children, you may also want to identify the populations of major countries of the world and indicate how few know the gospel of Jesus Christ.

You may want to identify the missionaries from your church or those where short-term mission trips have gone from your church. Place map stickpins in the appropriate locations. Talk about the missionaries from your church or those with whom you have personal acquaintance.

As you study the different countries where missionaries have gone in lesson 11, you will want to refer the children back to the world map and the locations of the countries across the globe.

Activity 4—Mini-Mission Trip for Children

Help your children gain a firsthand understanding of missions by engaging in a mini-mission trip. Arrange in advance with a children's home or retirement home in your community to have your children visit and share about Jesus. This may be done by reciting memory verses, singing "Jesus Loves Me," recitations, etc.

In this manner, the children can gain a firsthand experience of telling others about Jesus.

Activity 5—Care Package for Missionaries

Identify missionaries with whom your church or school has some relationship. It is particularly helpful if the families have children. Find out what needs they have. You may discover their needs by communicating through e-mails, letters, or fax transmissions. Or just identify items that the missionary children might like to have.

Prepare the package and send to the missionaries. Help the children see that they are contributing to the missionaries sharing the gospel with other people in faraway lands.

Activity 6—Contact with Mission Agencies

The mission of the church to a lost world is extremely important in today's world to fulfill God's call to reach all persons for Christ. You need to impress this upon your children. To gain additional understanding, contact the mission organizations that are sponsored by your church or denomination.

As an example, among Southern Baptists the missionary organization is the International Mission Board. You will find access to missionaries on the field for whom your class members can pray and support. You will find opportunities and help for structuring a mission program in your school or church. Their Web address is www.imb.org.

Other mission organizations will provide similar information. Check with your pastor or denominational representative. You may also find a very helpful resource for evangelical missions in the following reference, *Mission Handbook,* edited by John A. Siewert and Dotsey Welliber, 18th edition (Wheaton, Ill.: Evangelism and Missions Information Service, 2000).

Activity 7—What are Missionary Families Like Today?

Read "Roger and Vicki Grossmann," "Missionary Service in Guatemala," and "Mission to Hueheutenango" in the handbook. Turn to Activity Sheet 7 and make copies of this questionnaire for the students in your class.

Talk about the life of a missionary family, the Grossmanns, in a foreign country. Read the story given in the section "Roger and Vicki Grossmann," told by Vicki Grossmann, which begins with "It was Sunday, December 19, 1994. . . ." The intent of this section is to provide students with an understanding of a "real" missionary family. They are not that different from the families represented by your students.

Have the students answer the questions. If the students are younger, you may want to read the questions aloud to them and have them discuss the answers. Talk with the students about what it must be like to be a missionary in a land far away from home.

You will find a map of Guatemala on Activity Sheet 8. Place Guatemala on the world map as well. You might want to make a transparency of this map. Use an overhead projector to project the map of Guatemala on the wall. Trace the outline on a sheet of posterboard and include it with your wall decorations for this lesson. The Grossmanns serve in Guatemala from Quetzaltenango, second-largest city in the country. It is located on the western side of Guatemala. (It is probably not necessary to provide this much detail to young children.) Label the map, "Guatemala—Where the Grossmanns Serve."

Activity 8—Map of Guatemala

You will find a map of Guatemala on Activity Sheet 8. You will want to enlarge the map on a copy machine. You may make a transparency and project it on a sheet of posterboard and hang on the wall. Trace the outline of Guatemala. Have the children in your class decorate and color the map. Label the map "Guatemala—Country Where the Grossmann Family Serves."

Be sure to show the children where Guatemala is located on the world map. Place it in context. This is not as important for younger children as it is for older children.

The capital city and largest city of Guatemala is Guatemala City. The second largest city is Quetzaltenango. It is located on the western side of the country. You can easily locate both of these cities in an atlas or encyclopedia.

You may want to further explore the culture of Guatemala in an encyclopedia. Help your children understand what life is like in the country of Guatemala.

Activity 9—Write a Letter to the Grossmanns or Another Missionary Family

Since you have read the story about one missionary family serving in Guatemala, you may want to write a letter of encouragement to them. Be sure to identify yourself, where you are from, and how you discovered them. Tell them that you are praying for them and their ministry there in the far-off country of Guatemala. They can be reached at the following e-mail address: rognvic@yahoo.com.

If you have specific families who are missionaries from your church, write a letter to them. Letters of encouragement are always welcome by missionaries as they serve Christ in a far-off land. Think about how you would feel about receiving mail from home.

Activity 10—Memorize Acts 1:8

To help your children understand the significance of the mission of the church, have them memorize Acts 1:8. You will want the children to write this verse in their Bible Verse Memory Books and illustrate it.

> *But you will receive power when the Holy Spirit has come upon you, and you will be My witnesses in Jerusalem, in all Judea and Samaria, and to the ends of the earth.*

WORKSHEETS FOR LESSON 10

ACTIVITY SHEET 1: WHAT IS A MISSIONARY?

Directions: Check all the statements that you agree with.

A missionary is one who . . .
____1. cares for other people.
____2. loves God.
____3. has lots of money to travel overseas.
____4. is called by God.
____5. wants to see the world.
____6. is willing to wear other clothes to be like the people.
____7. is willing to give up some of the comforts of home for God.
____8. has lots of talent in music and preaching.
____9. wants to tell others about Jesus.
____10. is willing to eat food from different countries, even when it does not taste as good as food from home.
____11. is afraid to travel to other countries across the world.
____12. has great skills as a doctor or a builder.

"We can reach our world, if we will. The greatest lack today is not people or funds. The greatest need is prayer." —Wesley Duewel, head of OMS International

"It is possible for the most obscure person in a church, with a heart right toward God, to exercise as much power for the evangelization of the world, as it is for those who stand in the most prominent positions." —John R. Mott

"We talk of the second coming; half the world has never heard of the first."—Oswald J. Smith

"Tell the students to give up their small ambitions and come eastward to preach the gospel of Christ." —Francis Xavier, missionary to India, the Philippines, and Japan

"The command has been to 'go,' but we have stayed—in body, gifts, prayer and influence. He has asked us to be witnesses unto the uttermost parts of the earth . . . but 99 percent of Christians have kept puttering around in the homeland."—Robert Savage, Latin American Missionary

"People who do not know the Lord ask why in the world we waste our lives as missionaries. They forget that they too are expending their lives . . . and when the bubble has burst, they will have nothing of eternal significance to show for the years they have wasted."—Nate Saint, missionary martyr

"We must be global Christians with a global vision because our God is a global God."—John Stott

"The mission of the church is missions."—Unknown

"Missions is the overflow of our delight in God because missions is the overflow of God's delight in being God."—John Piper

"You can give without loving. But you cannot love without giving."—Amy Carmichael, missionary to India

"Someone asked, 'Will the heathen who have never heard the gospel be saved?' It is more a question with me whether we—who have the gospel and fail to give it to those who have not—can be saved."—Charles Spurgeon

"God uses men who are weak and feeble enough to lean on him."—Hudson Taylor, missionary to China

"The gospel is only good news if it gets there in time."—Carl F. H. Henry

"Let my heart be broken with the things that break God's heart." —Bob Pierce, World Vision founder

"No reserves. No retreats. No regrets."— William Borden

"The reason some folks don't believe in missions is that the brand of religion they have isn't worth propagating."—Unknown

"No one has the right to hear the gospel twice while there remains someone who has not heard it once." —Oswald J. Smith

"The Bible is not the basis of missions; missions is the basis of the Bible."—Ralph Winter

"The Great Commission is not an option to be considered; it is a command to be obeyed."—Hudson Taylor

"The spirit of Christ is the spirit of missions. The nearer we get to Him, the more intensely missionary we become."—Henry Martyn, missionary to India and Persia

"He is no fool who gives up what he cannot keep to gain that which he cannot lose."—Jim Elliot, missionary martyr who lost his life in the late 1950s trying to reach the Auca Indians of Ecuador

ACTIVITY SHEET 2-B: MAP OF THE WORLD

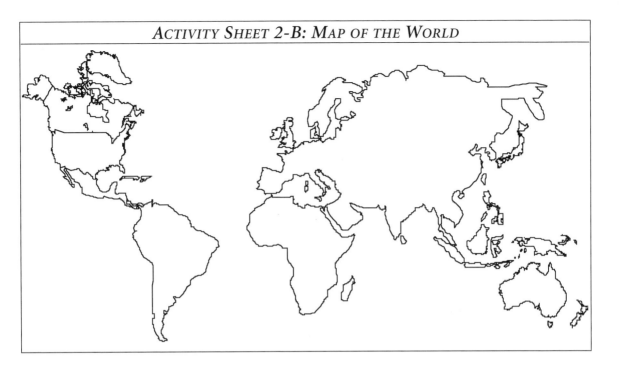

ACTIVITY SHEET 7: QUESTIONS ABOUT A MISSIONARY FAMILY TODAY

Directions: Answer the following questions:

1. In what country are the Grossmans serving as missionaries?

2. Where is Guatemala located?

3. How many children are part of their family?

4. As a nurse, how does Mrs. Grossmann help the people in Guatemala?

5. From the story of Adam, how do you think he was led to talk with the nurse from America?

6. What part did God have in helping Adam?

7. How did the help he received help him to become a follower of Jesus?

8. What were some things that prepared the Grossmanns for missionary service?

9. Dr. Grossmann was called to start churches. How did God allow a church to start in that area?

10. What is a major problem for missionaries in helping people to grow in the newfound Christian faith after they become Christians?

ACTIVITY SHEET 8:
MAP OF GUATEMALA

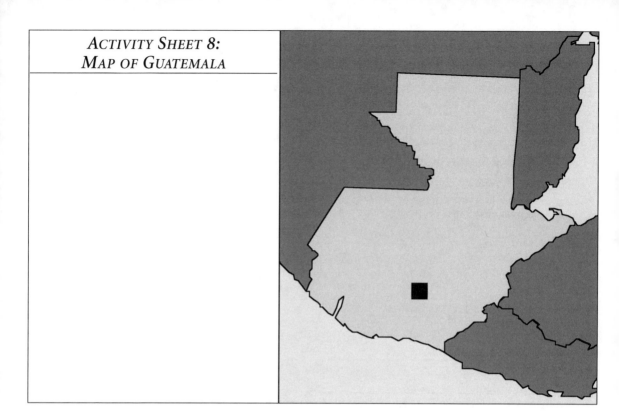

Readings from the Parent/Teacher Handbook: Their Christian Heritage, Vol. 2: "Christian Missions"

OBJECTIVES

By the end of this lesson, the learner should be able to

- understand why missionaries went to far-off lands in the 19th and 20th centuries, and
- identify and describe selected missionaries from the past:

    William Carey
    David Livingstone
    Lottie Moon

IDENTIFICATIONS

Concepts

Great Commission—Christ's command to go and teach and preach the gospel to the ends of the earth

Malaria—a disease carried by mosquitoes that still is one of the most significant diseases worldwide

People

William Carey: British Baptist missionary to India, who is credited with being the father of modern missions

David Livingstone: missionary from Scotland, who opened up the vast continent of Africa

Henry Stanley: newspaper reporter, who came to find Dr. Livingstone

Lottie Moon: Baptist missionary to China

Places

India: country with a vast population; located south of China and Nepal, surrounded by the Indian Ocean

Africa: huge continent south of Europe, bordering the Atlantic Ocean on the east and the Indian Ocean on the west

Zambezi River: river in Africa; followed by David Livingstone to its source

Westminster Abbey: cathedral in London, England, where David Livingstone is buried

Virginia: native state in the USA for Lottie Moon

Tengchow: city in China where Lottie Moon served as a missionary

MATERIALS NEEDED

Parent/Teacher Handbook: Their Christian Heritage, Vol. 2

Activity Sheets for Lesson 11
Crayons and markers
White paper for drawing
Lined paper for writing
Roll of shelf paper or butcher paper
Masking tape and plastic tape
Reusable adhesive
3x5-inch index cards
Tempera paints
Construction paper
Scissors
Card stock paper for duplication

LEARNING ACTIVITIES FOR LESSON 11

Activity 1—Time Line for the History of Missions

Turn to Activity Sheet 1. Have the students work in small groups and make a time line. Cut sheets of poster board in half. Each of the groups may take two or three of the events on Activity Sheet 1 and make a poster with the time period, the event, and a picture of that event. Show a connection among the events by running a string of yarn the length of all of the posters. It is not necessary to include all detail, only the main epochs of missionary strategy to show the changes that have occurred over the centuries. Mission work has always been part of the church throughout its history. But probably during the first two centuries and during the last two centuries, the church has been more mission minded than at any other stage.

Activity 2—Story Spin Wheel
Read the story of William Carey in the handbook. Tell the story of this pioneer to your class. Discuss what his missionary service meant to the people of Serampore, India.

In advance of this session turn to Activity Sheets 3-A and 3-B in lesson 6. Duplicate the two spin wheel parts on sheets of card stock paper. Have the children cut out the two parts. Then fasten the top sheet to the bottom with a brass paper fastener.

Have the children turn the top sheet so that the line from the first third of the opening is vertical. Use masking tape to hold the sheets on the desk in place. In the first third, write:

William Carey—

Born in 1761

Apprenticed to a cobbler

Another apprentice, John Warr, witnessed to Carey and led him to Christ

Married Dorothy Plackett

Carey began to preach and study Greek

Move the top sheet spin wheel to the second area and write:

William Carey became concerned about people dying in sin elsewhere in the world.

He wrote a book to encourage people to go to the foreign mission field.

The Baptist Missionary Society was looking for volunteers to go to India.

Carey volunteered to go to India with his family.

They encountered disease and Carey's son died and later his wife died.

Move the top sheet spin wheel to the third area and write:

Carey translated the Bible into six Indian languages.

Carey married Charlotte; she helped him open schools.

Carey baptized more that 1,400 converts.

Carey never returned to England.

Carey died in 1834.

Talk about the story in review. God does not call all of us to missionary service, but He does call upon us to be witnesses for Him. Recall what Jesus said:

You will be My witnesses in Jerusalem, in all Judea and Samaria, and to the ends of the earth. (Acts 1:8b)

William Carey served in Serampore, India. The city is north of Calcutta on the eastern side of India. You will find a map of India on Activity Sheet 2. Place India on the world map as well. You might want to make a transparency of this map and project the image of India on the wall. Trace the outline on a sheet of posterboard and include it with your wall decorations for this lesson. Label the map, "India—Where William Carey Served as a Missionary."

Activity 3—Map of India and Mission of William Carey
William Carey served in Serampore, India. The city was located north of Calcutta (now Kolkata) on the eastern side of the country, near the border of Bangladesh. Today Kolkata has a poplulation of excess of thirteen million and is the ninth largest city in the world. You will find a map of India on Activity Sheet 2.

You will find an atlas on your CD-ROM encyclopedia helpful for this activity. Enlarge the map on a copy machine and duplicate copies for each member of the class. Locate the city of Kolkata and label it. Entitle the map, "India—the Country where William Carey Served as a Missionary." Have the children color the map.

You will also want to help the children understand where the city of Kolkata and the country of India are located on the world map, found in lesson 10, Activity Sheet 2-B.

Activity 4—Life of David Livingstone: Missionary to Africa

Read the story of David Livingstone in the handbook. Tell the story of this great missionary doctor to your class. Discuss what his missionary service meant to those who came after him to the huge continent of Africa.

On Activity Sheet 4 duplicate the graphic organizer chart, "Life of David Livingstone—Missionary to Africa." Tell the story of David Livingstone to your class. Have the children fill in the Beginning, Middle, and End chart for the Livingstone's life.

Here are the facts to include:

Beginning—

    Born in Scotland in 1813

    Worked in a cotton mill

    During his college years he became interested in missions.

    He became a medical doctor.

    Livingstone went to Africa.

    He married Mary Moffat.

    Livingstone became upset because he had few converts.

Middle—

    Livingstone felt that God was leading him to explore the continent of Africa.

    Wanted to open the interior of Africa to end the slave trade and open it to the gospel.

    His wife and child died.

    Livingstone returned to England and was praised for his exploration.

End—

    Livingstone went back to Africa to continue his exploration.

    Livingstone became very ill and almost died.

    He continued his adventures and exploring.

    Livingstone opened up the continent of Africa to the gospel.

    He became very ill and died in 1873.

You will find a map of Africa on Activity Sheet 5. Place Africa on the world map as well. You might want to make a transparency of this map. Use an overhead projector to project the image on the wall. Trace the outline on a sheet of posterboard and include it with your wall decorations for this lesson. Livingstone explored from Cape Town, South Africa, north to the Zambezi River and east to the Indian Ocean. He also explored north and west to Luanda, just south of the place where the Congo River flows into the Atlantic Ocean. (Probably, this detail is not necessary for young children.) Label the map "Africa—Where David Livingstone Served as a Missionary and Explorer."

Activity 5—Map of Africa and the Missionary Journeys of David Livingstone

You will find a map of Africa on Activity Sheet 5. Livingstone explored from Cape Town, South Africa, north to the Zambezi River and east to the Indian Ocean. He also explored north and west to Luanda, just south of the place where the Congo River flows to the Atlantic Ocean. Probably, this much detail is not necessary for young children. But give them a general idea of the locations where Livingstone explored.

You will find a CD-ROM encyclopedia helpful. You may also search online on the Internet for resources on the travels of Livingstone.

Enlarge the map and duplicate enough copies for each member in the class. Have the children color the map and label it "Africa—Where David Livingstone Served—Explorer and Missionary."

You will also want to help the children understand where Africa is located on the world map.

Activity 6—Bookmarks for William Carey and David Livingstone

Children will enjoy designing a bookmark for each of these two great missionaries. If you make a folding bookmark, (see Activity Sheet 6 for pattern) they will have room to write a brief story of the missionary on the bookmark. Use 8$\frac{1}{2}$x11-inch card stock. Cut the sheet of card stock in half. Then fold the 4$\frac{1}{2}$-inch strips in half. Then trim 1$\frac{1}{2}$ inches from the bottom of the bookmark. An example of a bookmark may be found on Activity Sheet 6.

On the front of the bookmark have the children draw or use stickers of an animal from India for William Carey. On the front of the bookmark, they can write the name of the missionary and his famous quote: "Expect great things from God; attempt great things for God." They can write information that they learned on the back about the missionary.

Follow the same procedure for David Livingstone. On the face of the bookmark, write one of his famous quotations: "Sympathy is no substitute for action." Decorate the front with the name of the missionary and animal stickers of animals from Africa, such as elephants, giraffes, lions, zebras, etc.

Activity 7—Interview with Lottie Moon

Read the story of "Lottie Moon—Missionary to China" in the handbook. Invite an adult (perhaps a parent of one of your children) to play the role of Lottie Moon. Ask her to read the story of Lottie Moon and (if possible) dress up in nineteenth-century dress. Have members of your class prepared to interview Lottie Moon with questions about her life. In this way, you may tell the story of Lottie Moon. You may find additional information on the Internet.

Here are some questions that the children may ask:
1. From what state in America did you come?
2. How did you grow up in your early years?
3. When did you become a Christian and who was influential?
4. How did you become interested in missions?
5. Where did you go as a missionary?
6. Did you go to a large city or a small town?
7. How did you get the children interested in your lessons?
8. What problems did you have?

9. How were you able to help the people?

10. Looking back over your life, what was important?

Activity 8—Map of China and the Missionary Work of Lottie Moon

Lottie Moon served in the country of China. You will find a map of China on Activity Sheet 7. Enlarge the map of China and duplicate enough copies for each child in your class. Have the children color the map and label the map of China with "China—Where Lottie Moon Served as a Missionary."

Lottie Moon served in Tenchow in Shantung Province on the Yellow Sea. For younger children, you probably do not have to provide great detail on the exact location. You can find additional information about Lottie Moon online through the Web site of the International Mission Board, www.imb.org.

Activity 9—What Is the Lottie Moon Christmas Offering for Missions?

The mission of the church to reach the world for Christ is far from complete. The International Mission Board of the Southern Baptist Convention maintains the largest mission force in the world today. The Lottie Moon Christman Offering is designed to support missions worldwide. You may learn more about this great enterprise to carry out the Great Commission by entering the Web site of the International Mission Board, www.imb.org.

Whether you choose to be involved with the IMB or some other mission organization, help your children to understand the importance of giving to carry the gospel to the ends of the world. You may want to talk with the children about giving to a mission project that will help others share the gospel to other boys, girls, men, and women across the world.

Activity 10—Memorize the Great Commission (Matthew 28:18b–20)

In the Great Commandment we are instructed what our character needs to exhibit. In the Great Commission, we are instructed on the task we are to carry out. Help the children memorize these verses as a part of what God asks us to do.

All authority has been given to Me in heaven and on earth. Go, therefore, and make disciples of all nations, baptizing them in the name of the Father and of the Son and of the Holy Spirit, teaching them to observe everything I have commanded you. And remember, I am with you always, to the end of the age.

Have the children write these verses in their Bible Verse Memory Books and illustrate them.

ACTIVITY SHEET 2: MAP OF INDIA

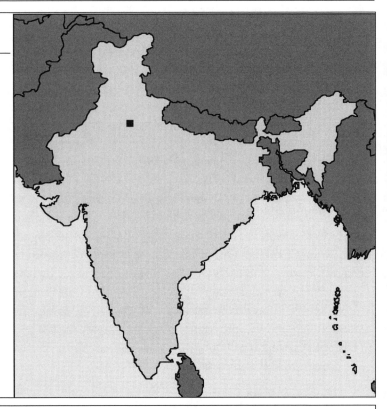

ACTIVITY SHEET 4: LIFE OF DAVID LIVINGSTONE—MISSIONARY TO AFRICA

Beginning

Middle

End

Activity Sheet 1: Missionary History

Time Line for Missionary Growth and Expansion

Christ to Constantine (AD 33–500)—Missionary Expansion of the Gospel

1. Paul takes the gospel to the Greek and Roman world.
2. Early Church missions (AD 100–313)
3. Emperor Constantine (c. AD 272–337) has a vision; he conquered in the name of Christ; he passed the Edict of Milan and made Christianity legal in the Empire.

Constantine to Charlemagne—Early Missions in Europe

AD 300–800—missionary expansion of the gospel

1. Ulfilas (AD 311–388) translated the Bible for the Goths.
2. Patrick (AD 396–493) evangelized Ireland.
3. Mohammed begins Islam—threat to the gospel.
4. Boniface (AD 680–755)—missionary to Germany
5. Monks responsible for preaching and teaching the gospel.
6. The Vikings (AD 800–1200)—hurt missionary endeavor and the gospel; killed people in churches, burned churches, sold monks to slavery; England and European continent devastated by Vikings, but paganism did not prevail.

Charlemagne to Luther—Medieval Missions in Europe (AD 800–1517)—Missionary Activity

1. Anskar (AD 801–854)—apostle to the north, but few visible results
2. The evil of the Crusades hurt missionary endeavor.
3. Francis of Assisi (1182–1226) lived the gospel, ministered to the Sultan in Egypt.
4. Martyrdom of Raymond Lull in northern Africa (1235–1315)—burdened for the Saracens

Luther to Carey (1517–1793)—Missionary Expansion and the Gospel

1. Count von Zinzendorf (1700–1760)—Moravian missionary
2. David Brainerd (1718–1747)—missionary to the North American Indians

Missionary Expansion (1793–1914)—Expansion and the Gospel

1. William Carey (1793–1834)—English Baptist missionary to India—European dominance of modern missions
2. David Livingstone (1813–1873)—missionary to Africa
3. Hudson Taylor (1832–1905)—missionary to China; American dominance of modern missions
4. Lottie Moon (1840–1912)—missionary to China
5. World Missions Conference, Edinburgh, Scotland (1910)

Modern Missions (1914–2000 and Beyond)—Changes in Missions

1. Beginning of missionary radio—1931
2. Post-World War II—World War II veterans bring world consciousness, growth of nationalism, decline of Western control, upsurge of Christianity in non-Western world.
3. Today we have vast new opportunities in communication and transportation.
4. New focus on "unreached people groups of 10/40 window"—population centers between 10° and 40° north latitude and urban population centers of the world.

ACTIVITY SHEET 5: MAP OF AFRICA

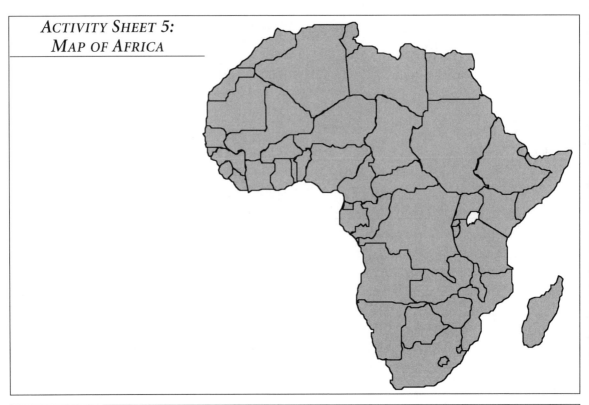

ACTIVITY SHEET 6: BOOKMARK

fold

ACTIVITY SHEET 7:
MAP OF CHINA

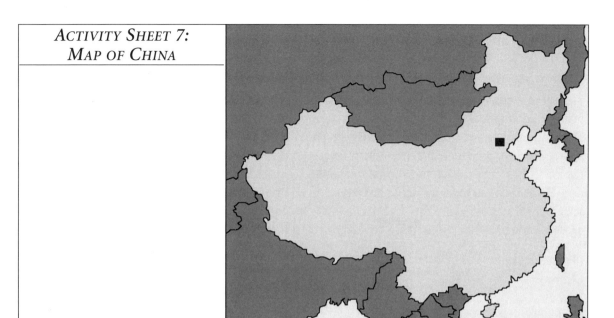

UNIT SUMMARY

This set of lessons will provide the learner with an introduction to the fine arts and to scientists from a Christian perspective. To help the learner gain an appreciation for aesthetic values from the perspective of a Christian orientation from past civilization. To help the learner gain an appreciation of science from scientists, who held a Christian point of view for their scientific research.

OVERVIEW

Objectives

By the end of this unit, the learner should be able to

- identify and describe the structure of a great cathedral as a church built to the glory of God in an age characterized by faith,
- identify and describe the furniture and other equipment that characterize the worshipful ambience of the cathedral,
- understand and appreciate the painting and sculpture that were used to decorate the interior of the great cathedrals and later of churches,
- understand and appreciate the aesthetically pleasing sounds that are associated with churches and cathedrals, beginning with the Gregorian chant and continuing to hymns and gospel songs, and
- identify and understand how science has contributed to our civilization and that it has not always been in conflict with Christian faith and belief. Rather, there have been scientists who have viewed their science in support of Christian faith, not in opposition to Christian faith.

Content Summary and Rationale

In past centuries, art, music, literature, and science have been affected positively by the Christian faith. Our children need to be given the opportunity to rightfully reclaim their heritage. It is only in recent times that the world has become increasingly secular.

To reclaim their heritage, children need to be exposed to good art, music, literature, and science. Far from denying the faith, in some cases they have been marshaled to support our Christian faith. We need to help children not to compartmentalize their Christian faith and remove it from the rest of life. Until the Renaissance, Christianity reigned as queen of the sciences. This unit seeks to present several of these subjects from a Christian perspective.

In this unit, we will examine architecture that was used by builders to the glory of God as they constructed the great cathedrals of the Middle Ages. The great cathedral edifices were aesthetically pleasing to God and man. We will also examine another form of art through painting and sculpture that were used to decorate the interiors of the great cathedrals of Europe. These artifacts were aesthetically pleasing to the worshipers, as they sought to worship God in surroundings that would lead them closer to God. Stained glass was employed to add to the aesthetic surroundings, but as it caught the rays of sunshine, it also contributed to the mystery of the presence of God in the great cathedral. The sounds that came from within the cathedral also added to the atmosphere of worship. They included the Gregorian chant to the hymns of the seventeenth and eighteenth centuries. We will examine some of these hymns as well.

Finally, this unit will examine the growth of science as it interfaces with Christian faith. Science has been suggested to be anti-Christian. This has not always been true. We will look at several scientists who have been believers and used their scientific discoveries to support Christian faith and belief.

Key Concept

Art, music, literature, and science in recent years have been removed from a Christian world and life view. In past centuries these disciplines were significantly related to Christian faith and belief. Our children need to become aware that their beliefs have been a major part of the culture until relatively recently, when the culture has tried to characterize them as anachronistic in the modern age. However, God's truth plays a strong role in our cultural heritage. Both we and our children need to recover that heritage.

Prior Knowledge Needed

Children have almost no knowledge or understanding of the Christian culture of past centuries. Prior knowledge is not expected in these areas. This will allow new knowledge to be established as part of the child's repertoire for the future.

RESOURCES FOR TEACHERS AND STUDENTS

- Buchanan, Edward, *Parent/Teacher Handbook: Their Christian Heritage, Vol. 2* (Nashville, Tenn.: Broadman & Holman, 2003).
- Butler, Trent, ed., *Holman Illustrated Bible Dictionary* (Nashville, Tenn.: Holman Bible Publishers, 2003).
- Dockery, David, ed., *Holman Bible Handbook* (Nashville, Tenn.: Holman Bible Publishers, 1992).
- An Encyclopedia—*World Book, Funk and Wagnalls, Britannica*, etc. (may use CD-ROM)

LESSON 12: CHRISTIANITY AND THE FINE ARTS

Readings from the Parent/Teacher Handbook: Their Christian Heritage, Vol. 2: "Christian Works of Art" and the subsection, "Medieval Building to the Glory of God." (Note: We covered subsection, "Christian Symbolism Found in the Catacombs" in lesson 5.)

OBJECTIVES

By the end of this lesson, the learner should be able to

- explain the purpose for constructing great cathedrals,
- identify and describe the great Gothic cathedral at York, England,
- discover the background of the cathedral at York,
- explore the variety of craftsmen who worked on the cathedral at York,
- define *Romanesque* and *Gothic*,
- explore the design of the inside of the cathedral at York,
- compare and contrast the cathedral with a neighborhood church building, and
- explain the use of stained glass in the cathedral, such as the Noah Window from the cathedral at Ulm, Germany.

IDENTIFICATIONS

Concepts

Cathedra—from a Greek word *cathedra* which means "chair" and today it is the bishop's chair

Cathedral—a very large church, usually in the shape of a cross and facing from the pulpit at the east to the main doors at the west

Anglican Church—state church of England

Romanesque—a form of architecture that was used from about the 10th to the 13th centuries and originated from the idea that it had its origin in the Romance languages from Latin; it has similarities to Roman architecture

Gothic—a form of architecture that allowed additional windows for greater light than the Romanesque architectural forms. It first appeared in the 12th century in France and later extended over much of Europe to the period of the Renaissance. At first *Gothic* was a derogatory term but now is much more appreciated as a unique and beautiful form of architecture.

Master builder—person responsible for the construction of the cathedral; probably an architect in our day

Masons—workers in stone

Carpenters—workers with skills in several building trades

Woodworkers—workers with wood

Glaziers—workers with clear glass and stained glass

Stained glass—glass colored for light to pass through

Ambulatory—walkway around the area that houses the high altar

High altar—the structure where sacrifices were made; in Christian churches it usually connotes a place where the Lord's Supper originates, remembering the sacrifice of Christ on the cross

Arcade—series of arches, supported by columns or piers

Cloister—open space; surrounded by an arcade

Clerestory—the uppermost range of windows in the church

Crossing—section of the church where the transepts cross at right angles with the main part of the church

Choir—part of the church that is set aside for the sung part of the church service

Flying buttresses—supports for the church, which carry the thrust of the weight of the roof to an outer wall buttress

Nave—western part of the church, where the congregation gathers

Piers—solid block of masonry used to support the structure

Lecturn—from the Latin word *legere*, which means to read. Scripture readings are done from the lecturn.

Pulpit—from the Latin word *pulpitum*, which means "a scaffold or platform"; in a church it is the elevated platform from which the pastor preaches his sermon.

Font—from the Latin word *fontes*, which means "fountain of water"; as used in the church, it is a container used for baptism.

Transept—the part of the church that crosses at right angles with the main part of the church between the nave and the choir

Vault—an arched roof or ceiling, usually constructed of stone

People

Paulinus: missionary who brought Christianity back to York, England

Edwin: most powerful king in England from Northumbria, who wanted to marry the Princess Ethelburga; she refused unless Paulinus was allowed to preach Christ in Northumbria. Edwin agreed and became a Christian.

Places

York, England: Medieval town in the northern part of England

Ulm, Germany: Medieval city in south Germany, center for arts and commerce; the residents voted to become Lutheran during the Reformation.

MATERIALS NEEDED

Parent/Teacher Handbook: Their Christian Heritage, Vol. 2

Activity Sheets for Lesson 12

Crayons and markers

Card stock duplication paper

White paper for drawing

Lined paper for writing

Roll of shelf paper or butcher paper

Masking tape and plastic tape

3x5-index cards

Plaster of Paris or a dough recipe

Tempera paints	Glue
Construction paper	Scissors
Paintbrush	Wax paper

1-inch square tissue squares of bright colors

LEARNING ACTIVITIES FOR LESSON 12

Activity 1—Dictionary Definition of Cathedral and Parts of the Cathedral

In the handbook read "Christianity and the Fine Arts," "Medieval Building to the Glory of God," "The Cathedral of York, England," "Building a Great Cathedral," and "Design of a Great Cathedral." You will find some terms that relate to the study of the cathedral on Activity Sheet 1. If your students are old enough to use a dictionary, have them define the following terms using the dictionary: cathedral, ambulatory, arcade, font, cathedra, clerestory, choir, flying buttress, crossing, transept, and nave. This is a good exercise, since the students do not like to practice dictionary skills, but this will allow them to do that in a way that is interesting.

Discuss with them the use of the dictionary. It includes pronunciation, parts of speech, definitions, and use of words in context. It may also include the etymology of the word.

If your students are not old enough to use the dictionary, you will need to help them with this activity. You will find definitions for the terms in the handbook under "Design of the Great Cathedral" and the sidebar "Interior of the Cathedral."

Activity 2—Ticket of Admission to the York Cathedral

In advance of this session, duplicate classroom quantities of tickets on cards stock duplicating paper. You will find the pattern for the tickets on Activity Sheet 2. Have the students cut out the tickets. If they are old enough, have them find the latitude and longitude lines for York, England, on a map. Enter the longitude and latitude numbers beneath the title. Then, under the longitude and latitude numbers, ask them to write a brief description of the cathedral at York. They may illustrate the cathedral in the block to the left.

If you have Internet access, use the ticket to get online with the official Web site for the York Cathedral. It may be found at the following Web address: www.yorkminster.org/index1.html. You will find pictures of the cathedral, other items of interest, and even audio clips of the magnificent choir at the cathedral.

Activity 3—Pyramid with Purposes of the Cathedral

Cut sheets of 8½x11-inch construction paper into 8-inch squares for each student. See the illustration on Activity Sheet 3. Fold the top corner of the construction paper down to the opposite corner. Do the same with the other corners. Have the students write the purposes for the cathedral on three of the four triangles. They may also decorate their pyramids. Open the folded paper and cut from the corner to the centerpoint on the left side of the blank triangle. Overlap the written triangle over the blank triangle and glue. The pyramid will stand up.

On the three sides of the pyramid, write the following items:

Side 1—Purpose 1

This is man's attempt to bring Christians closer to God.

The cathedral replaces the Tabernacle and the Temple for worship of God.

Side 2—Purpose 2

The cathedral is built in the shape of a cross.

This is the most important symbol of Christianity.

Side 3—Purpose 3

The cathedral was built to last for a very long time.

The beauty symbolizes how God created everything beautiful.

The large space in the cathedral speaks of God's awesome being.

Activity 4—Time Line for the York Cathedral

The history of York goes back at least two thousand years. Give a brief synopsis of the history of the cathedral. Then have the children answer questions about the past years of the cathedral. You will find the history, on Activity Sheet 4-A. The questions are on Activity Sheet 4-B. Duplicate copies of each and distribute to the members of your class.

Activity 5—Identifying the Furniture of the Cathedral

Read "The Furniture of the Cathedral" in the handbook. Become familiar with the furniture of the cathedral. If you are not very familiar, you might consult a dictionary, encyclopedia, or the Web site for York Cathedral for additional information.

Talk with the children about the furniture that is present in the cathedral. On Activity Sheet 5 you will find sketches of the pieces of furniture in the cathedral. Have the children name each of the pieces of furniture and write the names in the space provided.

Activity 6—Matching Builders of the Cathedral with Their Occupations

Read "Building a Great Cathedral" in the handbook. Discuss the different types of occupations that were employed in building the cathedral.

Have the students complete the matching exercise on Activity Sheet 6. Talk about the significance of occupations for building Christian churches in the Middle Ages. For additional help, consult a CD-ROM encyclopedia.

Activity 7—Comparing Characteristics of a Cathedral with Your Church

With the coming of the Reformation in the sixteenth century, there was a significant change in the way churches were structured. Martin Luther centered the service on the preaching of the Word. Anglican and Catholic churches continued to center the service on the Lord's Supper. As a result, you may find that your church is quite different from one of these great cathedrals. After looking at the characteristics of the cathedral, find the similarities and list the differences that exist. You may want to write these on a large sheet of paper. For younger children, make this a class exercise and write the characteristics on the chalkboard. Here are some of the characteristics of cathedrals:

- Generally cathedrals are made of stone.
- Cathedrals took many years to build.
- They have lasted many hundreds of years.
- Cathedrals have an altar for the Lord's Supper to remember Jesus' sacrifice.
- They normally have paintings and candles.

- They have stained glass windows.
- They have statues and sculptures.
- They have a baptismal font.
- They have small chapels for prayer.
- They have the choir separated from the congregation.
- Generally cathedrals are very large.

- The cathedra (or bishop's chair) is located in the cathedral.
- Their main purpose was to worship God.
- They have pulpits for preaching.
- A sermon is part of the service.
- Singing is part of the service.

Now select the characteristics that are present in your church. What are the similarities? What are the differences? Why do these differences happen?

Activity 8—Matching Quiz Review of Cathedrals

Turn to Activity Sheet 8 and duplicate classroom quantities of the review matching quiz. After you have studied the material together, ask the children to complete the quiz.

Activity 9—Make a Stained Glass Window

Mix 3 tablespoons of glue with $1/4$ cup of water. (It will appear about as white as milk). For each child, cut out two stained glass window frames found on Activity Sheet 9. Lay one frame on wax paper. Lay one 1-inch square of tissue at a time in the middle and along the sides of the frame. Dip your brush in the glue-and-water mixture and paint over the tissue square so that it is smooth but not too wet. Continue laying the tissue squares down with the glue-and-water mixture, similar to a collage.

After you have totally filled all the space in the middle of the frame and along the edges, lay the other frame on top of the sheet to sandwich all tissue squares in between the frames. Glue the other frame in place on top. Allow the tissue squares to dry completely before removing the wax paper. Hang the "stained glass window" on a window. Allow the sun to shine through. Look at the beauty of the colors coming through your "stained glass window."

Activity 10—Visit a Cathedral

Visit a cathedral in a large city near you. Given what you know about cathedrals, the trip will provide practical reinforcement to the insights that your students have gained from this study. In New York City, for example, there are the Cathedral of St. John the Divine (nondenominational), the Cathedral of St. Thomas (Episcopal), and St. Patrick's Cathedral (Catholic). In Washington, DC, there are the National Cathedral (Episcopal) and St. Mary's Cathedral (Catholic). There are other very good examples of cathedrals in other cities as well.

Activity 11—Memorize Psalm 96:8–9

This speaks of the majesty of entering the house of the Lord. It is appropriate to worship in the cathedral. The cathedral builders intended to ascribe glory to the Lord. Memorize Psalm 96:8–9:

Ascribe to the LORD the glory of His name; bring an offering and enter His courts.
Worship the LORD in His holy majesty; tremble before Him, all the earth.

Be sure to have the children write these two verses in their Bible Verse Memory Books and illustrate them.

ACTIVITY SHEET 1: DEFINITION OF TERMS FOR YORK CATHEDRAL

Cathedral

Cathedra

Choir *(Note: For "choir" the first definition is not the one you want. This one is a definition that makes this part of a church building).*

Ambulatory *(Note: For "ambulatory" the definition must be understood in relation to a part of the building).*

Arcade

Font

Clerestory

Flying buttress

Nave *(Note: This may not be the first definition given).*

Transept

Crossing

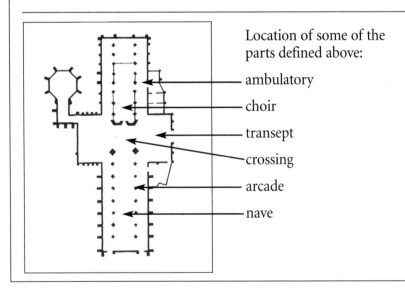

Location of some of the parts defined above:

— ambulatory

— choir

— transept

— crossing

— arcade

— nave

ACTIVITY SHEET 2: TICKET TO YORK CATHEDRAL

Directions: Describe the cathedral in the section of the ticket that states "Ticket to Visit the Cathedral." Draw a picture of the cathedral in the box at the left. Then cut out the ticket.

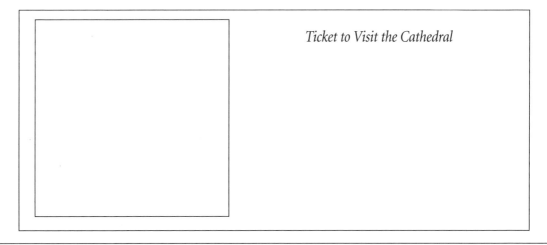

Ticket to Visit the Cathedral

ACTIVITY SHEET 3: PYRAMID WITH PURPOSES OF THE CATHEDRAL

Directions: Make a pyramid from a square of construction paper. Write or draw on the pyramid. Fold along the dashed lines and cut on the solid line. Overlap the bottom triangles and glue.

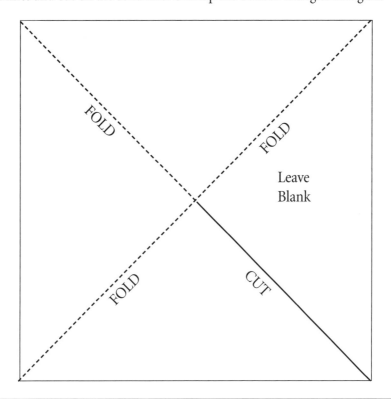

ACTIVITY SHEET 4-A: TIME LINE FOR THE CATHEDRAL

Year AD	Event
306	Constantine the Great was proclaimed emperor in York in the basilica under the present site.
627	Edwin was baptized in a wooden church, probably the first cathedral in York.
1069	The Anglo-Saxon cathedral was burned by the marauders from the north.
1080–1100	Thomas of Bayeux built a new cathedral, the remains of which can still be seen today along the walls.
1170	Choir was replaced by a choir with aisles.
1200–1253	The Cathedral was expanded, using a Norman-Romanesque style of architecture.
1407–1465	Central tower suffered damage and was rebuilt.
1472	Present building was rededicated.

ACTIVITY SHEET 4-B: GUIDE FOR DISCUSSION ABOUT THE HISTORY OF THE CATHEDRAL

Directions: Answer the following questions.

1. How many years did it take to complete the cathedral?

_____

2. Who was crowned Roman emperor in the West in the basilica?

_____

3. When was the cathedral rededicated?

_____

4. Who was baptized in the basilica?

_____

5. Who built the Norman-Romanesque cathedral?

_____

6. Why was the central tower rebuilt?

_____

ACTIVITY SHEET 5: FURNITURE OF THE CATHEDRAL

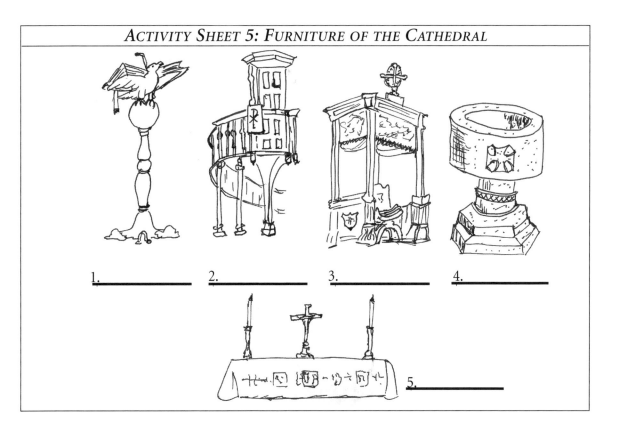

1._____   2._____   3._____   4._____

5._____

ACTIVITY SHEET 6: MATCHING REVIEW OF THE CATHEDRAL BUILDERS

Directions: Match the description in the right column with the occupation in the left by placing the correct letter on the line provided.

___1. Master builder

___2. Masons

___3. Carpenters

___4. Glaziers

___5. Day laborers

___6. Sculptors

___7. Metalworkers

a. make stone statues for the cathedral

b. heated silica to 3000°F to make windows for the cathedral

c. served as the overseer and had knowledge of geometry and mathematics

d. worked with many projects involving wood in the cathedral

e. responsible for cutting stone; one of the biggest jobs for the cathedral because it had to be fitted together without mortar

f. did the many unskilled jobs that were needed in the building of a great cathedral

g. these men worked with lead for the roof and brass for furnishings

ACTIVITY SHEET 8: MATCHING QUIZ

Directions: Match the lettered items at the right with the numbered items in the left column.

___1. Flying buttresses
___2. Gothic
___3. altar
___4. nave
___5. choir

a. section of church for choir
b. place of sacrifice; today Lord's Supper
c. form of architecture
d. piers outside the church to provide support
e. section of the church for congregation

Match the following:

___6. ambulatory
___7. arcade
___8. crossing
___9. pulpit
___10. transept

f. arms of the cross
g. midsection where transepts cross the nave
h. platform for pastor to preach
i. aisle that goes around the choir
j. aisle that goes around the nave

ACTIVITY SHEET 9: MAKING A STAINED-GLASS WINDOW FRAME

Cut around the outside and cut out the center. (Cut 2 frames for each child.)

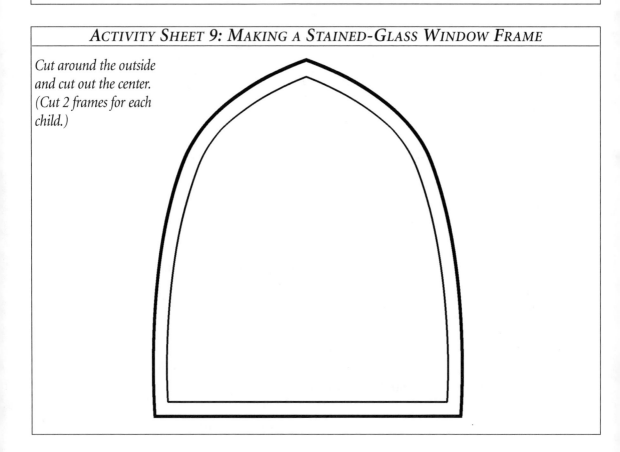

Readings from the Parent/Teacher Handbook: Their Christian Heritage, Vol: 2: "Christian Painting and Sculpture"

OBJECTIVES

By the end of this lesson, the learner should be able to

- understand the way the artist uses a two-dimensional surface with colors and shapes to convey his message,
- examine different styles of painting that tell the artist's story in different ways at different times,
- demonstrate appreciation for *Enthroned Madonna and Child* of the 13th century,
- contrast *Mérode Altarpiece* of the annunciation with *Enthroned Madonna and Child,*
- examine Michelangelo's *Pietá* sculpture, showing Mary at the death of Jesus,
- compare *Alba Madonna* of Raphael with the other paintings,
- compare and contrast Rembrandt's *The Hundred Guilder Print* with *Forest Scene* of Jacob van Ruisdael, and
- discover a very different approach to painting in *Peaceable Kingdom* by Edward Hicks

IDENTIFICATIONS

Concepts

two-dimensions—height and width, but no depth
color—a product of light that makes different objects appear distinct from each other
shape—differing forms
texture—smoothness or roughness of the surface
spiritual quality—relating to the sacredness of an object
tryptich—painting with three panels; two panels are hinged and may close over the center panel
Pieta—representation of Mary sorrowing over the dead body of Jesus
Madonna—artistic representation of the Virgin Mary
Etching—a design produced on a metal plate by having acid eat at the places the artist does not want to appear on the print
Tree of Life—same as the Tree of Knowledge in the Garden of Eden; it provided life.

Tree of Death—medieval idea of a tree that was the opposite of the Tree of Life

People

Robert Campin: painter from Flanders
Michelangelo: Italian artist; the greatest sculptor and painter of all time
Raphael: Italian Umbrian painter (1483–1520); one of the greatest painters of the High Renaissance
Rembrandt: Dutch painter (1606–1669) from Leiden; known for his masterful technique
Jacob van Ruisdael: Dutch painter (1628–1682) known for his landscape painting
Edward Hicks: American native painter (1780–1849) who is best known for his sixty different versions of the peaceable kingdom, expressing his Quaker views
William Penn: Quaker founder of Pennsylvania

Places

Tournai, Belgium: home of Robert Campin
St. Peter's Basilica, Rome: largest basilica in the world; at the Vatican
National Gallery of Art, Washington, DC: excellent art museum in America's capital
Metropolitan Museum of Art, New York City: greatest art museum in America
Holland: home of Rembrandt and van Ruisdael
Langhorne, PA: home of Edward Hicks

MATERIALS NEEDED

Parent/Teacher Handbook: Their Christian Heritage, Vol. 2
Activity Sheets for Lesson 13
Crayons and markers
White paper for drawing
Lined paper for writing
Roll of shelf paper or butcher paper
Masking tape, plastic tape, reusable adhesive
3x5-inch index cards
Plaster of Paris or a dough recipe
Construction paper
Art prints or slides (optional)
Tempra paints

Activity 1—Define Terms for This Lesson

Read "Christian Painting and Sculpture" in the handbook. Try to read this material in one sitting in order to see the differences that exist among the paintings and the sculpture.

Write the following vocabulary words on the chalkboard. Then for each word, write both a correct and an incorrect definition.

After you have written the words and the definitions on the chalkboard, ask the students to think about the words and their meanings. Ask them to decide which is the correct definition of the word according to the information in the handbook. Have them vote by raising their hands for the first definition or for the second definition. Erase the incorrect definition. For older students, have them write the words in their notebook. For younger students, you may just want them to differentiate between the right and wrong definitions.

The words and the two definitions are the following (the correct definition is indicated with an asterisk *).

Texture—
   *Definition 1—the surface feeling of smoothness or roughness
   Definition 2—the inner core of an object
Etching—
   Definition 1—a design that is painted on a surface with a narrow paintbrush with lines
   *Definition 2—a design that is created by using acid on metal to remove unwanted parts
Pieta—
   *Definition 1—Mary, mother of Jesus, grieving and holding her dead Son
   Definition 2—Dead body of Jesus lying limp as His body was removed from the cross
Madonna—
   *Definition 1—Mary, mother of Jesus, shown in a painting or sculpture
   Definition 2—person who is a singer today in the United States
Tryptich—
   *Definition 1—a painting with three panels; the two outside may close across the center panel
   Definition 2—a poster that has three parts and hangs on a wall
Shape—
   Definition 1—feeling of an object
   *Definition 2—form of an object
Color—
   Definition 1—absence of light that causes objects to appear differently
   *Definition 2—product of light that makes objects different from other objects

Activity 2—Questioning Strategy

In the handbook read "*Enthroned Madonna and Child,*" "*Merode Altarpiece,*" and the "*Alba Madonna.*" You will find black and white reproductions of the paintings in this volume.

It is important for your children to think carefully about an art object if they are going to gain the most from an art lesson. This is true, whether the art is sacred or secular. Before you start in class, design your questions. It is through questions that students are challenged to see things that they would otherwise miss in an art piece. Take some time yourself and answer the questions that you will ask the students. To be sure, your answers will exceed what your students will be able to do, but you still need to think through the same kinds of questions that the students will consider.

Have copies of the paintings—*Enthroned Madonna*, *Mérode Altarpiece*, and *Alba Madonna*—for the students to view. You can obtain prints of *Enthroned Madonna* and *Alba Madonna* from the National Gallery of Art, 2000B South Club Drive, Landover, MD 20785. For general information call (202) 737-4215. A print of *Merode Altarpiece* can be obtained from the Metropolitan Museum of Art, 1000 Fifth Avenue at 82nd Street, New York, New York 10028-0198. For general information call (212) 535-7710.

You can also view these paintings, and additional paintings in each of the collections, on the Web sites of the above museums. The National Gallery Web site is www.nga.gov. The Web site for the Metropolitan Museum of Art is www.metmuseum.org.

Have your students look at each of the three paintings. Ask your students the following questions:

1. What do you see in these paintings? What similarities and differences exist? For each painting, the artist has provided us with his or her view of the world. People from different time periods may be included. Painting is different from photography, especially in this respect.

2. Who are the figures in this painting? What do the figures represent? How important are persons to the total composition of the painting? Consider the people; do they come from different time periods? If so, why did the artist do this?

3. How did the artist give you a sense of space in which the objects are presented? On this two-dimensional surface of width and height, how did the artist give you a sense that there may have been depth as well? Consider the ways in which color, lines, and shapes are used.

4. How does the artist make you feel that the painting is complete and finished? How are the objects in the painting arranged? Composition is the way these parts are arranged to form unity or completeness.

5. How do the details of the painting affect the message that the artist is trying to convey? You will need some help with this question. You will find the help you need in the sections about these paintings in the handbook.

6. In the first question, we suggested that you look at the painting and try to gain as many details as possible. Then we focused on various parts of the painting. Now return to the first question. What do you see differently?

Whenever you approach a new work of art, these questions will help you understand and gain meaning that the artist is trying to convey. For some of the specific details, you may need to consult help from an encyclopedia, art book, or online. You might not be aware of why the artist did certain things. In our day, the reasons may not be readily apparent, but if you had lived at the time the artist produced the painting, they would be easily understood. For example, in *Mérode Altarpiece*, the inclusion of the donor and his wife could only have occurred for a short period of time. The conventions of medieval painting would not have allowed their inclusion. If the painting were done later, they would have been presented in a different way. For this kind of information, you will need to seek help from other resources.

Activity 3—Pyramid Comparison of Three Paintings
Using the pattern from Lesson 12, Activity Sheet 3, make a pyramid out of construction paper. Compare and contrast these three pictures: *Enthroned Madonna*, *Mérode Altarpiece*, and *Alba Madonna*. You might suggest that class members write something comparable to the following:

Enthroned Madonna
- Byzantine 13th century
- Flat surface—2-dimensional
- Gold gives it value

- Hung in a church over flickering candles
- Bright colors
- Spiritual and devotional value

Mérode Altarpiece
- Tryptich from the 15th century
- Sponsors are in the left panel
- Objects in room contribute to meaning

- In a private home for prayer and devotion
- Shows the Annunciation by the angel to Mary
- Joseph in carpentry shop in the right panel

Alba Madonna
- Painted in a circle, from the 16th century
- Hung in a private home in Spain

- Mary, Jesus, and John the Baptist form a pyramid
- Countryside scene with John the Baptist looking to Jesus, who holds a cross

Activity 4—*The* Pietá *of Michelangelo*
Read "*Pietá*" in the handbook.

Have your students study the *Pietá* before they read the section. Ask the following questions, which are given in the handbook. Record their responses on the chalkboard.

Who are the main figures in this sculpture? What is the meaning of the expression on the face of the woman? Why is the man on her lap limp as a lifeless form? Is there a spiritual meaning to this sculpture? What are the feelings caused by the sculpture? How do you feel about the sculpture? What kind of material do you suppose Michelangelo used to create this sculpture?

After the students have analyzed the sculpture to the extent that they can, tell them the story of this sculpture. Talk about the dark sadness that is evident in Mary's face. What does that tell you about her feelings? How would you have felt if you had been in her place? Recall the words of the prophet, Simeon, from Luke 2:34–35. How were they fulfilled? What can we learn from the sculptor's portrayal of Jesus' limp body in the arms of His mother, Mary? A color version of the statue can be found at www.statue.com/michelangelo-pieta.html.

Activity 5—*Compare and Contrast the artists: Campin, Michelangelo, and Raphael*
Have your students research these three artists—Robert Campin, Michelangelo, and Raphael. If you have access to an encyclopedia, this would be a good source. Have the students report on their findings at the next class session.

For younger students, you may find it helpful to provide information for them. Below are simple paragraphs that tell about their lives.

Michelangelo was an Italian artist. He was probably the greatest artist of all time. He lived between 1475 and 1564. He was a skilled sculptor, painter, and architect. He sculpted the *Pietá*. His most famous painting was the ceiling of the Sistine Chapel in Rome. He was the architect for the dome of St. Peter's Basilica, the largest basilica in the world. He worked in Florence, Bologna, and mostly in Rome.

Raphael was also an Italian painter. His father had been a painter before him. He was born in 1483 and lived to 1520. He had a traditional art education and completed altarpieces for churches in Umbria and Tuscany. He had to relearn his trade when he came to Rome. In Rome Raphael did his greatest work for two popes. Raphael painted *Alba Madonna*.

Robert Campin was Flemish, born in Tournai, Belgium, in 1378. He lived until 1444. Campin did not sign any of his pictures. He was more like the medieval artists, since they did not sign anything either. Many paintings, like *Merode Altarpiece*, have been assumed to come from his brush. The great Flemish artist Roger van der Weyden trained with Campin. Campin's work is clearly northern Renaissance in style and shows much more of a devotional bent than do the works of the Italian Renaissance painters.

Compare and contrast the works of each of these three artists. What do you like about each of the paintings? What do you dislike? How do they each make you feel? Do they cause you to worship God? Discuss.

Activity 6—Compare Rembrandt's Hundred Guilder *Etching with van Ruisdael's* Forest Scene

Ask your students to research the lives of these two Dutch artists—Rembrandt and Jacob van Ruisdael. Both lived about the same time. Have the students report at the next class session. As in the case of Activity 5, for younger students, you may need to help them to understand the lives of these two great Protestant artists. Below are two short paragraphs to describe their lives.

Rembrandt van Rijn was born in Leiden, Holland, in 1606. He trained under Pieter Lastman in Amsterdam. From there he worked in both Leiden and later in Amsterdam. Rembrandt is the most famous Dutch artist of the seventeenth century for both painting and etching. He did many biblical subjects, mythical subjects, genre, still life, and landscapes. Many artists adopted his techniques. Rembrandt died in 1669.

Jacob van Ruisdael was born in Haarlem, Holland, in 1629. At first he worked in his own hometown. But by 1666 he had moved to Amsterdam. His landscape painting was learned from his father, and his waterfalls were learned from his cousin. They were both painters. Unfortunately, in his later years Ruisdael returned to Haarlem, where he died tragically insane in 1681.

Look at the two paintings. You may want to duplicate the questions for *The Hundred Guilder* etching of Rembrandt and the *Forest Scene* of Jacob van Ruisdael. You will find the questions on Activity Sheet 6. Have the students study the two paintings. Answer the questions. Compare the paintings.

The Hundred Guilder can be found at www.louvre.frl/louvrea.htm and the *Forest Scene* can be found at www.nga.gov.

*Activity 7—*Peaceable Kingdom *by Eward Hicks*

Look carefully at *Peaceable Kingdom*. There are more than sixty extant paintings of this subject. Why did the Quaker, Edward Hicks, create so many different paintings of this one subject? Remember that Hicks was a Quaker, and as such, he was a pacifist. The passage of Scripture that was used by Hicks was Isaiah 11:6: "The wolf also shall dwell with the lamb, and the leopard shall lie down with the kid; and the calf and the young lion and the fatling together; and a little child shall lead them" (KJV).

Ask the questions about this painting from Activity 2 above. A color version of the paiting can be found at www.nga.org.

After you have completed your analysis of the questions from Activity 2, ask the children to find as many of the animals as they can. List them on the chalkboard. There are at least the following animals in Hicks's paintings: cattle, lion, bear, goat, leopard, wolf, tiger, and sheep. Why does the artist include both native American Indians and Quakers? What does this tell us about God's plan for the future?

Activity 8—Wordfind on These Works of Art

As a review activity, have copies of the wordfind on Activity Sheet 8 for these works of art available for the students in your class. Ask the students to write the word in the blank provided. Then they may complete the wordfind.

Activity 9—How Do These Works of Art Help Us Grow Spiritually?

We have discussed previously the role of art as a reflection of the culture from which the art came. God has given us an aesthetic side of our personalities so that we may enjoy good art. Good Christian art appeals to our aesthetic nature. The art and the symbols help us remember what God has done for us. Reading helps us become aware of what God is communicating to us. Art can serve the same purpose. It appeals to our emotions and our spiritual sensitivity.

Have students form small groups according to which painting or sculpture they enjoyed most. Have them select that piece of art and tell why they enjoyed it most. Help them use the questions of analysis from Activity 2 on the previous page. Encourage them to discover the reasons why they chose that particular piece of art. What is it about that piece of art that had instrinsic appeal? Have the students discuss this in their small group. When all have finished, have one person from each group tell why the group enjoyed that particular work of Christian art.

Activity 10—Field Trip to an Art Museum

Take the class on a field trip to an art museum or history museum in your community. Art museums have exhibits of art artifacts from time periods of the past and present. Many provide hands-on activities for children. There are usually self-guided tours through the museum that will focus upon materials of special interest. Remember to observe closely the objects on display. What has made them worthy of note? From what time period did they come? Compare them with similar objects from different time periods and note similarities and differences. This can provide an excellent learning experience for children.

If you are located near a large city, like New York, Chicago, Washington, DC, Cleveland, or Los Angeles, there are excellent art museums for field trips. Even some smaller cities have excellent museums, like Minneapolis or Raleigh. Many universities have excellent collections also.

Of particular note is the Metropolitan Museum in New York City. It also operates the Cloisters at Fort Tryon Park, which is the only museum devoted exclusively to medieval art in the United States. The National Gallery of Art in Washington, DC, is also of particular value. The collection is arranged chronologically from the Middle Ages to the present.

Activity 11—Memorize Psalm 19:1–2

Aesthetic appreciation is something that has been given to us by God. He has provided us with the beauty of nature. These things are provided for our enjoyment. Memorize Psalm 19:1–2:

The heavens declare the glory of God, and the sky proclaims the work of His hands.
Day after day they pour out speech; night after night they communicate knowledge.

Have the students write the verse in their Bible Verse Memory Books and illustrate it.

ACTIVITY SHEET 6: QUESTIONS FOR REMBRANDT'S PAINTING, THE HUNDRED GUILDER PRINT AND RUISDAEL'S FOREST SCENE

Questions for The Hundred Guilder Print—
What do you see in this print? Who are the many characters? Who is the main character? Why are so many people pictured in this print? How do the people on the left side differ from the people on the right side? What do the facial expressions tell you about the people? Can you find the donkey in this print? Why do you suppose that the artist used the etching technique to create a print instead of painting to carry his message?

Questions for Forest Scene—
Is this a Christian religious painting? Is this painting simply a beautiful country forest scene? Is there a deeper meaning to this painting? How does this painting differ from all of the other works of art that we have seen so far? What are the main elements of this painting? Are there any people in this painting? If there are people, what are they doing and why? What story do you think the artist is trying to tell in this painting?

ACTIVITY SHEET 8: WORDFIND FOR CHRISTIAN PAINTING AND SCULPTURE

Directions: Complete the wordfind using the words below:

Ruisdael	Michelangelo	Jesus	Gabriel
Altarpiece	Mary	Rembrandt	Peaceable
Joseph	Raphael	Campin	Hicks

```
K P C O N I F K Q Q E E G Q Y
C X H Y F S A A L Y T I T F F
F N L H L T D N A R B M E R U
M J T X P L F N I E I Z C H B
T I A A A E C E I P R A T L A
X W L K R O S Z I L M Y R A M
C B A W N A J O E J P A C U U
V V X Y N S P A J U R F C N X
C Z Z N K U D H G N S I L I Y
O R D C K S Y K A L A H Y Y A
Z G I V I E L B A E C A E P E
N H T U Y J R O X J L K E Z Y
M K R Q X H I A L E I R B A G
N O L E G N A L E H C I M P Z
J L E I O Z Y J V F I W F X Q
```

1. In the *Enthroned Madonna and Child* painting, the two main persons pictured are _____ and _____.

2. The *Mérode* has three panels. The center panel pictured the angel _____ telling Mary of the coming birth of Jesus. This painting was done by Robert _____. On the right panel, _____ is seen in his carpenter's shop.

3. This famous artist is the one who sculpted the *Pietá*.

4. The circular painting of Mary, Jesus, and John the Baptist was done by _____.

5. Jesus' healing and preaching to the crowd was done by the artist _____van Rijn.

6. Jacob van _____ used *Forest Scene* to show the good and bad choices people make every day.

7. The painting _____ *Kingdom,* which shows a lion, a tiger, and other animals, was done by Edward_____.

LESSON 14: CHRISTIAN HYMNS AND SPIRITUAL SONGS

Readings from the Parent/Teacher Handbook: Their Christian Heritage, Vol. 2: "Christian Hymns and Spiritual Songs"

OBJECTIVES

By the end of this lesson, the learner should be able to

- examine the development of spiritual music in the Bible and in the church today,
- identify the role of music in Christian worship today,
- demonstrate understanding of the life of John Newton, hymn writer,
- discover the rich beauty of John Newton's hymn "Amazing Grace,"
- understand the heritage of the great Christmas carol "Silent Night," and
- respond to the aesthetic beauty of "Amazing Grace" and "Silent Night."

IDENTIFICATIONS

Concepts

Psalm—sacred songs that were used in Jewish worship and compiled in the Book of Psalms

Anthem—spiritual song; often from Scripture and sung antiphonally

Hymn—a song of praise to God; usually not directly from Scripture

Gregorian chant—plain song or chant that has free rhythm and limited scale

Emotions—our feelings that are affected by music

Olney Hymns—hymns published while Cowper and Newton were at the Church in Olney

People

John Newton: hymn writer (1725–1807); coauthored *Olney Hymns* and wrote "Amazing Grace"

William Cowper: hymn writer (1731–1800), coauthored *Olney Hymns*

Joseph Mohr: priest who wrote "Silent Night" (1792–1848)

Places

St. Mary's Woolnoth Church: church where Newton pastored to his eightieth year

St. Nicholas Church in Oberndorf, Austria: church where Mohr was assistant priest and wrote "Silent Night"

MATERIALS NEEDED

Parent/Teacher Handbook: Their Christian Heritage, Vol. 2

Activity Sheets for Lesson 14

Crayons and markers

White paper for drawing

Lined paper for writing

Masking tape and plastic tape

3x5-inch index cards

Tempera paints

Construction paper

Audiotapes

Musical instruments (optional)

Tape recorder or CD player (optional)

LEARNING ACTIVITIES FOR LESSON 14

Activity 1—Music as a Part of Worship

Read "Christian Hymns and Spiritual Songs" in the handbook. Singing has always played a significant role in the worship of God, even from the time of the ancient Jews. Both choral anthems and congregational singing have played a part.

To help children understand the importance of this aspect of worship, turn to Activity Sheet 1-A. This sheet explains the role of singing in the temple, synagogue, cathedral, and in our local churches today. On Activity Sheet 1-B there are discussion questions that will help the children focus on the use of church music in the past and present.

Activity 2—How Does Music Enhance Worship?

If you have not read the introduction to "Christian Hymns and Spiritual Songs" in the handbook, please do so now. Talk about worship. The word means to ascribe praise and honor to God. In a previous lesson, we mentioned that the first mention of worship in the English language came from the Lindisfarne Gospels, from England about AD 950. Lindisfarne was a monastery. You may find a description and picture on the Web site for the British Library at http://www.bl.uk/.

Turn to Activity Sheet 2. Copy this Yes/No activity sheet for the members of your class and distribute. Discuss with the children the answers they choose. If the children are very young, you may want to simply discuss the questions without an activity sheet.

Activity 3—The Life of John Newton

Read in the handbook, "Amazing Grace, John Newton, London, 1779." Tell the story to the members of your class.

Duplicate copies of the puzzle on Activity Sheet 3. Have the students complete the puzzle.

Activity 4—Printing and a Manuscript, "Amazing Grace"

You may wish to try your hand at another manuscript for printing. If you have access to a computer with different font types and a color ink-jet printer, you can create a manuscript in a matter of minutes that will demonstrate some of the beauty and significance of printing in today's world. You will find the words for "Amazing Grace," by John Newton.

Choose a type, such as Script MT Bold or experiment with other fonts. They are available at the top of the screen in your word processor. You can also change the size of the font in the little window to the right of the font style. You may find a border from computer images or find a border at a craft store to cut out and place the manuscript behind it as a frame. A color ink-jet printer will produce the manuscript and the border (if you have access to borders on your computer). This would be a good project for your students to complete, take home, and frame.

Activity 5—Selecting a Favorite Hymn or Christian Song

If you are near Advent, Christmas, Easter, or Pentecost when you teach this lesson, select hymns from your hymnbook that are appropriate to the holiday. Have your class sing the hymns. Discuss the meaning of the hymns that you sing. Help the children to see that there is more to hymn singing than just trying to remember the words from rote memory. If you do not have hymnbooks available, ask your church if you may borrow enough for your class during this lesson.

If you are not near one of the Christian holidays, select several hymns and spiritual songs for your class to sing. In advance of the session, you can probably find each song and information about the composer on the Internet. Work to help your children to appreciate good Christian music. Taste in music is acquired. If you are going to help them, it will mean that you will have to take many opportunities during the school year to help the children develop that taste. Don't give up; it is worth the fight.

Activity 6—Sequence the Events of "Silent Night"

Read in the handbook, "Silent Night! Holy Night!, Joseph Mohr, Oberndorf, Austria, 1818." Tell the story to the children in your class.

In advance of this session have copies of Activity Sheet 6 duplicated. Give these to the children. Help them sequence the events, if they are younger. If they are older, you may have them work individually to complete the activity sheet.

Activity 7—Picture of the Scene of "Silent Night! Holy Night!"

Give the children a sheet of construction paper. Ask them to draw the little church at Oberndorf, Germany, where the pastor wrote that special Christmas song, "Silent Night! Holy Night!"

There are several scenes that might be drawn. You may want the children to take different scenes, so that you may display the entire story. Here are some possibilities:
- Joseph Mohr visiting the home of the family with the newborn baby in the rough cradle.
- Joseph Mohr walking home on the snowy, starlit night.
- Joseph Mohr, in his study, writing the words to the song.
- Franz Gruber writing the music to the song.
- Playing the song on Christmas Eve in the church at Oberndorf.
- Fritz Mauracher repairing the organ for the church.
- Women's group singing at Leipzig Fair.
- Serviceman coming home after the war to the United States and bringing the song to his church.

Activity 8—Background to the Story of the Song, "Jesus Loves Me"

Hymn stories can be very interesting. "Jesus Loves Me" is one of the best-loved songs by children. The story behind the song is especially interesting. Although it was written well over one hundred years ago, it is by far one that is beloved by children around the world. Even other religions have appropriated the words. Missionaries have reported hearing the words in a Buddhist temple, "Buddha loves me." Read the story behind this great gospel song using Activity Sheet 8.

Tell the story to the children in your class. When you are finished, sing this beloved song and have the children illustrate the meaning of the song to them. Give each child a sheet of construction paper to draw their picture. The background of the song from Scripture is derived from Mark 10:16: "After taking them in His arms, He laid His hands on them and blessed them."

Activity 9—Musical Instruments

It is beyond the scope of this book to describe and teach musical instruments. However, if you have triangles, drums, cymbals, etc., available in your classroom, you might use them in this activity. It will help the children appreciate musical instrumentation and rhythm.

Use the instruments to play a Christian song like "Onward Christian Soldiers" or "Stand Up, Stand Up for Jesus." You may use a tape, CD, or a piano to provide the background music.

If you do not have any musical instruments, you can make some rhythm instruments by using pans and a wooden spoon, plastic plates with beans between the plates, and a bell that will ring.

Activity 10—Take Your Class to a Concert

There is no substitute for firsthand experience. Take your class to a concert of Christian music. Expose them to good sacred music. Most cities have excellent orchestras. Around Christian holidays, they often perform religious concerts, such as Handel's *Messiah*. You can often obtain group rates that make the concert affordable. If you cannot go to a concert hall, check about the possibility of taking your class to a good church performance in your area.

Activity 11—Memorize Ephesians 5:19–20

Singing is a blessing from the Lord. Today's verses speak about the joy of music in our hearts and lives. Paul and his travelers would sing, even when they were in prison for their faith. Have your students memorize Ephesians 5:19–20:

> *Speaking to one another in psalms, hymns, and spiritual songs, singing and making music to the Lord in your heart, giving thanks always for everything to God the Father in the name of our Lord Jesus Christ.*

Conclude this activity by having the children copy the verses in their Bible Verse Memory Books and illustratating them.

ACTIVITY SHEET 1-A: MUSIC AS A PART OF WORSHIP

Music was used in the Old Testament during the worship service. In an era before literacy, singing and chanting of sacred texts helped in the memorization of those texts. The Psalms were compiled in order to provide a sacred hymnal. It is clear that David put the sons of the Kohathites in charge of the music. They were all Levites. This is found in 1 Chronicles 6:31ff.

Levites were responsible for singing and for playing instruments. The singing many times was antiphonal, which means that one group sang part and the next part was sung by another group. At other times it was responsorial, which means that a soloist sang and another group responded. The Talmud indicates that there were particular psalms that were used on specific days of the week.

When the Jewish people were taken into captivity, they developed the synagogue as a place of worship and study. As time passed, they used a cantor for the purpose of leading the worship. You may find Jewish music online at http://members.aol.com/israelmidi.

The early church used singing for worship as well. Recall that Paul and some of his companions were singing from their prison cells. Some of the early church fathers wrote against singing because it was often used along with pagan sacrifice. Music with instruments was also shunned, since it was often associated with immoral behavior.

Gregory the Great has been credited with changing the worship and particularly the music of the church. It has been assumed that Gregory gave us the chant known as the Gregorian chant. It can be very beautiful. The Gregorian chant was taken by the monks of the Middle Ages and used throughout their worship services. Different types of chants were used by the monks. You might want to play some excerpts from a Gregorian chant. You may find the Gregorian Chant in manuscript and music formats at the La Trobe University library medieval music database at http://www.lib.latrobe.edu.au/Audio-Visual/Stinson/medmusic.htm.

With the changes that took place in the Renaissance, 1400–1600, music again came back in vogue. Instruments were used. In the Reformation, music played an important part. Recall the high value that Martin Luther placed upon music. As a former monk, Luther knew that music could govern human emotions. He used music freely as part of worship. Luther wanted Christian people to be able to sing in their native language, not Latin. Music skills were part of a good education. They were taught to students in the university and used in the weekly services. You may find "A Mighty Fortress Is Our God" at http://www.cyberhymnal.org/htm/m/i/mightyfo.htm.

From 1600 to 1800 both the Roman Catholic Church and Protestant churches used music to attract and hold worshipers. Music was used to affect an emotional response on the part of the worshiper. The oratorio made its appearance. Music and dramatic content were combined to affect the listener. It is a means for teaching Christian truth.

Johann Sebastian Bach lived from 1685 to 1750. For more than 130 years before Bach, his family had been involved in the music of the Lutheran Church in Eisenach, Germany. Without a doubt he is the greatest composer that the West ever produced. He wrote extensively. His compositions fill 82 CD ROMs. To listen to Bach, go to the midi files through the J. S. Bach home page at http://www.jsbach.org/.

The great cathedrals have their own choirs and music resources. Music is an essential part of the music of our churches. You may find music from the York Cathedral on their Web site at http://www.yorkminster.org/.

When the Pilgrims came to the New World in 1620, they brought the Psalter with them. They were clearly nonconformist and brought that independence with them. It has affected American church music ever since. American revivalism has affected American church music through the camp meeting. African-American music has affected American church music through the spirituals. More recently, the Charismatic movement has greatly affected the use of gospel songs in church. Many of the popular hymns can be found and played on http://www.cyberhymnal.org/.

It is a good idea to afford your children the opportunity to listen to different types of church music. You may supplement or replace this music with CD-ROMs or cassette tapes of different types of church music.

ACTIVITY SHEET 1-B: MUSIC AS A PART OF WORSHIP— QUESTIONS FOR DISCUSSION

1. How did Jewish music affect the development of early church music?

2. How would you describe a Gregorian chant? What did you like or dislike about the Gregorian chant? Why?

3. What was the music of the Reformation like? How did it change from medieval music?

4. What happened to music in the period 1600 to 1800?

5. Who was the greatest composer? What did he do?

6. How would you describe the music from the cathedral?

7. What did the Pilgrims do with music? How has that affected church music today?

8. Why is good church music important, even today?

ACTIVITY SHEET 2: HOW DOES MUSIC ENHANCE WORSHIP?

Directions: Answer the questions by circling YES or NO.

YES   NO   1. Music does not affect our emotions and is not important to the worship experience in church.

YES   NO   2. Music was used by the Jews in the ancient worship of God in the Temple.

YES   NO   3. God is honored by the use of good music in the church.

YES   NO   4. The best kind of music is what is popular today.

YES   NO   5. Beautiful music can be heard in cathedrals, like the one in York, England.

YES   NO   6. Singing in church is all right, but we should not use instruments to accompany the singing.

YES   NO   7. Organ music is better for worship than any other type of music.

YES   NO   8. I feel closer to God when I sing in church.

YES   NO   9. I like to sing in church.

YES   NO   10. I do not like the singing that we do in church.

Directions: Complete the puzzle to spell AMAZING GRACE

Sentence clues for the puzzle—
John Newton was born in London, _____. His _____ taught him the way of faith. His mother died when he was seven and he went to sea with his_____. He was not interested in God or any _____ grace. Later, he joined the _____ navy and had his own ship. He became very _____ and _____ as a slave trader. He sometimes wished that he could believe in _____, but he loved his sin too much. One day he almost drowned but was _____. He finally remembered what his mother had taught him. He _____ to accept Christ. He gave up his ship. He married Mary _____. He then began to _____ and write hymns. One of the hymns that he wrote was "Amazing Grace."

Puzzle letters: A, M, A, Z, I, N, G, G, R, A, C, E

Directions: Put the events in the right order by placing the correct number in the space provided.

___1. Mohr and Gruber sang this new Christmas song to their little church at Oberndorf, Germany, on Christmas Eve 1818.

___2. The song made its way to the United States after World War I; servicemen heard it in Germany and brought it to America.

___3. Joseph Mohr visited in the home of a woodcutter and saw a new baby boy in a rough-hewn cradle. After walking home that cold starlit night in the snow, he was inspired to write the song.

___4. Mauracher asked for a copy of the music and took it to a women's group. They sang it at the Leipzig Fair. It became popular throughout Germany.

___5. After writing the words to "Silent Night! Holy Night!" he took the words to his friend Franz Gruber to put it to music.

___6. Sometime later, when Fritz Mauracher was working on the organ in the little church at Oberndorf, he asked Gruber to test the organ. Gruber played "Silent Night! Holy Night!"

ACTIVITY SHEET 8: STORY OF "JESUS LOVES ME"

Anna Bartlett Warner and her sister Susan lived near the Hudson River, near the United States Military Academy at West Point, New York. On Sunday they would teach the army cadets and focus on their moral character. They made a significant impact at the military academy. (When they died years later, their home was made a national shrine and they were buried with full military honors.)

Their father, a widower, had been a prominent New York attorney. When he died, the young women had to find a way to support themselves. Both had some talent for writing. Susan had written a best-seller, *The Wide, Wide World*, second at the time in popularity only to *Uncle Tom's Cabin*.

But it was Anna who wrote a book that would affect the lives of hundreds of thousands of persons over the next century and a quarter. She wrote a lesser-known book, *Say and Seal*. The book told the story of a boy named Johnny Fax. Johnny was dying. (In the 1860s, the mortality rate for children was very high). Mr. Linden, a friend of Johnny's, would repeat a poem that would comfort Johnny Fax. That poem was "Jesus Loves Me."

Dr. William Bradbury was born in Maine. He loved children and wanted to find a song that would speak specifically to children and tell them about the love of Jesus for them. Many of the songs of that day were dreary and did not help children to find the love of Jesus. Bradbury became associated with Lowell Mason. Mason has been known as the father of the American public school and was a prominent publisher of church music.

Bradbury served as a minister of music in several significant churches. Bradbury found the words of Anna Bartlett Warner's poem in her book *Say and Seal* and put them to music. He wrote the chorus to the four verses and published the song along with a number of other Christian and secular songs. "Jesus Loves Me" has become the most significant song for children to tell them of the love of Jesus.

Readings from the Parent/Teacher Handbook: Their Christian Heritage, Vol. 2: "Science and Christian Faith"

OBJECTIVES

By the end of this lesson, the learner should be able to

- discover the contributions that science has made to our lives today,
- identify and describe three important scientists who believed science supported God's creative work in the universe,
- develop an appreciation for scientists Johannes Kepler, Sir Isaac Newton, and Robert Boyle, and
- discover the miracle of God's creative activity in the world.

IDENTIFICATIONS

Concepts

Astronomer—one who observes objects and matter outside of our atmosphere

Mathematician—one who specializes in the science of numbers

Calculus—a method of mathematical computation involving logic or symbolic logic

Gravitation—attraction of a smaller object toward a larger object, such as the downward pull of an object toward earth

Telescope—an instrument with lenses through which the viewer can see distant objects magnified by means of the refraction of light rays

Microscope—an instrument that magnifies the size of infinitesimally small objects

Chemistry—science that deals with the composition, structure, and properties of substances and the transformation of those properties when changes occur

Boyle's Law—a volume of gas at constant temperature will vary inversely with the pressure exerted on it

People

Johannes Kepler: German astronomer who helped us understand the way planets move in the heavens

Copernicus: Polish astronomer who discovered that the earth revolves on its axis around a stationary sun

Sir Isaac Newton: English mathematician and physicist who wrote *The Principia*, one of the bases for modern science

Robert Boyle: British physicist and chemist who discovered Boyle's Law

Places

Cambridge University, Cambridge, England: University where Newton studied and taught

Ireland: home country of Robert Boyle

MATERIALS NEEDED

Parent/Teacher Handbook: Their Christian Heritage, Vol. 2

Activity Sheets for Lesson 15

Crayons and markers

White paper for drawing

Lined paper for writing

Roll of shelf paper or butcher paper

Masking tape and plastic tape

3x5-inch index cards

Tempera paints

Construction paper

Telescope (optional)

Microscope (optional)

Science computer programs (optional)

LEARNING ACTIVITIES FOR LESSON 15

Activity 1—What Science Has Contributed to Our Lives

Read in the handbook, "Science and Christian Faith." You will find the parents and teachers' introduction to this section especially helpful.

Prepare copies of the questionnaire "What Science Has Contributed to Our Lives" for your class. This questionnaire is on Activity Sheet 1. Have the students think about the positive contributions that science has made. If your students are younger, you may simply want to talk through the items that are on the questionnaire. If they are older, they can check the appropriate items.

Talk about the contributions that science has made to our world.

Activity 2—Nature Hike

Take your students on a nature hike. If you have a nature walk in a state or county park in close proximity to your school, you may utilize that resource. Usually, the state or county has park rangers available to talk with your students. Normally, if you are bringing a group, you will need to make reservations in advance.

If you do not have access to a nature walk, prepare your own nature walk in your local neighborhood. If you live in a city, there is likely a park available. If you live in a rural or suburban neighborhood, map out in advance the trail that you plan to follow with the children. You will want to take them along a shallow brook or stream, since the water is usually teeming with life. Be very careful to sharpen their observation skills as they look at the beauty of nature. They need to look very closely.

This activity is best done in spring, summer, or fall. It can be done in winter, but you will not find as many life forms to observe at that time of the year. Observe the insects and other creatures that God created. Be sure to help the children see the flora—trees, plants, flowers, etc.—as well as the fauna—animal life forms. As you observe the world God created, help the boys and girls appreciate how wonderfully beautiful God made the environment in which we live. The physical sciences of botany and biology help us better understand this environment by careful observation.

Activity 3—Research and Report

In the handbook read "Johannes Kepler, 1571–1630," "Sir Isaac Newton, 1642–1727," and "Robert Boyle, 1627–1691." You may want to use some additional resources, such as an encyclopedia, CD-ROM encyclopedia, online Web sites, etc. For Web sites that will provide biographical information, see Activity 5 below. If you are working with younger children, skip this activity and proceed to Activity 4.

Divide the class into three small groups and have each group work with one of these scientists—Kepler, Newton, or Boyle. Have them do library research about the life of the scientist for whom they are responsible. When was he born? What were his childhood and education like? Where did he go to school? What scientific discoveries did he make? How important were those discoveries? What was his belief in God? When did he die?

Have the students write their answers on notebook paper. Have them come together and discuss the scientist for whom they were responsible. Summarize their results. Have one member of each group report to the class about their findings.

Fill in anything that the students left out. Proceed to the matching quiz in the next activity.

Activity 4—Matching Quiz for the Lives of Three Scientists

In the handbook read "Johannes Kepler, 1571–1630," "Sir Isaac Newton, 1642–1727," and "Robert Boyle, 1627–1691." In class you should talk about each of these important scientists and their contribution to our understanding of science today.

Then have the students complete the matching quiz on Activity Sheet 4. For younger students, you will need to do this orally and perhaps note reasons on the chalkboard. Discuss the answers with them.

Activity 5—Picture and Brief Explanation of the Scientist's Belief in God

Provide your students with a sheet of construction paper. Using markers, have the students draw a picture of each of the scientists. Write a very brief description of each. Pay particular attention to their belief in God and the appropriate use of science by each of the scientists.

From the School of Mathematics and Statistics at the University of St. Andrews, Scotland, you can find a picture and biography of Johannes Kepler. The Web site is located at http://turnbull.mcs.st-and.ac.uk/history/Mathematicians/Kepler.html/.

From the same source, you can find a picture and biography of Sir Isaac Newton. The Web site is located at http://turnbull.mcs.st-and.ac.uk/history/Mathematicians/Newton.html/.

From the same source you will find a picture and biography of Robert Boyle. The Web site is located at http://turnbull.mcs.st-and.ac.uk/history/Mathematicians/Boyle.html/.

Activity 6—Microscope and Telescope Activity

If you have access to a microscope and a telescope, have the children experience the opportunity to look through each.

With the telescope, your children can see things up close that are very far away. *Caution:* Make sure they do not look at the sun! It can burn the retina permanently. But they may look at the moon if it is visible. They may look at buildings or other objects that are far away. Talk with your students about the fact that with the telescope we can see things that God has created that are very far away. While they look small to us, the stars are larger than the earth where we live. They are very far away. God's universe is very large. We cannot even imagine how large it is.

But God did not only create things that are large. He created things that are infinitesimally small. We use a microscope to look at things that are very small and cannot be seen with our eyes alone. If you have a microscope, you can prepare several slides in advance for the children to inspect.

If you do not have access to a telescope or microscope, there are several alternatives. The simplest alternative is to send your students to the library or online to find the results of looking through a telescope and a microscope.

For the telescope, there is an excellent NASA Web site where you can view the galaxies, planets, and outer space from your computer. It may be found at http://www.nasa.gov/. There are many activities for children that may be found on this Web site.

For the microscope, there is a good Web site that shows pictures of different objects under an electron microscope. This is the Boston Museum of Science. You will find the science museum at http://www.mos.org/. There are more science exhibits online at the museum also.

Have children compare the findings for the telescope and the microscope. Be sure to point out that God's creation is very large, but it is also just as small. We worship a great God.

Activity 7—Stargazing into the Heavens

One of the best ways to view the stars in the heavens is through a computer program. One such program is Starry Night Backyard. There are also other versions. You can find out about their programs on their Web site at http://www.starrynight.com/. Similar products are also available from other vendors. This approach allows your children to see the heavens without the cost of an expensive telescope. It will also point out specific phenomena that you may want to see as well. Be sure to relate the findings back to the creation of God in His vast universe.

Other science programs that you may want to explore include the human body, biology, zoology, chemistry, physics, etc. For homeschooling families, it may be worthwhile to purchase several of these science programs. Such programs may be used throughout the schoolyears.

Other possibilities include A & E Television Network's productions of videotapes. For example: *Sir Isaac Newton*, *The Gravity of Genius*, and other of their scientific programs. Many of these may be found at stores like the Discovery Store or video stores.

Activity 8—Life Cycle of an Insect

For this activity you will need to have available one of several research tools, like an encyclopedia, a CD-ROM encyclopedia, or a science textbook that deals with insects. Provide your children with a sheet of construction paper. Have them look in one of the research tools for the life cycle of a butterfly.

There are four stages in the life cycle of a butterfly:

Egg stage, where the eggs are laid by the mother on a leaf and held there by a sticky substance. The leaf serves as food for the next stage.

Larva stage, where the caterpillar hatches and feeds on the remains of the egg and on the leaves. The caterpillar has a head and twelve segments of its body. It spends its time eating and growing.

Pupa stage, where the caterpillar is full grown. At this stage the caterpillar finds the underside of a leaf. It spins a silk thread until it is completely covered. The pupa is inside the caterpillar. During this stage the caterpillar is dormant. But great changes, known as metamorphoses, are occurring to the body of the caterpillar. The time period may take six to eight months or more.

Adult stage, where it eventually emerges from the pupal shell as an adult butterfly. It takes the butterfly about thirty minutes to spread its wings and fly.

Have the children draw the four stages of the butterfly. This is a magnificent example of the beauty in nature that God has provided for us to enjoy. Talk with the children about the beauty of nature. In the summer, you may want to start a butterfly collection. You can find instructions in an encyclopedia.

Activity 9—What I Would Like to Ask a Scientist

After you have studied all of this material on science, ask the children what they would like to ask a scientist. Remind them that the material that they have studied is in relation to Christian faith. God is the Creator and Sustainer of all that is in the universe. Have them list three questions that they would like to ask. For younger children, you might want to make the list for the class on the chalkboard.

List the three questions:

1. I would like to know . . .
2. I would like you to tell me . . .
3. I would like to have you explain . . .

If you have a scientist who is a member of your church, invite that person to respond to the children's questions. You might want to obtain the questions first and then take them to your guest. Be sure that your guest understands that we are concerned that children have a deep understanding of God as Creator and Sustainer of the universe. This should be a good experience for both the children and the guest.

Activity 10—Field Trip to a Science Museum

Most large cities have excellent science museums. In cities like New York, Chicago, and Washington, DC, there are excellent science museums for field trips. Even some smaller cities have excellent science museums. Many universities have excellent science museums as well. These resources can supplement your teaching in this area and provide students with firsthand experience of the wonders of science. Be sure to visit the museum yourself first, if possible. If there are exhibits that are controversial, with a large emphasis on evolution, you may want to think about how you will present that to the class before you go and after you return. But do not let that be a reason not to go.

Activity 11—Memorize Psalm 33:6–9

Lead your children to memorize Psalm 33:6–9. This is an excellent poetic statement of the work of God in creation. If you are working with younger children, have them memorize only the first verse of this passage.

> *The heavens were made by the word of the LORD,*
> *and all the stars, by the breath of His mouth.*
> *He gathers the waters of the sea into a heap;*
> *He puts the depths into storehouses.*
> *Let the whole earth tremble before the LORD;*
> *let all the inhabitants of the world stand in awe of Him.*
> *For He spoke, and it came into being;*
> *He commanded, and it came into existence.*

Complete this activity by having the children write the verses in their Bible Verse Memory Books and illustrate them.

ACTIVITY SHEET 1: WHAT SCIENCE HAS CONTRIBUTED TO OUR LIVES

Directions: Check the items that are appropriate to the contribution that science has made to our lives.

___1. Great artworks that will help us enjoy our world more.

___2. Exploration of the South Pole by scientists who lived there for the duration of the winter.

___3. Automobiles for transportation to our sporting events at school.

___4. Dishwashers to clean our dirty dishes so that we do not have to wash them by hand.

___5. Washers and dryers for cleaning our dirty clothes from playing outside in the mud.

___6. Computers for us to play games and watch digital movies.

___7. Great works of literature that will give us insights about life.

___8. Rockets to explore outer space and place a man on the moon.

___9. Medical science that can help us understand why we have a stomachache and what to do about it to make the ache go away.

___10. Historians that can take us back to understand past civilizations.

___11. Archaeologists to discover many of the facts of the Bible that we do not understand.

___12. Meteorologists to study the weather and predict what will happen on the day we want to take a picnic in the park.

___13. Digital color television sets to allow us to view the awesome colors of nature at different seasons of the year.

___14. Modern military equipment that will save the lives of many of our soldiers in battle.

___15. Newspapers that will tell us what is happening elsewhere in the world today.

Directions: Match the descriptions of the scientists from the list below with the names listed below by writing the correct letter in the space provided. There will be more than one description to match to the scientist's name.

_____1. Johannes Kepler

_____2. Sir Isaac Newton

_____3. Robert Boyle

Descriptions:

a. German astronomer
b. went to Cambridge University
c. lived in Oxford, near Oxford University
d. invented the mathematical science of calculus
e. believed our better understanding of the universe helps us see how God constructed it
f. educated by a tutor and spent time in Venice
g. built his own understanding of the laws of gravity on the work of a man who came before him
h. oldest of the three scientists
i. had a stroke that left him partially paralyzed
j. believed in the Creator God of the Bible
k. born in Ireland
l. created first reflecting telescope
m. Lutheran Christian
n. belonged to the Royal Society
o. had some difficulty with the Augsburg Confession
p. used a compressor to build pressure for gases
q. European mathematician Leibnitz created trouble for him

ANSWERS TO ACTIVITY WORKSHEETS

LESSON 1
Activity Sheet 1
1. i 2. d 3. g 4. a 5. j 6. b 7. c 8. f 9. e 10. h

LESSON 2

Activity Sheet 1
1. Priest
2. Levites
3. Prophets
4. Scribes
5. Pharisees
6. Sadducees
7. Essenes
8. Zealots

Activity Sheet 2
1. They were a group of people who were known for their hospitality and healing. They were found in all towns in Palestine. They had a special community in Quamran.
2. They had to sell all that they had and had to live pure lives to join the Essene community.
3. They were known for hospitality and healing.
4. The Book of Discipline was a book that told about the way of life of the Essenes.
5. It was found in a cave by the Dead Sea in 1947 after 2,000 years.
6. A boy threw a stone into a cave and it made a noise when it hit the jar that held the scroll.
7. Ancient manuscripts of the Bible.

Activity Sheet 3
1. False
2. True
3. False
4. True
5. False
6. False
7. True
8. True

Activity Sheet 4
Pharisees:
Strictly followed the Oral Law
Kept every letter of the Law of God,
   given by Moses
Best known religious group
Sadducees:
Did not believe in the resurrection
Conducted the trial of Jesus before
   the High Priest
Did not believe in Heaven or Hell
Both the Pharisees and Sadducees:
Religious leaders
Opposed Jesus
Had political power

Activity Sheet 9

LESSON 3

Activity Sheet 2-B
1. True
2. False
3. False
4. True
5. True
6. True
7. False
8. False
9. True
10. True

Activity Sheet 4
1. Solomon
2. permanent
3. furniture
4. larger
5. God
6. Nebuchadnezzar
7. gold
8. money materials
9. five hundred
10. Temple
11. Romans
12. Wailing Wall

Activity Sheet 9
Across:
2. tabernacle
4. incense
6. holy
7. showbread
8. priest
9. sabbath
Down:
1. candlestick
3. laver
5. cherubim
10. temple

LESSON 5

Activity Sheet 5

Name	Purpose
1. New Year	Jewish
2. Atonement	repentance
3. Tabernacles	grape
4. Lights	lights
5. Lots	Esther
6. Passover	grain
7. Pentecost	Law

LESSON 4

Activity Sheet 6
Scapegoat
Fast
Holy
Jonah
Reconcile
Mercy
Death
Sin
Set

LESSON 6

Activity Sheet 5
1. *Confessions*
2. knuckles
3. Rhetoric
4. Monica
5. school
6. Christ
7. Hippo
8. God

Activity Sheet 8

LESSON 7

Activity Sheet 6
Check numbers:
2, 3, 4, 6, 7

LESSON 8

Activity Sheet 1
Across:
2. Moravian
4. Charles
6. aldersgate
7. Oxford
8. revival
Down:
1. ordained
2. Methodist
3. Susanna
5. Georgia

Activity Sheet 2
1. b   6. a
2. a   7. a
3. c   8. a
4. b   9. c
5. a   10. a, b

Activity Sheet 5

Raikes	Women
Gloucester	Ragged
Prison	Clean
Children	Hair
Sunday	Bible
School	Died
Jail	America

LESSON 9

Activity Sheet 9

Children	Murder
God	Marriages
Him	Steal
Name	Neighbors
Day	Covet
Honor	Worshiped

Activity Sheet 3
1. E—Intercession
2. B—Thanksgiving
3. A—Praise
4. E—Intercession
5. D—Petition
6. C—Confession
7. D—Petition
8. A—Praise
9. B—Thanksgiving

LESSON 10

Activity Sheet 1
Check numbers:
1, 2, 4, 6, 7, 9, 10
Number 4 is the most important.

Activity Sheet 7
1. Guatemala
2. Central America, below Mexico
3. Three—Josh, Melanie, and Nathaniel
4. She provides medical help.
5. He had no one else to turn to for help.
6. God miraculously healed Adam.
7. Like a child, Adam trusted Christ. Adan would not have known Christ as his personal Savior, if he had not been led to Jesus by the missionary.
8. They were raised in Christian homes, where they came to know Jesus as their personal Savior. They felt God's call on their lives. They went on a mission trip to Haiti during college. Vicki became a nurse and Roger went to seminary. They spent time with missionaries from Guatemala. Roger and Vicki were willing to follow Christ.
9. Rudy and Douglas became Christians and their lives changed. As a result of their testimonies, seventy people came to know Christ in Huehuetenango.
10. Illiteracy is a major problem. This means that most people can't read and write.

LESSON 12

Activity Sheet 4-B
1. 250 years
2. Constantine
3. 1472
4. Edwin
5. Norman conquerors
6. Foundation crumbled

Activity Sheet 5
1. lectern
2. pulpit
3. cathedra
4. baptismal font
5. altar

Activity Sheet 6
1. c
2. e
3. d
4. b
5. f
6. a
7. g

Activity Sheet 8
1. d   6. i
2. c   7. j
3. b   8. g
4. e   9. h
5. a   10. f

LESSON 13

Activity Sheet 8

LESSON 14

Activity Sheet 2
1. NO
2. YES
3. YES
4. NO, not necessarily
5. YES
6. NO
7. NO, not necessarily
8. Hopefully, that is a YES
9. Hopefully, that is a YES
10. Hopefully, that is a NO

Activity Sheet 6
3, 5, 1, 6, 4, 2

Activity Sheet 3
1. England
2. mother
3. father
4. amazing
5. British
6. sinful
7. greedy
8. God
9. rescued
10. prayed
11. catlet
12. preach

LESSON 15

Activity Sheet 1
Probably the following have not been as affected by science directly: 1, 7, 10, 15   But, even these have been affected by the way we explore literature, art, etc.

There is not very much in our world that has not been affected in some way by science.

Activity Sheet 4
1. Johannes Kepler
   e, h, a, m, o, and j
2. Sir Isaac Newton
   g, j, q, l, b, d, and n
3. Robert Boyle
   k, f, c, p, n, i, and j